D0147240

Reproducing Gender?

Reproducing Gender? charts the development of a theory of gender relations, built up over the last twenty years. This theory has been highly influential in establishing the importance of sociology of women's education for the study of society. It demonstrates the power of feminist educational theory and research and its role in creating new political and academic agendas.

Taking gender codes as a key concept, this book explores gender relationships at all levels of schooling. It brings together political, social and cultural theories to understand continuity and change in gender and education. Major issues include:

- changes in the nature of the school curriculum
- the co-education debate
- schooling and youth cultures
- families and schools
- the state and feminist educational politics
- patterns of male amd female educational achievement

Madeleine Arnot, widely considered to be a pioneer in the field of gender and education, brings together for the first time in a single volume her most influential writings. This book will be essential reading for students and academics in the areas of gender studies, women's studies, educational policy, sociology and history of education.

Madeleine Arnot is Reader in Sociology of Education and a Fellow of Jesus College, University of Cambridge.

Reproducing Gender?

Essays on educational theory and feminist politics

Madeleine Arnot

London and New York

First published 2002
by RoutledgeFalmer
11 New Fetter Lane, London EC4P 4EE

Simultaneously published in the USA and Canada
by RoutledgeFalmer
29 West 35th Street, New York, NY 10001

RoutledgeFalmer is an imprint of the Taylor & Francis Group

Typeset in Goudy by Taylor & Francis Books Ltd
Printed and bound in Great Britain by Biddles Ltd,
Guildford and King's Lynn

British Library Cataloguing in Publication Data
A catalogue record for this book is available from the British Library

Library of Congress Cataloging in Publication Data
Arnot, Madeleine.
Reproducing gender? : essays on educational theory
and feminist politics / Madeleine Arnot.
p. cm.
Includes bibliographical references and index.
1. Gender identity in education. 2. Sex discrimination in education.
3. Feminism and education. I. Title.
LC212.9 .A76 2002
305.3'07–dc21 2001048411

ISBN 0–750–70899–9 (hbk)
ISBN 0–750–70898–0 (pbk)

For Basil

Contents

Preface

This book is dedicated to the memory of Basil Bernstein who, as my doctoral supervisor in 1972, led me along a difficult and rocky path. I began my academic career teaching his theories and I have returned to his work time and time again to rethink the social relations which I observed. Bernstein challenged me at every stage in my academic career to rise above the detail of human experience and try to make sense of the social order. His belief in the power of sociology as a discipline remains central to my understanding of education. This book represents my response to his challenge.

Over the last twenty-five years so many people have helped me to develop my thinking and understanding that it is impossible to name them all. I do hope that I am not offending friends and colleagues by naming those to whom I owe especial thanks for the part they have played in supporting my work in the field of gender and education. At a time when gender was a marginal 'Cinderella' in sociology of education I owe a particular debt to Len Barton who organised the annual Westhill Conferences on sociology of education to which he invited me to talk on numerous occasions; to Kathleen Weiler as editor of *Journal of Education* at Boston University who gave me a number of opportunities to position myself within the American field of critical social theory; to James Donald who, when editor of *Screen Education*, commissioned my first article on gender; and to Rosemary Deem who asked me to contribute to the first gender and education collection.

My colleagues Roger Dale and Geoff Esland at the Open University argued with and supported me through the difficult days of the 'new sociology of education' and the emergence of political economy. I have the fondest memories of those exhilarating times. With their help, publishing under the name of Madeleine MacDonald, I cut my teeth on writing units and editing course readers for Open University courses and, in particular, for the infamous *Schooling and Society* course.

Feminist educationalists internationally have supported each other through various eras, both modernist and post-modernist. I owe an enormous debt to Miriam David and Gaby Weiner for years of extraordinary intellectual companionship and sisterhood and to Jo-Anne Dillabough for her friendship and exceptionally challenging encounters with my work. Other fellow travellers in these periods of change provided me with invaluable critical engagements and years of delightful shared experiences. I am therefore particularly glad to have worked alongside such leading feminists as: Carol Adams, Jean Anyon, Sandra Acker, Jill Blackmore, Maude Blair, Gloria Bonder, Sara Delamont, Jane Gaskell, Jane Kenway, Janet Holland, Wendy Luttrell, Diana Leonard, Sue Lees, Pat Mahony, Sue Middleton, Heidi Mirza, June Purvis, Diane Reay, Sheila Riddell, Susan Semel, Parlo Singh, Maria Subirats, Lyn Yates and Cecile Wright, among many others. I owe thanks too for the patience of my co-researchers who tolerated the intensity of my enthusiasm: Kiki Deliyanni, Roula Ziogou, Amparo Tomé, Helena Araújo and Gabrielle Ivinson for our highly enjoyable years of research together on European projects on citizenship and on masculinity and to Mary James, John Gray, Jean Rudduck and Gerard Duveen for their colleagueship on the OFSTED project.

Support comes in many forms and it would be remiss, therefore, if I did not express my thanks particularly to the following: Michael Apple, John Beck, Bob Connell, Tony Edwards, Phil Gardner, Gerald Grace, Terry McLaughlin, Joe Muller, Rob Moore, Paul Olson, Alan Sadovnik, John Thompson, Geoff Whitty and Peter Woods, among many others, who have taken the trouble to offer moral support and intellectual interest in my work. Malcolm Clarkson commissioned this book in the late 1980s and his daughter Anna Clarkson of RoutledgeFalmer Press waited over ten years for its completion. I thank them both for their limitless patience. My gratitude to Barbara Shannon and Rosemary Millen for their help in putting this book together. There has been no-one more forbearing or more caring than my family, Robin, Kathryn and Adam, for whom simple thanks are just not enough.

Acknowledgements

I am grateful to the following for granting permission to reprint:

'Socio-cultural reproduction and women's education', in R. Deem (ed.) *Schooling for Women's Work*, Routledge, 1980. Permission granted from RoutledgeFalmer Publishers, Cheriton House, North Way, Andover, Hampshire SP10 5BE.

'Cultural reproduction: the pedagogy of sexuality', *Screen Education*, 32/33 (1979), pp. 141–52. Permission granted from *Screen*, Gilmorehill Centre, University of Glasgow, Glasgow G12 8QQ.

'Schooling and the reproduction of class and gender relations', in L. Barton, R. Meighan and S. Walker (eds) *Schooling, Ideology and the Curriculum*, Falmer Press, 1981. Permission granted from International Thomson Publishing Services Ltd, Royalties Department, Cheriton House, North Way, Andover, Hampshire SP10 5BE.

'A cloud over co-education: an analysis of the forms of transmission of class and gender relations', in S. Walker and L. Barton (eds) *Gender, Class and Education*, Falmer Press, 1983. Permission granted from International Thomson Publishing Services Ltd, Royalties Department, Cheriton House, North Way, Andover, Hampshire SP10 5BE.

'Male hegemony, social class and women's education', *Journal of Education*, 164, 1, Winter (1982), pp. 64–89; reprinted in L. Stone (ed.) *The Feminism Reader*, Routledge, 1994. Permission granted from *Journal of Education*, Boston University, School of Education, 605 Commonwealth Avenue, Boston, MA 02215.

'Schools and families: gender contradictions, diversity and conflict', *Journal of Education*, 166, 1, pp. 5–24; reprinted in K. Weiler (ed.) *What Schools Can Do: critical pedagogy and practice*, SUNY Press, 1992. Permission granted from *Journal of Education*, Boston University, School of Education, 605 Commonwealth Avenue, Boston, MA 02215.

'A crisis in patriarchy? British feminist educational politics and state regulation of gender', in M. Arnot and K. Weiler (eds) *Feminism and Social Justice in Education: international perspectives*, Falmer Press, 1993. Permission granted from International Thomson Publishing Services Ltd, Royalties Department, Cheriton House, North Way, Andover, Hampshire SP10 5BE.

Extracts from 'Feminism, education and the New Right', in M. Arnot and L. Barton (eds) *Voicing Concerns: sociological perspectives on educational reform*, Triangle Books, 1992. Permission from Triangle Books, P.O. Box 65, Wallingford, Oxfordshire OX10 OYG.

'Sociological understandings of contemporary gender transformations in schooling in the UK', printed with permission from the UK–Japan Education Research Forum, September 2000.

'Basil Bernstein's sociology of pedagogy: female dialogues and feminist elaborations', in K. Weiler (ed.) *Feminist Engagements*, RoutledgeFalmer, 2001. Permission granted from Taylor & Francis Inc., 29 West 35th Street, New York, NY 10001.

'Gender relations and schooling in the new century: conflicts and challenges', *Compare: A Journal of Comparative Education*, 30, 3, October (2000), pp. 293–302. Permission granted from Taylor & Francis Ltd, P.O. Box 25, Abingdon, Oxfordshire OX14 3UE.

Figures 1 and 2 from J. Marks, *Girls Know Better: Educational Achievements of Boys and Girls*, Civitas, 2001. Permission granted from Civitas: Institute for the Study of Civil Society, the Mezzanine, Elizabeth House, 39 York Road, London SE1 7NQ.

Figure 3 from M. Arnot, M. David and G. Weiner, *Educational Reforms and Gender Equality in Schools*, Research Discussion Series no. 17, Equal Opportunities Commission, 1996. Permission granted from the Equal Opportunities Commission, Arndale House, Arndale Centre, Manchester M4 3EQ.

Table 2, Department for Education and Skills (DfES) at http://www.standards.dfes.gov.uk/genderandachievement/2000-data-5.html. Permission granted by Her Majesty's Stationery Office (HMSO).

Tables 3 and 4 from M. Arnot et al., *Closing the Gender Gap*, Polity Press, 1999. Permission granted from Blackwell Publishers, 108 Cowley Road, Oxford OX4 1JF.

1 Gender codes and educational theory

An overview

This book charts my contribution over the last twenty-five years to the emerging field of gender scholarship in education. This is a field which comprises some of the most sophisticated research in education. It engages with diverse theoretical problematics and explanatory frameworks; it develops its own methodological approaches; and it actively engages with the concerns of practitioners and students in a range of educational contexts and settings (from early years schooling through to higher education and adult education). The richness and originality of the field of gender and education research lies in its commitment to social analysis linked to critical praxis.

Theorising gender relations in education is a complex and dynamic project. Since the 1960s, gender research within education has had an extraordinary momentum as national and local policy-makers responded to the demands for better education for women. The impact of the women's movement in the UK and abroad has resulted in a multitude of local initiatives in school around the concept of equal opportunities. These interventions have drawn upon a range of feminist academic discourses and have been influenced by a range of political philosophies and agendas. Not suprisingly, feminist educationalists continually reflect on the relationship between social movements, political action and social inequalities.

I have contributed to this emerging field by attempting to develop a sociological theory of gender relations that is both critical and interpretative. My concern has been the ways in which gender relationships work within the social order. Arguably, the task of contributing to any field of study is made easier if the parameters and problematics of the discourse are made explicit. Over the period, I have therefore engaged with the sequence of theoretical (and often critical) encounters between sociology of education and feminist studies of education, looking to see what connections are made between gender relations and the education system. I have also put forward a range of conceptual and discursive frameworks, most notably a theory of *gender codes*, to help focus and advance the field of gender studies.

Like others in the field, I have been fortunate in being able to draw upon the insights gained from the rich multitude of large and small, national and international research projects on gender issues in education. The explosion of feminist studies has generated original insights into gender relations in education, more often than not critically challenging mainstream conceptual frameworks, understandings and explanations. I have also gained by addressing the plethora of audiences for such work. Like others of my generation working in higher education on gender and education, I have engaged with national and international academic debates, central government agencies, local government, schools, teachers, teacher educators and students. It has been important to relate the theory of gender relations explicitly to educational policy-making and practice. Theoretical understandings are best framed not just by social scientific academic discourses but also by pragmatic and practical considerations. One of the clear guiding principles of feminist studies and the women's movement has been the use of theory to ground social reform.

The selection of articles in this volume offers the opportunity to consider the strengths and weaknesses of social and cultural reproduction theory for the study of social inequalities. This volume does not cover all the issues I have worked on, but the articles selected represent my commitment to understand how power and social control work within the educational system and how social relations are produced, reproduced and transmitted through schooling. The central theme (hence the title of the collection) is the contribution which social and cultural reproduction theory can offer to an understanding of the relationship between social class, race and gender relations in schooling and society. Over the last twenty-five years, I have attempted to:

- construct a sociological theory of gender that accounts for, among other things, the transmission historically of specific sets of gender relations in education;
- explore theoretically the relationship between gender, race and class as social and educational inequalities;
- theorise the interface between gender relations, feminist politics and the state by considering contemporary policy-making at central, local and institutional levels;
- assess critically the construction and the power of feminist educational approaches as democratic discourses and social reform movements; and
- assess contemporary sociological theory in the light of gender transformations in late modernity.

I shall first describe the context in which these interests developed and then the ways I have used social and cultural reproduction theory for the study of gender.

Academic positioning

The principles which govern my work reflect my positioning within the field of sociology of education. Although trained in the 'master narratives' (Lather, 1992) of sociology, I consistently question whether such narratives can adequately address the specific nature of women's position in society and the specificities of female education. My first degree in sociology at Edinburgh University offered a training in positivist social science and an inculcation into modernist social theory. Theories of social class, stratification and mobility were critical to the project, as were theories of the social division of labour promoted by, for example, Emile Durkheim, Karl Marx and Max Weber. I learnt that at the heart of the sociological imagination can be found a concern with the nature of the social order and the processes of social change.

Later, as a doctoral student under the supervision of Basil Bernstein at the Institute of Education, London University (1973–5), I was influenced by the 'new sociology' of education which highlighted a number of key questions: How does society sustain itself economically, politically and culturally? What are the key forces of change? What role does educational knowledge play in such processes? Working directly on Bernstein's theories of educational codes in the early 1970s, I explored the historical relationship between symbolic structuring of educational knowledge and a class-based society. In my doctoral study of the Scottish university curricula, I focused on the complex connection between educational and social change, trying to use Bernstein's concepts of classification and framing of educational knowledge. Thus, even before attempting an analysis of gender and education, I had chosen a sociological agenda which privileged the structure of educational knowledge, its institutional forms and its relationship to social context.

My first teaching post in the Open University gave me access to a further set of theoretical dimensions and perspectives, many of which centred upon the relationship between structure and agency, between macro- and micro-processes of power and control, between individual and collective political agency. Of central significance at the time was the neo-Marxist political economy of education (or social reproduction theories) which privileged the education–economy relationship. The work of Althusser (1971) and Bowles and Gintis (1976) were central to this project. Such macro-social theories were complemented by theories of cultural reproduction (especially that of Bernstein, 1977, and Bourdieu and Passeron, 1977) since they focused on the cultural formation of identities and forms of consciousness, derived from the social division of labour (MacDonald, 1981).

My work was also influenced by changing political climates. For example, Chapters 2 to 6 which were written between 1980 and 1984 reflect a period in which the illusions of liberal democracy were being challenged by sociologists concerned about the continuing strong influence of social class inequalities, despite the post-war promises of meritocracy. These chapters address the illusions of gender neutrality and the image of social progress generated by social democracy. The post-war period with its weak ideals of equality of opportunity had not delivered gender equality in education or in employment or in the family. The initial purpose of critical feminist research, therefore, was to expose the ways in which the educational system transmitted and sustained gender inequalities and the ways in which male dominance of educational privileges related to the forms of social class dominance reproduced through the school system. These early chapters illustrate some of the perspectival differences and conflicts within the field of gender and education at that time, especially between liberal theories of socialisation and Marxist political economy.

By the late 1970s and early 1980s, sociologists of education in the UK turned to address the role of the state in education. In 1979 the election of a new government under Margaret Thatcher with a clear anti-egalitarian stance was a pivotal moment for the sociology of education, since it forced the discipline onto the defensive (Arnot and Barton, 1992). In this new context, it became important to conceptualise the role of the state in relation to gender relations. Education feminists were able to contribute (although they were not often given full recognition for their contribution) a gender perspective to the emerging sociology of the state. Chapters 8, 9 and 10 highlight the changing role of the UK government in the 1980s and 1990s in relation to gender and the lessons to be learned from feminist encounters with state action. In these chapters, it is possible to see the complex processes of change involved in what appeared to be the 'modernising' of gender relations – processes which engaged in an elaborate interaction between, on the one hand, the state regulation of gender and, on the other, feminist educational politics engaging the state. Making sense of the work of teachers, government and, latterly, media discourses became the main focus of much feminist educational debate – a debate heavily shaped by its parochial/national concerns.

Post-structuralist and post-modernist feminists also redefined the political terrain in the late 1980s and early 1990s. This feminist work drew heavily on Foucault (1970, 1979) – for example, see Davies (1989, 1993), Walkerdine (1990) and Dillabough and Arnot (2001) for a discussion of this tradition. Reflecting the social fragmentation of society under the New Right, the uneven effects of economic restructuring on women's and men's position, and the individualising/personalising consequences of globalising economies, feminist theory challenged the modernist categories of social class, gender and race. 'Changing of the subject' involved the deconstruction of policy regimes and discourses by highlighting the complexity involved in the formation of identities, subjectivities and performance. My focus in Chapters 8 and 9 on policy discourses and the discursive framing of youth identities reflects such interests.

By the end of the 1990s, a new Labour government under Tony Blair was voted into office. While sustaining both the economic and educational policies of the New Right, including the marketisation of schools and the standardisation of pupil performance, the new government set about redefining the political agenda to include a concern for poverty, social inclusion and social inequalities. Sociologists of education started to return to structural/materialist frameworks in order to offer more complex understandings of why patterns of social inequalities remained intact despite the shifting, more fluid nature of late modernity. Chapters 10 to 12 reflect this recent search for theoretical frameworks which can offer a structural/materialist analysis of education and the cautious return to social and cultural reproduction theories of the 1970s. Below

I describe in more detail my own contribution in response to these political and theoretical developments.

Social and cultural reproduction theory

By the mid-1970s, sociologists of education challenged liberalism and particularly the social democratic educational reforms of the post-war period for their failure to reduce social class inequality. Not only were social class patterns of educational achievement, especially unequal access to higher education, shown to be maintained (Halsey, Heath and Ridge, 1980; Goldthorpe et al., 1980), but patterns of class privilege were increasingly being connected to the organisation of schooling. The structure of the curriculum, the selection of educational knowledge and the ideologies of teaching, learning and assessment were identified as important contributors to such patterns of social class reproduction.

The major themes of what was called the 'new' sociology of education were expressed in the language of power, of social control and even of domination and oppression. Sociological analyses investigated the political framework of schooling by exploring the relationships between, for example, education, the economy and the state. Similarly, the sociology of culture (whether of the curriculum or of youth cultures) focused attention on the role of class cultures, especially the contribution which cultural conflict played in class struggle. At the heart of these studies lay the task of moving away from the 'naive possibilitarianism' (Whitty, 1974) of sociological analyses which failed to take account of the impact of the social structure on the form and content of school experiences. Arguments were put forward that schooling might, in effect, be unable to deliver even such limited goals as promoting equality of opportunity, especially if schools were designed precisely to maintain social inequalities in the interests of the dominant social classes or 'capital'. Debates concerning the nature of the relationship between the power structure and education ranged from stressing, at one extreme, the determining force of the economy or, alternatively, proposing the relative or even 'delegated' autonomy of schooling (Bourdieu and Passeron, 1977; Hall, 1981).

Such critiques were highly controversial, not least because of the references to the 'hidden' and even 'unconscious' structuring of the educational system. Critical sociologists wanted to delve beneath the taken-for-granted reality of schooling, to go behind the detail of student–teacher interaction in the classroom in order to uncover the class-based ideologies of intelligence and the legitimation of particular class cultural styles of teaching and learning. Behind such everyday practices, it was assumed that deeper 'codes' or principles (Bernstein, 1977; Bourdieu and Passeron, 1977) which governed the organisation of schooling could be found. The goal was to discover whether a connection existed between such educational principles (and the ideologies which sustained them) and the principles and ideologies governing economic production and class relations. Whether structurally or culturally, education was analysed as a major site for the 'reproduction' of the class structure and its unequal relations of power. Theories of social and cultural reproduction attempted, in their different ways, to relate the structure of society to the principles which governed collective and individual action or, put another way, to link a material analysis of the political economy to forms of class consciousness, ideology and practice.

In 1977, I contributed to this debate in a critical exposition of the work of social and cultural reproduction theorists for the infamous Open University course *Schooling and Society* (MacDonald, 1977). I reported the conceptual understandings of, for example, Marx and Engels (1970), Gramsci (1971), Althusser (1971), Freire (1972) and Durkheim (1964) alongside the work of social reproduction theorists such as Bowles and Gintis (1976) and cultural reproduction theorists such as Bernstein (1977) and Bourdieu and Passeron (1977). This review taught me that:

> The assumption underlying most of the 'reproduction' theories is that education plays a mediating role between the individual's consciousness and society at large. ... The individual acquires a particular awareness and perception of the society in which he [she] lives. And it is this understanding and attitude towards the social order which constitutes his [her] consciousness. ... The different emphases placed ... on social order or social change, on macro levels or micro processes, on structural or interactional features, derive from a variety of conceptions of the ability or inability of individuals and social classes to act in and upon the social world. In the context of educational strategies for change, these [reproduction] theories have different implications, for in each a particular relationship between schooling and society is postulated.
>
> (MacDonald, 1977, p. 60)

However, it was never clear whether such theories could account for the maintenance of the status quo as well as adequately identify the various forms of contradictions, struggle and conflict to be found within any social institution or social formation. What indeed were the origins of alternative ideologies, of counter-hegemonies or even of 'dominated' cultures? Clearly the critical analysis of schooling would have to examine the broader political relations surrounding schooling. In 1981, like a number of others (e.g., Hall, 1981; Johnson, 1981), I had turned to the work of Gramsci to break away from the pessimism of early versions of reproduction theory. I took the view that:

> While most [reproduction] theorists argue that situations of conflict and negotiation exist, they tend not to identify the ways in which such situations are catered for and responded to within education. ... If it is accepted that education provides the stake and site of class struggle, then any educational theory must surely be concerned to identify how ... class struggle is resolved in different historical periods ... . Perhaps with such an analysis we may become aware of the consistency of contradictions and the exceptional

> *occurrences of social equilibrium* … . [This would] mean developing an understanding of how stability occurs despite conflict, how order is maintained over and above the force for change. Any system of reproduction in so far as it operates within a cultural hegemony must be struggled for, won and maintained in the context of opposition.
>
> (MacDonald, 1981, pp. 103–4)

Without such concerns for social conflict and change, theories of social or cultural reproduction were vulnerable to the charge of excessive functionalism and of economic determinism, of setting up a far too simple and mono-causal account of schooling. The development of the sociology of youth cultures and the sociology of the school offered data about school life that could not easily fit into reproduction theory. Cultural production – the formation of cultural identities, sub-group cultures and cultural mediations of power – was established as part of that critical sociological agenda. Youth cultural studies also revealed the diversity of school experiences, some of which were hard to squeeze into the simple dichotomies of white, male, middle- and working-class cultures. Furthermore, ethnographic work offered insights into the ways in which schools produce social relations. The relationships, therefore, between macro-structures and micro-processes were clearly more complicated and contradictory than those assumed by early versions of class reproduction theory. Similarly, more complex reproduction theory was generating new questions about the production of meanings and the structuring processes involved in the curriculum (for an overview see, for example, Arnot and Whitty, 1982).

Other challenges to class reproduction theory were also being mounted outside the boundaries of sociology of education which, in terms of gender relations, were to have direct significance. In 1966, Juliet Mitchell (1966) had identified a range of functions which the family, and particularly women in the family, played in reproducing the social relations of production and the work force. Three years later, the Marxist feminist Margaret Benston argued that 'women as a group have a definite relation to the means of production and that this is different from that of men' (Benston, 1969, p. 118). The difficulty of explaining women's unpaid domestic labour and its relationship to capital became the key theme of what was called the 'domestic labour debate' (MacDonald, 1981). Underlying this debate was an attempt to identify the specifics of women's position in the class structure and, at the same time, to develop a Marxist theory of social class that abandoned its male biases.

The problem of relating class to gender or, put another way, of Marxism to feminism initially received considerable attention. Such debates, although never resolved, had significance for educational theories structured around concepts of social class and class relations. The time was ripe for reconsidering the gendered assumptions behind class reproduction theory in education. And one of the ways of reconsidering such assumptions was through a critical analysis of existing male theories of schooling. Such theories could not account adequately for the patterns of female education and address female concerns in education. However, if the role of gender as an organising principle of social hierarchy and social inequalities was to be fully understood, it required more than the study of the experience of one sex in isolation from the other. In 1980, a theory of gender relations in education was needed that could deliver a sophisticated account of schooling equivalent to that provided by social class theorists (Connell, 1987). Such a theory would analyse the gendered nature of the contexts, structures and micro-processes of schooling, as well as offer conceptual understanding of feminist educational theorisation and the discursive framing of feminist political agendas.

The articles reprinted here demonstrate how I analysed the interconnections and the contradictions between patriarchy and capitalism, as two power structures, within schooling. I analysed the ways in which the structure and culture of schooling was shaped by both sets of social relations. In tackling this project I was well aware that gender or 'race' could not just be 'added onto' class analysis, without becoming guilty of what O'Brien (1984) called 'commatisation' (the process of listing class comma gender comma race) – in other words, the failure to investigate the relationship between these three sets of relations. Some re-evaluation of the concept of social class was clearly necessary. This was made easier by the wealth of new data on the patterns of male and female employment, the structure of the labour market, patterns of social mobility, theories of the family and the history of the housewife. My contribution to these theoretical discussions was to put forward the concept of gender codes.

Gender code theory

Chapter 2 represents my first attempt to define a theory of gender and class relations. Using the insights of feminist theorists such as Veronica Beechey (1978) and Heidi Hartman (1979), I differentiated between the material bases of patriarchy and capitalism, and emphasised the historical specificity rather than universal nature of gender relations. It was important to explore the potential contradictions that might arise between these two separate relations.

> The contradictory nature of women's position in society, rather than being resolved through schooling is more likely to be accentuated …
>
> (MacDonald, 1980, p. 25)

The correspondence principle advocated by Bowles and Gintis (1976) could not offer the subtlety of insight needed to understand the cultural and symbolic processes of schooling, nor indeed the forms of cultural/political engagements of youth with such hegemonising practices. Bernstein's theory, in contrast, focused attention on the ways in which symbolic relations of schooling are shaped by the selection and organisation of knowledge and its forms of transmission. Chapter 2 adopts this approach by establishing the concept of a 'gender code' as the mode of transmission of gender relations through school knowledge/pedagogic structures. Derived from Bernstein's concept of educational codes, the concept of gender codes distinguished between the principles of *gender classification* (similar to Bronwyn Davies' (1989) concept of gender dualism) which reflected gender power relations and the gendered *framing* of classroom interaction in which students learnt the extent to which they could negotiate gender identities. The effect of the gender code transmitted through the structures and processes of schooling would be found in the formation of an individual's gender identity, experience and property.

The concept of the gender code was greatly enriched by the cultural theory of Pierre Bourdieu. I was already familiar with Bourdieu and Passeron's theory of habitus, cultural capital and cultural reproduction through education (MacDonald, 1977). Chapter 3 demonstrates how Bourdieu (1977), in *Outline of a Theory of Practice*, recognised the role of gender relations in shaping primary and secondary pedagogic contexts and, at a deeper level, individual habits of thought, customs and practice (habitus). In contrast with most sociologists of education who had focused almost exclusively on secondary education as the transit point for entry into paid employment, Bourdieu's analysis of the Kayble society in Algeria provided a salutary reminder of the importance of not neglecting informal education, especially 'domestic pedagogic work' which is usually performed by women in the family. Recent work on mothering provides ample evidence of the significance of female child-rearing practices for social identities (Steedman, 1987, 1988; New and David, 1985; Walkerdine and Lucey, 1989; Davies, 1993; Reay, 1998).

Sexual identities were also signalled in Bourdieu's theory – suggesting that key to any analysis of gender was both the sexual division of labour and the division of sexual labour (i.e., biological reproduction). At that point in time, work on sexual identity was largely underdeveloped, especially within sociology of education. The concept of 'gender' in the 1970s and early 1980s seemed to encapsulate all 'sexed' subjectivities and experiences. Little use was made of psychoanalytic theories in the study of education in contrast to media studies, feminist film and art history. It took authors such as Nancy Chodorow (1978, 1979) and Bob Connell (1983, 1987) to apply such theories to notions of gender 'socialisation'. Second, Bourdieu's concepts of *body hexis* and the 'domestication of the body', described in Chapter 3, also pre-dated the later attention that was given to bodily representations of gender. The concept of *body hexis* captured nicely the relationship between social subjectivity and biological presence – a relationship later explored independently by Connell (1983) in the context of masculinity, but more recently by others in the field (see Mac an Ghaill, 1994, 1996; Connolly, 1998; Epstein and Johnson, 1998; Middleton, 1998). Third, Bourdieu's theory of the processes of cultural reproduction also offered important conceptual insights for the sociology of the curriculum. His notion of the 'dialectics between objectification and embodiment' offered a new perspective on the relationship between structure and agency which took account of a learned physical presence, not merely the process of acquiring the principles for the organisation of work nor, indeed, just the acceptance of gendered expectations and conventions. By bringing Bourdieu's work into gender and education studies, I hoped to stress the importance of a structural (rather than attitudinal) theory of gender socialisation.

Chapter 4 represents my first attempt to consider the role of the curriculum in relation to the concept of gender codes and the formation of class and gender identities. I used this opportunity to think through the implications of Bourdieu's and Bernstein's theories of culture in the context of the secondary school curriculum with its structural divisions, its gendered images of specific subjects and its ideological content. Remembering Bourdieu's notions of *internalisation* and *externalisation*, I noted the following processes:

> The transference of femininity, for example, from the student to the school subject and back again to the student exemplifies the process of objectification and embodiment.
>
> (MacDonald, 1980, p. 37)

The process of *gender attribution* described in this article seemed to relate closely to Bernstein's notion of *recontextualisation* whereby familial or community values were introduced and reshaped by schooling. Here family-based concepts of masculinity and femininity were recontextualised into specific academic subjects/disciplines that were thought appropriate for each gender. This concept allowed for the fact that the forms of femininity and masculinity generated in the school (i.e., pedagogic gender identities) could differ from family- and community-generated identities. The *recontextualisation of gender* could be described as the ways in which the notions of appropriate behaviour for each sex are converted into appropriate academic disciplines. Thus the representation of different masculinities and femininities in school texts and curriculum subjects could be understood not as part of any behaviourist model of attitude socialisation but rather as important aspects of the much more complex processes of gender identity formation. Arguing strongly against a notion that gender identity is unitary and fixed, I highlighted the contradictions and tensions at the heart of processes of identification.

Gender code theory could also help interpret the role of different types of school as sites for the transmission of social relations. In the UK, public controversy surrounding co-education and the arguments for single-sex education in the mid-1980s fascinated me. From the work of, for example, Lavigeur (1980) and Shaw (1976, 1980), one could see that co-education provided a particularly important example of how class and gender relations dovetailed together historically. It offered, therefore, a fascinating case study to consider the changing modes of class and gender transmission and reproduction. Shaw (1980) had argued that mixed schools were more likely to maintain the distinctiveness, the boundaries and the polarisation between the sexes – a view that resonated with the structuring principles associated with gender codes. In Chapter 5, I set the co-educational debate in its historical context and identify the different ways gender relations might have been transmitted to members of different social classes through mixed and single-sex schools. I took the view that the 'sex structure' of the school was significant not because one was more 'liberating' than another, but because different types of school represented different ways of transmitting gender relations. Here, I drew inspiration from Bernstein's (1977) concept of *modalities of transmission* as the key to such differences in educational provision for working-class and middle-class pupils. Such historical research challenged the assumptions concerning the communality of women's experiences. Like post-structuralists later, I argued that the apparent *unity* of women's experiences (upon which radical feminist analysis based their critique of co-educational schools) was premised on the 'myth of female classlessness' (Bernstein's (1996) concept of a 'mythological discourse' would have been relevant here).

One of the conclusions I reached in my analysis of the co-educational debate was that: 'a separate strategy for one sex does not, in my view, challenge the overall reproduction of dominant gender relations' (Arnot, 1983a, p. 87). The consequences of co-education for boys was until recently a lost dimension of feminist analysis. It was somewhat contentious to raise the problem of boys' education when the women's movement had defined itself as struggles *for* and *about* women. Although many sociological studies of schooling had concentrated on boys' education (almost to the exclusion of girls), surprisingly there were, at that time, few studies of masculinity as a gender form. Similarly the men's movement had not had the same impact as that found in the United States, with the result that 'men's studies' had not developed in any substantial way in Britain. I recognised that there was no coherent theory of masculinity except in so far as it pointed to male psychological difficulties in being the 'oppressors' or in being especially exploited by capitalism as the primary wage earner in the family (Arnot, 1983b). The concept of gender codes suggested that feminist analyses should focus on how boys might be taught the structural divisions between public/private, family/work and male/female worlds. I later explored whether boys have a different relationship to these divisions compared with girls (ibid.).

In the mid-1980s, critics argued that gender code theory needed to develop a concept of male power (Mahony, 1985; Yates, 1987). Here Gramsci's theory of class hegemony appeared to have most potential, especially since it drew attention to the historical specificity of power relations and their complexity. The concept of *hegemony* discussed in Chapter 6 suggested that the conditions for such a congruence of class and gender relations in education were provided by a bourgeois hegemony – that is, the cultural domination of the working classes by the bourgeoisie, who attempted

> to gain the consent of women to a definition of femininity which locates their primary role as keepers of the home with only secondary involvement in waged work. Also the consent of men has to be won to a definition of masculinity which involves their leaving their homes to go out to work and to be responsible for the family income.
>
> (MacDonald, 1981, p. 31)

The notion of *male hegemony* within the concept of gender codes opened up the theory of educational transmission to the possibilities of both the production, not just the reproduction, of gender differences and the possibilities of challenges. Gender code theory needed to recognise the active nature of learning and the points at which gender conflict and power struggles could occur. Not only were girls and women to be understood as actors within their own socialisation but it was possible to theorise contestations over dominant gender definitions which would generate competing gender codes (or codings). Bernstein's work again provided the timely reminder that the 'recognition of principles does not determine the realisation (i.e. practice), it can only set limits on it' (Bernstein, 1977, p. 155). The concepts of bourgeois and male hegemony made it possible to conceptualise the creation of alternative principles, or counter-hegemony.[1] In the event, the late 1980s and 1990s saw precisely the development of counter-hegemonic notions of femininity and challenges to male hegemonic control of women (see Chapters 8 and 9).

Gender code theory also needed to address the relationship beween the family and school. In Chapter 7, I argued that the conceptual dichotomies between, for example, private/public, between family/work and their association with male/female divisions which had framed sociological discourse, were particularly evident in the political economy approach in sociology and its privileging of male spheres. As a result of using such classifications, the educational, family and work experiences of women and male private lives were excluded from a male-centred framework which almost exclusively concentrated on the public lives of men, especially in paid employment. Although Bernstein and Bourdieu separately had signalled the significance of the family as a depository of language, culture, identity and dispositions, they had not explored in any depth the critical distance they saw between the specific cultural identities and experiences within the family and those found within schooling.

The highly influential study *Making the Difference* (Connell et al., 1982) bore close resemblance to my thinking. Where I was developing concepts of bourgeois and male hegemony and gender codes, these authors described the 'hegemonising practices' of the school and 'gender regimes'. So similar were our concepts that some sociologists have collapsed the two sets together (Acker, 1987). In many ways, we were addressing what Bourdieu (1993) called 'institutional habitus' of schools from a gender perspective. The portrayal in this Australian research of the mediated relationship between the family and the school strengthened the analysis of primary and secondary pedagogic work (Chapter 3) and the recontextualisation of gender (Chapter 4). In Chapter 7, I returned to these themes to think about 'gendered practices' in family–school relationships – this time considering the need of individuals to use particular concepts of masculinity and femininity that *work in practice* in the context of class membership. I argued that such gendered practices (which were not far from the concepts of gender performativity developed later by Walkerdine (1990) and Butler (1990)) were developed within social and material constraints and were the forms of expression of particular sets of social relations. It was these practices that were recontextualised in the school. The school's definitions of gender practices, therefore, might be constantly in tension with those of students' families, and students would have to act as 'go-betweens'.

If patriarchal relations were to be considered seriously, then the possibilities of the family shaping the structure of schooling (especially early education) and the adult destinations of both boys and girls also had to be built into the analysis. Later, Steedman (1987, 1988), Walkerdine and Lucey (1989) and others were to show the strong links between mothering and teaching and the construction of the teacher as 'othermothers' (Foster, 1993). More recently, as school competition and parental choice became part of the government reform programme, sociologists highlighted the significance of family gender values (for parents and children) as mediators of class and race patterns of education (Carby, 1982; Phoenix, 1987; Mirza, 1992; David, West and Ribbens, 1994; Reay, 1998). This break with economic determinism and its overriding interest in the transition from school to work represented another important shift away from the model of social reproduction developed in the 1970s. Reintegrating family culture into the analysis of schooling allowed for the possibility of exploring gender identities and aspirations created in different class-based and ethnic family cultures.

By the late 1980s, however, the analysis of gender transmission was seriously disrupted by major interventions of the state in education. At first, the significance of UK government reforms of the curriculum and organisational reforms for gender relations was not clear. Weiner (1993) described a 'shell-shocked sisterhood' which had not anticipated the power of the state in restructuring social relations in other than egalitarian ways. It was unclear initially how and whether gender relations would be reinforced, interrupted or reformed by government educational restructuring. From a sociological perspective, the new political agenda suggested that what was needed was a theoretical reconceptualisation of the relationship between schooling and society that could take account of the interface (both material and discursive) between gender politics and the state.

New gender codes: gender politics, gender relations and the state

Education feminism in the UK was, to some extent, a grassroots movement which challenged both the central and local state to reform schooling and thus gender relations (Weiner and Arnot, 1987). By the end of the 1980s, women's studies emphasised the need to analyse the role of the state in order to understand fully women's oppression. It was unclear what the intervention of the state meant in this area. Earlier I had asked:

> Does state policy represent capital's interests *and* those of men, or does the state attempt to reconcile the interests of both? Or is the state an independent actor and arbiter in the conflict between the demands of the economy

> for female wage labour (albeit at low cost), on the one hand, and the expectations of men for their unpaid 'servicing' by womenfolk in the home, on the other? Alternatively, is the state a progressive force in so far as it can attempt to break down the more blatant aspects of sexual inequalities? … there is still much more work to be done in accounting for the ideology and practice of the state in defining women's education.
>
> (MacDonald, 1981, p. 94)

The expansion of state education meant more education for girls, even if the nature and content narrowed their horizons or did not compare favourably with the education provided for boys. At the same time, the state education system had attempted to maintain the sexual division of labour and class and race inequalities through educational provision (Arnot, 1985, 1986a, 1986b). Yet male-centred policy analysis had failed to offer a viable sociological theory as far as state action was concerned. It neglected to address feminist policy analysis of the patriarchal basis to the welfare state (and arguably also the analysis of the racialised state (Troyna and Williams, 1986; Troyna and Carrington, 1990)). The role of women, too, as policy-makers, whether as teachers, adminstrators or as members of key government agencies, tended not to be taken into account. Unlike Australia where educational feminists had become 'femocrats' working with state bureaucracies, women in the UK were represented by their absence in policy-making. Hence not only was the significance of policy change for gender relations ignored within analysis of capitalism but so too were the forms of political activism associated with feminism and the women's movement in advanced industrial societies in the late twentieth century.

Feminist educational programmes had encouraged reformist state policies and direct intervention into the social relations of schooling. However, the new model of the state in education represented by Margaret Thatcher's government, although strongly interventionist, was hostile to the notion of egalitarianism. The challenge for sociologists was to be able to develop theoretical frameworks which could grasp the historical continuities and transformations associated with New Right education reforms. Chapters 8, 9 and 10 in this volume represent attempts to use gender code theory to explore the significance, intentions and effects of the new policy regimes of the 1980s and 1990s. In a sequence of articles (Arnot, 1986b, 1989, 1989–90; Arnot and Blair, 1993), I tentatively explored, from the point of view of both gender and race, the conflicts between centralisation and local autonomy, between compulsion or freedom of choice, between universalism and positive discrimination. Such dimensions were important in differentiating particular national responses to egalitarian reforms. I also focused attention on the counter-hegemonic struggles (Weiler, 1987) of feminist teachers and academics, which provided fascinating insights into the role of the state in education. Looking back to the 1980s, an era of considerable feminist political pressure on government, it was possible to see feminist attempts to win power for women either by degendering strategies (reducing the strength of gender classification) or by weakening the framing – allowing girls more opportunity to negotiate their identities. At the same time, under the New Right, the state was actively strengthening knowledge boundaries and more tightly controlling pedagogic transmission.

Chapters 8 and 9 offer a sociological perspective on attempts to transform the gender codes of schooling both from the perspective of the women's movement and the state. Chapter 8, for example, highlights the significance of gender relations as *integral* to New Right political discourses. The restructuring of gender relations (new gender codes) was part of the transformation of the social order. The chapter shows that the Conservative government's attempts to restore Victorian values in family life had been a response to challenges to such values, but these attempts were overridden by the state's commitment to monetarist and laissez-faire economic policies. Thus, paradoxically, while there was a reassertion of traditional class-based male values, the possessive individualism which was nurtured in this era of reform was to have considerable impact on girls' education. Chapter 8 argues, rather controversially, that a 'crisis in patriarchy' (a hegemonic crisis) not just a crisis in capitalism was one of the major reasons for the development of New Right education politics. Feminist educational politics had been highly significant in unsettling the patriarchal relations which were part of the social fabric.

The contradictions within each historical period are especially significant for any theory of social change – contradictions especially between official 'mythologising discourses' and the realities of educational inequalities. Gaby Weiner, Miriam David and I developed this theme in *Closing the Gender Gap* (Arnot, David and Weiner, 1999) where we discussed the complex ambitions of welfarism, the personal and political conflicts of Margarat Thatcher, and the highly significant but often unintended effects of a range of government policies which disrupted and reformed gender relations in the late twentieth century. A sociological interpretation of the consequences for the reproduction of gender relations of the shift in gender performance patterns in the UK is offered in Chapter 9. The redistribution of educational credentials at the same time as the retention of male-centred knowledge structures and dominance suggested a complex interaction between transformed educational and gender codes.

Bernstein (1996) argued that schooling could create both retrospective and prospective identities. Strong gender classifications as an organising principle had been challenged by feminists who, arguably, put forward what I called 'integrative gender codes' which were prospective in nature. The principles underlying the modified gender code involved the weakening of gender boundaries and identities within compulsory education (−C) and greater opportunities for negotiated gender identities (−F). Male–female relations were to be reframed in ways that undermined the legitimacy of male control over women's lives. However, as I argue in Chapter 8, these ideals were mediated by the strengthening of male-centred forms of knowledge and pedagogic modes which sustained elite (predominantly white) male educational advantage. The complex effects of such restructuring were to be found in the differentiated gender patterns in compulsory and post-compulsory schooling.

Social class and race inequalities are still as significant in contemporary social formations. The transformation of class and ethnic relations represented by new policy climates was central to our book *Closing the Gender Gap* (Arnot, David and Weiner, 1999) where we explored changes in male and female patterns of schooling in specific groups. In Chapter 10, which was written to commemorate the twenty-fifth anniversary of the publication of *Schooling in Capitalist America* (Bowles and Gintis, 1976), I argue that the political economy approach represented in this seminal text had rightly grounded the study of education in the economy. However, it had failed to explore the ways in which *intra-class* relations (such as gender or race) could become the site of social change. Despite improvements in the number of qualifications achieved, despite massive reforms of the school system in the name of standards and despite more recent attempts at alleviating the effects of poverty, poor schools and declining communities, class divisions are still extensive and destructive of the opportunities for working-class youth. By drawing on contemporary youth cultural studies, I argue that the modality of gender reproduction has now changed. Class distinctions and identities appear to have reinforced or reworked the traditional identities of boys, while girls in different class positions have negotiated economic and family change and the school equality reform movements by identifying with the processes of individualisation (described, for example, by Ulrich Beck (1992)). I argue that, while the reproduction of working-class girls' class position through education remains indirect (although now through the discourses of feminism and individualisation), the reproduction of upper middle-class girls is now direct.

The reform of gender relations within the last twenty-five years traced through these chapters demonstrates a complex story of social continuity and social change, with class patterns being reproduced and gender patterns within those class patterns being transformed both discursively and materially.

Retheorising gender

The theoretical and methodological premises of social and cultural reproduction theory are rationalistic and more often than not structural. Developing a theory of gender within such a framework inevitably has its limitation. As Jo-Anne Dillabough and I argued, such rationalistic theories

> explained women's oppression on the basis of the authority of reason or on a corresponding theory of rationalism which ultimately reaffirmed the gender binary (i.e. male power over women) in educational thought. Rationalist approaches either charted linear relationships between, on the one hand, individual behaviours (e.g. gender roles, female characteristics) and women's oppression or, on the other hand, female marginality and what were often described as 'rationally' organised and deliberately controlled social structures (e.g. state or the market).
>
> (Dillabough and Arnot, 2001, p. 33)

Some of these rationalistic theories developed what Connell (1987) described as *intrinsic explanations*, since they tried to explain gender differences by referring to the intrinsic qualities of individuals (e.g., self-esteem or sex differences). In contrast, *extrinsic* versions of rationalistic theories such as my own early work tend to focus on the social basis of power relations in the polity. State structures, relations of production and the public sphere all figure in the manner in which gender is understood in education from an extrinsic perspective.

These essentially modernist explanations of women's education or gender relations were seriously challenged by the development of post-structuralist and later post-modernist sociological and social-psychological accounts of gender identities. By the mid-1980s, the fragmentation of the movement was considerable (Rowbotham, Segal and Wainwright, 1979; Segal, 1987, 1989; Weiner, 1994). Education feminisms had been seriously affected by tensions between different perspectives, as well as challenged by the emergent post-structuralist approaches. There was much debate about whether the category 'girl' could and should be sustained in feminist academic and political work (Middleton, 1998; Lather, 1992). The 'umbrella' (Acker, 1987) of equality of opportunity which sheltered stronger egalitarian approaches (Weiner and Arnot, 1987; Arnot, David and Weiner, 1999) was replaced by the new politics of identity and concerns about the framing of racialised feminist discourses which had constructed black women and girls as 'other' (e.g., Amos and Parmar, 1981; Carby, 1982; Bryan, Dadzie and Scafe, 1985; Brah and Minhas, 1985; Mirza, 1992). In this tradition, black feminists challenged the dominance of rationalistic theorising in education which they perceived to be eurocentric and ethnocentric. Black women were found to inhabit 'other worlds' in which their desire for inclusion is strategic, subversive and ultimately far more transformative than reproduction theory suggests (Mirza and Reay, 2000).

Influenced greatly by Foucauldian theory (Foucault, 1970, 1979), the *relational* conceptual frameworks put forward in the 1990s serve to:

> break down theoretical foundations and particular sets of power relations which lead to 'local' understandings of gender in education. They also attempt to capture the fluid nature of gender as a temporality which is embedded in the power of language rather than merely charting universal laws about women's experience in the broadest sense.
>
> (Dillabough and Arnot, 2001, p. 33)

By the end of the twentieth century, feminist studies of education had extended its theoretical terrain and its concerns. At the same time, it has not necessarily formulated what Bernstein called a *generative theory* that could move from the particular to the general. There is still a need to develop not just an internal language of description which can adequately account for events at the micro- and macro-levels, but an external language of description that can then frame hypothesis and research questions. Such a generative theory would give feminism a more epistemologically powerful 'vertical' knowledge structure which would allow knowledge to become more scientific, more cumulative and hence less reliant on the forms of knowledge generated through segmental voices in society. In Chapter 11, I return to reconsider the theoretical possibilities of Bernstein's sociology of pedagogy and the basic tenets of his theory of educational transmission for the study of gender, revisiting the concept of gender code, the nature of female pedagogic work and the gendering of pedagogic discourses. By asking leading female Bernsteinian scholars about the significance of his theory for their work, I was also able to discover how others conceptualise his contribution to the study of gender relations in education and society. These intellectual engagements (including my own) and the nature of the agenda show how Bernstein theorised the pedagogic forms associated with gender relations, the role of feminism as a knowledge structure and the role of education in creating new social identities. Yet again I saw the power of his theoretical project in delving systematically and analytically into the nature of the social and symbolic order, the production and transmission of knowledge, and political struggles for the control over social identities and relations. Again, I was reminded of the ways in which education represents the transmission of elaborated codes of the middle classes and the role which a new transformed education might play in the reproduction of social inequalities.

The collection of articles concludes with my own perspective on the challenges which face the women's movement in the new century. In Chapter 12, I argue that a new egalitarianism will emerge which involves the micro-inequalities of gender, class and ethnicity, and which is framed within the language of flexibilisation, individualisation and social fluidity. While some will hold on to traditional identities, others will take advantage of opportunities to break with the past. The worlds of men and women appear to be spiralling away from each other with major consequences for gender relations in the public and private spheres. Drawing on the insights of Ulrich Beck, I argue that sociologists of education might need to focus more systematically the new social conditions of a globalised world and the new political conditions which are likely to be developed.

Summary

Sociological theory of gender in education has moved a long way since the 1970s. There are now far more sophisticated understandings of differentiated gender identities and complex interconnections with social class, ethnicity and sexuality. The development of deconstructional feminisms such as post-structural and post-modern feminism has provided sociologists concerned with gender with both the methodological incentive and the theoretical spur to consider its own discursive framing. Sociological theorising, therefore, has had to engage with the limitations of its own 'master' narratives (Lather, 1992). However, the processes of critical reflection should not necessarily lead to the abandonment of some of the central concerns of the discipline which provide it with its rationale and focus. Earlier I argued that this rationale was a commitment to understand the underlying continuities in social order and the nature and significance of changes in the social structure.

My contribution within the field of sociology of education has been to interpret the role which gender relations play within society, both as forces of stability and disruption. In the 1970s, my concerns were, like those of many other feminist sociologists, to understand how gender relations were reproduced by schooling to the extent that the patterns of sex segregation in the labour market and the domestic divisions of labour remained largely intact over periods of considerable economic change. Understanding the role of the state in these processes became a project in itself, not least because of the women's movement's attempt to transform state modes of regulation and to use its potential in promoting more equitable sets of gender relations in society at large. The extent to which such a movement for social reform succeeded is most clearly seen in the extent of the backlash, with its concerns for establishing male advantage rather than promoting greater equality.

Feminist sociologists of education in the last thirty years have been caught up in the demands that they must generate 'grand theory' on a scale equivalent to the master narratives of the discipline and at the same time they have been encouraged to engage actively with the needs and insights of practitioner worlds and to help 'give voice' to those girls and young women who were historically silenced by the social system which shaped their lives. Sociological studies of gender and education have also had to chart a difficult course in relation to liberal democratic and socialist thought and feminist political discourses. In this book, I have indicated the route that I have taken through such conflicting and ambitious demands. It has been a route which has given me privileged access to the extensive research of feminist educationalists, policy-makers, teachers and students. Feminist sociologists have struggled against their marginalisation by the parent discipline, but at the same time they have always had a guaranteed audience. Gender identities, after all, are at the heart of the social formation. And it is this centrality which guarantees the future of gender education theory and feminist politics.

Notes

1 The usefulness of the concept of male hegemony in education can be seen most clearly in Weiler's (1987) research on women teachers working for a change. Here, she uses the concept to explain teachers' struggles to set up a counter-hegemony through feminist practice. Similarly Acker (1989, p. 310), in her study of British teachers and feminist politics, uses the concept of hegemony to ask 'how, when and why teachers do challenge the hegemony or conversely why so often they do not'.

References and further reading

Acker, S. (1987) 'Feminist theory and the study of gender and education', *International Review of Education*, 33, 4, pp. 419–35.

—— (1989) *Teachers, Gender and Careers*, Lewes: Falmer Press.

Althusser, L. (1971) 'Ideology and ideological state apparatus', in *Lenin and Philosophy and Other Essays*, London: New Left Books.

Amos, V. and Parmar, P. (1981) 'Resistance and responses: the experiences of black girls in Britain', in A. McRobbie and T. McCabe (eds) *Feminism for Girls*, London: Routledge & Kegan Paul.

Arnot, M. (1983a) 'A cloud over co-education: an analysis of the forms of transmission of class and gender relations', in S. Walker and L. Barton (eds) *Gender, Class and Education*, Lewes: Falmer Press.

—— (1983b) 'How should we educate our sons?', in R. Deem (ed.) *Co-education Reconsidered*, Statonbury: OUEE.

—— (ed.) (1985) *Race and Gender: equal opportunities policies in education*, Oxford: Pergamon Press.

—— (1986a) *Race, Gender and Education Policy Making*, Module 4 E333, Milton Keynes: Open University Press.

—— (1986b) 'State education policy and girls' educational experiences', in V. Beechey and L. Whitelegg (eds) *Women in Britain Today*, Statonbury: OUEE.

—— (1989) 'Crisis or challenge? Equal opportunities and the National Curriculum', *Education Review*, 3, 2, pp. 7–13.

—— (1989–90) 'Consultation or legitimation? Race and gender politics and the making of the National Curriculum', *Journal of Critical Social Policy*, 27, pp. 20–38.

Arnot, M. and Barton, L. (eds) (1992) *Voicing Concerns: sociological perspectives on contemporary education reforms*, Oxford: Triangle Books.

Arnot, M. and Blair, M. (1993) 'Black and anti-racist perspectives on the National Curriculum and government education policy', in A. King and M. Reiss (eds) *The Multicultural Dimension of the National Curriculum*, London: Falmer Press.

Arnot, M. and Whitty, G. (1982) 'From reproduction to transformation: recent radical perspectives on the curriculum from the USA', *British Journal of Sociology of Education*, 3, 1, pp. 93–103.

Arnot, M., David, M. and Weiner, G. (1999) *Closing the Gender Gap: postwar education and social change*, Cambridge: Polity Press.

Arnot, M., Gray, J., James, M. and Rudduck, J. (1998) *A Review of Recent Research on Gender and Educational Performance*, OFSTED Research Series, London: The Stationery Office.

Beck, U. (1992) *Risk Society: toward a new modernity*, London: Sage.

Beechey, V. (1978) 'Women and production: a critical analysis of some sociological theories of women's work', in A. Kuhn and A.M. Wolpe (eds) *Feminism and Materialism*, London: Routledge & Kegan Paul.

Benston, M. (1969) 'The political economy of women's liberation', *Monthly Review*, 21, 4, pp. 13–27.

Bernstein, B. (1977) *Class, Codes and Control*, vol. 3, London: Routledge & Kegan Paul.

—— (1996) *Pedagogy, Symbolic Control and Identity: theory, research, critique*, London: Rowman & Littlefield.

Bourdieu, P. (1977) *Outline of a Theory of Practice*, Cambridge: Cambridge University Press.

—— (1993) *Sociology in Question*, London: Sage.

Bourdieu, P. and Passeron, J.C. (1977) *Reproduction in Education, Society and Culture*, London: Sage.

Bowles, S. and Gintis, H. (1976) *Schooling in Capitalist America: reform and the contradiction of economic life*, London: Routledge & Kegan Paul.

Brah, A. and Minhas, R. (1985) 'Structural racism or cultural difference: schooling for Asian girls', in G. Weiner (ed.) *Just a Bunch of Girls*, Milton Keynes: Open University Press.

Bryan, B., Dadzie, S. and Scafe, S. (1985) *The Heart of the Race: black women's lives in Britain*, London: Virago.

Butler, J. (1990) *Gender Trouble: feminism and the subversion of identity*, New York and London: Routledge.

Carby, H. (1982) 'White women listen! Black feminism and the boundaries of sisterhood', in Centre for Contemporary Cultural Studies (eds) *The Empire Strikes Back*, London: Hutchinson, in association with the CCCS.

Chodorow, N. (1978) *The Reproduction of Mothering*, Berkeley: University of California Press

—— (1979) 'Feminism and difference: gender relations and difference in psychoanalytic perspective', *Socialist Review*, 9, 4, pp. 51–70.

Connell, R.W. (1983) *Which Way is Up? Essays on Class, Sex and Culture*, London: Allen & Unwin.

—— (1987) *Gender and Power: society, the person, and sexual politics*, Melbourne: Allen & Unwin.

Connell, R.W., Ashenden, D.J., Kessler, S. and Dowsett, G.W. (1982) *Making the Difference: schools, families and social division*, London: Allen & Unwin.

Connolly, P. (1998) *Racism, Gender Identities and Young Children. Social Relations in a Multi-ethnic, Inner City Primary School*, London: Routledge.

David, M.E., West, A. and Ribbens, J. (1994) *Mother's Intuition? Choosing secondary schools*, London: Falmer Press.

Davies, B. (1989) 'The discursive production of male/female dualism in school settings', *Oxford Review of Education*, 15, 3, pp. 229–41.

—— (1993) *Frogs and Snails and Feminist Tales*, Sydney: Allen & Unwin.

Dillabough, J. and Arnot, M. (2001) 'Feminist sociology of education: dynamics, debates and directions', in J. Demaine (ed.) *Sociology of Education Today*, London: Palgrave.

Durkheim, E. (1964) *The Division of Labour in Society*, London: Macmillan.

Epstein, D and Johnson, R. (1998) *Schooling Sexualities*, Buckingham: Open University Press.

Feminist Review (1984) *Many Voices One Chant: Black feminist perspectives* 17 (Autumn).

Foster, M. (1993) 'Other mothers: exploring the educational philosophy of black American women teachers', in M. Arnot and K. Weiler (eds) *Feminism and Social Justice in Education: international perspectives*, London: Falmer Press.

Foucault, M. (1970) *The Order of Things: an archaeology of the human sciences*, London: Random House.

—— (1979) *Discipline and Punish: the birth of the prison*, London: Vintage Books.

Freire, P. (1972) *Pedagogy of the Oppressed*, Harmondsworth: Penguin.

Goldthorpe, J.H., with Llewelyn, C. and Payne, C. (1980) *Social Mobility and Class Structure in Modern Britain*, Oxford: Oxford University Press.

Gramsci, A. (1971) *Selections from the Prison Notebooks*, trans. Q. Hoare and G. Nowell Smith, London: Lawrence & Wishart.

Hall, S. (1981) 'Schooling, state and society', in R. Dale, G. Esland, R. Fergusson and M. MacDonald (eds) *Education and the State*, vol. 1, *Schooling and the National Interest*, Lewes: Falmer Press.

Halsey, A., Heath, R. and Ridge, J. (1980) *Origins and Destinations: family, class and education in modern Britain* Oxford: Oxford University Press.

Hartmann, H. (1979) 'The unhappy marriage of Marxism and feminism: towards a more progressive union', *Capital and Class*, 8, pp. 1–33.

Johnson, R. (1981) *Education and Popular Politics*, Unit 1 E353, Milton Keynes: Open University Press.

Lather, P. (1992) *Getting Smart*, London: Routledge.

Lavigeur, J. (1980) 'Coeducation and the tradition of separate needs', in D. Spender and E. Sarah (eds) *Learning to Lose: sexism and education*, London: Women's Press.

Mac an Ghaill, M. (1994) *The Making of Men: masculinities, sexualities and schooling*, Buckingham: Open University Press.

—— (ed.) (1996) *Understanding Masculinities*, Buckingham: Open University Press.

MacDonald, M. (1977) *The Curriculum and Cultural Reproduction*, Units 18/19 E202, Milton Keynes: Open University Press.

—— (1980) 'Socio-cultural reproduction and women's education', in R. Deem (ed.) *Schooling for Women's Work*, London: Routledge & Kegan Paul.

—— (1981) *Class, Gender and Education*, Block 4 E353, Milton Keynes: Open University Press.

Mahony, P. (1985) *Schools for the Boys: coeducation reassessed*, London: Hutchinson.

Marx, K. and Engels, F. (1970) *The German Ideology*, trans. C.J. Arthur, London: Lawrence & Wishart.

Middleton, S. (1998) *Disciplining Sexuality: Foucault, life histories, and education*, New York: Teachers College Press.

Mirza, H. (1992)*Young, Gifted and Female*, London: Routledge.

Mirza, H. and Reay, D. (2000) 'Redefining citizenship: Black women educators and "the third space"', in M. Arnot and J. Dillabough (eds) *Challenging Democracy: International Perspectives on Gender, Gender Education and Citizenship*, London: RoutledgeFalmer.

Mitchell, J. (1966) 'The longest revolution', *New Left Review*, 40 (November–December), pp. 11–37.

New, C. and David, M. (1985) *For the Children's Sake*, Harmondsworth: Penguin.

O'Brien, M. (1984) 'The commatization of women: patriarchal fetishism in the sociology of education', *Interchange*, 5, 15/2, pp. 43–60.

Open University (1976) *Schooling and Society*, E202, Milton Keynes: Open University Press.

Phoenix, A. (1987) 'Theories of gender and black families', in M. Weiner and M. Arnot (eds) *Gender Under Scrutiny*, London: Hutchinson.

Reay, D. (1998) *Class Work: mothers' involvement in their children's schooling*, London: University College Press.

Rowbotham, S., Segal, L. and Wainwright, L. (1979) *Beyond the Fragments: feminism and the making of socialism*, London: Virago.

Segal, L. (1987) *Is the Future Female?*, London: Virago.

—— (1989) 'Slow change or no change? Feminism, socialism and the problem of men', *Feminist Review*, 31 (Spring), pp. 5–21.

Shaw, J. (1976) 'Finishing school – some implications of sex segregated education', in D.L. Boiler and S. Allen (eds) *Sexual Divisions in Society: process and change*, London: Tavistock.

—— (1980) 'Education and the individual: schooling for girls or mixed schooling – a mixed blessing', in R. Deem (ed.) *Schooling for Women's Work*, London: Routledge & Kegan Paul

Spender, D. (1987) 'Education – the patriarchal paradigm and the response to feminism', in M. Arnot and G. Weiner (eds) *Gender and the Politics of Schooling*, London: Hutchinson.

Steedman, C. (1987) 'Prisonhouses', in M. Lawn and G. Grace (eds) *Teachers: the culture and politics of work*, Lewes: Falmer Press.

—— (1988) 'Mother made conscious: The historical development of a primary school pedagogy', repr. in M. Woodhead and A. McGrath (eds) *Family, School and Society*, London: Hodder & Stoughton, in association with the Open University, pp. 82–95.

Troyna, B. and Carrington, B. (1990) *Education, Racism and Reform*, London: Routledge.

Troyna, B. and Williams, J. (1986) *Racism, Education and the State*, London: Croom Helm.

Walkerdine, V. (1990) *Schoolgirl Fictions*, London: Verso.

Walkerdine, V. and Lucey, H. (1989) *Democracy in the Kitchen: regulating mothers and socialising daughters*, London: Virago.

Weiler, K. (1987) *Women Teaching for Change: gender, class and power*, South Hadley: Bergin & Garvey.

Weiner, G. (1993) 'Shell-shock or sisterhood? English school history and feminist practice', in M. Arnot and K. Weiler (eds) *Feminism and Social Justice in Education: international perspectives*, London: Falmer Press.

—— (1994) *Feminisms in Education: an introduction*, Buckingham: Open University Press.

Weiner, G. and Arnot, M. (1987) 'Teachers and gender politics', in M. Arnot and G. Weiner (eds) *Gender and the Politics of Schooling*, London: Hutchinson.

Whitty, G. (1974) 'Sociology and the problem of radical educational change', in M. Flude and J. Ahier (eds) *Educability, School and Ideology*, London: Croom Helm.

Yates, L. (1987) *Curriculum Theory and Non-sexist Education*, unpublished Ph.D. thesis, School of Education, La Trobe University, Australia.

2 Socio-cultural reproduction and women's education

Within a capitalist mode of production, patriarchal relations which are characterised by male–female hierarchy and dominance assume specific historical forms at the economic, political and ideological levels. Even though patriarchal forms of control existed prior to the advent of capitalism, the economic and social subordination of women has, nevertheless, become an integral element of the capitalist social formation. This is not to assume that they constitute an essential ingredient necessary for the survival of that system, but rather to recognise that they figure as one of its central organising principles. In the capitalist economy, patriarchal relations have a specific material base in, for example, the separation of the family from the production process, in the economic dependence of women on men. In this chapter, therefore, I shall attempt to develop an analysis of women's education which relates the form and content of schooling to women's position in such societies. The emphasis will be upon the way in which schooling produces both classed and sexed subjects, who are to take their place in a social division of labour structured by the dual, yet often contradictory, forces of class and gender relations.

Despite the diversity of material and forms of analysis now available for the study of women's education, there is one consistent overriding concern. The essential unity of purpose in this research is the establishment of the sociology of women's education on the academic agenda. The pressure which this research exerts upon existing accounts of schooling takes the form of demanding recognition for the ways in which schooling constructs, modifies and transmits specific definitions of gender and gender relations to each new generation, within and across class boundaries. The challenge inherent in these analyses is to reassess current explanations of schooling which have glossed over or ignored the existence of the sexual division of labour within the school and its impact in determining the relations between the family, schooling and the labour processes.

It is my intention in this chapter to reassess two major bodies of theory, to investigate their limitations and to suggest how they may be reformulated in the light of new evidence. I shall concentrate on what have been called the theories of social reproduction and those of cultural reproduction of the class structure. Within the first tradition I shall focus on the work of Althusser (1971) and of

Bowles and Gintis (1976), within the second on the work of Bernstein (1977 with the aim of using these theories as the basis for an explanatory model of t forms of women's education within societies which are both capitalist and patriarchal.

Schooling and the reproduction of the labour force

In the work of Althusser and Bowles and Gintis, one finds the initial premise that education plays a central, if not critical, role in the reproduction of a capitalist mode of production. As outlined by Althusser, there are essentially two aspects to this process. First, there is the reproduction of productive forces; and, second, perhaps more importantly, there is the reproduction of the social relations of production.

In the analysis of the reproduction of productive forces, Althusser points to the fact that if any social formation is to reproduce itself, it must ensure not merely that its labour force is available in sufficient numbers (through biological reproduction and immigration), but also that it must be diversified, adequately skilled and competent to work within a given social structure. Historically, the reproduction of the work force was provided by 'on the job' training and apprenticeship schemes. Under capitalism, outside institutions, such as the educational system, increasingly have taken over the task of providing workers with basic skills such as literacy and numeracy. Further, the educational system equips future workers with the appropriate attitudes for work, which include acceptance of the rules of good behaviour, 'respect for the socio-technical division of labour and ultimately the rules of the order established by class domination' (Althusser, 1971, p. 127). Individuals, he argues, are placed in a certain relation to the existing social order – relations of 'subjection to the ruling ideology or mastery of its practice' (p. 128).

These parameters may also be found with the analysis of Bowles and Gintis's *Schooling in Capitalist America* (1976). Here they stress the importance of educational structures as selective and allocating devices for the social reproduction of the class structure. The function of school, they argue, is to produce a differentiated, stratified and conforming work force, adjusted in personality and character, equipped with the necessary skills and competencies to work in the socio-economic division of labour.

In analysing the labour force found within the US economy, Bowles and Gintis recognise, under capitalism, the tendencies for the labour market to segment, and point out the segregation of the primary and secondary labour markets. The primary segment they locate predominantly in the corporate and state sectors, where jobs are characterised by relatively high wages, job ladders and opportunities for promotion. Within this segment, there are likely to be high levels of job security and workers' unionisation. In the secondary labour market there are relatively low wages, little workers' unionisation, low levels of job security and little chance of promotion and training. Within this labour market are to be found the most oppressed groups, which in the US are 'blacks',

Puerto Ricans, Chicanos, native Americans, women, the elderly, the young and *other minority groups* (my emphasis, Bowles and Gintis, 1976, p. 67).

By classifying women as yet another minority group, Bowles and Gintis fail to analyse labour market segmentation as one of the most significant features of the integration of the sexual division of labour and in particular of patriarchal power structures within the very nature of the capitalist formation. They thus gloss over the presence of a sex-segregated labour force within and across the binary division of primary and secondary labour markets. Particularly in the US there is a process of 'ghettoization' of the female labour force in the secondary labour market.[1]

Further, there exists a sexual division of labour within each segment, where women are typically employed in jobs that have subsequently been defined as stereotypically 'feminine' occupations, whether it is because of their assumed manual dexterity (e.g., textiles), their domestic interests (food processing, health care, cleaning, etc.) or their vocation in providing personal services (teaching, social work, etc.). What characterises women's location both within and between these different labour markets is their inferior position with regard to wages, training prospects and promotion. Although Bowles and Gintis recognise that capitalism has adapted and utilised pre-existing 'social prejudices' such as racism and sexism, they neglect to give any material basis to what in their analysis appear to be exogenous ideological factors. Any theory of education which seeks to account for the form of schooling in terms of the mode of reproduction of the work force, I would argue, must recognise the structure of male–female dominance relations as integral and not subsidiary organising principles of the work process.

Within this framework, it is essential that we recognise the pattern of specifically female employment as different from that of men. The changing definitions of jobs from 'masculine' to 'feminine' and vice versa are one aspect of the dynamic nature of women's position in society. At one level this is mediated, as shown by Ashton and Maguire (1980), by the attitudes, expectations and ideology of employers, who operate and realise historically specific conceptions of female employees, their abilities and their personalities (diligence, lack of boredom with routine tasks, dexterity).

These conceptions, however, while appearing as an independent variable in the process of employee selection, are core features of the pattern of use of female labour within the economy. As Beechey (1978) has argued, capital acquires certain advantages in the employment of female labour within certain sectors of the labour force. The two major advantages she identifies relate to the dual location of women within the family and the production process. First, when all members of a workman's family are employed, the value of labour power is lowered as the costs of reproduction (e.g., nurturance, household and health care) are spread over all members of the population. Second, the value of female labour is less than that of men since women have less training and are not expected to pay the full costs of the household, as it can be assumed that they will be supported by their menfolk. Women are not expected to bear the costs of their own reproduction, therefore employers may also pay less than the value of female labour, since women are defined as subsidiary workers, financially dependent on men within a patriarchal family.

The hiring of female labour, while it has its advantages, also poses dilemmas for capital, especially in the employment of married women workers. The greater the use of married women in wage labour, the more threatened is the effective performance of their work as domestic labourers within the family. The separation of waged from domestic labour, of production from consumption, of the economy from family life is not merely a facet of the development of capitalism but also constitutes one of the elements of the process of reproduction of that system. Women's services within the family as wife, mother, servant, therapist and so on are critical aspects of the reproduction of the labour force.[2] The tension therefore exists within capitalism in maintaining an appropriate balance between the need for certain types of labour power, on the one hand, and, on the other, the continued functioning of the patriarchal nuclear family, which services and reproduces the labour force outside the production system.

Any account of the relationship between schooling and the structure of the labour force must therefore take into account the differing positions of women and men within the social formation. It must furthermore take heed of the advice that:

> the central feature of women's position under capitalism is not their role simply as domestic workers, but rather the fact that they are *both* domestic and wage labourers. It is this dual and contradictory role that imparts a specific dynamic to their situation.
>
> (Coulson, Magos and Wainwright, 1975, p. 60)

It is important to recognise the existence of class differences operating within the female labour force, which determines not merely the sort of jobs which women are likely to find themselves in, but also their relation to the means of production. Within the working class, women workers bear the same relation to the means of production as working-class men, since they own only their own labour power to sell on the labour market. At the other extreme, women within the capitalist class might well have a different relationship to the means of production than their menfolk. While their fathers and husbands are more likely to own and control capital directly, buying the labour of others, these women may indirectly benefit from and live off the accumulation of family wealth without any necessity to work for an income. With the breaking down of patrilineal inheritance and the rights of women to own independent property, potentially more women of this class can become actively involved in the production process as owners of capital, shareholders and employers. They are still represented in very small numbers in the structures of management and control. For the majority of these women, the relation to the means of production is one of indirect ownership and control. In the professional middle classes, while the men are likely to become the ideologists or the managers of capital, the women, located primarily in the 'caring' professions, may be a major source of what Bernstein (1977d) called the 'agents of symbolic control', presenting the 'soft' face of capitalism in the welfare and educational agencies. It is important, therefore, to recognise the difference between the forms of women's education found in the private and state schools, and further to relate the forms within them not just to women's labour but also to their future class position.

What Bowles and Gintis have tended to assume is that, within the differential forms of schooling catering for different sectors of the wage labour force, both sexes experience on the whole similar conditioning. Carter, in the same tradition of political economy, is more careful about assuming similarities, even though he does not attempt an analysis of the differences.

> The structural relation of school experience to subsequent labour market experience for women is very complex and does not exactly replicate the relation that obtains for men. For instance, many women achieve good grades, graduate from high school and still obtain only secondary jobs. To understand the relationship of women to existing job structures, we must consider not only the structure and ideology of schooling but also the structure and ideology of the family. To avoid confusing the analysis with too many details, we have ignored the circumstances peculiar to the experience of women.
>
> (Carter, 1976, p. 180)

What becomes clear from the study of forms of women's education, particularly in terms of curriculum and examinations, is the different routes the two sexes take through the educational system. For the working-class girl, often allocated to the curriculum streams of the 'less able', requiring courses in 'everyday life' and 'citizenship', basic training in skills and non-examination courses, the experience is orientated towards a future domestic role rather than waged labour. Training is directed towards domesticity, with courses in household crafts such as cooking and sewing added to a diluted academic curriculum. As Wolpe (1974) has shown, the 'common code' in British government planning in education has been founded on the assumption of gender differentiation with the belief that women's primary role in society is to become wives and mothers, despite the fact that large numbers of women become workers outside the home. There is an assumed dichotomy between the world of work, which is taken as the primary goal and interest of boys, and the world of the family and marriage, as the future desire of girls. The educational motto of 'preparation for life' takes on specific meanings in the ideological climate of patriarchy. The results can be seen in the alignment of forms of education for socially defined and attributed gender roles.

The patterns of working-class girls' schooling (though this may appear contradictory, given the presence of working-class women in the labour force) may have a certain logic. By regarding marital and maternal roles as primary goals in life, working-class women are likely to treat work within social production as a peripheral and secondary concern. This focusing upon domestic life for personal fulfilment, which is encouraged rather than discouraged by the educational system, may partially explain why women are prepared to accept employment in the worst, lowest-paid jobs within the secondary labour market. The provision of a form of schooling for domesticity may be one of the ways in which the conditions are ensured for the continued existence of a female reserve army of labour and an unskilled, cheap, female labour force. Such a form of schooling would also contribute indirectly to the reproduction of capitalism by encouraging a female domestic labour force, responsible for the biological reproduction and the nurturance of workers.

For the middle classes, school experience is different but no less contradictory. The overt ideology of equal opportunity and equality between the sexes, although realised by the equal range of curriculum options made available to both sexes and the expressed liberalism of the teachers, may well run counter to the hidden curriculum of the school, which perpetuates the ideology of femininity as synonymous with wife and mother. Even where the school is geared more towards careers, the assumption can often be identified in teachers' attitudes and their guidance on choice of school subjects, that girls' careers are best found in typically 'feminine' professions, such as medicine, education, social work and so on. Ironically too, these girls may well receive sufficient academic qualifications to proceed to higher education and full-time careers which later come into conflict with their concept of marital life. Particularly within the professional middle classes, one finds a strong belief in motherhood as a professional full-time job that requires the mother to be at home with her children, responsible for the reproduction of the class culture by her domestic pedagogic work and capable of responding to the demands made upon her by the schools.[3]

In the case of working-class girls, the ideology of sex differences, and the naturalness of the sexual division of labour between home and work, is often overt, with only minimal recognition of the necessity for or the desire of these girls to take up paid employment. In the education of the middle-class girl, the situation is reversed. There is often a recognition of the desirability that women should achieve academically, in order to obtain some work fulfilment and career prospects; this is set against the likelihood that once married they will have much greater financial security and less need to work either for money or for fulfilment, given motherhood. In both cases, the ideology of femininity and the acceptance of the sexual division of labour act as a filter for the continued presence of women in certain types of labour with specific expectations and attitudes to work.

Gender and the social relations of production

If we turn now to the reproduction of the social relations of production (i.e., the class relations operating within the structuring of the labour process) we find the kernel of analyses of schooling by Althusser and Bowles and Gintis. Both see the reproduction of the social relations found in the production process as the central function and determining force in the shape of schooling within capitalism. For Althusser, the educational system is the dominant ideological state apparatus which processes each school population in accordance with, and in preparation for, the class structure and class power relations. The process is one of selective socialisation where groups of children, on the basis of their class origins, are given different types and amounts of education through which they acquire certain types of knowledge and know-how, as well as particular ideological predispositions. Theoretically these acquisitions allow them to cope with and adapt to the work relations and authority structures in specific locations in their production process. Some children will thus be prepared for their future role as the exploited, with an apolitical, national, ethnical or civic consciousness. Others will learn how to give orders and enforce obedience, in expectation of their future role as agents of exploitation (employers, managers) or agents of repression (police, army). The third major category will acquire the ability to manipulate ideologies and forms of consciousness. Within the seemingly neutral context of the school, 'the relations of production in a capitalist social formation, i.e. the relations of exploited to exploiters and exploiters to exploited, are largely reproduced' by a 'massive' inculcation of the ideology of the ruling class (Althusser, 1971, p. 148). In this rudimentary framework, Althusser concentrates upon class domination with no mention of the ways in which patriarchal ideology is transmitted in the school, mediating and contextualising the ruling ideology of class domination within the structures of sexual oppression. A question he forgets to ask is: Are women ever inculcated with the ideology suited for the agents of exploitation or repression? If any ideology is most likely to be acquired by women, it is that of the exploited, with relatively few trained to become professional ideologists.

In the work of Bowles and Gintis (1976), the reproduction of the social relations of production occurs through their presence in structural equivalents in the social relations of schooling. The form of socialisation, rather than being ideological, is one of experience of the social relations and authority structures of schooling which mirror those to be found in future work places. In elaborating what they call the 'correspondence principle', they identify a structural homology between the hierarchy of the teacher–pupil relations and that of the supervisor/manager over the worker, which reproduces the authority structures and forms of control characteristic of class relations:

> Specifically, the social relationships of education – the relationships between administrators and teachers, teachers and students, students and students, and students and their work – replicate the hierarchical division of labour. Hierarchical relations are reflected in the vertical authority lines from administrators to teachers to students. Alienated labour is reflected in the student's lack of control over his or her education, the alienation of the student from the curriculum content, and the motivation of school work through a system of grades and other external rewards rather than the

> student's integration with either the process (learning) or the outcome (knowledge) of the educational 'production process'.
>
> (Bowles and Gintis, 1976, p. 131)

Beyond this aggregate level, Bowles and Gintis point to the different forms of education and internal organisation of schools, which prepare children for different levels within the occupational structure. While the lowest levels are likely to emphasise rule-following and close supervision, the middle and higher levels of education provide greater space for initiative, moving from discipline and direct control to more independent activity. These levels are to be found not merely in the various tiers of the educational system but also within streamed schools. The implications of these structures are the attunement of each generation to the behavioural norms required by the levels of the capitalist production process, which are internalised in the 'types of personal demeanour, modes of self presentation, self image and social class identifications which are the crucial ingredients of job adequacy' (ibid.).

In this analysis of schooling, there is little recognition of the potential correspondence between patriarchal authority structures and the hierarchy of male over female within the social relations of the school and of the work processes. This might be due to the fact that Bowles and Gintis define sexual inequality and prejudices as external to the operation of capitalism. They point out that

> [the] smooth control over the work process requires that the authority structure of the enterprise respect the wider society's prejudices. In particular socially acceptable power relationships must be respected.
>
> (Bowles and Gintis, 1976, p. 98)

They suggest, but do not develop the point, that a strong case could be made that the form and strength of both racism and sexism are closely related to the particular historical development of class relations in the US and Europe.

Furthermore, they do not analyse the ways in which sexual power relations have become integral features of capitalist work structures. The control of women workers by male managers, for example, may be found mirrored in the sexual hierarchy of the school's division of labour, with a male headteacher and inspectors and a large female teaching force. Within the fragmentation of knowledge, one can also find the stratification of knowledge reproducing the hierarchy of male over female with particular school subjects and disciplines classified as 'masculine' or 'feminine' (Harding, 1980, and Weiner, 1980), which contribute to the acceptance of students of the sexual divisions within the labour force. In the classroom, the authority of the teacher may also be affected by sex. In the primary school, the teacher's authority is more likely to be similar to that of the mother (i.e., personalised), while at the university level the model is one of paternal authority, based upon status and position.[4]

This sexual division of labour in school knowledge and among the teaching staff is perhaps one of the ways in which women become attuned to the dual forms of control found within their specific work locations. For example, within an office the form of control between male bosses and their female secretaries is likely to contain elements of paternalism. In industry, as Gee found, the form of control of the female work force was a combination of patriarchal and capitalist management practices. She concludes:

> The sexual division of labour underpinned by the patriarchal structure of the family and the division of labour in detail, brought together under factory discipline and management, means for women a dual form of control in the work place.
>
> (Gee, 1978)

The implication of this dual form of control within the work place is that women are expected to be both docile to management and docile to men. Such a training in obedience and subservience can be seen located in the educational system, which expects high degrees of conformity not only to the school norm of a good pupil but also to the definition of femininity, as the research on the hidden curriculum of schooling has shown.[5]

Further, socialisation into both class and gender identity is also found within the family, where, as Bowles and Gintis point out,

> Despite the tremendous structural disparity between family and economy – one which is never really overcome in capitalist society – there is a significant correspondence between the authority relationships in capitalist production and family child-rearing … . The male-dominated family, with its characteristically age-graded patterns of power and privilege, replicates many aspects of the hierarchy of production in the firm.
>
> (Bowles and Gintis, 1976, p. 144)

Interestingly here, they notice the existence of patriarchy as one potential element in the authority structures of production. While they have not accounted for the ways in which schooling may reproduce, at an ideological and structural level, the sexual division of labour, they do analyse very briefly the role of the family in this context:

> First, wives and mothers themselves normally embrace their self concepts as household workers. They then pass these on to their children through the differential sex role-typing of boys and girls within the family. Second, and perhaps more important, children tend to develop self concepts based on the sexual divisions which they observe around them. Even families which attempt to treat boys and girls equally cannot avoid sex role-typing when the male parent is tangentially involved in household labour and child-

> rearing. In short the family as a social as well as biological reprod unit cannot but reflect its division of labour as a production unit. T typing, unless countered by other social forces, then facilitates the subm- sion of the next generation of women to their inferior status in the wage labour system and lends its alternative – child-rearing and domesticity – an aura of inevitability, if not desirability.
>
> (Bowles and Gintis, 1976, p. 144)

It would appear that if we are to understand the ways in which women are prepared to take their assigned place within capitalism in the family and in the labour force, we need to investigate the processes of gender construction in both the family and education. As David (1978) argued, it is time to look at the family–education couple as the dual determining agencies of reproduction of sexual divisions within the social formation.

Cultural reproduction

With this in mind, I shall now turn to the theories of cultural reproduction and specifically to the work of Basil Bernstein,[6] who analyses education in terms of the contribution it makes to the cultural reproduction of the class structure. This work emphasises the importance of the culture of the curriculum and the social and moral order of the school. Unlike the social reproduction theories, which stress the economic inequalities of class societies, Bernstein emphasises the mediation of the family between class origin and school as the critical source of cultural inequality. Not concerned with the inheritance of economic capital, he develops his analyses around the concept of symbolic property (language, cultural tastes, manners) and educational property in the form of certificates and diplomas. Although Bernstein does not specifically address the question of gender differentiation within schooling, his theory makes available conceptual tools which can be usefully employed in the analysis of gender relations in schooling. According to Bernstein,

> Educational knowledge is a major regulator of the structure of experience. From this point of view, one can ask 'How are forms of experience, identity and relation evoked, maintained and changed by the formal transmission of educational knowledge and sensitivities?'
>
> (Bernstein, 1977c, p. 85)

In investigating this question, Bernstein concentrates upon the ways in which schooling reproduces the social order through the categorisation of pupils by age, sex and social class. This categorisation lies embedded in the structuring of knowledge and also in the form of pedagogy, the spatial organisation of the school and the evaluation criteria. The two critical features of school experience are to be found in the form of classification (the construction and maintenance of boundaries between different categories, their interrelations and stratification) and framing (the form and degree of control within pedagogic relations, between teacher and taught).

Using this theoretical framework, it is possible to investigate the ways in which schooling transmits a specific *gender code* whereby individuals' gender identity and gender roles are constructed under the school's classification system. The boundaries between the appropriate activities, interests and expectations of future work for the two sexes are maintained, and the relations and hierarchies between the two are determined by such a gender code.

In traditional schools one may find a strong boundary between the definitions of masculinity and femininity, which will be reinforced by the application of this principle to the spatial organisation of the school, school uniforms, classroom activities and curriculum subjects. This will be implemented through specific pedagogic relationships where the framing is strong. The child's behaviour will be evaluated according to sex-appropriate criteria (e.g., 'that is quite good for a girl', 'little girls don't do that'). In this type of school, the teacher in the classroom is most likely to operate distinctions between male and female children in terms of their notion of a 'good pupil', their expectations of ability and educational success, and their form of discipline. This form of pedagogy would most likely occur in societies or communities where the sexual division of labour in the home and in the work environment was strongly demarcated. As Clarricoates (1980) found in her research, the classification of gender roles was strongest and most overt in schools serving industrial or agricultural communities where sexual differentiation at the economic and ideological levels was strong.

In schools serving either the suburban middle classes or the semi-skilled or skilled occupational groups on a council estate, the classification of children by gender was weakened in the spatial arrangements and types of education which girls and boys received. It was nevertheless to be found within the classrooms, despite the ideology of equal opportunity. While gender may not have been the major organising principle of the school structure, it was still operative in the context of pupil control (i.e., strong framing). In none of the primary schools studied by Clarricoates could one say that the gender code was characterised by weak classifications (i.e., equality between the sexes) and weak frames (freedom to negotiate the definitions of gender). Given that a strong sexual division of labour exists within capitalism, it is not surprising that the dominant gender code of schooling in Britain is that of strong classification, which reproduces the power relations of male–female hierarchy, and strong framing, where teachers play a large part in determining gender definitions and control. Within this dominant code, one may of course always find 'codings': particular expressions of the dominant ideology which may attempt to weaken gender roles.

The dominant code can be 'interrupted'[7] by single-sex schools in which, without the presence of one sex, the gender boundaries are blurred and the form of gender control weakened, as Shaw (1980) has shown. Nevertheless, children within this type of schooling will still acquire the principles of gender classification by the very existence of a division of schools based upon sex difference. Once such pupils have reached higher education, they will be confronted with the academic sexual division of labour (Rendel, 1980) and the realities, after graduating, of the labour market and career prospects (Chisholm and Woodward, 1980).

The constraints which limit the possibility of weakening gender classifications and patriarchal structures are manifold, especially since they are, as has been previously argued, integral elements of the capitalist mode of production. That is not to say that reforms are not possible. One starting point must certainly be the breaking down of gender roles within the family and the patterns of child-rearing. As Bernstein argues,

> To the extent that the infant/primary school fails to utilize age and sex as allocating categories, either for the acquisition and progression of competencies *or* for the allocation of pupils to groups and spaces, the school is weakening the function of these categories in the family and the community.
> (Bernstein, 1977d, pp. 129–30)

In particular, such restructuring is likely to affect the mother's domestic pedagogic work. This process could be accomplished by a series of educational reforms including the re-education of teachers, the editing and selection of textbooks, the monitoring of classroom practice and curriculum guidance, and the availability of all curriculum options for both populations of schoolchildren.

Just as it is certain that these reforms would make an impact upon sexual inequalities, especially at the level of gender identification of children, it is also certain that the reproduction of sexual division is not a smooth, unproblematic process. The setting up and transmission of sex stereotypes as a form of social control does not necessarily imply that individuals become what the stereotype demands. As Fuller (1980) has shown, West Indian black girls strive for academic achievement and, by doing so, resist the stereotypes of 'blackness' and 'femininity'. Operating a delicate balance between resistance and acceptance of school norms, they walk a tightrope between conformity to school discipline and conformity to the racial and sexual stereotypes.

In the case of white working-class girls and boys, the mediation of class and gender categorisation takes different forms. As Willis (1977) has shown in his research into the behaviour and attitudes of working-class boys, these 'lads' celebrate their masculinity against school norms of docile, conforming and diligent pupils. By labelling such pupils as effeminate and 'cissies', the 'lads' affirm their pugnacious and physical masculinity in an anti-school culture. They thus confirm their respect for their masculine identity, derived from their families and peer group, and see its fulfilment in hard, physically demanding manual jobs. According to Willis, the 'lads' therefore invert the mental–manual hierarchy to match the male–female hierarchy. As he describes it,

> This important inversion, however, is not achieved within the proper logic of capitalist production. Nor is it produced in the concrete articulation of the site of social classes of two structures which in capitalism can only be separated in abstraction and whose forms have now become part of it. These are patriarchy and the distinction between mental and manual labour. The form of the articulation is of the cross-valorization and association of the two key terms in the two sets of structures. The polarization of the two structures becomes crossed. Manual labour is associated with the social superiority of masculinity, and mental labour with the social inferiority of femininity. In particular manual labour is imbued with a masculine tone and nature which renders it positively expressive of more than its intrinsic focus in work.
>
> (Willis, 1977, p. 148)

Mandy Llewellyn (1980), on the other hand, together with other researchers such as McRobbie (1978) and Sharpe (1976), reveals that the definitions of femininity can act both as prison and as an escape route for working-class girls. Because they are female, their academic failure is legitimated, their success treated as unusual luck or a result of overdiligent, hence 'boring', effort. Femininity as constructed within the school does not encourage achievement or ambition in the academic world; rather it directs the girls to external goals of being good female companions to men. In this sense it runs counter to the prevailing ideology of education, which stresses academic achievement, intelligence and material success in later life.

The concept of femininity can provide working-class girls with the weapons with which to fight a class-determined education when the realities of working-class life-chances are recognised for what they are. By searching for emotional and personal fulfilment in domestic life and motherhood, the girls can turn away from the frustrations of school life and alienating employment. They themselves judge academic success not as masculine but rather as 'unfeminine' on the assumption that 'bluestockings' do not find husbands or boyfriends and therefore will fail as women. The effect, similar to the result from the resistance of working-class lads, is to invert the hierarchy of productive over domestic labour, although they leave unchallenged the hierarchy of male over female. School resistance is individualised, unlike that of the working-class boys, yet it also derives from peer-group culture and families' (particularly the mothers') definitions of femininity.

Paradoxically, then, while the school may not succeed in transmitting gender definitions which can merge easily with prescribed class identities, pupils may still acquire gender identities which prepare them indirectly for their future class position.

Conclusions

In conclusion, what I have attempted to show is that the theories of cultural and social reproduction, despite their limitations,[8] still raise interesting questions for the sociology of women's education. By looking specifically at the educational experience of women, we are forced to modify any simple correspondence theory of the relations between schooling and work. The contradictory nature of women's position in society, rather than being resolved through schooling, is more likely to be accentuated; if women *are* prepared for certain types of waged labour, they are often only prepared indirectly. Furthermore, we need to ask the question what relation, if any, does the 'gender code' of schooling have to the patriarchal relations in domestic life and in the production process? We also need to find out more about the forms of resistance to, and negotiation of, definitions of gender through class cultures and peer groups inside and outside the school.

Finally, while there is much more research required before we can say we understand women's education, this work should not preclude any of the very necessary programmes for breaking down sexual discrimination in our education system.

Notes

1 See, for example, Hartmann (1979). For Britain, see Barron and Norris (1976); Bosanquet and Doeringer (1973); Wolpe (1978); Ashton and Maguire (1980).
2 This area is now subject to what is commonly referrred to as the 'domestic labour debate'. For good summaries of this debate, see Himmelweit and Mohun (1977) and Fee (1976).
3 For an analysis of middle-class women's relation to 'progressive' primary schooling and the contradictions this poses for them, see Bernstein (1977d) and Chamboredon and Prévot (1975).
4 The distinction between personalised and positional authority is derived from Bernstein (1977a).
5 For a good summary of this research, see Lobban (1978).
6 See especially Bernstein (1977c).
7 This concept derives from Bernstein's analysis of 'progressive' primary schools (1977d), where 'interruption' is defined as a change in the form of transmission and reproduction of the dominant code.
8 For further analysis of the theories of cultural and social reproduction, see MacDonald (1977).

References and further reading

Althusser, L. (1971) 'Ideology and ideological state apparatuses', in *Lenin and Philosophy and Other Essays*, London: New Left Books.

Ashton, D. and Maguire, M. (1980) 'Young women in the labour market: stability and change', in R. Deem (ed.) *Schooling for Women's Work*, London: Routledge & Kegan Paul.

Barron, R.D. and Norris, G.M. (1976) 'Sexual divisions and the dual market', in D.L. Barker and S. Allen (eds) *Dependence and Exploitation in Work and Marriage*, London, Longmans.

Beechey, V. (1978) 'A critical analysis of some sociological theories of women's work', in A. Kuhn and A.M. Wolpe (eds) *Feminism and Materialism*, London: Routledge & Kegan Paul.

Bernstein, B. (1977a) *Class, Codes and Control*, vol. 3, 2nd edn, London: Routledge & Kegan Paul.

—— (1977b) 'Open schools – open society?', in *Class, Codes and Control*, vol. 3, 2nd edn, London: Routledge & Kegan Paul.

—— (1977c) 'On the Classification and Framing of Educational Knowledge', in *Class, Codes and Control*, vol. 3, 2nd edn, London: Routledge & Kegan Paul.

—— (1977d) 'Class and pedagogies: visible and invisible', in *Class, Codes and Control*, vol. 3, 2nd edn, London: Routledge & Kegan Paul.

Bosanquet, N. and Doeringer, P.D. (1973) 'Is there a dual labour market in Great Britain?', *The Economic Journal*, 83: 421–435.

Bowles, S. and Gintis, H. (1976) *Schooling in Capitalist America*, London: Routledge & Kegan Paul.

Carter, M. (1976) 'Contradiction and correspondence: analysis of the relations of schooling to work', in M. Carnoy and H.M. Levin (eds) *The Limits of Educational Reform*, New York: McKay.

Chamboredon, J.C. and Prévot, J. (1975) 'Changes in the social definition of early childhood and the new forms of symbolic violence', *Theory and Society*, 2, 3: 331–50.

Chisholm, L. and Woodward, D. (1980) 'The experiences of women graduates in the labour market', in R. Deem (ed.) *Schooling for Women's Work*, London: Routledge & Kegan Paul.

Clarricoates, K. (1980) 'The Importance of Being Ernest ... Emma ... Tom ... Jane. The perception and categorization of gender conformity and gender deviation in primary schools', in R. Deem (ed.) *Schooling for Women's Work*, London: Routledge & Kegan Paul.

Coulson, M., Magos, B. and Wainwright, H. (1975) 'The housewife and her labour under capitalism: a critique', *New Left Review*, 89, January–February, pp. 59–81.

David, M.E. (1978) 'The family–education couple: towards an analysis of the William Tyndale dispute', in G. Littlejohn, B. Smart, J. Wakeford and N. Yuval Davis (eds) *Power and the State*, London: Croom Helm.

Fee, F. (1976) 'Domestic labour: an analysis of housework and its relation to the production process', *Review of Radical Political Economics*, 8, l: 1–8.

Fuller, M. (1980) 'Black girls in a London comprehensive school', in R. Deem (ed.) *Schooling for Women's Work*, London: Routledge & Kegan Paul.

Gee, M. (1978) 'The capitalist labour process and women workers', paper presented at the Conference of Socialist Economists, Bradford, Yorkshire.

Harding, J. (1980) 'Sex differences in performance in science examinations', in R. Deem (ed.) *Schooling for Women's Work*, London: Routledge & Kegan Paul.

Hartmann, H. (1979) 'Capitalism, patriarchy and job segregation by sex', in Z. Eisenstein (ed.) *Capitalist Patriarchy and the Case for Socialist Feminism*, London: Monthly Review Press.

Himmelweit, S. and Mohun, S. (1977) 'Domestic labour and capital', *Cambridge Journal of Economics*, l, pp. 15–31.

Llewellyn, M. (1980) 'Studying girls at school: the implications of confusion', in R. Deem (ed.) *Schooling for Women's Work*, London: Routledge & Kegan Paul.

Lobban, G. (1978) 'The influence of the school on sex-role stereotyping', in J. Chetwynd and O. Hartnett (eds) *The Sex Role System*, London: Routledge & Kegan Paul.

MacDonald, M. (1977) *Curriculum and Cultural Reproduction*, E202, Milton Keynes: Open University Press.

McRobbie, A.L. (1978) 'Working class girls and the culture of femininity', in Women's Studies Group (eds) *Women Take Issue: aspects of women's subordination*, London: Hutchinson, in association with the CCCS.

Rendel, M. (1980) 'How many women academics 1912–76?', in R. Deem (ed.) *Schooling for Women's Work*, London: Routledge & Kegan Paul.

Sharpe, S. (1976) *Just like a Girl*, Harmondsworth: Penguin.

Shaw, J. (1980) 'Education and the individual: schooling for girls, or mixed schooling – a mixed blessing?', in R. Deem (ed.) *Schooling for Women's Work*, London: Routledge & Kegan Paul.

Weiner, G. (1980) 'Sex Differences in Mathematical Performance: a review of research and possible action', in R. Deem (ed.) *Schooling for Women's Work*, London: Routledge & Kegan Paul.

Willis, P. (1977) *Learning to Labour*, Farnborough: Saxon House.

Wolpe, A.M. (1974) 'The official ideology of education for girls', in M. Flude and J. Ahier (1976) *Educability, Schools and Ideology*, London: Croom Helm.

—— (1978) 'Education and the sexual division of labour', in A. Kuhn and A.M. Wolpe (eds) *Feminism and Materialism*, London: Routledge & Kegan Paul.

3 Cultural reproduction

The pedagogy of sexuality

The incorporation of Pierre Bourdieu's work into what is loosely termed the 'Marxist perspective' within Anglo-Saxon sociology of education is doubtless one reason for the steady growth of his reputation. This has been a highly selective process, as Annette Kuhn has already pointed out in *Screen Education*,[1] and it is in a popularised and often distorted form that many of his concepts – 'cultural capital', 'symbolic violence', 'mis-recognition' – have passed into everyday sociological speech. Also, the stress on works such as *Reproduction in Education, Culture and Society* (written in collaboration with J.-C. Passeron) has been at the expense of other equally important texts like the *Outline of a Theory of Practice*, where the theoretical premises of Bourdieu's theory of cultural reproduction can be found.[2] In part, this emphasis may reflect the strict division of academic labour in this country between sociology proper and anthropological analysis. In the *Outline*, Bourdieu draws upon a study of the Kayble society in Algeria to analyse, among other features, the nature of primary pedagogy in a non-literate society where early education takes place within the familial and community environment. *Reproduction*, although it too is concerned to relate symbolic classifications and cultural forms to the social structure and its power relations, concentrates on the mechanisms of social and cultural reproduction within institutionalised education in an advanced capitalist social formation. (Specifically, it investigates the role of the high-status arts faculties in French universities.)

This difference also suggests another reason for the neglect of the *Outline*. The central theme in sociological critiques of education tends to be the relationship between institutional schooling and the social division of labour – in particular, the extent to which formal education contributes to the reproduction of the class structure and the labour force. Informal and, in particular, domestic pedagogic work are given far less attention. Furthermore, the reproduction of the *sexual* division of labour is relegated to the family as a separate ideological (state) apparatus; schooling contributes to this only through a process of confirmation. In treating these factors as 'secondary', such critiques often attribute to the sexual division of labour a minor role in the formation of social inequalities and identities. Sexual oppression (when not wholly neglected) tends to be subsumed into the broader context of economic exploitation, thus avoiding the need to explain how particular forms of patriarchal relations operate within specific modes of production. This position would not only find it difficult to incorporate Bourdieu's anthropological studies; it also has clear limitations for socialists and teachers alike. In the first place, it assumes that any political strategy must concentrate on the abolition of class and relegates sexual oppression to a 'post-revolutionary' problem. In the second, in reaction to liberal beliefs, it leads to the argument that education can only play a minor role within such a strategy; economic upheaval and reformation are seen as the necessary conditions for radical social change.

However, the growth of feminism as a political movement and as an academic discourse has directed interest back to the ways in which pedagogy within formal and informal instructional contexts contributes to the reproduction of the sexual division of labour at both the socio-economic and cultural levels. Complex questions now arise. What role do the practices and discourses at work in educative contexts (such as the family, the community, the media, schools) play in forming and transmitting sexual identities, gender attributes and sexual power relations? Does schooling contribute to the reproduction of a particular mode of biological reproduction, as well as the social/sexual division of labour? What role can education play in a movement for the breakdown of existing gender categories and definitions of sexuality? Attempts to answer these often shift uncomfortably between biological, psychological and sociological explanations. The debate has also been marked by a split between psychoanalytic explanations of the unconscious formation of sexed subjectivity and sociological accounts of the impact of the social construction of gender at the conscious level of 'learned' identity. This is not a controversy I can deal with here, but it does seem clear that some synthesis between psychoanalysis and Marxism is needed as a precondition of the productive synthesis of the sexual struggle and socialist strategy. Thus, in their summary of the complexities of this debate, Steve Burniston, Frank Mort and Christine Weedon point to:

> [the] necessary task of tracing, concretely, the relationship between historically specific forms of sex/gender identity (including their unconscious representation), the material practices which structure the acquisition of that identity (the media, the educational system, the labour process and primarily the mode of kinship/familial organisation) and the organisation of economic and social relations which constitute the mode of production.[3]

They also stress the particular need to analyse the family/kinship structures and the processes of ideological socialisation through which sexual identity is learned. Sexual structures, they argue, contribute (socially and unconsciously) to the maintenance of the specific form of social relations necessary for the biological reproduction of labour power, and hence the reproduction of the mode of production.

Bourdieu's *Outline of a Theory of Practice* also looks at the role of pedagogic work in the cultural reproduction of sexual structures. It is in this context, then, that I want to re-examine his work: for, although theories about class identity and experience, sex roles and gender identification abound in current thinking about education, the element of specifically sexual identity is noticeably lacking. The 'product' of schooling is still often represented as a social subject without a biological presence (be it physically ascribed or socially attributed). The *Outline* and *Reproduction*, taken together, can offer a way into the analysis of education and sexuality, and in this chapter I shall begin by looking at the concept of habitus in so far as it represents the locus of class and sexual identities. I shall move on to an analysis of the sexual division of labour in terms of the distribution of cultural capital and forms of resistance to class domination through language and culture.

Habitus

More than any other of Bourdieu's concepts, habitus reveals the influence of Durkheim's analysis of the ways in which symbolic classifications reproduce the categories and structural hierarchies of society. It is most fully elaborated in the *Outline of a Theory of Practice*, where Bourdieu argues that sociology should be an experimental science of the 'dialectic of the internalisation of externality and the externalisation of internality'.[4] This externality refers primarily to the material conditions of existence characteristic of a class condition, which are themselves the product of 'casual series' such as biological and social determinisms. Although they may be relatively independent, within a determinate historical conjuncture these series are brought together, in the last analysis, by the economic base. The objective structures produce habitus – the systems of durable (lasting), transposable (adaptable and generalisable) dispositions. These patterns of thought generate practices and representations which, in turn, reproduce those objective structures of which they are themselves a product. So the habitus is a 'socially constituted system of cognitive and motivating structures'[5] which is overdetermined (that is, doubly determined) as it reproduces its own conditions of existence. It structures and determines patterns of thought, perception, aspirations, the sense of the possible, the impossible and the probable. It represents the condition for the production of forms of behaviour, forms of communication and cultural practices.

The trouble with sociologists, according to Bourdieu, is that they have ignored the dialectical relationship between objective structures and the cognitive motivating structures, or else, suffering from 'genesis amnesia', they have forgotten that objective structures are themselves products of historical practices. They therefore find difficulty in relating together different subsystems – an example would be the relationship between the mode of human reproduction (monogamy, polygamy), the economic mode and educational systems. Because they cannot recognise the *structural homology* which (Bourdieu argues) exists between these diverse systems, sociologists fall into the trap of dichotomising structure and practice, score and performance, essence and existence. Bourdieu, therefore, stresses the need to recognise that objective structures (he cites language and the economy as examples) reproduce themselves in the form of lasting dispositions in individuals who have been subjected to the same conditioning by being placed in the same material conditions of existence. All biological individuals who are the product of these objective conditions are the supports of the same habitus. Although Bourdieu accepts the impossibility of *all* members of the same class having the same experiences in the same order, he nevertheless points out that:

> each member of the same class is more likely than any member of another class to have been confronted with the situations most frequent for members of that class.[6]

He also suggests that habitus makes coherence and necessity out of accident and contingency: for example,

> the equivalences it establishes between positions in the division of labour and positions in the division between the sexes are doubtless not peculiar to societies in which the division of labour and the division between the sexes coincide almost perfectly.[7]

In a class society, then, all the products of these agents will:

> speak inseparably and simultaneously of his [or her] class – or more precisely his [or her] position in the social structure and his [or her] rising or falling trajectory – and his (or her) body, or more precisely, all the properties, always socially qualified, of which he or she is the bearer – sexual properties of course, but also physical properties, praised, like strength or beauty, or stigmatised.[8]

In such ways three core classification systems, always historically determined, are reproduced by the habitus – the structure of class relations, the structure of sex relations and the structure of age relations.[9]

The relatively autonomous universe of family relationships contains, *par excellence*, the sexual division of labour as well as 'domestic morality, cares, strifes, tastes' which are formed through economic and social necessity in particular historical circumstances and which are produced by a determinate class position; and it is here, in the early educational experiences of family life, that the child's habitus is formed. This 'habit-forming force' becomes the foundation of perception and appreciation in all subsequent experiences – educational action may transform early training but, according to Bourdieu, it can never totally reverse its effects. In societies where education has not been institutionalised as a specific autonomous practice with specialised agents, pedagogic work takes place in a 'symbolically structured environment' by the whole group. Learning is then a process of acquiring *practical* mastery of the principles of the social formation. A social grammar of behaviour, thought, symbols and language is acquired through practical experience, without attaining a level of discourse (here referring to principles of abstraction and generalisation) which characterises *symbolic* mastery. The child imitates not 'models' but actions, acquiring a system of social meanings and values, a body language of gestures, postures and expressions, the use of implements and tools, a form of speech, a way of talking. In short, the child acquires a certain subjective experience of the social world which is *embodied* in the presentation of self as a physical and social being.

In thinking about pedagogy and sexuality, embodiment is one of Bourdieu's most valuable concepts. It directs analysis of cultural/symbolic forms towards the creation of a physical as well as a social presence and identity as a political process.[10] 'Embodiment' prevents the 'domestication of the body' being lost in a purely sociological account of socialisation. The awareness of the sexual classification of male and female within this analysis appears to be a primary element in the constitution both of self and furthermore of the social world; it also allows Bourdieu to integrate both social and sexual identities in his analysis of primary pedagogic work.

Even more important, though, is Bourdieu's identification of the dialectic between the biological and social world, *the dialectic of embodiment and objectification.* In his investigation of the Kayble's symbolic system, he puts forward a theory of the structural homology between the sexual division of labour (in particular male and female functions in biological reproduction) and what he calls the mythico-ritual oppositions. Socially constructed categories such as masculine and feminine are not merely objectified in the classification of cultural phenomena, but are also embodied in the individuals operating that classification system. As Bourdieu explains:

> It is in the dialectical relationship between the body and a space structured according to the mythico-ritual oppositions that one finds the form *par excellence* of the structural apprenticeship which leads to the embodying of the structures of the world, that is, the appropriating by the world of a body thus enabled to appropriate the world. In a social formation in which the absence of the symbolic product-conserving techniques associated with literacy retards the objectification of symbolic and particularly cultural capital, inhabited space – and above all the house – is the principal locus for the objectification of the generative schemes; and, through the intermediary of the division and hierarchies it sets up between things, persons and practices, this tangible classifying system continuously inculcates and reinforces the taxonomic principles underlying all the arbitrary provisions of this culture.[11]

Within the household/home, in the relationship particularly between the mother and the father, in their asymmetry and antagonistic complementarity, the child acquires the principles of both the *sexual division of labour* (the division between male and female forms of labour) and *division of sexual labour* (the division of labour in biological reproduction). Within the Kayble society, Bourdieu found homologous oppositions between the concepts of male and female, the right and left hands, religion and magic, external space (the place of assembly, the market, the fields) and internal space (the house, the garden, the fountain). The classification of the social environment, of material objects, of time and space, reproduces in objectified form the biologically based yet socially constructed categories of sexual differences, and in particular the social definition of sexuality.

Individuals relate to each other according to the same principles as those governing the organisation of space, time and objects because they are the product of the same generative schema. The child, experiencing his or her body and the social environment, acquires in terms of the same concepts:

> the relationship between man and the natural world and the complementarity and opposed states and actions of the two sexes in the division of sexual work and the sexual division of work, and hence in the work of biological and social reproduction.[12]

One symbolic opposition which Bourdieu draws from the Kayble is between the *centrifugal* male orientation and the *centripetal* female orientation. This provides not only the principle for the organisation of domestic space but also the principle for the relationship of each of the sexes to their bodies and their sexuality. Such an opposition, he argues, can also be found in European societies dominated by male values which assign men to politics, history and war, and associate their sexuality with prowess and sublimation. Women are assigned to the hearth, the novel and psychology, and given a relation to their sexuality which tends to exclude reference to specifically female sexual interests, dominated as it is by male values of virility. In Bourdieu's view, though, the relationship of individuals to their own and others' bodies cannot be treated as merely the product of sexuality. The body (defined biologically) and the natural world are 'set in order' by what Melanie Klein called a 'body geography' or cosmology. The child's initial encounter with its mother's and father's bodies is the experience both of biological *and* mythopoeic oppositions (like gender roles). As Bourdieu argues:

> The child constructs its *sexual identity*, the major element in its social identity, at the same time as it constructs its image of the division of work between the sexes, out of the same socially defined set of inseparably biological and social indices. In other words, the awakening of consciousness of sexual identity and the incorporation of the dispositions associated with a determinate social definition of the social functions incumbent on men and women come to hand with the adoption of a socially defined vision of the sexual division of labour.[13]

Bourdieu ascribes to formal 'secondary pedagogic work' the confirmation and limited restructuration of the initial habitus, the individual's mental structure predetermined by early familiarisation with the structural hierarchies of class, sex and age relations. Within schooling, the practical mastery of such classifications, learned through domestic pedagogic work, is transformed into symbolic mastery of the abstract and generalisable principles of culture, language, tastes, style and so forth. The effectiveness of secondary pedagogy is a function of the distance between the type of early habitus and that transmitted by the school – so the domestic sexual division of labour is thus a crucial factor in the formation of the child's habitus and its ability to receive and appropriate the cultural message of the school. The implication of this theory is that, in terms of the sexual division of labour, the school can only reproduce sexual structures and has a very limited capacity for restructuration. Traditional visible pedagogies are based on the acquisition of strong individual identities which reinforce age and sex classifications. One only has to remember how traditional schooling differentiates pupils in terms of spatial organisation (segregated schools, seating arrangements), physical appearance (uniforms, clothes, etc.), activities (sports, tasks, curriculum subjects) and manners (ways of talking, sitting, standing, etc.) to recognise the likely impact upon the child's social and physical awareness of self. On the other hand, the many feminist teachers who believe that progressive education can change or diminish sex stereotyping would probably endorse Basil Bernstein's argument that invisible pedagogies 'are likely to weaken such classifications and inasmuch as they do this, they transform the concept of the child and the concepts of age and sex status.'[14]

Bernstein also suggests that the school can act back upon the family – that the relationship between the two institutions is interactive rather than unidirectional:

> to the extent that the infant/primary school fails to utilise age and sex as allocating categories *either* for the acquisition and progression of competencies *or* for the allocation of pupils to groups and spaces, the school is weakening the function of these categories in the family and the community.[15]

Such schooling would have an impact on the mother's domestic work, particularly in the upper classes. She will be encouraged to adopt a new pedagogic style (as in the professional organisation of play and activities) and new forms of interaction with her child (on the basis of the child's personality, for example, rather than a rigid model of patterns of growth and sexually stereotyped behaviour). J.-C. Chamboredon and J. Prévot reach similar conclusions from their study of progressive French primary schools.[16] What remains unclear, though, is the effect these schools are likely to have on the domestic pedagogy of the working-class mother. In his research on *Class and Conformity*, Melvin Kohn has found that gender distinctions (such as expectations of cleanliness, good manners and happiness for girls as against ambition, dependability and school success for boys) are more likely to be found in working-class than middle-class families. In particular, he discovered that 'working-class mothers draw precise distinctions between what is behaviourally proper for boys and for girls' whereas these distinctions were largely irrelevant for the middle-class mothers in his sample.[17] The distance between the habitus acquired by a child within a traditional household and that represented in a progressive primary school may be too great to have any real impact. For Bourdieu, then, the reformulation of gender and sex roles would depend on changes within the sexual division of labour in the home and so, in the final instance, in the economy.

The beneficial effects of 'progressive' schooling on sexual structures will also be constrained by its place in the educational system. This form of pedagogy is most common in schools staffed mainly by female teachers and responsible for very young children – that is those closest to the traditionally female environment of the home. In cultivating 'expressive spontaneity', creativity and the development of personality rather than individuality, it emphasises what is regarded in our society as essentially female (emotional, inward looking, personal). Secondary schooling, in contrast, is oriented towards the *outer* (male) world of work, not inner development – it is centrifugal rather than centripetal. Its forms of legitimate knowledge are public, not private – factual knowledge is valued above personal experience. Thus there is a tension. Although progressive pedagogy may help to break down sexual stereotypes, the division between a primary 'spontaneist' approach and more authoritarian and 'instrumental' secondary education may actually reproduce the normative division between production (male) and consumption (female), between the male preserve of work and the female preserve of the family and domestic labour. In other words, the sexual division of labour is affirmed as the child acquires the principles underlying the classification of the two forms of pedagogy. This process of reproduction is reinforced by the sexual basis of teachers' authority. Given the role of women in early pedagogic work (mothers and primary school teachers), Bernstein suggests that it is the middle-class mother who 'provides the model for the pre-school, infant school teacher.'[18] In the secondary and university sectors, the male model of authority prevails (as headteacher, professors) even where, as in secondary schools, there are large numbers of female teachers. Bourdieu actually quotes Freud as the source of the idea that the teacher's authority is based on the concept of the father.

> We understood now our relations with our teachers. These men, who are not even fathers themselves, became for us paternal substitutes. That is why they struck us as so mature, so inaccessibly adult, even when they were still very young. We transferred onto them the respect and hopes the omniscient father of our childhood inspired in us, and we started to treat them as we used to treat our fathers at home.[19]

It is likely, therefore, that the child learns not merely its own placing in the sexual structure but also the principles governing sexual power relations – the equation of maleness with high status, dominance and authority. Against this, though, Chamboredon and Prévot argue that the division of labour between the sexes, particularly the assigning of cultural power to the woman and economic power to the man in the French upper classes, is one of the mechanisms ensuring the *integration* of the two forms of pedagogy.

The general trend towards the integration of a spontaneous liberalism and technocratic ideology within the upper class takes on a specific form in pedagogical matters. I would suggest that two main devices permit the resolution of potential between the trend towards spontaneity and the traditional more authoritarian tendencies. The first one is accomplished through the division of labour between sexes, the spontaneist elements being accorded to the feminine. The second is accomplished through relegating these elements to different stages of life and the school career, with the spontaneist elements being predominant during the period of pre-school education.[20]

Summary

To summarise, then, Bourdieu's structural analysis raises questions about three major aspects of the processes through which the sexual division of labour is culturally reproduced:

1 the internalisation (or embodiment) of the domestic divisions of labour together with the homologous symbolic classifications of tasks, objects, function, time and space mediated through the family and school contexts;
2 the structural reproduction of the male/female hierarchy and male dominance through the recognition of the sexual nature of teachers' authority at different levels of schooling and the different forms of pedagogy operating at these levels, in the transition from the domestic to the productive spheres;
3 the reproduction of the masculine/feminine social and sexual identities through different educations in instrumental/expressive skills, public/private knowledge, discipline/spontaneous creativity. Within this framework the impact and origins of the hierarchical stratification of academic disciplines in the context of both class and gender relations are also important.

Before looking at Bourdieu's account of how institutionalised schooling contributes to the reproduction of the socio-sexual division of labour, it is worth examining how useful the concept of habitus is in theorising the constitution of gender and sexuality. Its advantage (particularly for a feminist analysis) is that it brings together the psychoanalytic and the sociological factors in this process and, by positing a dialectic between the two levels of determination, avoids either biological determinism or purely ideological analysis. It also moves away from the subjective/objective dichotomy to an interactive relationship between the two forms of experience. Yet, however all-encompassing and complex the concept of habitus may seem, it still has limitations. The particular conjunctures of symbolic and material structures identifiable in Kayble society made it possible for Bourdieu to establish equivalences in sets of classification systems. But can such equivalences be discovered in a highly differentiated class society?

The model of primary pedagogic work within a non-class society needs to be refined before it can be applied to domestic pedagogy in families of different social classes. Given the lack of any centralised authority having the force to impose one set of legitimate definitions of gender, representations of sexuality or a particular domestic division of labour, such social constructs are the product of struggle – both class struggle and sexual struggle within the context of historically specific power relations.

These elements seem to be lost in Bourdieu's analysis, and he offers no account of social change in the cultural arena. The cultural reproduction of class and sexual identities appears to be a 'deep' unconscious process which, although materially determined, is unlikely to be broken. He seems to discount the possibility of change through recognising one's own habits of thought, perception and action, which potentially could lead to a radical programme of action for 'breaking' the sexual and economic divisions of labour instead of just restructuring them. Such an 'awakening' could only be the product of changed material circumstances, the causes of which remain unspecified. There are thus two dangers in using a concept such as habitus. The first is that it is hard to establish the nature of its existence and the forms it may take in different historical conjunctures. Instead of offering a theory of learning, Bourdieu deduces the impact on individuals' consciousness of economic, symbolic and sexual structures; this crucial but untested deduction represents the weakest point in his theory of social order. Second, haunting his theory is the implication that any planned programme for change (through educational reform, for example) can have little impact against such social determinism, whether it be class or sexual domination.

Cultural capital

At the heart of Bourdieu's analysis of how formal schooling reproduces class inequalities and power is his concept of *cultural capital.* Again the family is crucial. Its position in relation to the class structure determines the form of cultural capital to be transmitted to the child, who inherits, through a process of 'familiarisation' and appropriation, not only particular linguistic and social competencies but such qualities as style, taste, manners and 'know-how' and also expectations about future chances, criteria of success and a particular relation to the dominant culture. Whereas a child born to the dominant class will have invested in it cultural 'funds' which can be exchanged for academic certificates and diplomas, working-class children have no such cultural capital to 'bank' in an alien school culture which reproduces the 'cultural arbitrary' of another social class.

A striking feature of Bourdieu and Passeron's empirical research in *Reproduction* is that, by defining cultural capital in terms of the *father's* occupation and education, they seem to accept that either a woman has no class culture or that her culture is not a significant feature of family pedagogy. The implication is that the sexual division of labour in domestic pedagogy ensures that only the man's culture is communicated: hence that cultural heredity operates only through the male line. A second theoretical assumption of their research is that for each given social class there is 'an equal distribution of linguistic capital … between the sexes'[21] – that both sexes within one class have the same amount of cultural capital. Neither of these assumptions is tenable (as Bourdieu's own later work shows). Without going into the debates about 'maternal deprivation' and the effect of mothers on the development and personality formation of their children – or even about Bourdieu's own contention that women (especially in the upper class) have 'cultural power' – it is self-evident that the idea that women are 'invisible' and have no impact upon the child's cultural experience is unacceptable. Against the assumption that cultural competencies are shared equally between the sexes, Bourdieu and Passeron themselves argue that the *relationship* to culture is as important as its form. Thus, they point out, female students often reveal a 'feminine' relation to the dominant culture, stressing 'sensitivity to the imponderable nuances of sentiment or a taste for the imprecise preciosities of style'.[22] That is why they are more likely to choose the literary, artistic or humanistic disciplines designated as 'feminine'.

In assessing the objective possibilities open to them, women may also be affected by a lower level of cultural and economic investment in their education (which could limit their chances of school success, as defined by the number and type of their examination certificates). They also face differential 'rates of conversion' of their diplomas on the academic and job markets. Their qualifications may be devalued as 'typically female' or allow access to occupations (like the teaching profession or social work) from which men have moved out, leaving them 'feminised'. In such ways, women's expectations of future possibilities are likely to be not only different from but 'lower' than men's. It is therefore necessary to qualify Bourdieu and Passeron's theory of reproduction to take account of the operation of the sexual division of labour in the creation and the nature of cultural capital.

In a recent article, Bourdieu has analysed the relationship of the sexes to language, a crucial component of dominant culture. Because they have a 'special interest in symbolic production' (a feature he does not explain), women can identify with the dominant culture without cutting themselves off from their own class (if it is not the bourgeoisie); nor do they run 'the risk of their transformation being taken as a change in both their social and sexual identity.'[23] To explain the comparatively unproblematic relation of women from dominated classes to the dominant culture, Bourdieu argues that mobility is given as a reward for docility in a class society; at the same time, within a male-dominated society, docility is represented as a dimension of an essentially 'feminine' social identity and a particular feminine relation to the body. Hence women who have acquired the socially prescribed disposition can relate to the dominant culture without negating their sexuality. Although this reasoning makes sense about women who associate domestic life with cultural activity (like the upper classes in France), it is unlikely that working-class girls will easily adopt the bourgeois 'finesse' of school culture. The conformity integral to traditional stereotypes of 'femininity' is not necessarily part of their actual disposition. In her work with one group of working-class girls,[24] Angela McRobbie has shown that their celebration of female sexuality (in clothes, make-up, going out with boys, etc.) is part of an anti-school culture, a resistance to the culture and the discipline of schooling.

Whether the association of docility with feminine dispositions is correct or not, it is clear that the dominant culture – or rather the participation in it of people from outside the dominant class – is designated as feminine or effeminate. The opposition between spiritual or sublimated symbolic culture and language and material physical culture, Bourdieu argues, is 'more or less perfectly congruent with the taxonomy which organises the division between the sexes'. To acquire this dominant culture demands docility, a 'feminine' disposition. Thus biological (male/female) and gender (masculine/feminine) determinations 'exert their influence on linguistic (or sexual) practices and imagery through the structure of homologous oppositions which organise the images of the sexes and the classes.'[25] Given this set of equivalences in the biological and cultural oppositions, Bourdieu interprets the resistance of the working-class male to the dominant culture as part of a class *and* sexual struggle. In acquiring dominant linguistic and cultural forms, what is at stake is not just the accusation of class disloyalty, but also the negation or repudiation of masculine sexuality defined in terms of virility, pugnacity and self-assertion. Taking on bourgeois culture – a way of speaking, self-presentation though gesture, dress and so forth – also implies a particular relation to one's body – hence the different names for parts of the body (the femininity and daintiness of *la bouche* against the roughness and violence of *la gueule*) in bourgeois and working-class speech. Recognising but *inverting* the classification between class cultures, says Bourdieu, working-class men celebrate their masculine sexuality and their physical (manual) culture by punctuating their language with 'coarse' and 'crude' words and 'broad and spicy' stories.

Paul Willis has identified a similar process in his analysis of the relationship between forms of labour power and patriarchy in *Learning to Labour*. The working-class 'lads' in his study were affirming their sexuality as well as their class identity through their resistance to the dominant school culture. In espousing manual labour and dismissing the 'ear 'oles' as conformist, effeminate 'cissies', they inverted the hierarchical distinction of mental over manual labour by transposing it to the hierarchy of male and female. As Willis explains:

> This important inversion, however, is not achieved within the proper logic of capitalist production. Nor is it produced in the division of labour spontaneously. It is produced in the concrete articulation on the site of social classes of two structures which in capitalism can only be separated in abstraction and whose forms have now become part of it. These are patriarchy and the distinction between mental and manual labour. *The form of the articulation is the cross-valorisation and association of the two key terms in the two sets of structures.* The polarisation of the two structures becomes

> crossed. Manual labour is associated with the social superiority of masculinity, and mental labour with the social inferiority of femininity. In particular manual labour is combined with a masculine tone and nature which renders it positively expressive of more than its intrinsic focus in work.[26]

Thus, both Bourdieu and Willis argue that the mode of production and class oppression are reproduced in part through the equivalence established between the mental/manual division of labour and between masculinity and femininity. This also, according to Willis, paves the way for the reproduction of male manual labour power within the working class. As for the reproduction of female manual labour, it is possible that by *inverting* the hierarchy of productive over domestic labour, working-class girls prepare themselves for both unskilled, low-paid work and unpaid domestic service. In neither case, then, would working-class men and women have to negate their culturally received sexual identity in the process of resisting class domination.[27] Boys 'achieve manhood' through hard physical work and girls 'become women' as wives and mothers. In both instances, forms of resistance to schooling which are based on the celebration of traditional sexual identities paradoxically confirm the cycle of reproduction. They undermine neither the sexual nor the social division of labour.

Conclusion

What emerges most clearly from an analysis of pedagogy and sexuality based (critically) on Bourdieu's concepts of habitus and cultural capital is the intricacy of the relationship between the sexual division of labour (biologically and socially constructed), the social division of labour, and forms of language, education and culture. Instead of counterposing feminist and materialist approaches, this makes it possible to theorise the constitution of classed and sexed subjects as a complex process of social and cultural reproduction in which the two structures of patriarchy and capitalism are dialectically integrated. The programmatic implication is the need to investigate further both the significance of the structural characteristics of schooling in the reproduction of both sets of power relations, and also the contradictions and complexities of the interrelations between class and sexual structures within cultural formations. So it is at the level of understanding institutional and familial pedagogies – and the relations between the two contexts of transmission – that this work is most useful. It is less clear what Bourdieu's type of analysis can offer in terms of thinking about a direction or a strategy for 'radical pedagogy'. If anything, it may leave the teacher with a sense of powerlessness, unable to do more than collaborate in the 'restructuration' of social and sexual classifications and identities, without being able to affect the material conditions which determine them. Although, as feminist and socialist teachers have argued, this is not a project to be dismissed, Bourdieu's implicit pessimism raises once again the question of the place of education in a broader political and cultural strategy.

Notes

1 Kuhn, A. (1978) 'Ideology, structure and knowledge', in *Screen Education*, 28, Autumn.

2 Bourdieu, P. (1977) *Outline of a Theory of Practice*, Cambridge: Cambridge University Press; Bourdieu, P. and Passeron, J.-C. (1977) *Reproduction in Education, Society and Culture*, London: Sage. For critical responses to *Reproduction*, see Kuhn, op cit.; Nice, R. (1978) 'Bourdieu: a "vulgar materialist" in the sociology of culture', in *Screen Education*, 28, Autumn; Swartz, D. (1977) 'Pierre Bourdieu: the cultural transmission of social inequality', *Harvard Education Review*, 4, 4, November, pp. 545–55; MacDonald, M. (1977) *Curriculum and Cultural Reproduction*, Units 18/19 E202, Milton Keynes: Open University Press.

3 Burniston, S., Mort, F. and Weedon, C. (1978) 'Psychoanalysis and the cultural acquisition of sexuality and subjectivity', in Women's Studies Group (eds) *Women Take Issue: aspects of women's subordination*, London: CCCS/Hutchinson, p. 128.

4 Bourdieu, 1997, p. 72.

5 Ibid., p. 76.

6 Ibid., p. 85.

7 Ibid., p. 87.

8 Ibid., p. 87.

9 Bourdieu writes:

> Social representations of the different ages of life, and of the properties attached by definition to them, express, in their own logic the power relations between age-classes, helping to reproduce at once the union and the division of those classes by means of temporal divisions tending to produce both continuity and rupture. They thereby rank among the institutional instruments for maintenance of the symbolic order, and hence among the mechanisms of the reproduction of the social order whose very functioning serves the interests of those occupying a dominant position in the social structure, the *men of mature age*.
>
> (Ibid., p. 165; my emphasis)

10 Bourdieu argues that physical bearing or *body hexis* is a political mythology realised. For example, sexual potency is inseparable from social potency. The manner of standing, speaking, coincides with a manner of feeling and thinking. Similarly language as an 'articulatory style' is a body technique which is one dimension of body hexis – namely, the expression of one's relation to the social world.

11 Ibid., p. 89.

12 Ibid., p. 91.

13 Ibid., p. 93.

14 Bernstein, B. (1975) 'Class and pedagogies, visible and invisible', in *Class, Codes and Control*, London: Routledge and Kegan Paul, vol. 3, p. 130. Bernstein distinguishes 'invisible' from 'visible' pedagogies by the following characteristics: (1) the control of the teacher over the child is implicit rather than explicit; (2) ideally, the teacher arranges the *context* which children are expected to rearrange and explore; (3) within this arranged context, the children apparently have wide powers over what they select, over how they structure and over the time-scale of their activities; (4) the children apparently regulate their own movements and social relationships; (5) there is a reduced emphasis upon the transmission and acquisition of specific skills; (6) the criteria for evaluating the pedagogy are multiple and diffuse – and so not easily measured.

15 Ibid., p. 129.

16 Chamboredon, J.-C. and Prévot, J. (1975) 'Change in the social definition of early childhood and the new forms of symbolic violence', in *Theory and Society*, 2, 3, pp. 331–50.
17 Kohn, M.L. (1977) *Class and Conformity*, Chicago, IL: University of Chicago Press, p. 22.
18 Bernstein, op. cit., p. 125.
19 Bourdieu and Passeron, op. cit., pp. 19–20.
20 Chamboredon and Prévot, op. cit., p. 334.
21 Bourdieu and Passeron, op. cit., p. 81.
22 Ibid., p. 78.
23 Bourdieu, P. (1977) 'The economics of linguistic exchange', in *Social Science Information*, 16, 6, p. 661.
24 McRobbie, A. (1978) 'Working class girls and the culture of femininity', in Women's Studies Group (eds) *Women Take Issue: aspects of women's subordination*, London: CCCS/Hutchinson.
25 Bourdieu (1977), op. cit., p. 662.
26 Willis, P. (1977) *Learning to Labour*, Farnborough: Saxon House, p. 148.
27 Among the middle classes the equivalence between the gender hierarchy and the mental/manual distinction is the reverse of that found in the working class. At this level, the 'mental' work of planning and management is considered a masculine activity, whereas more 'manual' occupations (secretarial, for example) are designated 'women's work'; middle-class women face the dilemma of trying to retain their 'femininity' in traditionally masculine occupations such as business, law and science.

4 Schooling and the reproduction of class and gender relations

In 1967, Quintin Hoare wrote:

> British education is from a rational point of view grotesque, from a moral one, intolerable and from a human one tragic … . Predictably, the Labour Party has at no time offered a global challenge to the present system. It has at most stood for its expansion and the elimination of some of its most flagrantly undemocratic features. It has never seriously threatened the most important of these: the continued existence of the public schools and sexual discrimination against girls in every type of school. Above all, it has never attacked the vital centre of the system, the curriculum, the *content* of what is taught.[1]

In 1980 these remarks are still valid not just for the Labour Party, but also for sociologists of education. This may seem a curious statement to make, particularly given the development of sociology of the curriculum over the last decade and the more recent flowering of feminist analyses of schooling within the discipline.

However, while the diversity and range of sociological theorising is considerable and its critical stance not disputed, I shall argue in this chapter that, first, what is still lacking in the studies of the curriculum is that 'vital centre' – the *content* of school subjects. The sociology of school texts has been left a minimal element, squeezed between the blocks of macro- and micro-studies of school structures and processes. The analyses of the ideology of textbooks and of the visual and literary resources teachers daily refer to and use in the classroom have been left with little critical evaluation, apart from that of journalists concerned about the bias in such material. Second, although there is now more research on patterns of sexual discrimination in schools, this research still retains a marginal status. By and large, it has not been integrated into the 'radical' critiques of schooling which tend to weight theories of education towards class analysis. There has been a noticeable neglect of race and sexual structures in schooling as integral and not subsidiary elements of capitalism. Interestingly, it is only when these latter hierarchies and inequalities are referred to, that there seems to be any need for the investigation of school texts. In these contexts, educational materials are studied as potential sources of ideological representations and prejudice.

My concern in this paper with these two forgotten subjects of school analysis is part of an attempt to answer the same central theoretical question. I am interested in the ways schooling may be involved in the processes of legitimation and hence of reproduction of class and gender relations under capitalism. Here, I shall focus specifically on the structure and content of school culture as represented by the curriculum. The position I shall take is, first, that one cannot isolate out one sex or one social class. One has to remember that these categories exist within a set of social relations. In particular, the category of gender, which is socially constructed, only has meaning when the concepts of masculinity and femininity are recognised as a pair which exist in a relationship of complementarity and antithesis.

Gender as social relations

Simone de Beauvoir[2] describes this relationship by using a Hegelian distinction between Subject and Other. Man is the Subject, the absolute, and woman is the Other. Within this duality, the definition of woman is constructed *relative* to man:

> The terms *masculine* and *feminine* are used symmetrically only as a matter of form, as on legal papers. In actuality the relation of the two sexes is not quite like that of two electrical poles, for man represents both the positive and the neutral, as is indicated by the common use of *man* to designate human beings in general, whereas woman represents only the negative, defined by limiting criteria, without reciprocity.[3]

The assumption I hold is that both class relations and gender relations, while they exist within their own histories, can nevertheless be so closely interwoven that it is theoretically very difficult to draw them apart within specific historic conjunctures. The development of capitalism is one such conjuncture where one finds patriarchal relations of male dominance and control over women buttressing the structure of class domination. In a wide variety of 'sites', such as the work place, the family, the law and the educational system, there are the hierarchies of class and also of sex. Further, in so far as class relations (in other words the division between capital and labour) constitute the primary element of the capitalist social formation, they limit and structure the form of gender relations, the division between male and female properties and identities. I do not believe that one can disassociate the ideological forms of masculinity and femininity, in their historical specificity, from either the material basis of patriarchy nor from the class structure. If one definition of femininity or masculinity is dominant, it is the product of patriarchal relations and also the product of class dominance, even though these two structures may exist in contradiction.

Within capitalism, the relations of class and gender take a unique form. They are brought together, for example, in the maintenance of capitalist social relations of production – where male dominance reinforces the authority of supervisors, managers and experts.[4] At a more fundamental level, the coincidence of these two structures facilitates the reproduction of the work force required by that mode of production. Biological reproduction of workers occurs within a particular family mode, which is characterised in capitalism by a patriarchal household, monogamy and a domestic sexual division of labour which delegates to woman the prime responsibility for child care and early education. Social reproduction of the work force occurs through the extension of this domestic division of labour (supposedly derived from the biological role of woman in child-bearing) to the division, within capitalism, between social production and the domestic sphere. A correspondence is maintained between the public and male worlds and between the private and female realms. This coincidence, I would argue, is one of the major factors in the reproduction of the male and female work force which, in the capitalist mode of production, is organised largely along the lines of sex segregation. The division between work and the family represents a 'split' or separation between production of commodities for exchange and the production of use values, such as food, garments and so on, for consumption in the family. However, this becomes 'misrecognised' or falsely perceived when it appears that the division is based upon the 'natural instincts and interests' of men in work and women in the family. Thus, the usefulness for capital of this division, and the additional superior status attributed to productive work because of its 'masculine' association, is hidden in the ideology of sex differences.

What it is important to recognise is that the congruence of these two structures is not natural but socially imposed and, as a result, has to be continually reinforced through the legal, political and educational agencies of the state if it is to be maintained.[5] The context of this imposition is that of bourgeois hegemony; of the attempt by the bourgeoisie to gain the consent of women to a definition of femininity which locates their primary role as keepers of the home with only secondary involvement in waged work. Also the consent of men has to be won to a definition of masculinity which involves their leaving their homes to go out to work and to be responsible for the family income. If such consent can be won, the ideological conditions are more likely to be ensured for the daily and generational reproduction of the wage labour force through the unpaid work of the wife and mother.[6] Also, the recruitment of working-class women is facilitated, because of their domestic commitments, into those occupations which require little skill, are badly paid, are often part-time and normally lack any prospects. Other advantages for capital also arise from this sexual division of labour across the divide of work and family life. Zaretsky,[7] for instance, suggests the psychiatric advantages of the family to capital by the alleviation of class aggression and alienation, through the 'hiving off' of the world of personal relations from the materialistic and harsh world of work. Women in the family can become a stabilising emotional force or alternatively the victims of male violence. Further, the state can be relieved of the responsibility of catering for such functions as early childhood care and education, sick nursing, care of the aged and so on. These can be delegated to the family and especially to women.

It is, therefore, within the context of bourgeois hegemony that we can understand the dominant pattern of state education where women have been implicitly oriented, if not overtly prepared, for domesticity and men for the world of work.[8] While schooling, for men, has been directed largely towards the discipline of the work place, the development of mass schooling for women has taken a different direction. As Davin[9] argues, if state education developed solely as a result of a need for a skilled work force or alternatively to educate a newly franchised working class politically, this could only explain the establishment of schools for men, as women did not fall into either category. Extending Johnson's argument[10] that the school was meant to compensate for a morally deficient family (held responsible for the decay in society), Davin presents the view that:

> a further aim of schooling was to impose on working-class children the bourgeois view of family functions and responsibilities. Education was to form a new generation of parents (especially mothers) whose children would not be wild, but dependent and amenable ...[11]

The bourgeois form of family which schools were to establish as a 'stabilising force' was composed of the male breadwinner, the dependent housekeeping wife and dependent children. In her analysis of Board School readers of the turn of the century, Davin concludes that:

> it is worth noticing that their tendency, both through the behaviour they advocated – unselfishness, compassion, devotion to housewifely industry and family duty – and through the situations which they presented as natural to women, was to direct girls towards an exclusively domestic role, even at the expense of school.[12]

We can understand the social relations of schooling not just as attempts to prepare for class obedience but also as attempts to prepare women for their role subordinate to men. In both the reproduction of the social relations of production and the work force, we must therefore recognise the *dual* locations of family and work, not just for women but for men as well. Education for one sphere has implications for men and women's roles within the other. For working-class men, the contradictions between these two worlds are clear: at school they learn to expect forms of control and discipline when they become workers but they also learn about the expected dominance of men in the home. In some way they have to balance and contextualise these two different behavioural repertoires. Working-class women, on the other hand, experience dual forms of control, both as workers and as women, and also the contradictions of trying physically and emotionally to cope with both domestic and wage work. The role of schooling in the reproduction of the capitalist mode of production, I believe, is not therefore just to do with the reproduction of a work force through basic skill training, nor is it just to do with reproduction of the social relations of production through the hidden curriculum of discipline and authority. The work of the school facilitates the maintenance *in the long run* of the work force and the social relations of production through the transmission of a set of gender relations, its association with the division between domestic and waged labour, and all the contradictions this entails.

Care must be taken, however, when generalising this to all stages of capitalist development. With the growth of corporate capitalism and the emergence of the welfare state we can see an increased intervention of the state and the economy into the privatised world of the family. Patriarchy, as a set of power relations, may well conflict with the structure of advanced capitalism. This can be seen in the case of Sweden, where the state has attempted, and yet failed, to combat sexual discrimination in families, the communities and the schools. The advantages to be gained by capital in the breakdown of patriarchal families would lie in the 'releasing' of married women from the home and domestic chores for waged work in the commodity production system.[13] Patriarchal structures in the families of different social classes also may have different relations to the labour process and capital. Dorothy Smith,[14] for example, argues that the family of the managerial classes has been incorporated into the bureaucracies of corporate capitalism. The family of the business executive (and in particular his wife) now stands in what she called a 'subcontractual' relationship to the corporate enterprise, transmitting its culture and values and reflecting its authority structures. Humphries,[15] on the other hand, argues that historically the working-class family stood in opposition to capital because in the protected world of home life the working class could maintain and transmit its own culture and values. The weakening not only of the boundaries between the family and the economy but also of the domestic division of labour among the middle classes has to some extent heralded attempts to break down sex segregation in the schools and to construct and transmit a new set of gender relations that are more appropriate for corporate capitalism.

The impression we have to keep is of the dynamics of class and gender relations through the development of capitalism but, more than that, it is important to remember the existence of class and sexual struggle. The dualities of capital and labour and male and female, constitute not only social dichotomies but also hierarchies upon which both material and symbolic power is based. Inside these hierarchies, class and sexual struggles are waged. If we wish to understand the role of schooling as one site of the reproduction of the socio-sexual division of labour, we must also be aware of the stakes of these *two* forms of struggle and their interrelations. Certainly there is now an interest in the forms of popular struggle over and in education, in forms of class resistance and the nature of the final compromises. However, this perspective has not really affected feminist analyses. There seems to be little recognition of sexual struggle particularly in the educational arena. If the history of education concerns winning the consent of women to their position in society, then surely there must also be a history of their dissent. There must be a history of women's fight ducation not merely as a means of social mobility but also of sexual libera-. More than that, there must be a 'hidden' history of women's class struggle ınd outside the classroom to resist and reflect bourgeois definitions of femi-ııı.ity transmitted with such persistence through every cultural agency.

The analysis of class and gender relations requires, I believe, a theory of 'identity formation' – the patterns and processes which define, limit and transmit the range of models available to individuals to identify with. I make no assumption that these structures will necessarily describe individual or group identities, but I do assume that they will represent social priorities and the cultural framework within which individuals acquire a sense of themselves. The mistake, I believe, that many theories of education make, is that they assume that social identities are formed through the experience of cultural forms without ever testing this. The experience can be as little as 'contact', as active as 'consumption' (such as the buying of a book or a record) or as deep as the process of 'unconscious internalisation' or 'acquisition' of structural principles. It is at this point that our theories of education are at their most deterministic and make their greatest theoretical leaps. The learner is assumed to be either passive or 'naked' in the sense of being unaffected or unformed by any previous experience, and therefore incapable of resisting social pressures. Further, what is noticeable is how often these theories assume that individuals are what they are supposed to become. The working class are often talked of as passive, quiescent, docile or uncritical because educationalists since the nineteenth century have argued for such, or because the school is seen to be a place of discipline and control. Yet, as Willis[16] so succinctly puts it, 'merely because capital would like to treat workers as robots does not mean they are robots'.[17] Similarly women in feminist accounts, whether they are sociological or historical, tend to take on the mantle of femininity and passivity without any struggle. In attempting to move away from biological determinism in the explanation of sex differences, such theories often fall into the trap of *social* determinism. There is a sense in which, in feminist writings, women are 'oversocialised'. Take, for example, this statement by Simone de Beauvoir,

> The passivity that is the essential characteristic of the 'feminine' woman is a trait that develops in her from the earliest years. But it is wrong to assert a biological datum is concerned; it is in fact a destiny imposed upon her by her teachers and by society.[18]

The formation of identity is a highly complex process which cannot be *assumed* to be successful at either the conscious or unconscious levels of learning. Ideally what we need is an analysis not just of the production and transmission of cultural messages but also of the reception of cultural messages before we can judge the impact of these forms. Further, it is important to understand the part played by school culture in a wider context. In an age of mass media and a wide variety of cultural agencies, we can no longer justify concentrating upon schools, in isolation, as the sole or even dominant creator of meanings, class and sexual identities, and consciousness. We need to investigate the relationship between 'external' cultural resources and internal school culture in both its complementary and antagonistic aspects. As Bernstein[19] has already pointed out, the consciousness of the ruling class and the consciousness of the working class are less likely to be dominated by the mode of education than by the mode of production. In contrast, it is the consciousness of the new middle classes (called by Bernstein 'the agents of symbolic control') which is constituted by the mode of education and only indirectly by the mode of production. This view is supported by Willis, who argues that the distinction between work and culture must be broken down, particularly in the analysis of male working-class identities. He claims,

> not only can work be analysed from a cultural point of view, but it must occupy a *central* place in any full sense of culture. Most people spend their prime waking hours at work, base their identity on work activities and are defined by others essentially through their relation to work.[20]

To recap: I have argued, first, that any analysis of class and gender relations in schooling must recognise the historical specificity of definitions of masculinity and femininity. They are socially constructed categories and power relations which are contained within, and defined by, the structure of class relations. In educational institutions one is likely to find, therefore, the imposition of gender definitions which are integral to the culture of the ruling class (e.g., aristocratic or bourgeois concepts of masculinity and femininity). These definitions represent one aspect of their effort to exert hegemonic control through schooling. Second, I have argued that there must be recognition of the forms of class and sexual struggle in terms of educational provision and in the processes of class and sexual identity formation through culture. Third, I have argued that one of the ways class and gender relations are produced under capitalism is through the separation of domestic and wage labour and its reproduction in schools.

In the next section of this chapter, I shall go back to the sociology of the curriculum to try to draw out elements of a theory of class and gender relations. The analysis will be, of necessity, exploratory. I shall concentrate on the structure of school culture first, and then move on to school texts.

School gender cultures

The first body of theory I shall look at is that of cultural reproduction, to see what a structuralist account of class and gender relations in schooling could look like. Within this category one can place Basil Bernstein's theory of educational codes and Pierre Bourdieu's work on cultural codes.[21] The theme here is that culture has, through education, been divided into two categories – the legitimate and the illegitimate. This dichotomy also reflects the division between public and private knowledge, between culture and common sense, between school knowledge and family and community experience. Further, the transmission through educational institutions of specific forms of culture does not merely ensure the reproduction of that culture but also of the class structure it supports. Culture, according to Bourdieu, symbolically:

> reproduces in transfigured and therefore unrecognisable form, the structure of prevalent socio-economic relationships – it produces a representation of the social world immediately adjusted to the structure of socio-economic relationships which are consequently perceived as natural, so contributing to the symbolic buttressing of the existing balance of forces.[22]

The structural division and relations between forms of knowledge, according to Bourdieu (and indeed Bernstein as well), is a far more significant aspect of the formation of social identities than the *actual* selection of knowledge and *its* hidden message. What is important is the acquisition of the rules and principles which govern the structural hierarchies of culture. Indeed for Bernstein[23] the word 'content' signifies merely how a period of time is filled in the school timetable. Thus a curriculum is defined 'in terms of the principle by which certain periods of time and their contents are brought into a special relationship with each other'.[24] What is central to Bernstein's analysis is whether a school subject has high or low status, whether it is compulsory or optional, and what relation it bears to other subjects in terms of the strength or weakness of its boundaries.

In both Bernstein's and Bourdieu's structuralist accounts of schooling, social identities are formed through a process of internalisation of three core classifications – those of age, sex and social class. The structures of age relations, sex relations and class relations are to be found, for example, in the family, the school and the work place. While their analyses of these classifications and their interrelations remain underdeveloped, one can still see what direction that analysis might take if we look at Bourdieu's *Outline of a Theory of Practice*.[25] In this study of the Kayble society in Algeria, Bourdieu identified structural correspondences between the sexual division of labour and symbolic oppositions.[26] The categories of masculine and feminine were found *objectified* in the dichotomies of the right and left hands or the division between religion and magic, between external space (such as the market and the fields) and internal space (the home). When children learn to use these structural divisions of gender and their objectified form in the divisions of time, space and objects, according to Bourdieu, the children also construct their social identity. This social identity is composed first of a sexual identity which is learnt through simultaneously experiencing the mother's and father's body as well as the sexual division of labour within the home. It is also made up by a whole system of social meanings and values, a body language of gestures, postures, and a physical bearing (what Bourdieu calls *body hexis*), a form of speech and a language. Children experiencing the structural organisation of the economic, the social and the cultural will learn to relate to their own bodies, to other individuals and to nature according to the same principles. For the female child among the Kayble, for example, the experience is one of learning 'inner-directedness' or what Bourdieu called a *centripetal* orientation. The male child, by contrast, will be 'outer-directed' – he will have a *centrifugal* orientation which will be expressed in outward displays of virility and by his involvement in work, politics and war. The process is what Bourdieu called *embodiment*, which determines not merely children's social identities but also their physical and sexual presence.

In terms of the relevance of this account for an analysis of institutionalised education, we need to ask the following questions. Is it possible to identify *similar dialectics of embodiment and objectification* in the culture of a class society? Is there any reality in talking of correspondences between the structure of gender relations, of masculinity and femininity, and the divisions of school knowledge? In the world of formal education, it is certainly not difficult to identify numerous sets of oppositions which divide and distance forms of knowledge and their associated activities. For example, we can find the dichotomies of public and private knowledge, politics and psychology, reason and emotion, science and art, technology and nature, reality and fantasy. Further, as Spender[27] has noticed, there are also the methodological distinctions between hard and soft data, objectivity and subjectivity. The difficulty is of judging, at more than a common-sense level, the relationship of these classifications to the social definitions of masculinity and femininity. As Roberts put it,

> How polarisation and dichotomisation affect thought systems is still open to much consideration. The 'we and they', the 'foe and friend', the 'reward and punishment' – the ubiquitous and fallacious paired opposites are obvious. What is unclear is the extent to which social sex polarisation provides the basis of such dualistic thinking.[28]

Certainly much of the literature on school subjects and sex segregation within the school, places great emphasis on the fact that some subjects are perceived as either masculine or feminine. The 'masculinity' of science or the 'femininity' of domestic science can be seen as contributing to the unwillingness of girls to choose the former and of boys to study the latter.[29] The question is, how does such characterisation occur which limits the range of choice of school subjects for the different sexes? Is it purely through the unconscious manipulations of teachers using restricted gender definitions or is it the effect of the different patterns of men and women's employment? Certainly both might enter the hidden curriculum of the school and affect the students' choice of subject. Bourdieu[30] suggests that the process of gender attribution to both students and academic disciplines is dialectical. The transference of femininity, for example, from the student to the school subject and back again to the student exemplifies the dialectic of objectification and embodiment:

> the objective mechanisms which channel girls preferentially towards the arts faculties and, within them, towards certain specialities (such as modern

> languages, art history or French) owe part of their effectivity to a social definition of the 'feminine' qualities which they help to form; in other words, to the internalisation of the external necessity imposed by this definition of feminine studies. In order for a destiny, which is the objective product of the social relations defining the female condition at a given moment in time, to be transmuted into a vocation, it is necessary and sufficient that girls (and all those around them, not least their families) should be unconsciously guided by the prejudice ... that there is an elective affinity between so-called 'feminine' qualities and 'literary' qualities such as sensitivity to the imponderable nuances of sentiment or a taste for the imprecise preciosities of style.[31]

In this description of the process, women's educational route becomes a self-fulfilling prophecy once one has imposed a specific definition of femininity. The question which one has to ask is, 'How do academic disciplines or school subjects change their gender?' Why do some subjects change from appearing masculine to being viewed as essentially feminine (e.g., social sciences) or alternatively change in the other direction (e.g., education)? The answer must lie, to a great extent, in the pressures exerted on the school and universities by the changing pattern of employment of men and women in the labour force. However, the attribution of gender to specific subjects is also part of class culture and its operation in the school is, I shall argue, one of the means for legitimating the structure of class domination.

In the family, the child learns the class-based definitions of masculinity and femininity, as well as a certain sexual division of labour. When the child enters the school this experience is challenged by a very specific set of gender relations – what I shall call, following Bernstein, a *gender code*.[32] The school's gender code sets up the categories of masculine and feminine, as well as the boundaries and relations of power between them. While variations of the dominant gender code are possible in different types of school,[33] what is transmitted is essentially the form of gender relations which is specific to the ruling class. It represents the morality of the bourgeoisie and, as Davin argued,[34] it legitimates as its ideal the bourgeois family form. In this sense, we can see the work of the school as involving the process of what Bernstein called *re-contextualising* where the familial form of gender relations is converted into that of the dominant class. Because of this process, the concepts of masculinity and femininity can be found to vary in different historic periods within schooling, affecting both the provision and the 'image' of school subjects. According to Bernstein, the informal everyday experience and everyday communication within the family and peer groups which shape social identities feed into and

> create procedures and performances fundamental to formal education. However, formal education also selects, and re-focuses and abstracts from such experiences and in so doing de-contextualises it.[35]

The process begins with this de-contextualising of the behaviours and competences invoked in the contexts of the home and community. They are thus freed from their dependence on these evoking contexts and, through a process of re-contextualising, become generalisable and abstract. Thus the 'practical mastery'[36] acquired through imitation of actions in the home is converted, if the process is successful, into 'symbolic mastery' of the school discourses. One of the aspects of this process in the context of class society is the re-contextualisation of definitions of masculinity and femininity into the class-based, and hence arbitrary, classification of school knowledge. The notions of appropriate behaviours for each sex is converted into the appropriate academic disciplines. Despite the actual availability of all subjects, girls and boys of different classes learn the new ideology of sex differences which mixes a theory of biological sex differences with expected gender differences of intelligence, ability, interests and ambitions, making it appear 'natural' that boys and girls should study different school subjects.

The process of re-contextualising, even of de-contextualising, may, however, not always be effective, especially where the family structure and culture differs considerably from the school. Let us look for a moment at the distinction between mental and manual labour which is integral to the capitalist labour process. In bourgeois culture it is transposed with the hierarchy of male over female – in other words mental labour is equated with the masculine and manual work or practical skills with the female. The dominant gender code within school is likely to transmit this pairing of two hierarchies. However, as Willis has shown in *Learning to Labour*,[37] working-class boys confronted with this dual structure have two choices – either they conform, with the result that they lose credibility with their own class and deny their masculine sexuality, or they can reject the message of the school. Significantly, the conformist or 'ear'ole' is labelled as 'effeminate' or 'cissy'. The 'lads', on the other hand, in their resistance to bourgeois culture, invert the school hierarchy of mental over manual, celebrating the manual and physical working-class masculinity. This inversion is in line with the family culture of the 'lads', and in particular with that of their fathers. Thus, in resistance, 'manual labour is associated with the social superiority of masculinity, and mental labour with the social inferiority of femininity'.[38] On the shop floor as well, this convergence of manual labour with masculinity has political repercussions:

> where the principle of general abstract labour has emptied work of significance from the inside, a transformed patriarchy has filled it with significance from the outside. Discontent with work is turned away from a political discontent and confused in its logic by a huge detour into the symbolic sexual realm.[39]

The failure of the school to 're-contextualise' the masculinity of these 'lads' into academic rather than physical displays has reinforced the probability of their occupational destiny and the diffusion of their class discontent. On the other hand, those 'ear'oles' who conformed have been swept into acceptance of bourgeois culture. In both cases, the resolution of the conflict between sexual and class identities and school culture helps contain opposition to school order and, later, to the class divisions of the mode of production.

In the case of working-class girls, the classification of mental work as male and manual work as female is less problematic, as it is often reinforced rather than resisted by the family culture. We must, however, be careful to distinguish between the application of the 'manual' category to working-class and middle-class women. In the case of the working class, manual labour either refers to the form of waged labour practised by this group of women or alternatively to their unpaid domestic labour. In this case the school will legitimate the equating of domesticity, of marriage and of motherhood with femininity. For the middle-class girl, manual labour can either mean skilled work in secretarial or administrative occupations or alternatively the more 'practical' professions such as social work or nursing. The forms of class resistance to the imposition of bourgeois definitions of femininity by working-class women takes the form of exaggerated celebration of domestic life and the overemphasis of 'female' interests.

Paradoxically, the work of Willis, McRobbie and Sharpe[40] has shown that these forms of class resistance to the school, which involve the celebration of working-class definitions of masculinity and femininity, have confirmed rather than broken down the cycle of class reproduction. *They undermine neither the sexual nor the social division of labour.* In both cases, mental labour and the high-status and high-income professions are delegated and legitimated as the preserve of the male bourgeoisie and, to a lesser extent, the female bourgeoisie. The formation of sexual identities in the home and the school are therefore critical elements of the reproduction of the class structure.

In summary, I have argued in this section that specific sets of symbolic classifications represent the essence of bourgeois culture. Further underlying these hierarchies of knowledge, together with their associated 'gender', is the attempt by that class to 'win the consent' through schooling of the working class to the dominance of capital, and to win the consent of women to the sexual division of labour in which men dominate.

The gendering of school texts

Let us now turn to the analysis of school texts. These texts represent a system of choices from the 'external' culture – whether we are talking about a body of literature, a range of photographs, a set of experiments drawn from the science departments of universities or history textbooks produced by educational publishers. Despite the diversity of resources available to teachers, the research on school texts reveals a pervasive ideology – that of legitimacy of the status quo. This message, according to Gerard MacDonald,[41] has become hidden in school textbooks which once were the vehicle for an overt ideology of conservatism based on religion.

> Textbooks present a particular ideological position which can best be described as the politics of stasis. The existing order, whether natural or social, is presented as what Marx calls an 'exterior fatality'. Textbook knowledge glosses or ignores the extent to which our world is a human project. It does not help towards either real understanding or real alternatives. Resigned quiescence is no longer an overt message in textbooks. Instead it has become their hidden agenda.[42]

School texts are characterised by their 'untouchable' and apolitical nature. They are received as the truths of a 'de-classed' cultural heritage. Whether we are talking about science[43] or social science[44] or literature[45] or music,[46] the analyses show the uncritical orientation of texts towards both the selection of 'facts' and their presentation within an ideology which leaves unchallenged the status quo. Children, if working class, are faced with a presentation of the real world which does not correspond to their 'lived' experience or, alternatively, with a view of the world as far too stable to be amenable to active reform.

What characterises most of the literature in the politics of school knowledge is the examination of the social relations of learning in which school texts are employed. The effect of such texts is found to lie in the alienation of working-class children not merely from the school and the realms of high culture but also from their own lived experience outside the school. When the music, the literature and the insights learned from the family and community are given secondary status within the school, when the child's language and culture are treated as illegitimate and the message of the classroom is that there is only one definition of truth and that is to be found in the textbooks, then class domination is at its strongest. Through the authority of teachers, the legitimacy of examination syllabuses and the social and material rewards which accompany scholastic success, the child, it is argued, learns the reality of a class society, even if unconsciously. Yet while the force of these analyses makes disbelief difficult, one must ask: What is the nature of the ideology which is transmitted through these texts? Is there no attempt to form social identities? Is it really the case that the working-class child is unlikely to acquire any sense of identity – only alienation – from school? There is little analysis of the actual representations of social class in texts, which makes it extremely difficult to answer these questions. Even Hardy's article on 'Textbooks and classroom knowledge'[47] is more concerned with the changing *form* of textbooks which have moved from presenting a body of knowledge to be taught to a new emphasis on the teaching of concepts and the development of understanding and activities. Most of the research on the content of school texts (rather than the form) has aimed at identifying potential sources of sexism and racism.

In terms of sexism, there are a number of studies of school and university texts which use several different methodologies – some quantitative and some qualitative. What they have in common is their interest in identifying the ways in which gender, and in particular women, are represented. If anything, most of the studies, especially the quantitative research, tend to assume the existence of a sexual division of labour and look for its representation in the subject matter. Also they search for consistency, rather than diversity, of images of women with the result that they identify the existence of sex-role stereotypes and gender stereotypes. In addition, there is little concern with class analysis so that the overall impression is that cultural forms exist purely within a patriarchal society without any impact from capital's involvement and control over agencies of cultural production. Whereas the sociology of school knowledge described above has neglected, by and large, this source of cultural domination and sexual oppression, feminist analysis of school culture and the mass media has, to a considerable extent, neglected the forms of class control in the production and transmission of knowledge.

The picture which emerges from these exploratory and rather descriptive studies is, nevertheless, not only interesting but also very depressing. While we might have thought that the gains won by women in political, economic and sexual spheres would be reflected in the cultural media, if anything this research shows just how deeply embedded are sexual ideologies and how 'conservative' they are. The impression gained is one of women's inferiority, her domesticity, her lack of intelligence, ability, sense of adventure or creativity. In the studies undertaken in the United States (where the majority of content analysis is found) and Britain, the analyses of school texts in, for example, domestic science,[48] history[49] and literature[50] are complemented by those at university level in such disciplines as sociology,[51] anthropology,[52] psychology,[53] political science[54] and community studies.[55] The message is still the same – there is a consistent distorted model of woman which not only misrepresents her activities in social life but does nothing to correct the social patterns of discrimination. From the fantasy world of children's books[56] to the male bias of academic disciplines which purport to be 'value-free', one finds a persistent pattern of representations of women which can only be construed as the ideological wing of patriarchy. This pattern has three basic elements:

1 Women suffer from invisibility – which one author called her 'symbolic annihilation'. Women are absent actors in the histories of Western civilisation. They do not appear as active participants in such diverse fields as history, politics, literature, drama or art. Except for the heroine who portrays the individualised rather than the collective struggles of women, most women are present in passive roles.
2 When women do appear, they are generally in low-status or 'second-rate' jobs. The occupations they fill are most likely to be traditional, limited in prospect and narrow in range. Even in children's reading schemes, in the world of fantasy, women's prospects are not much better. Lobban,[57] for example, found in her study of children's readers that, in contrast to the thirty-three occupations shown for adult men, only eight were available for adult women – mum, granny, princess, queen, witch, handywoman about the house, teacher and shop assistant. However, what is more important is that women do not appear in employment nor in typically female jobs in

the ratio in which they are actually found in the economy. If anything there is an under-representation of women in paid work with an over-representation of their financial dependence on men. Spence[58] noticed this in the case of British magazine photographs:

> The visual representation of women as not having to work, as the glamorous property of men, harks back to the tradition of bourgeois painting. It effectively displaces the idea that women *do* work, and so inhibits their sense of themselves as workers. In fact according to the Equal Opportunities Commission, women make up 37 per cent of the paid work force.[59]

The image of the female is no less arbitrary and distorted. What is interesting is that the differences between the sexes appears to increase as they move from childhood to adulthood. Take, for example, Dohrmann's conclusions[60] from a study of children's educational television programmes:

> The male child is accorded the most laudable pattern: ingenuity, achievement, bravery-rescue. The female child, while rewarded and achieving, is also a follower, an object of insult, and helpless. The adult female is even more uniformly passive, adding routine service, incompetence, and admiration of others to her behavioural repertory. The adult male excels in rewarding, performing occupationally-related tasks, putting others down and picking them up in the rescue role.[61]

3 There is an over-riding emphasis on women's domesticity. The message comes across not as any subtle or hidden code but rather with a degree of repetition that can only be described as ideological bombardment. The assumption first of all appears to be that women have never left the home and, if they had, it must have been unwillingly. This is then limited even further by the portrayal, for example, of women in advertisements selling the products of those two 'feminine' locations in the home – the kitchen and the bathroom.[62]

This pattern can be traced from television drama to commercials, from newspapers to magazines to comics.[63] Against this background of cultural invasion into the home and the community, the school takes its place as just one competitor for the right to present the legitimate gender model that the child is encouraged to follow. In the United States, it is already the case that young children spend more time watching television than in school. Thus we cannot say that the message of the school is the only source of class and sexual identity formation nor, indeed, necessarily the dominant one. Yet the amount of time and effort spent on school texts is considerably greater than that spent on a short television programme, a magazine that is only read once, an advertisement glanced at in the street. What we can suggest is that the message of school texts is most likely to represent in its purest form the ideological statement of the ruling class or, at least, those values which it considers essential to transmit. Because of this, I believe, it is extremely important that we analyse school texts in all their variety.

The tools for such analysis are being developed to a large extent outside the sociology of education. It is impossible to delve too deeply here into a vast body of literature which covers content analysis, semiotics, cultural histories and so on. However, what I would like to do is to make some observations and draw some conclusions from this research. First, what is interesting about this research on culture is that it reveals a considerable split between the world of the family and that of work. Certainly, the equation between women and the home and men and public life appears to be carried in most media. If any message exists, it is the ideology of this division. Cultural texts are therefore a further 'site' for the reproduction of the 'dual spheres', reinforced not just by the ascription of gender to each sphere but also by the re-contextualising of masculinity and femininity in each setting. For example, the image of women in the daytime serial in the United States was found to be different to that shown in the evenings. The image offered to the housewives in the daytime represented one of the strongest characterisations of women on television:

> The woman of the daytime serial is above all a human being. She is liked and respected by her male acquaintances, not merely sought as an adjunct to male activities and interest. She is a responsible member of a family structure, exercising judgement and offering support to parents and children alike. Her opinions are solicited and acted upon. She enjoys the friendship of other women.[64]

In television commercials in the United States, another difference was noticed in the portrayal of masculinity. In this vivid description, one finds the distinction between the image of the man at home and the man in the world outside:

> The image of the American man in TV commercials as muscular, knowledgeable, dominating, independent, sexy, cosmopolitan, athletic, authoritative and aggressive exists only when he is seen away from his family. In embarrassing contrast the American father and husband is portrayed as passive and stupid, infantile and emasculated … . But outside the house, trouble is what he is looking for. Swift as a panther, stealthy as a cougar, free as a mustang he speeds to his rendezvous with status, independence and violence.[65]

The definitions of femininity and masculinity which we find in cultural texts are not then simple, homogenous stereotypes but rather ideological products which, if they are pulled together with all their contradictions into a coherent pattern, represent one aspect of bourgeois hegemony. The existence of a dominant gender code does not, however, rule out the possibility of dominated or subordinated codes which reshape the dominant message of patriarchy into the requirements of specific audiences. This process of re-contextualising *within* one cultural form can be seen most clearly in Frith and McRobbie's research into popular forms of music.[66] Here, without all the statistical manipulations of content analysis, they identify two 'ideological' models of gender relations. The first exists in rock music primarily for a male audience. Masculinity is portrayed by the 'rampant destructive male traveller, smashing hotels and groupies alike ... '. Women, in the eyes of these men, are:

> either sexually aggressive and therefore doomed and unhappy or else sexually repressed and therefore in need of male servicing. It's the woman, whether romanticised or not, who is seen as possessive after a husband, anti-freedom the ultimate restriction.[67]

Teenybop music, in contrast, played to a largely female audience of housewives and female factory workers, presents a different model of sexuality. As the authors argue,

> If cock rock plays on conventional concepts of male sexuality as rampant, animalistic, superficial, just-for-the-moment, teenybop plays on notions of female sexuality as being serious, diffuse and implying total emotional commitment ... . It is men who are soft, romantic, easily hurt, loyal and anxious to find a true love who fulfils their definition of what female sexuality should be about.[68]

Frith and McRobbie argue that within each musical form one can find a range of models or definitions of sexuality, mediated by the words of the song, the rhythms and beat of the music, the packaging and image of the singer or group. What their analysis reveals is the complexity of the ideological struggle to define and contain sexual identities within the framework of class culture.

This complexity can also be found in McRobbie's analysis of the schoolgirl magazine *Jackie*.[69] Here she uses semiology to provide a method for such research, a form of analysis which has become increasingly popular in cultural studies. The advantages of this form of analysis are that it has

> more to offer than traditional content analysis if only because it is not solely concerned with the numerative *appearance* of content, but with the messages which such 'contents' signify ... . Quantification is therefore rejected and replaced with understanding media messages as *structured wholes* and combinations of structures, polarities and oppositions are endowed with greater significance than their mere numerative existence.[70]

As a result, she is able to draw out five different subcodes of femininity which relate to beauty, fashion, pop music, personal/domestic life and romance. What is important here is that the magazine is examined not just as a social product but also as an active agent in the *production* of new meanings. The problem therefore is not one of trying to fit these representations of women to the realities of their lives but rather to recognise the ideological 'work' carried out by these texts in the *reconstruction* rather than the reproduction of gender definitions and relations.

By analysing the combinations of various representations of femininity or masculinity within one set of texts, one is also more likely to be made aware of the contradictions which can arise between different gender definitions. Take, for example, the contradictory sets of female ideals: the capable consumer housewife versus the dependent incapable wife; the insatiable temptress and the passive sex object; the all-embracing earth mother versus the childlike doll. Another example can be found in the excellent analysis of 1950s texts in three domains (motherhood, education and sexuality) by the Birmingham Feminist History Group.[71] Here they located the ideological struggle between the liberal concept of equal opportunity and the bourgeois ideal of separate spheres for each sex, which was resolved in the 1950s in the ideology of the two sexes being 'equal but different'. Further they identified the contradictory pressures upon married women both to return to work and to act as efficient and dedicated wives and mothers. Thus the apparent 'unity' of the 1950s collapsed under their scrutiny into 'contradictions, tensions and divisions'. They found that:

> There was no one representation of women; but the struggle for primacy of one set of representations concerned with marriage, home and family, is systematically victorious throughout our period.[72]

Conclusions

What I have argued is that not only must we be aware of the complexity of definitions of gender relations in culture but that we must recognise the role of culture within hegemony. The question I believe we should be asking is not just what relation do the representations found within texts bear to 'lived' relations but also what is the relevance of that message for capital? The struggle to define and contain sexuality is no less a problem for capital than containing the force of class opposition and preparing the working class for the rigours of the work place. Indeed, as Gramsci argues in the notes on 'Some aspects of the sexual question',[73] the two facets of hegemony are often inextricably linked. Sexual relations, the definitions of morality, of masculinity and femininity, are historically constructed under immense odds. First, according to Gramsci,

> The history of industrialism has always been a continuing struggle (which today takes an even more marked and vigorous form) against the element of 'animality' in men. It has been an interrupted, often painful and bloody process of subjugating natural (animal and primitive) instincts to new more rigid norms and habits of order, exactitude and precision which can make

> possible an increasingly complex form of collective life which are the necessary consequence of industrial development.[74]

Sexual instincts have undergone the greatest degree of repression from society, according to Gramsci. Within this history, the 'aesthetic' ideal of women has oscillated between the concept of 'brood mare' for reproduction and 'dolly' for sport and pleasure. The biological reproduction of the work force necessary to support an 'unproductive' sector of the population (due to age and ill health) is one of the problems connected with women's position. If this ratio is unbalanced, then a further problem for hegemony is posed.

The history of hegemonic control over relations between the sexes has been fraught with crises which have affected mainly the middle classes and sectors of the ruling class. After each period of Puritanism, Gramsci argues, there is a crisis of libertinism which only marginally affects the working class – through the corruption of their women. However, what is important in Gramsci's argument is that gender relations, or more specifically sexual relations, are linked to the methods of production and patterns of work within a mode of production. For example, he links the relative stability of sexual unions among the peasants to the system of agricultural work in the countryside. With the introduction of Fordism, the rationalisation of work, Gramsci argued, made it important that the working classes held a new sexual ethic – that of monogamy.

> The truth is that a new type of man demanded by the rationalisation of production and work cannot be developed until the sexual instinct has been suitably regulated and until it too has been rationalised.[75]

The rigorous discipline of work demands discipline of the sexual instincts and with it, according to Gramsci, comes the strengthening of the ideology of the family and the stability of sexual relations. The reason for the 'Puritanical' interventions of the industrialists, such as Ford, into working-class families (controlling the consumption of alcohol and 'womanising') could be found in the necessity of reproducing the work force in fit-state for the discipline of the new work methods. Capital needed to preserve 'outside of work, a certain psycho-physical equilibrium which prevents a physiological collapse of the worker, exhausted by the new methods of production'.[76]

In these brief notes Gramsci argues that not only are the relations between the sexes historical products, related to the development of capitalism, but also that these relations are areas in which consent has to be won. To create and make new moralities 'second nature', to win consent for the arbitrary division of social life into male and female worlds of public and private activities, is no easy task and perhaps that is why there is such ideological bombardment from educational and cultural agencies of the state. It is not that capital has *succeeded* in creating classed and sexed subjects, suitably adjusted to the rigours of work in the home and the work place, but rather that no day can go by without it *trying*.

Notes

1 Hoare, Q. (1967) 'Education: programmes and men', *New Left Review*, 32, p. 40.
2 de Beauvoir, S. (1972) *The Second Sex*, Harmondsworth: Penguin.
3 Ibid., p. 15.
4 See Hartman, H. (1976) 'Capitalism, patriarchy and job segregation by sex', *Signs: Journal of Women in Culture and Society*, 1, 3, part 2 (Spring), pp. 137–69, and Gee, M. (1978) 'The capitalist labour process and women workers', paper given at the Annual Conference of Socialist Economists in Bradford.
5 See Land, H. (1978) 'Who cares for the family?', *Journal of Social Policy*, 7, 3, pp. 257–84.
6 For a brief summary of the 'domestic labour debate' which analyses the economic implications and advantages to capital of women's household work, see Fee, T. (1976) 'Domestic labour: an analysis of housework and its relation to the production process', *Review of Radical Political Economics*, 8, 1, Spring, p. 108.
7 Zaretsky, E. (1973) *Capitalism, the Family and Personal Life*, New York: Harper Colophon Books.
8 Dyehouse, C. (1977) 'Good wives and little mothers; social anxieties and school girl's curriculum 1890–1920', *Oxford Review of Education*, 3, 1, pp. 21–36; Sharpe, S. (1976) *Just Like a Girl*, Harmondsworth: Pelican; Deem, R. (1978) *Women and Schooling*, London: Routledge and Kegan Paul; Wolpe, A.M. (1977) *Some Processes of Sexist Education*, London: WRRCP pamphlet; Wolpe, A.M. (1976) 'The official ideology of education for girls', in M. Flude and J. Ahier (eds) *Educability, Schools and Ideology*, London: Croom Helm; Delamont, S. and Duffin, L. (eds) (1978) *The Nineteenth Century Women*, London: Croom Helm (articles by Delamont).
9 The 1869 Franchise Act created approximately a million new voters, none of whom were women (see Davin, A. (1979) 'Mind you do as you are told, reading books for board school girls', *Feminist Review*, 3, pp. 89–98).
10 Johnson, R. (1970) 'Educational policy and social control in early Victorian England', *Past and Present*, 49, pp. 96–113.
11 Davin, op. cit., p. 90 n. 9.
12 Ibid., p. 98.
13 The state also acted against patriarchal family structures during the two world wars, by encouraging the employment of women in wage labour. The child care facilities established during this period were later to be closed down when women were directed back to the home.
14 Smith, D. (1975) 'Women, the family and corporate capitalism', *Berkeley Journal of Sociology*, XX, pp. 55–90.
15 Humphries, J. (1977) 'Class struggle and the persistence of the working class family', *Cambridge Journal of Economics*, 3, 1, pp. 241–58.
16 Willis, P. (1979) 'Shop floor culture, masculinity and the wage form', in J. Clarke, C. Critcher and R. Johnson (eds) *Working Class Culture*, London: Hutchinson.
17 Ibid., p. 187.
18 Quoted in J. Freeman (1970) 'Growing up girlish', *Trans-Action*, 8, November–December, pp. 36–43.
19 Bernstein, B. (1977) 'Aspects of the relation between education and production', in *Class, Codes and Control*, London: Routledge and Kegan Paul, 2nd edn, vol. 3.
20 Willis, op. cit., p. 186 n. 16.
21 For a critical analysis of the work of Bernstein and Bourdieu, see MacDonald, M. (1977) *Curriculum and Cultural Reproduction*, Block 3 E202, Milton Keynes: Open University Press.
22 Bourdieu, P. (1971) 'The thinkable and the unthinkable', *Times Literary Supplement*, 15 October, p. 1,255.
23 Bernstein, B. (1977) 'On the curriculum', in *Class, Codes and Control*, London: Routledge and Kegan Paul, 2nd edn, vol. 3.

24 Ibid., p. 79.
25 Bourdieu, P. (1977) *Outline of a Theory of Practice*, London: Cambridge University Press.
26 For an outline of this theory, see MacDonald, M. (1979) 'Cultural reproduction: the pedagogy of sexuality', *Screen Education*, 32–33, Autumn–Winter, pp. 143–53.
27 Spender, D. (1978) 'Educational research and the feminist perspective', paper presented at the British Educational Research Association Conference, Leicester University, April.
28 Quoted in ibid.
29 See, for example, Kelly, A. (1975) 'A discouraging process: how girls are eased out of science', paper presented at the Conference on Girls and Science Education, Chelsea College, 19–20 March; Wynn, B. (1977) 'Domestic subjects and the sexual division of labour', in G. Whitty, *School Knowledge and Social Control*, Block 3 E202, Milton Keynes: Open University Press.
30 Bourdieu, P. and Passeron, J.-C. (1977) *Reproduction in Education, Society and Culture*, London: Sage.
31 Ibid., p. 78.
32 For a description of gender codes, see MacDonald, M. (1980) 'Socio-cultural reproduction and women's education', in R. Deem (ed.) *Schooling for Women's Work*, London: Routledge and Kegan Paul.
33 Clarricoates, K. (1980) 'The importance of being earnest … Emma … Tom … Jane … : the perception and categorisation of gender conformity and gender deviation in primary schools', in Deem, op. cit.
34 Davin, op. cit.
35 Bernstein, B. (1977) 'Aspects of the relation between education and production', p. 30.
36 For the distinction between practical and symbolic mastery, see Bourdieu (1977) *Outline of a Theory of Practice* and Bourdieu and Passeron (1977) *Reproduction in Education, Society and Culture*.
37 Willis, P. (1977) *Learning to Labour*, Farnborough: Saxon House.
38 Ibid., p. 148.
39 Willis, P. (1979) 'Shop floor culture, masculinity and the wage form', op. cit., p. 198.
40 Willis, P. (1977) *Learning to Labour*; McRobbie, A. (1978) 'Working class girls and the culture of femininity', in Women's Studies Group (eds) *Women Take Issue*, London: CCCS/Hutchinson; Sharpe, op. cit.
41 MacDonald, G. (1976) 'The politics of educational publishing', in G. Whitty and M. Young (eds) *Explorations in the Politics of School Knowledge*, Driffield: Nafferton Books.
42 Ibid., p. 223.
43 Young, M. (1976) 'The schooling of science', in Whitty and Young, op. cit.
44 Whitty, G. (1976) 'Studying society: for social change and social control', in Whitty and Young, op. cit.
45 Hand, N. (1976) 'What is English?', in Whitty and Young, op. cit.
46 Vulliamy, G. (1976) 'What counts as school music?', in Whitty and Young, op. cit.
47 Hardy, J. (1976) 'Textbooks and classroom knowledge: the politics of explanation and description', in Whitty and Young, op. cit.
48 See Wynn, op. cit.
49 Trecker, J.L. (1971) 'Women in US history high school textbooks', *Social Education*, March, pp. 249–60, 338. Anyon, J. (1979) 'Ideology and United States history textbooks', *Harvard Educational Review*, 49, 3, August, pp. 361–86.
50 Wolff, C.G. (1972) 'A mirror for men: stereotypes of women in literature', *Massachusetts Review*, 13, pp. 205–18. See also articles in S. Stacey, S. Bereaud and J. Daniels (eds) (1974) *And Jill came Tumbling After*, New York: Dell.

51 Ehrlich, C. (1971) 'The male sociologist's burden: the place of women in marriage and family texts', *Journal of Marriage and the Family*, 33, August, pp. 421–30.
52 Slocum, S. (1975) 'Woman the gatherer: male bias in anthropology', in R. Reuter (ed.) *Toward an Anthropology of Women*, New York: Monthly Review Press.
53 Weisstein, N. (1971) 'Psychology constructs the female', in V. Gornick and B.K. Moran (eds) *Women in Sexist Society*, New York: Basic Books.
54 Bourque, S. and Grossholtz, J. (1975) 'Politics as unnatural politics, political science looks at female participation', *Politics and Society*, Winter, pp. 225–66.
55 Frankenberg, R. (1976) 'In the production of their lives, Men (?) sex and gender in British Community Studies', in D.L. Barker and S. Allen (eds) *Sexual Divisions and Society*, London: Tavistock.
56 See, for example, Lobban, G. (1975) 'Sex roles in reading schemes', *Educational Review*, 27, 3, June, pp. 201–10; Weitzman, L.J. et al. (1976) 'Sex role socialisation in picture books for pre-school children', in *Sexism in Children's Books*, Children's Rights Workshop No. 2, London: Writers and Readers Publishing Co-op; Dixon, B. (1977) *Catching them Young (No. 1); Sex, Race and Class in Children's Fiction*, London: Pluto Press; Women on Words and Images (1975) *Dick and Jane as Victims*, P.O. Box 2163, Princeton NJ 08540.
57 Lobban, G. (1978) 'The influence of the school on sex role stereotyping', in J. Chetwynd and O. Harnett (eds) *The Sex Role System*, London: Routledge and Kegan Paul.
58 Spence, J. (1978) 'What do people do, all day; class and gender in images of women', *Screen Education*, 29, pp. 29–45.
59 Ibid., p. 31.
60 Dohrmann, R. (1975) 'A gender profile of children's educational TV', *Journal of Communication*, 25, 4, pp. 56–65.
61 Ibid., pp. 62–3.
62 See, for example, Courtney, A.E. and Whipple, T.W. (1974) 'Women in TV commercials', *Journal of Communication*, 24, 2, pp. 110–18.
63 For good summaries of research, see Busby, L.J. (1975) 'Sex role research on the mass media', *Journal of Communication*, 25, 4, pp. 107–31, and UNESCO (1979) 'Mass media: the image role and social conditions of women', *Reports and Papers on Mass Communication*, 84.
64 Downing, M. (1974) 'Heroine of the daytime serial', *Journal of Communication*, 24, 2, p. 137.
65 Bardwick, J.M. and Schumman, S.I. (1975) 'Portrait of American men and women in TV commercials', *Psychology*, IV, 4, pp. 18–23, quoted in Busby, op. cit., p. 116.
66 Frith, S. and McRobbie, A. (1978) 'Rock and sexuality', in *Screen Education*, 29, Winter, pp. 3–20.
67 Ibid., p. 7.
68 Ibid., p. 7.
69 McRobbie, A. (1978) '*Jackie*: an ideology of adolescent femininity', CCCS Occasional Paper No. 53.
70 Ibid., p. 11. For other examples of semiotics, see CCCS Women's Studies Group, 'Images of women in the media', CCCS Occasional Paper No. 3.
71 Birmingham Feminist History Group (1979) 'Feminism as femininity in the nineteen fifties', *Feminist Review*, 3, pp. 48–65.
72 Ibid., p. 64.
73 Gramsci, A. (1971) *Selections from the Prison Notebooks*, trans. Q. Hoare and G. Nowell-Smith, London: Lawrence and Wishart.
74 Ibid., p. 298.
75 Ibid., p. 296.
76 Ibid., p. 303.

5 A cloud over co-education

An analysis of the forms of transmission of class and gender relations

In 1948 John Newsom,[1] then a school inspector, in his book *The Education of Girls* expounded the view that girls' education should reflect the fact that:

> Women possess certain particular needs based on their particular psychology, physiology and their social and economic position … . The fundamental common experience is the fact that the vast majority of them will become the makers of homes, and that to do this successfully requires the proper development of many talents.[2]

Girls, according to Newsom, constituted a single and more or less homogeneous group since they shared a common interest and a main vocation in domesticity. The ideals of education should, therefore, reflect this future destination of women and stress the *complementarity* yet *differences* between the sexes. Schooling for girls and boys should be, in the rhetoric of the 1940s, 'equal but different', and should stress the development of individual talents and interests. As Bland, McCabe and Mort have pointed out, Newsom's book provided an early example of the attempt to overcome the contradiction between an ideology of child-centred education with its progressive ideals of individual development and the assumption that all girls were destined to a collective and identical future as 'homemakers'.[3] Yet the book is also an interesting example of yet another problem which has faced educationalists in the nineteenth and twentieth centuries. In his book, Newsom reaches a point where, having demarcated the necessary division between the sexes, he has to recommend a school structure that would fulfil the conditions for the reproduction of such a sexual division of labour. He asks the question: should boys and girls in all their heterogeneity be educated together, or should they be separated during school life? He concludes:

> As far as the children are concerned there is no satisfactory evidence from which to deduce whether co-education is more generally suitable than segregation. It is a matter of opinion rather than exact knowledge. True it is rarely contended that children of primary age should be separated according to sex, but at the secondary stage there is no generally accepted

> theory on the subject. If there are enough boys and girls to establish separate schools, then that course is followed; if there are not sufficient for proper organization then a mixed school is provided. In certain circles, however, a cloud 'no bigger than a man's hand' [sic] is forming, a cloud whose contention is that between twelve and fifteen boys and girls are better apart. Puberty comes earlier to girls and they are already 'interested in boys' when boys are still going through the last happy period of barbarism when they regard girls as a nuisance if not with positive distaste. Once the change from childhood to physical maturity is accomplished, it is held that they can be brought together again with profit. I do not know how far this theory is supported but it presents a fascinating field for detailed research … . If there were any possibility of the main contention of this book becoming operative, that of planning of girls' education according to their needs instead of slavishly copying the education of their brothers, there would be an additional reason for temporary segregation. It is all very difficult.[4]

In this chapter I shall show that there is just as much confusion today and just as little research on this issue as in the 1940s. It is still 'all very difficult'. Newsom's decision about the merits of co-education is representative of the general decision of policy-makers. For example, in 1945 the Ministry of Education's pamphlet *The Nation's Schools* could not recommend a fixed doctrine as to the provision of mixed or single-sex schools.[5] As it was desirable and advantageous for boys and girls to learn 'to know and respect each other's point of view', co-education was desirable within primary education. But in the area of secondary education, there were the rival advantages of single-sex schools. Since it was already agreed that at adolescence boys and girls *should* be separated for physical training and major games and that, at this age, their needs and interests ran further apart, single-sex schooling appeared to be the most logical structure. At the level of further education, the mixing of the sexes was again desirable. Therefore, the recommended form of reproduction of the division of the sexes through education was to vary according to the different *age* of the pupils and the different types of schooling offered in the primary, secondary and tertiary sectors. One might explain this by noticing that, in the primary schools, the gender divisions to be reproduced were those found within the domestic sphere where brothers and sisters mix together freely; while in the secondary schools the preparation was for the sexual division of labour found within paid employment and a gender-divided labour market. By the time students reached further education, they could be safely brought together since the patterns of gender differentiation would have been largely settled.

The debate over the relative merits of each type of school has a long and forgotten history, forgotten perhaps because it is an issue that appears only to concern women. This is especially the case today, since it is only feminists and those agencies concerned with the equality of the sexes which have become involved in the discussions as to the advantages and disadvantages of each form of schooling. The traditional and the socialist histories of education have marginalised women's educational experiences and have assumed that the discussion of female education is something that can occur without reference to, or influence upon, male or class histories of education. Thus the issue of what Weinberg[6] called the 'sex structure' of schools is an absent or well-hidden aspect of these accounts. However, if we are not to treat gender categories as natural organising principles of educational research and gender relations as only referring to female education, then we have to investigate the sets of gender relations made available, through a class-determined educational system, to *both* men and women. Thus what I would like to show in this chapter is that the issue of whether to support single-sex or co-educational schools is broader than the current feminist concern of attempting to help girls study science subjects (to help them compete as equals with boys) or to help girls enter university and male occupations. It is an issue which involves analysing the differences between class-based notions of education in the state and private sector and the reproduction of the socio-sexual division of labour under capitalism.

I shall trace the outlines of what I have called the 'hidden' history of co-education in the context of a pattern of educational policy-making which assumed that boys' and girls' education should be different. In a patriarchal society, such a pattern of policy-making was hardly surprising. However, it also led to various problems in the nineteenth century and in the twentieth century, since it posed the question: how does one place two different types of education (one for each sex) within *one* state system of education? Second, how does one locate female class differences in an educational system designed to reproduce the seemingly more important set of class relations – those of men and male occupational hierarchies? The solutions to such policy dilemmas were to utilise the ideology of *female domesticity*, as female historians have shown.[7] Where the two processes of class and gender reproduction collude historically is in the attempted imposition through schooling of a bourgeois family form that entailed the social construction of the female housekeeping wife dependent upon a wage- or salary-earning husband. Second, it involved the development of the *myth of female classlessness* which blurred or covered over the differences of educational provision for girls of different social classes.[8]

The dual impact of these two ideological aspects of the processes of reproducing dominant class and gender relations led not to a single educational structure but to a variety of school structures. The history of schooling reveals the range of alternative 'sex structures' available at any one time, as well as the class factors involved in their provision. Thus while one might want to talk about a dominant *gender code* in education,[9] reproducing dominant bourgeois gender relations, one must also be aware that in different historical periods and for different social classes there may be a variety of *modalities of transmission* of those gender relations.

In the context of the English state system of education, the most influential modality of transmission of class and gender relations has been that exemplified by the private single-sex grammar school. However, by the late 1960s the two systems of education had diverged significantly, with the majority of state comprehensive schools offering co-education and the majority of private secondary schools retaining their single-sex status. I shall argue that the development of such co-educational comprehensive schools did not represent, despite its progressive image, a challenge to the reproduction of dominant gender relations but rather a modification of the *form* of their transmission. In the second part of the chapter, therefore, I look at the critiques and defence of co-education and the ways in which class factors have become submerged in the debate over the merits or disadvantages of mixed schooling. It is no surprise to me, for instance, given the history of co-education, that (as Jenny Shaw points out) the paradox of the British model of mixed comprehensive secondary school is that 'by its own criteria of success its most promising pupils persistently underachieve'.[10] 'How is it', she asks, 'that girls, who begin their school career with what appears to be a flying start over boys, being as much as two years ahead in reading and in physical and psychological maturity, come to leave school with far fewer qualifications?'[11] The suggestion here is that such schools do not offer equality of opportunity to boys and girls alike, but rather that they actually close the door on or 'harm' girls by their detrimental effects.[12]

Co-educational comprehensives historically were meant to reproduce life within a 'normal' heterosexual world, and it is the reproduction of this world that feminists have responded to. In the final part of the chapter I look very briefly at the various responses of feminists to the nature of such an educational goal. I look at the critiques they offer to mixed schooling and the implications of each perspective in terms of how far they may realistically expect to break down gender inequality by the educational reforms they suggest.

The hidden history of co-education

It is generally assumed that co-educational schools only became an issue in the 1970s, especially after the report of the Department of Education and Science on 'Curricular differences for boys and girls' found that girls were more likely to achieve a broader education and make less sex-stereotyped decisions of subject choice in single-sex schools than in mixed ones.[13] Certainly that report can be seen as the contemporary catalyst to much more interest being taken in the advantages and disadvantages of mixed schools. However, the relative merits of this form of schooling had been challenged as early as the 1920s when women teachers realised that mixed schools might well involve a reduction of their promotion prospects, especially since most mixed schools had a male head and female teachers were generally limited to teaching infants, girls and specialist domestic-type classes.[14] As it is impossible to trace the intricacies of this history of co-educational schools without more research and more space, I will therefore confine myself here to the broadest of patterns which appear to be significant.

The development of co-educational schools had been patchy in the nineteenth century, and to a large extent was determined by the social-class background of the pupil clientele.[15] The increasing provision of girls' private schools, both day schools and boarding schools, repeated in many ways the style and ethos of boys' schools. They attempted to emulate their academic norms as well as provide for the distinctive requirements of middle-class and aristocratic girls. In 1864 the Taunton Commission recommended that the proper development of middle-class girls' character was provided by the establishment of girls' day schools, even though a Mr Hammond who gave evidence to them reported that he had found no noticeable difference of attainment in the two sexes when taught in mixed schools. During the nineteenth century several notable girls-only public schools were set up, modelled upon the boys' public boarding schools: for example, St Leonards, St Andrews (1877), Roedean (1885), Godolphin School (1886), Wycombe Abbey (1896) and Sherborne (1899).[16] These schools restricted their entry to girls of specific social class (through the procedures of social selection and the setting of high fees) to a greater extent than the girls' day schools under the aegis of the Girls' Public Day Schools Company. The main pattern of education of the bourgeoisie was therefore largely that of single-sex education which entailed a segregation of the sexes based upon a differentiation of the roles of men and women of that social stratum.

Certainly, at one level, it was convenient to establish single-sex girls' schools since the boys' schools were already so well developed. On the other hand, single-sex schooling more easily catered for the reproduction of the bourgeois gender relations in which, as Judith Okeley argues,[17] girls were prepared more for the marriage market than the labour market.

> girls are protected for a future marriage contract within an elite whose biological and social reproduction they ensure. They have no economic and political power independent of males such as their fathers, and later their husbands and sons.[18]

Thus the advantages of attending a public school for girls are not found in the economic advantages of access to the high-status professions, nor indeed necessarily access to universities. Rather, they lie in the acquisition of the cultural capital of that social class and of maintaining the possibility of marrying into it, through the social network the schools give access to. Thus, as Okeley writes, in this social stratum:

> boys' and girls' educations are not symmetrical but they are *ideologically interdependent*. That considered female is partly defined by its opposite: that which is considered to be male. The characteristics of one institution are strengthened by their absence in the other. Qualities primarily reserved for one gender will have a different meaning in the institution of the opposing gender. The two educations are also linked in practice since, in adulthood, individuals from the separate institutions will be united in marriage for the consolidation of their class. As members of the same social class the girls

> and boys may share similar educational experiences but as members of different gender categories some of their educational experiences may differ.
> (my emphasis)[19]

What single-sex schools offered to the bourgeoisie was the chance to provide *different but equally privileged* educations for its sons and daughters, maintaining the appropriateness of a rigid sexual division of labour between public and private worlds, between male paid employment and female family responsibilities. Further, single-sex schools by their physical segregation of the sexes provided the conditions for the maintenance of female adolescent virginity and the preservation of the concept of bourgeois marriage. The reproduction of heterosexuality as the norm of sexual relations ironically required the setting up of single-sex environments, which always contained the dangers of sponsoring homosexual relations among staff and pupils. Yet while homosexuality among boys in particular was a well-known occurrence in boys' public schools, it did not appear to threaten the stability of the bourgeois family form in a way that mixing of the sexes at adolescence might have implied. As Turner argues,

> the reason why the middle class insisted on a social and educational barrier between boys and girls was because they feared that sexual misbehaviour was an inevitable consequence of co-education.[20]

Thus while the dominant form of transmission of the sexual division of labour among the bourgeoisie – single-sex schools – allowed for the reproduction of class cultural unity, it also provided for the reproduction of intra-class gender differentiation which maintained the notion of the bourgeois family form of salary-earning husband and dependent housekeeping wife who would provide the only legitimate heirs to the economic and cultural wealth of that social class.[21] However, the development of co-educational schools was beginning to be officially encouraged for the middle classes: for example, the Bryce Commission in 1895 took the view that there were too few endowed and proprietory schools which were mixed. The Commission used the experience of the United States, where co-education had been flourishing, to argue that:

> this system has been tried with so much success in other countries, and to some extent in Great Britain itself, that we feel sure its use may be extended without fear of any undesirable consequences, and probably with some special advantages for the formation of character and general stimulus to intellectual activity.[22]

By 1898, the most famous co-educational boarding school, Bedales, had opened its door to girls. However, the popularity of single-sex schools in the private fee-paying sector was to hold its own well into the latter part of the twentieth century. By 1968 the Public Schools Commission found that out of 273 public schools in England and Wales there were only three mixed public schools, accounting for 1162 out of 105,000 pupils.[23] In the maintained sector, by contrast, 58 per cent of secondary schools were co-educational, catering for 60 per cent of secondary pupils. The Commission felt that the high number of single-sex private schools was more a reflection of the 'intentions of their founders and the conventions of their day' than the current parental attitudes in the late 1960s. They suggested that:

> many parents would welcome co-education either for its own sake or so that brothers and sisters may attend the same school where this would be more convenient than attending separate schools.[24]

The objection to co-education they saw as linked to boarding education and the fear of sexual relationships developing between male and female pupils. Such fear they felt to be exaggerated and argued instead that if girls were to have equal opportunities with boys, they could only receive these through co-educational schools.

Today, there are many more mixed private secondary schools. Some boys' schools have brought girls into all 'forms' and others have let girls into the sixth form only.[25] However, as a recent report in *The Sunday Times* showed,[26] the introduction of mixing in these schools has not threatened the reproduction of gender relations at either the academic or sexual level. Girls are being recruited either to take the arts subjects which boys do not choose to study, particularly at advanced levels, or to provide entertainment for boys who also might be distracted from their homosexual activities. Interestingly, the penalty for a boy and girl found in bed together is expulsion, while a lenient view tends to be taken of homosexual activities in such schools. As *The Sunday Times* reporter commented:

> This puts the schools in the curious position of turning a blind eye to an illegal activity (homosexual relations between persons under 21) while maintaining severe sanctions against a perfectly legal one (heterosexual relations between persons over 16).[27]

Male teachers also felt the advantages of the presence of girls in such mixed public schools. One, for example, claimed that the major benefit of introducing girls into previously boys-only private schools was a 'rediscovery of a relaxed normality'. Unfortunately the nature of this 'normality' can be seen in the following statement of another teacher:

> I couldn't face going back to the intensity of a single-sex school. I'd rather leave teaching. Did you notice this morning? I went into the classroom and the girls saw straight away that I'd had a haircut and they commented on it. They'll mention your tie as well. It keeps you on your toes: in the old days masters wore the same ties for the whole term.[28]

The dominant form of reproduction of bourgeois gender relations (until recently when it has been modified) has been that of single-sex schools which were based upon the principle of children's exclusion and protection from contact with other social classes and from contact with the opposite sex. Education was meant to train boys for their future roles as leaders of the country and as patriarchs, and to train girls for their future roles as wives and mothers of the members of that social class. In this way single-sex schools made possible a division of labour which gave both boys and girls of that social class privileges, as well as ensuring the reproduction of the gender hierarchy specific to that social class. In this context a specifically bourgeois notion of femininity was transmitted to the girls that differed from those aspects of femininity taught within state secondary schools. While to the outsider the concepts of femininity in the private- and state-sector schools may appear to be very similar, as Lucy Blandford found, ex-public school girls in 1977 were acutely sensitive to the signs of class difference between themselves and girls from state grammar schools. These differences can be seen in the following extracts from Blandford's interviews:

> At ten a public school girl has already learned how to handle servants: that particular distance that the upper classes keep from inferiors and each other, is imbibed early. At school a girl soon learns that one doesn't talk to the kitchen staff: in the hols she learns how much to tip staff and how to do it unselfconsciously when she goes away (and these days, how not to register surprise if there's no staff to tip, times being what they are). As one grander type puts it 'You can always tell a grammar school girl who has married well by the fact that she's a fraction too familiar with her servants and rather uncomfortable with yours.'[29]

> Can a state-school girl pass herself off as The Real Thing? There's a moment of embarrassed surprise. 'When she's young', says Sal … 'any pretty woman with a good figure can dress herself up and pass herself off as anything. But when she gets older, she inevitably reverts to type.' Nicki describes a well-turned-out, well-educated and ambitious state-school girl as a 'cultured pearl, not a real pearl.'[30]

In contrast to this history, many co-educational schools were available to the children of the working classes by the mid-nineteenth century. The early charity schools set up by the bourgeoisie to educate poor children in the 'rudiments' of education and to provide a training in 'morals and good conduct' were often mixed. June Purvis has documented the variety of forms of educational provision available to working-class girls from 1800 to 1870, noticing that a large number of National Society schools were mixed.[31] The evidence she collected suggested that girls attained a higher academic standard in the 3Rs, especially in arithmetic, when in mixed schools and taught by male teachers. Problems arose if girls were in mixed schools with infants, since female pupils might be asked to help care for and teach the younger children as unpaid helpers. In 1858, the Newcastle Commission reported that of the 1,895 schools they had inspected nearly half were mixed, of which 10 per cent were mixed infant schools. Only 18.1 per cent were girls' schools and 22.2 per cent were boys' schools.[32] With the passing of the 1870 Education Act, a state system of national elementary schools became established, bringing together, as Purvis has pointed out, not just the fragmented system of educational provision but also the principles of class and gender differentiation and controls which had characterised the voluntary schools run by the bourgeoisie for the working classes. This Act did not attempt to establish the principle of equal education for all social classes; nor did it attempt to establish an equal education for boys and girls.

> For working class girls … the provision of a state system of national education meant a renewed emphasis on education for motherhood rather than education for employment, a renewed emphasis that was especially pronounced in the latter decades of the century when grants were made for the teaching of cookery and laundry work. But not all working class girls experienced such a state system since school attendance was not made compulsory until 1880 and not made free until 1891.[33]

Thus, despite the fact that many elementary schools were co-educational (about half in 1900), gender differentiation in the working classes was not seriously challenged. As Purvis' research shows, whatever the form of schooling it was always assumed that the female sex should be prepared for the private sphere of the home, while boys would be prepared primarily for activities outside the home, in paid employment. Separate schools, separate departments or separate classes were established for boys and girls, and in each type of school *gender-specific curricula* were taught. Therefore, a range of alternative school sex-structures was offered to the working classes, the choice being affected to a certain extent by the regional catchment area since single-sex schools were more likely to flourish in towns, while mixed schools were needed in the scattered populations of rural areas. However, it is important that behind the pragmatics of policy decisions, there was little identification of the concept of *gender mixing* with that of *identical training* for boys and girls. Co-educational schools generally meant that the different educations for boys and girls were 'mixed together' rather than integrated into a common form of schooling.

Sex-segregation could involve the physical separation of boys and girls through total exclusion in boarding schools, such as those provided by and for the middle classes, or it could involve the separation of day schools by sex, or it could involve the separation of teaching classes and subjects for boys and girls *within* one building. For example, the 1903 Code established, according to David,[34] separate 'classes' in different school subjects. The basis was set for the unity and diversity of male and female working-class education within one type of school. The production of class identity was provided through the common courses that boys and girls took as a 'preparation for adult life', which was generally referred to by the 'neutral' concept of 'citizenship'. In the higher elementary schools these were English language and literature, elementary maths, history and geography. Separate courses, on the other hand, could then reproduce the sexual division of labour. Boys were trained for their futures not just as manual workers through such vocational courses as technical drawing and woodwork, but also for their role as future fathers, that is, wage earners and heads of households. Girls were prepared for their future roles as economically dependent mothers and domestics within the working class.

The growth of secondary schools involved the financial necessity of producing larger schools. This led, according to David, to more mixed secondary grammar schools, where women teachers tended to be excluded from headships and the teaching of male adolescents. Not surprisingly many women teachers were in favour of single-sex schools and a differentiation of curricula for boys and girls, since it was only in this sort of educational provision that they stood any chance of promotion, a career, responsibilities and control over education. The numbers of mixed secondary schools, however, were still small.

By 1919, only 224 out of 1,080 secondary schools recognised as efficient were co-educational.[35] The motto 'education for one's station in life' involved class and gendered concepts of adult destiny that did not easily lead to co-education as a progressive ideal, but rather accepted it as a pragmatic necessity in certain circumstances. Put another way, the protection that upper-middle-class girls had from contact with the male sex was a possible sacrifice in the development of a sparsely funded state educational system. The compromise was to make sure that the sexes did not mix physically in any sports and to provide a range of separate classes for boys and girls within secondary schools. In the development of secondary education, what we can find is a diluted and modified version of the reproduction of bourgeois gender relations for those who could not afford the full cost of private education.

Concern over co-education was shown in the Report of the Consultative Committee of the Board of Education on the *Differentiation of the Curriculum for Boys and Girls Respectively in Secondary Schools* in 1923.[36] This report did not see the issue of co-education as part of its brief; nevertheless, in an appendix it collected the views of its witnesses upon this topic. Significantly, criticism of co-educational schools came largely from women witnesses. They argued that mixed schools were in fact boys' schools with girls in them, that women teachers and girls had no chance to get involved in the running of the school, that girls were shy in the presence of boys and that girls in girls' schools reached a higher standard than in co-educational schools. Sexual attachments were also a problem between male teachers and female pupils. (All these criticisms, interestingly, are the same as those made of mixed schools today.)

While the issue was not resolved in this report, what was evident was the tension between a desire to maintain the internal unity of class experience as well as the *diversity* of different sexes and different social classes. Were the sons and daughters of the working class to receive broadly similar educational experiences or would boys receive an education in common with boys of another social class, and working-class girls with their counterparts in the bourgeoisie? This tension and its resolution are still a matter of contention. Socialist historians emphasise the collective 'lived experience' of the working class in contrast with that of the bourgeoisie. On the other hand, feminists have stressed the differences between boys' and girls' schooling. While identifying class differences, they have, nevertheless, talked of a *domestic ideology* which, within a patriarchal context, has displaced class differences and *united* the subordination of daughters of the bourgeoisie and working classes. The impact of an educational ideology which is *familial* in orientation and domestic in practice (across the divide of state and private education) is supposed to have reduced the effect of class divisions among women to the extent that gender is primary.

My own view is that the *ideology of femininity, of family and domesticity has hidden the female class divisions within education.*[37] While vocational ideology (that is, an education for different occupational statuses) reveals, in far more explicit form, *male* class differentiation within state schooling, domestic ideology has more successfully involved a 'misrecognition' of the action of state and class power. In this sense, one reading the history of female education could assume that women were untouched by the class nature of society, except in so far as they married into different social classes. There is a danger that in focusing too exclusively upon gender divisions, apart from the class history of education, the *myth of female classlessness* will be perpetuated. This myth is one found in state policy. As a result, within government reports one can find the variety of ideological solutions found to the problem of positioning a specifically 'female' education within the *structure of male class relations* within education, especially within those dealing with the tripartite division of secondary schools. The underlying ideological premise was that schools should prepare boys in different ways for their future places within the occupational hierarchy; meanwhile girls of different social classes were being prepared in different ways in different types of school for that other hierarchy – the sexual hierarchy of family life. Thus working-class girls received a diet of cookery, sewing and domestic science courses and middle-class grammar school girls learnt the range of languages, literature, history and artistic accomplishments necessary for a future marital life.

The new rhetoric of 'social engineering' by the 1970s changed the focus of girls' education somewhat, since it recognised that girls were indeed likely to go into paid employment – especially when single. The co-educational comprehensive school in many ways represented a new solution to the problem of class and gender inequalities in society, in that it placed all pupils in one school and theoretically encouraged children to follow courses according to their own 'interests and needs'. Pupil freedom of choice now seemed to be the way to alleviate class and gender inequalities. In this context co-educational schools acquired a new 'progressive' image which was not really challenged until the 1970s.

Historically, as we have seen, boys and girls were rarely offered a *common curriculum* since the premise of educational policy-makers and schools was that girls should receive a different education from boys. It was hardly surprising, therefore, that when the programme of comprehensivisation was developed, encouraging co-educational schools, the assumption of gender differentiation was retained underneath the new ideology of free choice and pupil needs. Instead of explicitly identifying all girls as a homogeneous group with identical needs, the reproduction of gender divisions could be left to the now historically internalised attitudes and gender ideologies of parents, teachers, careers officers, employers and finally the students themselves. In this sense the assumptions of male superiority and female domesticity (being unchallenged) were encouraged, albeit more implicitly, to prevail. The form of reproduction of gender relations became therefore more hidden and less conscious, surrounded as it was by the ideology of ability, 'achievement-motivation' and individual freedom of choice.

Critiques and defence of co-education

I shall now discuss the contemporary debate over co-education, which has many similarities with the views expressed in the 1920s by female witnesses to the Report of the Consultative Committee of the Board of Education.[38] The catalyst for recent discussion of the value of co-education was the 1975 Sex Discrimination Act, which attempted to eliminate discrimination on the grounds of sex in areas where women have been prevented from achieving social and economic equality with men, as well as the DES survey on the 'Curricular differences for boys and girls' published in the same year.[39] The latter, conducted by the HM Inspectorate on primary, middle and secondary schools, revealed the extent of gender differentiation practised in schools. There was a variety of discriminatory practices based upon the assumption that boys and girls had different interests, abilities and futures. Schools were shown to be structured in such a way that children of different sexes were prepared for different roles in adult life and were encouraged to expect gender differentiation as normal. The reason given for such differentiation was not academic but that it was 'normal practice' (that is, it was a convenient long-standing organisation or financially necessitated). The most important effect of such practices was found in the pattern of boys' and girls' curricula – the subjects they were offered, those they chose to study and those taken by boys and girls for examination. Curricular options were offered differentially for boys and girls, especially in secondary schools. These included physical education, crafts (such as home economics, needlework, woodwork and metalwork) and the more academic subjects such as languages, physics and chemistry. The effect of such differentiation was that girls could be found clustered in the arts subjects, leaving boys in the majority in the 'hard sciences'.

However, the important revelation of this report was that the *provision* of different curricular subjects did not determine *choice*. What appeared to be important in affecting choice of subjects was whether the school was mixed or single sex. Thus in single-sex schools, girls were more likely to take science subjects and boys more likely to choose languages and the arts than in mixed schools. The choice of 'academic' subjects was also affected at A-levels where 'any correlation between the sex of the pupil and the popularity of a subject is markedly greater in mixed schools than in single-sex schools'.[40] The tendency was for single-sex schools to weaken the gender patterns of subject choice, particularly as far as girls and science were concerned. These findings were supported by other pieces of research, such as King's study of mathematics teaching in mixed and single-sex schools[41] and Omerod's on subject choice.[42] However, despite this evidence that girls and boys received less stereotyped educations in single-sex schools, the DES survey did not argue that boys and girls *should* be educated either separately or together. It argued that *'the findings would be misinterpreted if used to argue the case for either single-sex or mixed schools'* (my emphasis) and advised a reconsideration of the curricular programmes of twelve- to sixteen-year-olds to ensure that 'the principal areas of the curriculum are open to all boys and girls in whatever kind of school they happen to be'.[43]

The report's hesitancy to recommend single-sex education may have been affected by the other findings which, to a large extent, have been ignored by recent commentators. In almost all single-sex schools there is very little variety for the non-academically oriented pupil. Craft and practical subjects follow very traditional patterns. As Eileen Byrne has pointed out, this lack of free access of girls to handicrafts and of boys to homecraft has important vocational effects.[44] Domestic economy has meant that girls are taught cookery and needlework as preparation for the home and not employment, while boys are taught handicrafts such as woodwork, metalwork and technical drawing which have more 'transfer value' and more conceptual elements than homecraft.

> The technical craft subjects ... unquestionably have a major educative value in their own right. Regardless of whether boys later became welders or craftsmen, woodwork, metalwork and technical drawing have several foundation and transfer values not characteristic of domestic economy. They reinforce spatial development and numerical concepts, involving mensuration and spatial relationships from the outset – the very areas in which girls are alleged to be innately weaker than boys and in which girls therefore need early reinforcement, not further deprivation ... . There is a clear causal relationship between girls' exclusion from the technical crafts and their almost total under-recruitment in the training and employment fields of construction, metal trades, electrical engineering, maintenance engineering.[45]

As Byrne pointed out, the exclusion from these subjects means that girls are most likely to see skilled work in these areas as masculine. The recent concern over the academic advantages of single-sex schools has generally been limited to a concern for girls taking O- and A-levels and for those who might attend university rather than enter skilled apprenticeships or further training in the engineering sciences. Yet the extent of gender differences in these craft subjects at CSE can be seen in the statistics. In 1978, for example, only 540 girls passed

CSE in metalwork compared with 50,493 boys; 2,126 girls took technical drawing compared with 73,461 boys.[46]

Second, the emphasis upon the gender differentiation of academic subjects covers the class bias of the school system, which is hidden within the findings of the report. The only factor other than gender which is referred to is that of the type of school, but the main body of the report does not discuss the differences between them. In the appendices the DES report shows that physics was offered to 90–100 per cent of grammar school girls (mixed and single-sex) but only 37 per cent of mixed secondary modern and 11 per cent of single-sex secondary modern school girls. While 33 per cent of girls in single-sex grammar schools and 29 per cent of mixed grammar school girls took physics, a paltry 3 and 4 per cent of girls in mixed and single-sex secondary modern schools did. The differences regarding *type of school* attended are critical to subject choice, especially in subjects such as physics, chemistry and other high-status 'academic' subjects. The greatest advantage of single-sex over mixed schools is in the comprehensive school group, and that difference is only 5 per cent more girls taking physics and 6 per cent more girls taking chemistry. Yet the differences regarding types of schools were not used in the report except as a means of statistically adjusting the data since most of the single-sex schools in the sample were grammar schools.

The differential impact of single-sex schooling on different social classes in different types of schools was investigated by Douglas and Ross using the National Survey of Health and Development data.[47] Here they found that the majority of middle-class children in their sample attended single-sex grammar schools while over half the manual working class attended secondary modern mixed schools. The sex-segregated grammar schools had the advantages of having small class sizes, more resources and high school-leaving age, with more of the pupils coming from middle-class homes than the mixed grammar schools. This applied especially to the boys' schools. Using class origins, type of school and the results of reading and mathematics tests administered at eleven and fifteen years, what Douglas and Ross discovered was that middle-class boys, and both boys and girls of the manual working classes, stayed on longer and got better O-level results if they attended single-sex rather than mixed grammar schools.

Middle-class girls, in contrast, were at a considerable advantage at mixed grammar schools, which might be because girls' grammar schools were under-resourced and the curricular options were limited. At grammar school level, therefore, the interests of middle-class girls opposed those of working-class girls. In the secondary modern schools again the middle-class girls stayed on longer in mixed schools than in single-sex schools, while for all other pupils there was no difference between co-educational or single-sex schools. Douglas and Ross leave the reader to decide whether the academic advantages of co-education for middle-class girls outweigh the disadvantages of mixed schools for all boys and working-class girls at grammar school level. Certainly there does seem to be a conflict between the results obtained here and those offered later in the DES survey. Unfortunately Douglas and Ross could not study the impact of comprehensive schools. The growth of co-educational comprehensive schools in contrast to the single-sex grammar school has certainly contributed to what Glennerster called the 'snob value' of single-sex schooling,[48] because if anything the single-sex direct grant schools had become even more restricted in social class intake – educating a 'special elite'. The data are totally insufficient to make an adequate assessment of the *academic* or the *class* advantages and disadvantages of co-education and single-sex schooling.[49]

Nevertheless, the concern for the academic disadvantages of co-education represents a re-evaluation of the operation of the ideology of equality of opportunity and its application to girls. More than that, it represents a challenge to the major premises of educational planning since the 1960s, especially since the growth of co-educational schools was accelerated by the reorganization of schooling along comprehensive lines. In 1975, some 87 per cent of state comprehensive schools were mixed; in contrast 74 per cent of state grammar schools were single-sex. All but 3 of the 174 direct grant schools were single-sex. (In Scotland, by contrast, only 4.8 per cent of all pupils in educational authority secondary schools were in single-sex schools.) By 1978 the pattern of English and Welsh educational provision in the maintained sector was as shown in Table 1.

Table 1 English and Welsh educational provision in the maintained sector, 1978 (no. of schools)[50]

	Boys	*Girls*	*Mixed*	*Total*
Primary	33	31	20,577	20,641
All middle schools	7	7	1,289	1,303
All secondary schools (excluding middle)	472	482	3,156	4,110
Modern	93	95	451	639
Grammar	114	118	73	305
Technical	6	7	6	19
Comprehensive	235	248	2,594	3,077
Other secondary	24	14	32	70

Needless to say, the opposition to the comprehensive ideal was sometimes fought by attacking its co-educational status. For example in the *Bristol Evening Post* in 1964 the concern over sexual promiscuity, so feared by the middle classes, again reared its head:

> One London co-education school headmaster considered his figures 'greatly improved' with only 16 pregnancies in a year among his 15 and 16 year old girls. The authorities at a large comprehensive co-educational school were shocked to discover that the babies of a number of girls found to be pregnant were actually conceived on the premises – at break times. Co-education brings sex right into the classroom.[51]

Yet according to Benn and Simon, in their study *Half Way There*,[52] there was no evidence of increased sexual promiscuity in mixed comprehensive schools. What they did find was a wide range of discriminatory practices restricting the principle of comprehensivisation – the freedom of pupils to choose those subjects that suited their interests. They were particularly concerned to discover the lack of access for girls to engineering subjects such as building, woodwork, navigation, physics with chemistry, surveying and technology courses. Half of the mixed schools limited some subjects to boys only and 49 per cent limited subjects such as catering, nursing, pottery, hygiene, jewellery making, domestic science and dancing to girls only. The future of effective comprehensivisation, in their view, was to *eliminate* such gender differentiation.

Support for genuinely co-educational schools came from a range of sources. The NUT, for example, stated in 1975:

> The Union recognises that the origins of separate education for boys and girls lie in the history and evolution of education. Schools traditionally educated boys and girls in ways which were intended to prepare them for quite separate and distinct roles in society as men and women: roles which were so different that the teaching methods and curricula were incompatible. Society has changed radically, however, and the pressures to give full equality to men and women in their work, their places in society and their responsibilities and commitments they face should be reflected in and catered for by the schools. To educate children in groups, segregated on the basis of difference of sex, is to effect an artificial separation which bears little or no relation to life at home or to society in general … . A pattern of education based on such separation and founded on concepts of allegedly distinguishable and incompatible needs of boys and girls no longer serves the interests either of society or of children.[53]

Thus while the current academic disadvantages of boys and girls within educational comprehensive schools might be recognised, the belief in the *transformative potential* of such schools (with, as Benn and Simon put it, an active attempt to change and improve those schools) was sufficient for some to continue to believe in the principle of mixing, albeit within a society still structured through class and gender inequality.

Yet support for the principle of mixing boys and girls in school came from other rather embarrassing quarters. Dale is famous for his three-volume study of the advantages of mixed and single-sex schools as seen by pupils and ex-pupils who were trainee teachers.[54] He stresses more than anything the social rather than the academic advantages of co-education, since mixed schools more effectively reproduce what he calls 'normal life'; boys and girls get to know each other; they are less likely to suffer from the extremes of character defects such as the aggression of boys and the 'cattiness' or 'bitchiness' of girls. Less harsh discipline and more friendly relations exist within the happy family atmosphere of such schools. Overall, he argues, co-education leads to greater happiness since it is a less 'unnatural' or distorted educational experience. As in all such studies, Dale is careful to refer continuously to the 'objectivity' of his research even though a good deal of his analysis rests upon interpretation of interview material. The concern for 'performance' is again the criterion of assessment, except that in this case it refers to social behaviour and attitudes.

His interpretation of his research data, as well as the limitations of his sample and style of inquiry, have been challenged by quite a few.[55] Perhaps the more sceptical response has been that offered by feminists who are aware of the conservative view Dale holds as to the differences between the sexes. In one paper he uses an analogy which he knew would infuriate 'members of the Women's Liberation Movement'.[56] He argues that men and women are biologically different not just in physiology but in temperament. Thus the aggression of men is compared with the 'bull who is master and defender of the herd while the cows peacefully graze and look after their offspring'. He argues:

> That men and women are complementary is a biological fact. That they also influence each other's conduct – from the gift of flowers to the hurling of the kitchen utensils – is an inevitable accompaniment of life in a bisexual world. A family has a father and a mother; lacking one of these each member feels incomplete and unsatisfied ... So it is with other institutions when they are one-sex – as we know from the homosexual activities in Public School and armed forces ... both the father figure and the mother figure are needed in our schools.[57]

For Dale, the advantage of mixed schools can be found precisely in their reproduction of life in a heterosexual world, in which men dominate and women learn to complement and subordinate themselves to men. With this image of 'normality' in mind, it is hardly surprising that co-educational schools are seen as nowhere near the ideal from a feminist position. The research of Michelle Stanworth, for example, confirms that it is the worst aspects of patriarchal relations which are reproduced within the mixed educational setting.[58] Girls have to cope with *devaluation* by teachers and by boys – teachers who cannot remember their names, who expect them to leave school and become good wives and mothers, or in the short term secretaries and nurses, and boys who see themselves as superior to the girls, who attract most of the teacher's attention, who ridicule the more academic girls and chase after the more amenable.

'Feminist' responses to co-education

I shall now look briefly at three different responses to the data and arguments collected so far. The 'feminist' responses have not been unified; they comprise what I see as three strands, each of which represents a different political position and a different concept of what education can do to reform or change gender relations. These three strands have the following features in common.

First, they seek an educational programme of reform which will lead to the *equality of the sexes*. They argue for the importance of education and its potential to change attitudes and behaviour. However, the nature of the goal differs. For some equality of the sexes means equality of power sharing, for others it means equality in difference, or equality of opportunity. The actual *elimination* of gender as a category in education as an overall goal is not really discussed by any of the three groups, and yet it is the one goal which Eileen Byrne argues (and I would agree with her) will challenge women's subordinate position at a fundamental level.[59]

Second, all the various perspectives simplify the argument to its most essential features – that of mixed versus single-sex schools. This is given legitimacy by the DES statistics which only use these two categories; yet as we have seen historically there is a wide range of difference in the type of gender differentiation in available forms of secondary schooling. Today we can find schools with boarding provision for both sexes or one sex only; schools with two sexes mixed together in the sixth form only; schools that are paired on one site; or mixed schools in which leisure activities are divided and curricular options are gender differentiated. Rather than discuss the different *levels of degrees* of mixing and sex segregation, what characterises nearly all the recent articles on this issue is their narrowing down of the discussion to the question: should boys be present or absent in the educational lives of girls? Physical segregation is the main issue rather than an overall assessment of when, where and how boys and girls are and could usefully be brought together or separated. Given the desire to change the sexist attitudes and practices of teachers, male pupils' behaviour and the stereotypical ambitions and self-evaluations of female pupils, the question needs to be asked: would a conscious explicit attack upon segregation, and a real attempt to reform teacher's ideology and practice, be more effective than increased or renewed sex segregation?

Third, there is more a concern to change the form of *female* education than to restructure boys' education in such a way as to 'interrupt' the socialisation of boys into prejudiced men. In this sense, co-education versus sex segregation remains a feminist issue without challenging, in the present, the attitudes of men. Gender relations become identified as a *female* rather than a male problem, and one which appears to have had no historical basis within the development of a capitalist and patriarchal society.

The liberal reformist perspective

The emphasis of this perspective (which is currently the most popular)[60] is on the academic failure of girls to achieve in science subjects, to get to universities and to receive a broadly based education. The assumption is that girls lack the motivation, the encouragement and the opportunity to break from the stereotyped notions of femininity and women's occupational futures. The attitudes of teachers, careers advisers, curricular texts and the pupils themselves must be challenged and opened out so that there is no division between female and male subjects, no association of non-femininity with academic success. The problem of girls' failure to enter any other than the most stereotypically female jobs is referred to as an 'educational problem', since if girls would only seize the opportunities offered in comprehensive schools, they could compete as equals with boys and men. Within this perspective is a belief in the individual nature of social mobility, of achievement and ambition. The problem for reformers, therefore, becomes one of breaking the hold of myths about women's role in society, of breaking the circulation of a sex-role ideology which is seen as both the cause and *effect* of women's inferior position. The solution to such female underachievement is to sponsor single-sex classes in a compensatory fashion, giving girls a chance to develop for themselves their spatial and mathematical abilities, without the competition of boys, and to encourage them to see science and technology as female occupational areas.

Such a perspective offers considerable optimism to teachers and educational planners since it gives practical and 'do-able' advice at the classroom level. Yet there are several difficulties in this viewpoint. The first is obvious: *does the separation of girls from boys actually change patriarchal relations* or does it merely give girls access to the male world of science in which they still might only become technicians and laboratory assistants? Even if girls were to receive identical qualifications to boys there is no guarantee that they will obtain the same jobs as boys. As Wolpe has pointed out,[61] qualifications do not guarantee occupational entry especially in an occupational world in which men's skills are defined as superior to women's and there is resistance from male-dominated employers and trade unions.

The idea of compensatory education for girls in single-sex classes has been taken up by the Equal Opportunities Commission, and by ILEA educational officers. Further, it receives support from the various schools which are already trying it out. What is not yet clear is which category of pupil is to be encouraged to attend single-sex classes (that is, A-level, O-level or CSE candidates). There also seems to be an assumption that if the pattern of boys' and girls' examination passes, subject choice and entry rates into further training and higher education matched, then equality of the sexes would be achieved. However, the problem here is that such a view ignores the *class inequalities* of education and tends to assume that class oppression should be shared equally. The school is left in a social and political vacuum without any reference to the history of educational provision which constructed the problem of gender differentiation in the first place. Paradoxically the school is expected to challenge the reproduction of gender relations even though it was itself set up precisely to reinforce this. The limits of any compensatory programme need to be recognised at the outset.

The conservative perspective

This position is most similar to that which has underpinned educational policy-making since the nineteenth century. Support for single-sex schools was justified, according to this perspective, because of the special role which women have as mothers and wives, which differentiates them from men. The ideology of equality of the sexes in this context has meant that boys' and girls' education should be different but equal. According to Sara Delamont,[62] in the nineteenth century feminists were divided into two camps – which she called the 'separatists' and the 'uncompromising'. The analogy here is with the separatists who argued for a special education for girls to prepare them for their uniquely feminine futures. An example of this view is to be found in Barbara Cowell's article.[63] She writes, 'if society is to benefit from the intellectual and emotional potential of women, we shall have to ensure that they retain without shame their different qualities', and this may well be achieved by a period of separate education. The conservatism of her view is best shown in the following quotation:

> There are few more grotesque sights than that of the supposedly intelligent woman who neglects her children, in that short period when they really need her care, in order to foster her own ambitions. Such neglect … breeds immense resentment in the next generation. Children with the resulting sense of deprivation spend the rest of their lives wresting from society, from their unfortunate partners, the special attention denied them in infancy.[64]

Girls, according to Cowell, should not be encouraged to *envy* men, just as the working class should not envy those with privilege. Further, they should not aim to study science since that is just helping to 'propel our civilization down the slippery slope into a completely materialistic way of life'.[65] The tendency of girls to copy boys and the tendency of women to aspire to the male world only lead, according to her, to unhappiness, high divorce rates and the too high expectations and vast disillusionment of women. In contrast, an emphasis upon gender specialities and differences would allow women to find solidarity among other women. This *solidarity* and the *polarity* it produces *between* men and women should be encouraged, in Cowell's view, through single-sex schools during adolescence when the physical, emotional and mental development of girls and boys differs.

What this position represents is a concern to reproduce the dominant set of gender relations through traditional forms of schooling, although Cowell is prepared to compromise with separate schools being on the same campus or very close together so that facilities for joining social functions can be provided. The model school for her is the old single-sex grammar school, since what was reproduced in such schools were traditional gender differences.

The radical feminist perspective

The most radical feminist position has recently been put in Sarah, Scott and Spender's article in *Learning to Lose*.[66] Using much the same data on mixed schools as the liberal reformist and conservative perspectives, these authors argue very forcefully against mixed schools on the basis that they are the main means of reproducing the patriarchal relations of domination. The academic and social relations of schooling, the atmosphere, the ideology of teachers and pupils all contribute to the subordination of girls. In their view it is the presence of boys which affects girls' low self-perception, low academic performance and narrow traditional feminine interests after school. The only way they can suggest to prevent such gender reproduction is through single-sex schools where the 'subversive potential' of schools can be appropriated for feminist practice. With an all-female teaching staff and a female head, girls will perceive that it is not impossible for women to hold power and to enter the male world of science. They will learn to appreciate feminine friendships and a sense of solidarity with each other. Through the cultivation of 'sisterhood', girls will be able to 'grow and develop their human potential, they will be in a much stronger position to resist oppression in the wider society'.[67] Further, single-sex schools could attempt to counteract the traditional patterns of socialisation the girls will have experienced in their homes. As Rosemary Deem summarises their case:

> the emphasis on academic learning in a single-sex school is not likely to convey to girls the impression that it is unimportant whether girls do well at school or not, a message which may already be conveyed to girls by their socialization and culture and not always contradicted in mixed schools.[68]

Sex segregation through schooling will not blur or eliminate the boundary between girls and boys but will allow girls to find their self-confidence and to learn how to challenge patriarchal relations. On the one hand, the absence of boys and their jokes, their ridicule of girls, their absorption of the teachers' energy, their competitive spirit and their aggression, and, on the other hand, the cultivation of feminist consciousness within all-girls' schools lead the authors to support the principle of sex segregation, without reference to the impact this might have upon boys. They recognise that what they are suggesting is radical, but do not think they are being utopian:

> We are assuming that universal single-sex education for girls would completely resolve the problem of sexism in education but in an age where co-education is heralded as a symbol of progress, it must be made clear that while it may represent progress for boys, for girls it represents a defeat rather than an advance.[69]

Conclusion

I have tried to show that the issue of co-education and single-sex schools is not just a contemporary but also a historical debate which has involved notions of what the relations between the sexes should be in an educational system which was already class divided. The use of single-sex schooling had been the major form of reproduction of gender relations – relations that constituted the bourgeois ideal of the family form, of male hierarchy and female dependency and subordination. Co-education represented a variation on that form of reproduction – never a radical alternative to the nature of the relations between the sexes. The pattern of educational provision was, therefore, essentially one of gender segregation and differentiation either physically or through the provision of separate classes, activities and curricular options. The nature of differentiation between boys and girls differed between social classes in terms of the type of subjects to be studied. For the working classes, the differentiation is most acute in the craft subjects studied; in the middle classes, the science and arts split was the most significant aspect of the gender divide. At no point historically was there an attempt to set up an equal (that is, identical) education for boys and girls.

The evidence for the impact of single-sex and mixed-sex schools must be taken in the context of the type of school discussed, the types of school subjects and the social-class origins of pupils before we can adequately decide on the basis of evidence rather than political perspective which type of schooling would benefit girls. Yet even then what will we say about the *education of boys*? The feminist ideals for girls' education, of whatever variety, do not leave a clear strategy as to how to overcome *male prejudicial attitudes* to women. The question remains, are patriarchal and sexist attitudes a female or a male problem? A separate strategy for one sex does not, in my view, challenge the overall reproduction of dominant gender relations. We may merely *interrupt* it by using, for our own purposes, a pre-existing form of schooling. Gender as a basis for allocating individuals will not disappear as an educational or a social variable if schools or classes are allocated to one or other sex, nor will the inequalities of social class, which distinguish the educational experiences and future work lives of working-class and middle-class girls. What the three perspectives offer are ways to change the *form* of reproduction of gender relations: they do not challenge the *causes* of what it is that is reproduced. In other words, they focus on changing the modality of transmission of gender relations without changing *what* should be reproduced. We do not surely want to change the nature of 'femininity' as a concept but rather to abolish it as a social construct into which children are socialised. But we can only do this by understanding the meaning and significance the concepts of gender have within patriarchal relations in the family and the waged labour process in advanced capitalism. There is a danger if we do not understand the location of schooling within this political and economic context that we will be naively optimistic in believing that educational reform can change society.

As a political strategy, the support for single-sex education should recognise that small single-sex schools are unlikely to receive resources equal to those of the larger mixed schools in the current climate, especially when it comes to the funding of expensive science, technology and craft courses. Nor are girls' schools likely ever to achieve equal status to boys' schools unless the economic and political basis of patriarchal relations is challenged, since within such relations what is 'female' will always be defined as inferior. Similarly, compensatory educational programmes will run into conflict with the closed nature of the labour market and its gendered structures.

The implications of feminist struggles over sex segregation for class struggles over education cannot be ignored or seen as separate. Single-sex schooling was part of the reproduction of class relations, in just as significant a way as were the different types of school and curricula provided through secondary schooling. The history of class reproduction, of class relations and bourgeois privilege includes, not as a marginal but as an integral feature, the reproduction of bourgeois family forms (of the norms of heterosexuality, female virginity and marriage) as well as particular concepts of masculinity and femininity which held together the gender division of labour within paid employment and family life. Support for single-sex schools or sex segregation, therefore, has class connotations. In particular, we may find ourselves pushed into a position of supporting the private single-sex schools against state comprehensives, irrespective of the class selection and privilege involved. Further, we have to be careful that we do not attack comprehensive schools for failing to achieve a programme of reform which, in my view, they were never designed to do – that is, restructure the relations between the sexes in such a way as to eliminate gender as an educational discriminator. Their historical role so far has been to facilitate different 'interests' and 'needs' without taking on the reform of those 'needs' and 'interests'.

Genuine equality of the sexes has not yet been an educational goal and if it is now to become one, should we not, first of all, set up major educational reforms in teacher education, in in-service training programmes to reshape teachers' classroom practice, redesign the curricula, rewrite text books and so on? Should we not try to re-educate parents and employers? Should we not try to uncover the hidden forms of reproduction of gender relations, especially those which underpin the ideologies of parental freedom of choice (which led middle-class parents to choose single-sex schools), of student freedom of choice and of teacher neutrality. In the context of such a programme of educational reform, in my view it will be the co-educational comprehensive schools that will have the resources to offer a more equal education to boys and girls and will have the facility for bringing to the fore the issue of gender discrimination and prejudice, for both male and female pupils and teachers.

Notes

1 Newsom, J. (1948) *The Education of Girls*, London: Faber & Faber.
2 Ibid., p. 110.
3 Bland, L., McCabe, T. and Mort, F. (1979) 'Sexuality and reproduction: three "official" instances', in M. Barrett, P. Corrigan, A. Kuhn and J. Wolff (eds) *Ideology and Cultural Production*, London: Croom Helm.
4 Newsom, op. cit. (Note 1), pp. 158–9.
5 Ministry of Education (1945) 'The nation's schools: their plan and purpose', Pamphlet No. 1, London: HMSO.

6 Weinberg, A. (1981) 'Non-decision making in English education: the case of single sex secondary schooling', paper presented at the British Sociological Association Conference, Aberystwyth.
7 David, M.E. (1980) *The State, Family and Education*, London: Routledge and Kegan Paul; Dyehouse, C. (1981) *Girls Growing Up in Late Victorian and Edwardian England*, London: Routledge and Kegan Paul; Burstyn, J.N. (1980) *Victorian Education and the Ideal of Womanhood*, London: Croom Helm; Purvis, J. (1980) 'Working class women and adult education in nineteenth century Britain', *History of Education*, 9, 3, pp. 193–212; Purvis, J. (1981) 'The double burden of class and gender in the schooling of working class girls in nineteenth century England, 1800–1870', in L. Barton and S. Walker (eds) *Schools, Teachers and Teaching*, Lewes: Falmer Press.
8 These points are more fully developed in Arnot, M. (1981) 'Towards a political economy of women's education', paper presented at The Political Economy of Gender Relations in Education Conference, OISE, Toronto; Arnot, M. (1982) 'Male hegemony, social class and women's education', *Journal of Education*, 164, 1, pp. 64–89.
9 See MacDonald, M. (1980a) 'Socio-cultural reproduction and women's education', in R. Deem (ed.) *Schooling for Women's Work*, London: Routledge & Kegan Paul; MacDonald, M. (1980b) 'Schooling and the reproduction of class and gender relations', in L. Barton, R. Meighan and S. Walker (eds) *Schooling, Ideology and the Curriculum*, Lewes: Falmer Press.
10 Shaw, J. (1974) 'Finishing school: some implications of sex-segregated education', in D. Leonard Barker and S. Allen (eds) *Sexual Divisions and Society: process and change*, London: Tavistock.
11 Ibid., p. 134.
12 See also Shaw, J. (1980) 'Education and the individual. Schooling for girls, or mixed schooling – a mixed blessing?', in Deem, op. cit. (Note 9).
13 DES (1975) 'Curricular differences for boys and girls', *Educational Survey No. 21*, London: HMSO.
14 David, op. cit. (Note 7).
15 Other factors included religion, since several mixed schools were set up by religious foundations (such as the Quakers) or by individual philanthropists. See Turner, B. (1974) *Equality for Some*, London: Ward Lock.
16 For a brief review of information on girls' schools, see Report of the Committee on Public Schools appointed by the President of the Board of Education (1942) *The Public Schools and the General Education System*, London: HMSO, ch. 8.
17 Okeley, J. (1978) 'Privileged, schooled and finished: boarding education for girls', in S. Gardener (ed.) *Defining Females*, London: Croom Helm.
18 Ibid., p. 109.
19 Ibid., p. 110.
20 Turner, op. cit. (Note 15), p. 182.
21 This argument ties into that presented in Engels, F. (1972) *The Origin of the Family, Private Property and the State*, London: Lawrence & Wishart.
22 Quoted in Lawson, J. and Silver, H. (1973) *A Social History of Education in England*, London: Methuen & Co., p. 344.
23 Public Schools Commission (1968) *First Report Vol. 1*, London: HMSO, para. 64.
24 Ibid., para. 301.
25 Rae, J. (1981) *The Public School Revolution*, London: Faber & Faber, suggests that 60 out of 210 Headmasters Conference Schools had admitted girls, of which 26 were fully co-educational. These figures have been challenged by Walford, G. (1982) 'The "dual student market" and public schools', paper presented at the BSA conference, Manchester. Walford suggests that of 211 HMC schools in Great Britain and

Northern Ireland in 1981, 46 were fully co-educational and at least 72 admitted some girls at sixth form only.

26 Wilby, P. (1981) 'A parent's guide to private education', *The Sunday Times Supplement*, 22 and 29 November.
27 Ibid., pp. 54–5.
28 Ibid., p. 53.
29 Blandford, L. (1977) 'The making of a lady', in G. Macdonald-Fraser (ed.) *The World of the Public School*, London: Weidenfeld & Nicolson, p. 204.
30 Ibid., p. 198.
31 Purvis (1981), op. cit. (Note 7).
32 David, op. cit. (Note 7), p. 36.
33 Purvis (1981), op. cit. (Note 7), p. 111.
34 David, op. cit. (Note 7), p. 137.
35 Turner, op. cit. (Note 15), p. 182.
36 Board of Education (1923) *Report of the Consultative Committee on Differentiation of the Curriculum for Boys and Girls Respectively in Secondary Schools*, 2nd impression, London: HMSO.
37 Arnot, op. cit. (Note 8).
38 Board of Education, loc. cit. (Note 36).
39 DES, op. cit. (Note 13).
40 Ibid., p. 16.
41 King, W.H. (1965) 'Experimental evidence on comparative attainment in mathematics in single sex and co-educational secondary schools', *Educational Research*, 8, pp. 155–60.
42 Omerod, M.B. (1975) 'Subject preference and choice in co-educational and single sex secondary schools', *British Journal of Educational Psychology*, 45, pp. 257–67.
43 DES, op. cit. (Note 13), p. 22.
44 Byrne, E.M. (1978) 'Equality of education and training for girls (10–18 years)', *Education Series No.* 9, Brussels: Commission of the European Communities.
45 Ibid., p. 42
46 DES (1976) *Statistics of Education*, vol. 1, *School Leavers CSE or GCE*.
47 Douglas, J.W.B. and Ross, J.M. (1966) 'Single sex or co-ed? The academic consequences', *Where*, 25 (May), pp. 5–8.
48 Glennerster, A. (1966) 'Comprehensive reorganization – will there be more co-ed schools?' *Where*, 26 (July), pp. 16–18.
49 For further confusing and inconclusive data, see Sutherland, M.B. (1961) 'Co-education and school attainment', *British Journal of Educational Psychology*, 31, 2, pp. 158–69; Wood, R. and Ferguson, C. (1974) 'Unproved case for co-education', *The Times Educational Supplement*, 4 October, p. 22.
50 DES (1978) *Statistics of Education*, vol. 1, *Schools*. In contrast, 1,046 independent schools were single sex out of 2,220 such schools.
51 Quoted in Hansard (1964) Debate on Grammar Schools, 27 November.
52 Benn, C. and Simon, B. (1972) *Half Way There*, Harmondsworth: Penguin.
53 Quoted in La Vigueur, J. (1977) 'Co-education and the tradition of separate needs', in D. Spender and E. Sarah (eds) *Learning to Lose*, London: Women's Press.
54 Dale, R.R. (1969) *Mixed or Single Sex School*, vol. 1; (1971) *Mixed or Single Sex School*, vol. 2, *Some Social Aspects*; (1974) *Mixed or Single Sex School*, vol. 3, *Attainment, Attitudes and Over-view*, London: Routledge & Kegan Paul.
55 See Deem, R. (1978) *Women and Schooling*, London: Routledge & Kegan Paul; Shaw, op. cit. (Note 10); Sarah, E., Scott, M. and Spender, D. (1980) 'The education of feminists: the case for single sex schools', in D. Spender and E. Sarah (eds) *Learning to Lose*, London: Women's Press.
56 Dale, R.R. (1975) 'Education and sex roles', *Educational Review*, 27, 3, pp. 240–8.
57 Dale (1969), op. cit. (Note 54), p. 114.

58 Stanworth, M. (1981) *Gender and Schooling*, Pamphlet No. 7, London: Women's Research and Resource Centre.
59 Byrne, E. (1978) *Women and Education*, London: Tavistock.
60 See Arnot, M. (1981) 'Cultural and political economy: dual perspectives in the sociology of women's education', *Educational Analysis*, 3, 1, pp. 97–116, for further discussion of this perspective, which I call the 'culture perspective' in sociology of education.
61 Wolpe, A.M. (1978) 'Girls and economic survival', *British Journal of Educational Studies*, 26, 2, pp. 150–62.
62 Delamont, S. (1978) 'The contradictions in ladies' education', in S. Delamont and L. Duffin (eds) *The Nineteenth Century Women*, London: Croom Helm.
63 Cowell, B. (1981) 'Mixed and single sex grouping in secondary schools', *Oxford Review of Education*, 7, 2, pp. 165–72.
64 Ibid., pp. 166, 65.
65 Ibid., p. 170.
66 Sarah, Scott and Spender, op. cit. (Note 55).
67 Ibid., p. 65.
68 Deem, op. cit. (Note 55), p. 75.
69 Sarah, Scott and Spender, op. cit. (Note 55), p. 70.

6 Male hegemony, social class and women's education

> At any given time, the more powerful side will create an ideology suitable to help maintain its position and to make this position acceptable to the weaker one. In this ideology the differentness of the weaker one will be interpreted as inferiority, and it will be proven that these differences are unchangeable, basic, or God's will. It is the function of such an ideology to deny or conceal the existence of a struggle.
>
> (Horney, 1967, p. 56)

According to Sheila Rowbotham in *Woman's Consciousness, Man's World* (1973), the concept of male hegemony, like that of female oppression, is not new, but then (as she also points out) it is one thing to encounter a concept, quite another to understand it. That process of understanding requires one to perceive the concept of male hegemony as a whole series of separate 'moments' through which women have come to accept a male-dominated culture, its legality, and their subordination to it and in it. Women have become colonised within a male-defined world, through a wide variety of 'educational moments' which seen separately may appear inconsequential, but which together comprise a pattern of female experience that is qualitatively different from that of men. These educational moments when collated can provide considerable insights into the collective 'lived experience' of women as women. For example, in the educational autobiographies of women edited by Dale Spender and Elizabeth Sarah (1980), what emerges is that in education women have 'learnt to lose' and, more than that, they have learnt *how* to lose, even though they may have had the ability to succeed academically. Through such experience they have learnt to accept that 'the *masculine* man is one who achieves, who is masterful: the *feminine* woman is one who underachieves, who defers' (Brewster, 1980, p. 11).

However, research into the experience of women in education also raises numerous problems, not just in terms of doing the research (e.g., Llewellyn, 1980) but also at the level of theorising about education and its relationship to the political and economic context. Here I shall focus upon existing work in British sociology of education to show the differences between two bodies of research into women's education which I call the cultural and political economy perspectives. I will also discuss the relationship between studies of women's education and Marxist theories of education. I will examine the interaction between class and male hegemony in education and then attempt to develop a different and very elementary framework within which to conceive of research questions in this area, as a starting point for a more cohesive study of class and gender. The problems raised through attempting to put together theories of two different structures of inequality will, at least, point to the *complexity* of combining, in everyday life, the demands of two sets of social relations and their interrelations.

In a previous paper (MacDonald, 1980b; Chapter 4 in this volume), I argued that both class and gender relations constitute hierarchies in which material and symbolic power is based. Inside these hierarchies, class and gender struggles are waged. If we want, therefore, to research the role of schools as one social 'site' in which the reproduction of the socio-sexual division of labour occurs, then it is necessary to be aware of the nature of these *two* forms of social struggle, the different stakes involved, and how such struggles are 'lived through' by individuals who negotiate terms within these power relations and who construct for themselves specific class and gender identities.

The need to describe the processes of gender discrimination in education and its effects – female subordination in the waged and domestic labour forces – is circumscribed by the political commitment to offer suggestions, proposals and programmes for educational reform which will help liberate women. However, that political cause should not allow us to stop at the immediate level of ethnographic or quantitative description and prescription. We need to go further and analyse in depth the processes of the *production* of gender differences both inside and outside schools, and to analyse the forms of gender reproduction which are inherent in, and not independent of, the patterns of class reproduction, class control and class struggles.[1] This political and economic context of gender reproduction sets the limits and influences the forms and outcomes of gender struggles. It critically affects the impact of any education reform and its effectiveness. In this paper, therefore, I shall retain my original position that:

> In so far as class relations (in other words the division between capital and labour) constitute the primary element of the capitalist social formation they limit and structure the form of gender relations, the division between male and female properties and identities. I do not believe that one can disassociate the ideological forms of masculinity and femininity, in their historical specificity, from either the material basis of patriarchy or from the class structure. If one definition of femininity or masculinity is dominant, it is the product of patriarchal relations and also the product of class dominance, even though these two structures may exist in contradiction.
>
> (MacDonald, 1980b, p. 30)

The analysis of the origins and nature of gender differences will make reference to the existence of a bourgeois and male hegemony which has controlled the development of female education. The concept of hegemony used here refers to a whole range of structures and activities, as well as values, attitudes, beliefs and morality, that in various ways support the established order and the class and male interests which dominate it. By putting the concept of hegemony rather than 'reproduction' at the fore of an analysis of class and gender, it is less easy in doing research to forget the *active* nature of the learning process, the existence of dialectic relations, power struggles and points of conflict, the range of alternative practices which may exist inside, or exist outside and be brought into, the school. Further, it allows us to remember that the power of dominant interests is never total nor secure. Cultural hegemony is still a weapon which must be continually struggled for, won and maintained. Women in this analysis must offer unconsciously or consciously their 'consent' to their subordination before male power is secured. They are encouraged 'freely' to choose their inferior status and to accept their exploitation as natural. In this sense the production of gender differences becomes a critical point of gender struggle and reproduction, the site of gender control.

Cultural and political economy perspectives

In contrast to studies in the United States, where a considerable amount of research has been carried out on gender socialisation, there is relatively little research on girls' and women's schooling in British sociology of education. It is almost as if the 'left-wing' stance of much British sociology of education has precluded investigation into the area of gender and race relations within schooling, even though these other structures of inequality are contained within, affect and even exaggerate the effects of class divisions, as Westergaard and Resler (1975), Byrne (1978) and King (1971), among others, have discovered. By and large, the analysis of gender divisions has developed separately from that of class divisions and still seems to have had little or almost no impact upon those who remain within the latter tradition. Even those who appear to have moved away from a strict 'correspondence' model such as researchers at the Centre for Contemporary Cultural Studies (CCCS) who now argue that one should recognise that schools face *two* directions – towards the family and towards the economy – have done little to rectify the gender bias of their analysis. In their new publication, *Unpopular Education* (1981), the analysis of state educational policy and forms of struggle at particular historical conjunctures very quickly leaves the study of parenthood and the relationship between class and gender-determined education on the sidelines.

Cultural studies, as Angela McRobbie (1980) has argued, are also guilty of being sex-blind since either they equate 'working-class culture' only with that of the male working class or they focus specifically on working-class boys and ignore the sexism inherent in their particular form of subcultural 'style' or version of masculinity.[2] In terms of classroom ethnography, which is still a major methodological tradition and strand within contemporary British sociology of education, the neglect of gender is even more noticeable and less excusable since it implies that the observer in the classroom is blind to the process of gender discrimination which, according to recent feminist work (e.g., Clarricoates, 1980; Delamont, 1970; Lobban, 1975), occurs most of the time in teacher–pupil interaction, classroom lessons, and pupil control in British primary and secondary schools. Fortunately, there is now a growing amount of research published, for example in Deem (1980) and Kelly (1981), which uses a variety of research techniques to investigate the process of gender ascription, labelling and discrimination in schools.

The development of work on gender in education in Britain, I believe, has employed what I have called the cultural perspective (Arnot, 1981). I have argued that those who use the cultural perspective focus upon the patterns of 'sex-role socialization', that is, upon the processes internal to the school which determine and shape the formation of gender identities.[3] Their concern is with educational 'underachievement', with the analysis of the overt curriculum and the hidden curriculum, with classroom interaction, with girls' attitudes to schools as well as with teachers' and career officers' attitudes to girls' futures. What this cultural perspective appears to have in common with the political economy model is that it also refers to the processes involved in the 'reproduction' of gender. However, 'reproduction' here is not a Marxist concept. Several critical differences distinguish the political economy and cultural perspectives – only a few of which I can cover here. Perhaps the most important difference is that cultural analysis concentrates upon *how* rather than *why* schools function to reproduce the patterns of gender inequality – the focus is therefore upon internal rather than external processes. The origin of these processes lies in the concept of 'sex-role ideology' (or some equivalent concept), yet, paradoxically, this ideology is also produced and reproduced in the school. It is thus both the *cause* and the *effect* of gender inequality, since each new generation of pupils in turn becomes the new generation of parents, teachers, employers and so on, carrying with them the assumptions of such 'sex-role ideology'. Therefore, what is portrayed is a vicious circle of attitudes in which the learnt attitudes of one generation constrain the new generation and so on. It is in this sense that the concept of 'reproduction' is used.

This work challenges traditional sociology of education to recognise the complexity of factors which are to be found in schools and which produce the educational, and later the social, inequality between men and women. These analyses make it difficult to hold any belief that we have achieved formal equality of opportunity within schools by eradicating overt forms of gender discrimination. Further, this challenge is directed towards state educational policy-makers who tend to gloss over the nature and extent of discrimination in education against women. The political orientation of much of this research is, therefore, to challenge the success of the programme for equality of opportunity and to demand that women receive genuine equal opportunity with men. With such a political goal and audience, researchers tend therefore not to address themselves to the radical sociological tradition within the sociology of education but rather aim to influence teachers, local educational authorities and the Department of Education and Science.

There are two results of such an orientation. First, even though it challenges official views of education, much of this literature takes for granted and uses the official ideology that schools are neutral agents in society and the official definition that if women do 'underachieve' relative to men, then it is an 'educational problem' and an 'educational solution' must be sought. Second, this literature does not search too deeply into the class basis of the inequality of opportunity from which boys suffer. Educational achievement in Britain is still closely correlated with the class origins of students. The implication then appears to be that girls should match the class differentials of educational achievement and access to occupations which boys experience. Equality of opportunity in this context therefore appears to mean similar class-based inequalities of opportunity for both men and women. One could say, equal oppression!

What the cultural perspective lacks is precisely the cutting edge which caused the development of Marxist reproduction theory in the first place – that of a need to provide a critique of educational policy and practice, to get behind the illusion of education's neutrality and the myth of equality of opportunity, and to explain the relationship of schools to the economy, dominant class interests, and the hierarchical structures of economic and cultural power. Ironically, what the cultural perspective gains by neglecting this analysis of the socio-economic context of schooling is its optimism, its belief in educational reform and teachers' practice. What it loses is an adequate political analysis of the context in which these reforms would have any impact and the constraints under which schools realistically operate. By failing to provide a critique of liberal ideology and its view of education, much of the research into gender appears to be undertheorised and to have little concern for the *origins* and the conditions of school processes or the *sources* of potential conflict and contradiction within gender socialisation.

Nevertheless, there are also several advantages in such cultural theory, particularly for the development of a feminist analysis of the operation of *male hegemony* in education. What such research can show is the unity of girls' experiences across class boundaries by focusing upon female education as a common experience *vis-à-vis* that of boys. Clarricoates (1980), for example, concludes from her research in four primary schools that 'the subordination of women is always maintained', even though femininity varies.

> All women, whatever their 'class' (economic class for women is always in relation to men – fathers and husbands) suffer oppression. It is patriarchy in the male hierarchical ordering of society, preserved through marriage and the family via the sexual division of labour that is at the core of women's oppression; and it is schools, through their different symbolic separation of the sexes, that give their oppression the seal of approval.
>
> (Clarricoates, 1980, p. 40)

The advantage of the alternative perspective, that of political economy, is precisely the reverse of cultural theories, since what this perspective can reveal is the *diversity* of class experience and the nature of *class hegemony* in education.[4] What becomes clear from this analysis is that working-class boys and girls do actually share some experiences in school, such as alienation from the school values of discipline and conformity, estrangement from school culture, and scepticism as to the validity of an ideology which stresses the possibility of individual social mobility. Admittedly, most of the research on social-class experience in schools has been conducted on boys, showing the homogeneity of their experiences within one social class (e.g., Corrigan, 1979; Hebdige, 1979; Willis, 1977). Empirically, there are very few studies of working-class or middle-class girls (Lambert, 1976; McRobbie, 1978; McRobbie and Garber, 1975; Nava, 1981; Sharpe, 1976). As Delamont (1970) and King (1971), among others, have pointed out, this is an under-researched area in the sociology of education as a whole. Most of the work in the political economy perspective has been theoretical or at a macro-level of analysis.

What researchers using this perspective have in common is their concern for constructing a theory of class and gender education and for bridging the gap between Marxist theories of class reproduction and theories of gender divisions.[5] Curiously in this work one finds perhaps more references today to the Marxist theories of social reproduction that were popular in the mid-1970s in British sociology of education than in any other body of current educational literature.[6] The aim of most of this Marxist feminist work is to develop a political economy of women's education which moves out and away from the limitations of a purely cultural theory of gender, and which addresses itself to questions about the determinants of girls' schooling as well as its processes and outcomes. The starting point for much of this work has tended to be social rather than cultural reproduction theory, and in particular the theory of Louis Althusser. The reason for this interest in Althusser's (1971) work on ideological state apparatuses is that he makes the distinction between the reproduction of the labour force and the reproduction of the social relations of production. Much of the domestic labour debate has focused attention upon the role of women in fulfilling the former function for capital through biological reproduction of the next generation of workers and the daily reproduction, through servicing, of the work force (e.g., Hall, 1980; Secombe, 1973). The question which concerns Marxist feminist sociologists of education is that of the role of schooling in the social reproduction of the female waged and domestic labour forces. The differential experience of boys and girls for the first time assumes particular importance in the analysis of the social reproduction of a capitalist labour force and capitalist social relations of production. Sexual divisions of labour which segregate women and men and maintain the male hierarchy within the work place and domestic life come into direct contact with the forms of class oppression and exploitation, as well as with class cultures of resistance, in these two sites.

Feminism and social reproduction theory

In the context of patriarchal capitalism, explaining the nature of women's education has also created a variety of problems for the analysis of class reproduction and it is these which encourage a reformulation of that theory.[7] Let me for a moment give two brief examples of how existing accounts of class reproduction through education must be modified to take account of gender difference. If we look at the explanations which have been offered for the rise of mass compulsory schooling in nineteenth-century Britain, we find none of them can adequately account for the fact that girls were educated at all. Why bother to educate girls in preparation for becoming a skilled work force when few women became such workers? Why educate women to be a literate electorate when they did not have the vote? If women were educated to become docile and conforming workers, why did they receive a different curriculum from boys – since their class position would have meant that working-class boys and girls had similar experiences? According to Davin (1979), none of these explanations of schooling can account for the particular pattern of girls' education. Instead one must recognise that what schools taught was the particular bourgeois family ideology in which women played a special role as dependent wife and mother. Davin argues that it was this need to educate girls into domesticity that encouraged educational policy-makers to establish schools for girls as well as boys. By limiting oneself to a strictly 'economic' or 'political' model of schooling, the saliency of family life within the concept of 'social order' would be missed entirely.

If we turn briefly now to the twentieth century, when human capital theory provided the ideological basis for so much of educational planning and decision-making, we find that even within this framework we cannot account for the development of women's education. If human capital theory did influence educational development to the extent that, for example, Bowles and Gintis (1976) suggest, then we understand that all children were prepared strictly for their future place in the work force. However, as Woodhall (1973) argues, human capital theorists used the concepts of 'investment in *man*' and 'manpower planning' with good reason, since they were mainly if not exclusively referring to men. Human capital theorists viewed women's education very differently from that of men. They saw it as:

> either a form of consumption, or an unprofitable form of investment given the likelihood that women have to leave the labour force after marriage, or may work short hours or in low paying occupations.
>
> (Woodhall, 1973, p. 9)

The returns in terms of cost–benefit analysis on women's education would therefore be low and hardly worth the effort. According to T.W. Schultz, himself a renowned human capital theorist,

> If one were to judge from the work that is being done, the conclusion would be that human capital is the unique property of the male population – despite all of the schooling of females and other expenditures on them they appear to be of no account in the accounting of human capital.
>
> (Schultz, 1970, pp. 302–3)

Can one then ignore the differential investment in men's and women's education and the different purposes for which schooling was meant? It must be remembered that the motto 'education for production' or 'education for economic efficiency and productivity' takes on specific meaning in the ideological climate of patriarchy.

If these explanations of the nineteenth- and twentieth-century development of schooling are inadequate to account for the rise of girls' schooling, then so are the theories which have used them as a basis for criticism, such as the work of Johnson (1970) and Bowles and Gintis (1976). Theories of class cultural control and the social reproduction of class relations are inadequate precisely because they have lost the sense of the specificity of class experiences in terms of gender. While there are similarities between members of each social class, there are also differences which often can give them common ground and shared experiences with members of another class (with whom they could potentially form alliances). The problem then becomes one of trying to sort out these similarities and differences. Certainly one way in which the analysis can be improved is through the recognition of the dual origins and destinations of female *and* male students – that of the waged and domestic labour forces and the sets of social relations within both the labour process and domestic life. Another way is to recognise that women's position within the hierarchy of class relations is different from that of men. There are far fewer women employers, managers, members of high-status professions and supervisors. Very few women are likely therefore to give orders and enforce obedience. Indeed they are more likely to be what Bernstein (1977) called the agents of 'symbolic control' (teachers, social workers) presenting the 'soft face' of capital rather than what Althusser (1971) called the 'agents of exploitation and repression'. Women therefore are not easily described by a concept of class structure that is defined by the distribution of male occupations and male hierarchies of control.

Another problem in theories such as that of Bowles and Gintis (1976) is that there is no identification and analysis of the reproduction of the patriarchal basis of class relations in the work place and in the school. They ignore the fact that so many women number in the ranks of what they call the 'secondary labour market' in a segmented labour force. If the principle of capitalist social relations of production is one of 'divide and rule', then one cannot ascribe sex segmentation of the labour force as a subsidiary principle of class division. In my view it is a major medium of class control and also the most visible form of the principle of 'divide and rule' (see MacDonald, 1981).

Bowles and Gintis did not really get involved in discussing patriarchal relations within the social relations of production and schooling because of their view that the reproduction of the sexual division of labour occurs primarily in the family, with the mother playing an active role. They argue that it is because the family is semi-autonomous and actively engaged in the reproduction of *gender* divisions and the private–emotional life of the family that capital has increasingly come to use the educational system as its primary agency for the reproduction specifically of the *class* structure and its relations. The thesis in *Unpopular Education* (CCCS, 1981) is similar; its authors argue that there are different social 'sites' for the reproduction of social relations which are hard to disentangle, especially in their combined effects.

> Nonetheless it is useful to think of 'the factory' (in shorthand) as the main site of class relations, and the family as strongly organised around relations of gender, sexuality and age.
>
> (CCCS, 1981, p. 25)

We have to be careful of this thesis of the physical and social separation of the two sites of reproduction precisely because it tends to result in giving legitimacy to research which ignores gender divisions in schools and work places and which assumes the production of gender all happens outside the school and factory walls. Second, this thesis begs the question of the nature of the relationship between class and gender divisions and between processes of class and gender reproduction which occur simultaneously in the family, the school and the work place. Third, implicit in this separation is the assumption that the family and the work place are indeed separate and distinct destinations for both men and women, and that their preparation for one location is different from their preparation for the other. But this separation is itself an ideological construction which has originated in the context of bourgeois hegemony (see Hall, 1980). It is extremely difficult to use such a dividing line for the destination of women, since for many the distinction is blurred in terms of the location of their productive work (e.g., domestic industries) and their time. The reproduction of family life and the domestic sexual division of labour could just as well be described as the reproduction of class position so far as women are concerned, especially if one wished to include housewives in, rather than exclude them from, a class analysis.

The family is indeed the site of gender reproduction, but it also reproduces class cultures, ideologies and values which are critical components of class relations. The simultaneous operation of these two processes means that specific class forms of gender divisions are constructed and reproduced in this site. Similarly the school is another site in which the two processes occur simultaneously. What is especially significant, therefore, is not the separation of the two sites, but rather the nature of family–school interrelations. (See David, 1978, who argues for the analysis of the 'family–education couple'.) The transition from the private world of the family and its 'lived' class culture into the public world of class divisions and sex segregation is one which is fraught with conflict between the 'familiar', received class and gender identities and those taught in the school. It is the process of transition that is the critical point at which we shall understand the ways in which the reproduction of both sets of power relations occurs. At the end of their school days, schoolchildren leave as young adults who despite their different class origins are meant to have learnt the more elaborated[8] and abstract definition of masculinity and femininity, and to have placed themselves, using such class and gender identities, in the hierarchies of the domestic and waged labour forces.[9]

The development of a Marxist feminist theory of gender education, like cultural theory, has been affected by the assumptions of the body of knowledge which it is criticising. It is unfortunate that much of the political economy of gender education has repeated many of the mistakes of social reproduction theory. I am thinking here of the four major problems which Johnson (1981) argues lie in the social reproduction model, requiring some modification of the model if it is to be used at all. He argues that social reproduction theory has a tendency toward functionalism, especially in so far as it does not refer to the reproduction of the contradictions and conflicts which are integral to the social relations of production and the points of class struggle arising during the process of capital accumulation. I would also add that Marxist feminist theories of social reproduction have a very real tendency to ignore any notion of gender struggle and conflict, of forms of gender resistance, of contradictions within the process of the social reproduction of the female waged and domestic work forces, and of the patriarchal relations in the family and the labour processes. They too suffer from inherent functionalism. Social reproduction theories conflate educational conditions with educational outcomes, giving the appearance that the rationales and rhetoric of state policy successfully determine the products of the educational system. This tendency is just as clear in cultural theories of gender as in the Marxist feminist analysis of the sexual division of labour. It would appear from such work that girls become 'feminine' without any problems. They acquire the mantle of femininity through the experience of the family and the school, and keep it for the rest of their lives. As a result, in searching historically for the common pattern of girls' schooling, there has been an overwhelming emphasis upon the pattern of subordination of girls through education, with very little emphasis upon the patterns of resistance and struggle. But one of the greatest women's struggles has been fought over the right of access to and social mobility through the educational system. The fight for the right to be educated represents the most public of gender struggles and yet in contemporary accounts of schooling it is either forgotten or relegated to a marginal event since it was, after all, a struggle by middle-class women for middle-class rights and privileges. And yet it had repercussions for all women. Also, in the analysis of contemporary education, the most visible of struggles over education and the most visible set of problems which confronts teachers is that of controlling working-class boys. The degree of attention paid by educationalists to the disciplining of boys, their degree of concern over male delinquency and truancy rates, is reflected in the amount of attention paid to working-class boys in sociological studies. There is considerable neglect of the more 'silent' forms of resistance by girls, whether such resistance takes the form of daydreaming (Payne, 1980) or of girls painting their nails in class (Llewellyn, 1980; McRobbie, 1978) or of 'non-attendance' at school (Shaw, 1981).

By ignoring gender struggles, Marxist feminist analyses of schooling fall into the trap of social determinism, even while rejecting as totally false other theories of determinism, such as the biological. Hence de Beauvoir can write:

> The passivity that is the essential characteristic of the 'feminine' woman is a trait that develops in her from the earliest years. But it is wrong to assert a biological datum is concerned: it is in fact a *destiny* imposed upon her by teachers and by society.
>
> (quoted in Freeman, 1970, p. 36; my emphasis)

Such determinism means that social reproduction theory suffers from a latent pessimism and can leave women, and women teachers particularly, with a sense of fatality and helplessness. In the case of feminism, the 'hold' of the system over women seems especially fatalistic in that women are, according to the CCCS (1981), 'doubly determined'.

> The position of women is doubly determined and constrained: by patriarchal relations and the sexual division of labour within the home and by their patriarchally structured position within waged labour outside.
>
> (CCCS, 1981, p. 156)

However, this can be put another way. What we can say is that the 'consent' of women is sought to their subordination in both the home and in the waged labour force, and it is on both these fronts that they fight against class and gender control. If we forget to refer to women's struggles, we also lose sight of the victories gained. Not surprisingly then, it is very hard to find an account of the political economy of women's education which points out the gains women have made in forcing their way through the barriers of social prejudice and the obstacles which men have placed in front of them to prevent their appropriation of male culture and of male-dominated professions, status and power. It must be remembered that access to education can be liberating even within a class-controlled system, since it is not only at the level of class relations that oppression occurs. What the Marxist feminist accounts lose sight of, because of their overriding concern for Marxist class categories, is that patriarchal oppression has its own dynamic and its own 'stakes' in gender struggles, and one of the most important ones has been access to, and achievement in, education as a source of liberation.

Contradictions in theories of gender education

Let us now for a brief moment look at the theoretical assumptions of the two traditions within the analysis of gender education and notice the contradictions which emerge between the different analyses. It is at these points of contradiction that research possibilities are opened up and new directions can be taken in the analysis of class and gender. Here I shall identify three major contradictions between the cultural and the political economy perspectives.

First, let us look at the different analyses of the relationship between the home and the school. Cultural theorists have argued that there is, by and large, a *continuity* between the home and the school. Gender socialisation appears to start at birth and continue undisturbed to adulthood. Gender definitions are not, therefore, class specific but societal in source and nature. Thus the school's role is to extend and legitimate the process begun at home, whatever the material circumstances of the particular family or community. The political economy perspective, on the other hand, stresses the importance of the *discontinuity* and distance between the culture of the home and the school. Working-class culture is seen as markedly different from the bourgeois culture transmitted in the school.[10] The school's role in this latter case is to select from class cultures and to legitimate only some cultural forms and styles. From this perspective, school knowledge is seen as attempting to ensure the ratification of class power in an unequal society which is divided by class conflict. If this is the case, it becomes improbable that *one* pattern of gender socialisation into *one* set of gender stereotypes extends across different class cultures and across the divide of family and school. What is more likely is that the family culture and gender definitions of the bourgeoisie are transmitted in the school and it is the middle-class child who will experience the least difficulty with gender roles taught in school. This view is given support not just by personal accounts of women such as Payne (1980), who was a working-class girl sent to a middle-class grammar school, but also by the class history of girls' education. Marks (1976), for example, shows how definitions of masculinity and femininity were prominent categories in the development of an English school system which was class divided. She argues that her analysis had shown that:

> notions of femininity vary both historically and between social classes; and [are shown] to be dialectically related to the changing roles of women in society.
>
> (Marks, 1976, p. 197)

Purvis' (1980, 1981) historical research also supports this view. She has shown that what was appropriate for one social class in terms of gender was not necessarily appropriate for another. What Purvis found was the imposition by the bourgeoisie in the nineteenth century of a different concept of femininity for the middle classes (the 'perfect wife and mother') from that imposed upon the working class (the 'good woman').

> The ideal of the 'good woman' may be seen … as an attempt by the bourgeoisie to solve the various social problems associated with industrialisation and urbanisation. The 'good woman' was a dilution of the higher status

> ideal of the perfect wife and mother and thus it may be interpreted as a form of 'intervention' into working-class family life, an attempt to convert and transmit that part of bourgeois family ideology that insisted that a woman's place was in the home, that she was responsible for the quality of family life and that her domestic skills were more important than, say, vocational skills that might be used in waged labour. The 'good woman' was, therefore, a form of class cultural control ... an attack upon the patterns of working-class motherhood and parenthood as perceived by the middle classes.
>
> (Purvis, 1980, p. 11)

The second contradiction which arises between the cultural and political economy theories is in terms of the expected effect and outcome of the education system. So much of the work on gender which has come out of the cultural perspective has stressed that the difference between Western European definitions of masculinity and femininity lies precisely in the fact that while femininity is defined as 'docility, submission, altruism, tenderness, striving to be attractive, not being forceful or bold or physically strong, active or sexually potent' (Loftus, 1974, p. 4), masculinity means being aggressive, independent, competitive and superior, learning to take the initiative, lead an active out-of-doors life and so on (Belotti, 1975). Yet according to Bowles and Gintis' (1976) version of social reproduction theory, or even Althusser's (1971), what working-class children, and in particular working-class boys, learn through schooling is to obey, to take discipline, to follow rules and to submit to hierarchy. They learn docility, which according to cultural theory is a 'female' gender attribute. How then do boys cope with this difference in social expectations?

It is impossible to answer this question at the present time since there has been so little research on the problem of class and gender as competing power structures within school environments. However, as I have argued above, it is more likely that there is a discontinuity between the home and the school as a result of class divisions. This will mean that working-class boys and girls will have to negotiate their way not just through class identities, but also through gender identities. Bourdieu (1977) has argued that the response of the working-class boy and man to the 'femininity' of bourgeois school culture is one of resistance through the use of 'coarse' language, manners, dress and so on. This reaffirms their class identity but also protects their masculinity from negation by the 'effeminate' style of bourgeois culture. On the other hand, according to Bourdieu, working-class girls can more easily negotiate school life and its values, since the feminine identity derived from their families also stresses docility and passivity. This analysis forgets the importance of the mental/manual division and the hierarchy of knowledge, not just in the school curriculum but also in the forms of girls' response to schooling. The inversion of the mental/manual division allows working-class 'lads' to celebrate their masculine identity (Willis, 1977), but a similar inversion also allows working-class women to celebrate their femininity through a rejection of male culture which stresses the value of hierarchies (particularly mental over manual work), objective versus subjective knowledge, and individual competition above cooperation (see Spender, 1980b).

Paradoxically then, femininity, the supposed essence of docility and conformity, can become the vehicle for resisting forms of class reproduction. By playing off one set of social expectations against the other, working-class girls can resist the attempts of schools to induce conformity. Unfortunately, like the forms of resistance of the 'lads' which confirm their fate as manual workers, the resistance of girls only leads them to accept even more voluntarily their futures as dependent and subordinate to men, and as semi- or unskilled workers with low pay and insecure working conditions, often in dead-end jobs. Furthermore, the forms of class resistance of neither working-class boys nor working-class girls are likely to negate their preconceived notions of gender derived from their families. If anything they may reinforce the patriarchal relations specific to that social class by granting it more social value and potency in class resistance.

The third contradiction between the two bodies of theory lies in their conceptions of the ideology of schooling. According to cultural theories, girls' educational 'underachievement' is a result of the fact that girls are 'taught how to fail'. Horner (1971) described the process of education as one in which girls learn to avoid and 'dread success', since it means becoming failures as women.[11] Alison Kelly (1981), in her study of girls' failure to study or be successful in science in schools, argues that the school actually discourages girls from achieving in these subjects in a variety of different ways. This process, which she calls a 'discouraging process', involves either not making science available to girls or putting them off through conscious advice or unconscious bias in favour of boys. In contrast to this rather negative view of schools, theories of class reproduction have argued that the dominant ideology of education taught through education is that of equality of opportunity. According to these theories, students are encouraged to see failure as individual, resulting from their lack of ability. Now this may be the case today where class is a hidden category of education practice and where the categories of educational divisions are in terms of high to low academic ability. However, it is still possible to find gender being used as a very explicit allocating device for curriculum design, options and routes, as well as for classroom organisation, the labelling of pupils and so on, in a way that is no longer socially acceptable with social class. It is also still possible to find girls' failure at school described as natural since 'she is only a girl'. Female students as a group can expect not to succeed and their collective failure is visible. Indeed, as Wolpe (1976) has argued, the official ideology of equality of opportunity was modified to fit the 'special needs or interests' of girls, so that it referred to future expectations of domestic life rather than the rewards to be gained from social mobility through better employment prospects.

The illusion of meritocracy, which Bowles and Gintis attacked as being prevalent in schools, must therefore be treated with caution, since it may only be an illusion of *male meritocracy* taught to the working class. What is even more interesting is that when the expansion of the universities occurred in

Britain in the 1960s, it was with some despair that Hutchinson and McPherson (1976) reported from their studies of Scottish university undergraduates that equality of opportunity had benefited middle-class women *at the expense of* working-class men. These women had, in their words, 'displaced' those working-class men who had successfully made their way through the school system and were knocking upon the university doors. There were therefore two 'competing' ideologies of equality of opportunity, not one. No concern was shown for the drastically low numbers of working-class women who reached the university and whose numbers were quoted as being 'stable' (hence uninteresting) *despite* the expansion of the university sector. The impression is gained therefore that class equality of opportunity refers to the male working class and gender equality of opportunity to middle-class women. Possibly the fact that working-class women have not gained by this opening up of opportunities is because their subjective assessment of their objective possibilities for entry into higher education and for social mobility has led them to limit their own education aspirations. Their assessment may well have 'penetrated' (to use Willis' term) the fact that meritocracy is for men. Perhaps, as Sharpe's (1976) study has suggested, they have accepted a more satisfying alternative – the ambition to become a wife and mother – rather than compete in vain for access to a male world.

Developing a theory of cultural production

Up until now, I have focused on some of the problems of using social reproduction theory to develop a feminist account of girls' schooling and have pointed out some of the dangers of not addressing oneself to the questions concerning the determinants of schooling under capitalism. Here I shall turn to theories of cultural reproduction, which I think have been ignored by feminists using either the cultural or the political economy perspective. It is possible that cultural reproduction theories have been avoided because the relevance of this work for a theory of gender is not obvious, especially since it appears to refer only to class. However, even though Bernstein's (1977, 1980) research has been adopted (and transformed) in the context of Marxist theories of education developed in the 1970s, I believe that his theory of classification systems, of the social construction of categories and 'classes' (in the neutral sense of social groups), can be very useful in developing a general theory of gender differences and relations and in setting out the premises for research in schools. I think that one can develop a theory of gender codes which is class-based and which can expose the structural and interactional features of gender reproduction and conflict in families, in schools and in work places. The idea of a gender code relates well to the concept of hegemony, since both concepts refer to the social organisation of family and school life where the attempt is made to win over each new generation to particular definitions of masculinity and femininity and to accept as natural the hierarchy of male over female, the superiority of men in society. The concept of code also allows one to develop a structural analysis of school culture which avoids seeing the problem of gender inequality as one simply of attitudes which have no material basis. The political and economic distribution of power between men and women in our society is reproduced through the structural organisation of school life, as one of its major agencies; yet schools are also the critical reproductive agencies of class cultures and their principles of organisation. In this sense gender codes can be related to an analysis of class codes in schools.

The first major premise of any theory of gender must be that gender categories are in a very important sense arbitrary social constructs. The arbitrary nature of their contents, both historically and in terms of social class, is the product of 'work' carried out by a variety of social institutions and agents (e.g., schools, churches, the mass media – teachers, priests, authors, film producers). The active nature of the production of a category called 'gender' is captured nicely in Eileen Byrne's definition:

> Gender is the collection of attitudes which society *stitches together* (dress behaviour, attributed personality traits, expected social roles, etc.) to clothe boys and girls.
>
> (Byrne, 1978, p. 254; my emphasis)

Gender classification differs from that of sex in the sense that whereas the former is totally socially constructed, the other is biologically based. However, what I believe they have in common is that, like the notions of male and female sex, gender is in fact an arbitrary dichotomy imposed upon what is essentially a continuum. The questions we have to ask then are how and why are gender categories constructed in the way they are? We obviously need a historical analysis to sort out the specificity of our particular version of this dichotomy, our principle of classification, so that we can seek the source of that principle in the changing class relations contained within educational history. Further, we need to look for alternative sources of gender division that can be found in those social classes which have not appropriated the medium of the school to transmit their principles of gender difference.

The second premise is that gender classifications are not universal, nor societal, nor are they static or simple. Indeed they are highly complex in the sense that in order to construct two seemingly mutually exclusive categories which can apply to any range of social contexts, considerable work has to be done to pull together or, as Byrne put it, 'stitch together' a diversity of values and meanings. The tension within each category is as great as that between each category. Think, for example, of the contradiction which women face in trying to make sense of such antagonistic images of femininity as being both dependable and dependent, of being a sexual temptress and sexually passive, of being childlike and mothering, and of being a capable and intelligent consumer as well as being politically and economically inept. Unfortunately, so much of the work identifying stereotypes in masculinity and femininity has focused on the consistency rather than the contradiction within these categories. The imposed compatibility of different 'narrative structures' in which girls have to construct a coherent female identity has to be 'worked at', rather than assumed to exist, in order to produce what Althusser might have called a 'teeth-gritting harmony'.

The third major premise is that gender categories are constructed through a concept of gender difference which Chodorow (1979) has argued is essential to the analysis of male hegemony. The hierarchy of men over women is based upon an ideology of gender difference which is manifested in the structural division of men and women's lives, their education, their dress, their morality, their behaviour and so on. The ideology may be founded upon a theory of supposed natural divisions. This ideology then successfully hides the fact that gender is a cultural variable and one which is constructed within the context of class and gender power relations. The source and nature of the imposition of gender differences is so concealed that the power of the dominant class and the dominant sex is increased by such unconscious legitimation.

Yet how is the consent won to particular arbitrary definitions of masculinity and femininity by both men and women, so that they treat such classifications as natural and inevitable? One of the ways in which male hegemony is maintained is obviously through schooling, where it is most easy to transmit a specific set of gender definitions, relations and differences while appearing to be objective. The opportunity to transmit a gender code is, however, not open to any social class, but rather to the bourgeoisie who have appropriated, more than any other class, the educational system for themselves. The dominant form of male hegemony within our society is therefore that of the bourgeoisie. That is not to say that the classification of gender used by the working class or the aristocracy has not entered the school. As we have already seen in the work of Willis and McRobbie, it is these categories and definitions of masculinity and femininity from the working class that provide the vehicle for classroom and social-class resistance. The aristocratic ideal of masculinity can be found in the English public schools, where the concept of the amateur sportsman, the gentleman and the benevolent paternal leader are in contrast to the grammar school bourgeois ideals of the hard-working scientist, scholar or artist. Matched to each ideal is its antithesis of 'non-masculinity': the complementary ideals of femininity – the hostess, the good wife and mother, the career woman and so on.

If we return very briefly to the separation of home and work discussed earlier, we can now relate it to the production of gender difference through a class-based classification system. Historically, as Davin (1979) and Hall (1980) have shown, the nineteenth century saw the development of the bourgeois family form (with its male breadwinner, its dependent housekeeping wife and dependent children) and its imposition upon the working class through educational institutions. Implicit in this social construction was the notion of two spheres which distinguished and segregated the world of women and men. This classification of male and female worlds was made equivalent to and imposed upon a further classification – that of work and family (or put another way, the distinction between the public world of production and the private world of consumption). This latter ideological construction, despite having a material basis as the continuing development of the factory and office systems, nevertheless has to be continually reinforced in day-to-day life. In this sense, the division between family and work which so many sociologists of education take for granted can also be seen as an *ideological* division which is part of bourgeois hegemony. The structural imposition of the gender classification upon this other division unites the hierarchy of class relations with that of gender relations since it allows for the exploitation of women by both men and capital. Hence the productive world becomes 'masculine' even though so many women work within it, and the family world becomes 'feminine' even though men partner women in building a home. As Powell and Clarke argue, this classification helps create the political and economic 'invisibility' of women:

> It is the dominant ideological division between *Home* and *Work* which structures the invisibility of women and not their real absence from the world of work. Their identification solely with the 'privatised' world of the family has masked, firstly, the historical (not natural – and for a long time very uneven) removal of work from the home, and secondly the continuing presence of working women. (It also masks the man's presence in the home.) Men and women do not inhabit two empirically separated worlds, but pass through the same institutions in different relations and on different trajectories.
>
> (Powell and Clarke, 1976, p. 226)

In understanding the differential experience of girls and boys in schools, we should pay particular attention to the way in which the school *constructs* a particular relationship between, for example, home and work and how it prepares the two sexes in different ways for these two destinations. Thus boys and girls are meant to learn a different relation to the bourgeois classification of public and private worlds, of family and work, of male and female spheres. Schools teach boys how to maintain the importance of those distinctions and to see their futures in terms of paid work. (There is little, if any, training for fatherhood in schools.) Boys are trained to acquire the classification in its strongest form, to make the distinction between work and non-work, masculinity and non-masculinity. Hence they avoid academic subjects which are considered to be 'feminine', 'domestic' and personal/emotional. Their masculinity is premised upon maintaining the distinctiveness of the two spheres, since it is in that hierarchy that their power is based. Girls, on the other hand, are taught to *blur* the distinction between family and work for themselves, to see an extension of identity from domestic activities to work activities, to extend their domestic skills to earn an income and to use their employment for the benefit of their domestic commitments rather than for themselves. Their construction of the work/family division differs from one which they accept as natural for men, and so they too maintain the classification even though it is not directly applicable to themselves. Thus, as Powell and Clarke (1976) point out, the dimensions of possible activity for both sexes are constructed around the oppositions of work/non-work, management/labour and work/leisure, but the opposition family/non-family overshadows all the others in the case of women.

We can describe through research the ways in which the schools structure the experience of boys and girls in such a way as to transmit specific gender classifications with varying degrees of boundary strength and insulation between the categories of masculine and feminine and a hierarchy of male over female, based upon a specific ideology of legitimation. Through classroom encounters where boys and girls experience different degrees and types of contact with the teacher, through the different criteria for evaluating boys' and girls' behaviour, and through the curriculum texts and the structured relations of the school, limits are set to the degree of negotiation of gender that is possible within the school. In this sense the school *frames* the degree and type of response to that gender code. What is relevant therefore is not just an analysis of the structural aspects of gender codes, but also the *form* of interaction within school social relations.[12]

Using a notion of gender code, we can recognise that while the school attempts to determine the identities of its students, it is also involved in a process of transmission in which the student takes an active role. First, the student is active in inferring the underlying rules from a range of social relations between men and women (between parents, teachers, pupils and so on). Students learn to recognise and make sense of a wide range and variety of contradictory and miscellaneous inputs, and the results are not always predictable, especially since they relate these school messages to the alternatives which they have experienced or derived from their families, their peer group, the mass media and so on. The student will undergo a process of actively transforming these various messages and will produce at the end, in a temporary sense, a constellation of behaviour and values which can be called 'femininity' or 'masculinity'. What the school attempts to do is to produce subjects who unconsciously or consciously consent to the dominant version of gender relations. This does not mean, however, that if it fails, patriarchal relations are challenged, since it must be remembered that in all social classes it is the men who are dominant and hold power.

Men and women become the embodiment of a particular gender classification by internalising and 'realising' the principle which underlies it. They externalise their gendered identities through their behaviour, language, their use of objects, their physical presence and so on. It is through this process of 'realisation' that the dialectics of objective structures and social action are created. In the process of producing classed and gendered subjects who unconsciously recognise and realise the principles of social organisation, the reproduction of such power relations are ensured. Thus individuals internalise the objective and external structures and externalise them, transformed but not radically challenged. The potential for rejecting such definitions is inherent within the process for, as Bernstein (1980) argues, the recognition of principles of classification does not determine the realisation (or practice); it can set the limits upon it. What appears to be a smooth process of repetition is in fact one in which the contradictions, the struggles and the experience of individuals are suppressed. As Bernstein (1980) has argued, 'any classification system suppresses potential cleavages, contradictions and dilemmas'.

The fact that there is a dominant gender code (i.e., that of the bourgeoisie) means that there are also dominated gender codes (those of the working class or different ethnic groups). The experience of learning the principles of the dominant gender code is therefore the experience of learning class relations, where working-class family culture is given illegitimate and low status at school. Interestingly, the form of class reproduction may occur through the very formation of gender identities which we have been talking about. Further class resistance may be manifested through resistance to gender definitions. However, and this is really a very important point, in neither the dominant nor the dominated gender codes do women escape from their inferior and subordinate position. There is nothing romantic about resisting school through a male-defined working-class culture. It is at this point that women across social class boundaries have much in common.

Concluding remarks

Briefly then, I think that any research in the area of women's education should have two essential features. First, it should recognise the existence of both class and male hegemony within educational institutions and the sometimes difficult relationship which exists between them. Second, it should be aware that any set of social relations, such as class or gender relations, constitutes a social dynamic in which the forces of order, conflict and change are contained. The process of what Freire (1972) called 'domestication' in the case of girls implies a dialectic of oppression and struggle against class-based definitions of femininity. It is the dual nature of that struggle which allows women to seek allies simultaneously in their own social class and among women in different social classes. Somehow our research must capture the unity *and* the diversity of the educational lives of women.

Notes

1 Production is used here to refer to the act of *social construction* either by institutions such as schools, the mass media and so on, or by individuals.
2 McRobbie is referring here to the work of Paul Willis (1977) and Dick Hebdige (1979).
3 Examples of a 'cultural perspective' are Kelly (1981), Frazier and Sadker (1973), Belotti (1975), Delamont (1970) and Lobban (1975).
4 Examples of a 'political economy perspective' are Barrett (1980), David (1978, 1980), Deem (1978, 1981), MacDonald (1980b, 1981) and Wolpe (1978a, 1978b). For full references, see Arnot (1981).
5 By social reproduction theory I am referring to the work of Althusser (1971) and Bowles and Gintis (1976).
6 It is interesting that, despite the development of the cultural theory of gender, the cultural reproduction theory found in Bernstein (1977) and Bourdieu and Passeron (1977) has not generally been used, or even referred to.

7 The most contentious area, which cannot be treated here, is obviously the appropriateness of using existing Marxist definitions of social class for describing women's economic and political position. For this debate see, for example, Barrett (1980), MacDonald (1981) and West (1978).
8 I am using Bernstein's (1977) concept here to show that in schools children are taught the middle-class cultural definition of gender that appears to be 'context independent' and thus neutral and generalisable.
9 This would obviously only occur in times of full employment. In the present context, being 'working class' and 'female' is often a qualification for unemployment.
10 See the introduction to Bernstein (1977).
11 Similar arguments are put forward in contributions to Spender and Sarah (1980).
12 See 'On the classification and framing of educational knowledge' in Bernstein (1977).

References and further reading

Althusser, L. (1971) 'Ideology and ideological state apparatuses', in *Lenin and Philosophy and Other Essays*, London: New Left Books.

Arnot, M. (1981) 'Culture and political economy: dual perspectives in the sociology of women's education', *Educational Analysis*, 3, pp. 97–116.

Barrett, M. (1980) *Women's Oppression Today*, London: Verso.

Belotti, E.G. (1975) *Little Girls*, London: Writers and Readers Publishing Cooperative; first published, Milan: C. Feltrienelli Editore, 1973.

Bernstein, B. (1977) *Class, Codes and Control*, vol. 3, 2nd edn, Boston and London: Routledge & Kegan Paul.

—— (1980) 'Codes, modalities and the process of cultural reproduction: a model', *Pedagogical Bulletin*, no. 7, University of Lund, Sweden: Department of Education.

Bourdieu, P. (1977) 'The economics of linguistic exchange', *Social Science Information*, 16, 6, pp. 645–68.

Bourdieu, P. and Passeron, J.-C. (1977) *Reproduction in Education, Society and Culture*, London: Sage.

Bowles, S. and Gintis, H. (1976) *Schooling in Capitalist America*, Boston and London: Routledge & Kegan Paul.

Brewster, P. (1980) 'School days, school days', in D. Spender and E. Sarah (eds) *Learning to Lose: sexism and education*, London: Women's Press.

Byrne, E. (1978) *Women and Education*, London: Tavistock.

Centre for Contemporary Cultural Studies (CCCS) (1981) *Unpopular Education: schooling for social democracy in England since 1944*, London: Hutchinson.

Chodorow, N. (1979) 'Feminism and difference: gender relation and difference in psychoanalytic perspective', *Socialist Review*, 9, 4, pp. 51–70.

Clarricoates, K. (1980) 'The importance of being earnest ... Emma ... Tom ... Jane. The perception and categorization of gender conformity and gender deviation in primary schools', in R. Deem (ed.) *Schooling for Women's Work*, Boston and London: Routledge & Kegan Paul.

Corrigan, P. (1979) *Schooling the Smash Street Kids*, New York: Macmillan.

David, M.E. (1978) 'The family–education couple: towards an analysis of the William Tyndale dispute', in G. Littlejohn et al. (eds) *Power and the State*, London: Croom Helm.

—— (1980) *The State, Family and Education*, Boston and London: Routledge & Kegan Paul.

Davin, A. (1979) 'Mind you do as you are told: reading books for boarding school girls 1870–1902', *Feminist Review*, 3, pp. 80–98.
Deem, R. (1978) *Women and Schooling*, Boston and London: Routledge & Kegan Paul.
—— (ed.) (1980) *Schooling for Women's Work*, Boston and London: Routledge & Kegan Paul.
—— (1981) 'State policy and ideology in the education of women, 1944–1980', *British Journal of Sociology of Education*, 2, 2, pp. 131–44.
Delamont, S. (1970) *Sex Roles and the School*, London: Methuen.
—— (1978) 'The contradictions in ladies' education' and 'The domestic ideology and women's education', in S. Delamont and L. Duffin (eds) *The Nineteenth Century Woman*, London: Croom Helm.
Frazier, N. and Sadker, M. (1973) *Sexism in School and Society*, New York: Harper & Row.
Freeman, J. (1970) 'Growing up girlish', *Trans-Action*, 8 (November–December), pp. 36–43.
Freire, P. (1972) *Pedagogy of the Oppressed*, Harmondsworth: Penguin.
Fuller, M. (1980) 'Black girls in a London comprehensive school', in R. Deem (ed.) *Schooling for Women's Work*, Boston and London: Routledge & Kegan Paul.
Hall, C. (1980) 'The history of the housewife', in E. Malos (ed.) *The Politics of Housework*, London: Alison & Busby.
Hebdige, D. (1979) *Subculture: the meaning of style*, London: Methuen.
Horner, M.S. (1971) 'Femininity and successful achievement: a basic inconsistency', in J. Bardwick, E.M. Douvan, M.S. Horner and D. Gutmann (eds) *Feminine Personality and Conflict*, Pacific Grove, CA: Brooks Cole Publishing.
Horney, K. (1967) 'The flight from womanhood', in H. Kelman (ed.) *Feminine Psychology*, Boston and London: Routledge & Kegan Paul.
Hutchinson, D. and McPherson, A. (1976) 'Competing inequalities: the sex and social class structure of the first year Scottish University student population 1962–1972', *Sociology*, 10, pp. 111–20.
Johnson, R. (1970) 'Educational policy and social control in early Victorian England', *Past and Present*, 49, pp. 96–113.
—— (1981) *Education and Popular Politics*, Milton Keynes: Open University Press.
Kelly, A. (ed.) (1981) *The Missing Half*, Manchester: Manchester University Press.
King, R. (1971) 'Unequal access in education – sex and social class', *Social and Economic Administration*, 5, 3, pp. 167–75.
Lambert, A. (1976) 'The sisterhood', in M. Hammersley and P. Woods (eds) *The Process of Schooling*, Boston and London: Routledge & Kegan Paul.
Levy, B. (1972) 'The school's role in the sex-role stereotyping of girls: a feminist review of the literature', in M. Wasserman (ed.) *Demystifying Schools*, New York: Praeger.
Llewellyn, M. (1980) 'Studying girls at school: the implications of confusion', in R. Deem (ed.) *Schooling for Women's Work*, Boston and London: Routledge & Kegan Paul.
Lobban, G.M. (1975) 'Sexism in British primary schools', *Women Speaking*, 4, pp. 10–13.
Loftus, M. (1974) 'Learning sexism and femininity', *Red Tag*, 7, pp. 6–11.
MacDonald, M. (1979–80) 'Cultural reproduction: the pedagogy of sexuality', *Screen Education*, 32/33, pp. 141–53.
—— (1980a) 'Socio-cultural reproduction and women's education', in R. Deem (ed.) *Schooling for Women's Work*, Boston and London: Routledge & Kegan Paul.
—— (1980b) 'Schooling and the reproduction of class and gender relations', in L. Barton, R. Meighan and S. Walker (eds) *Schooling, Ideology and the Curriculum*, Lewes: Falmer Press.

—— (1981) *Class, Gender and Education*, Milton Keynes: Open University Press.
McRobbie, A. (1978) 'Working class girls and the culture of femininity', in Women's Studies Group (ed.) *Women Take Issue: aspects of women's subordination*, London: Hutchinson, in association with the CCCS.
—— (1980) 'Settling accounts with subcultures: a feminist critique', *Screen Education*, 34 (Spring), pp. 37–49.
McRobbie, A. and Garber, J. (1975) 'Girls and subcultures', in S. Hall and T. Jefferson (eds) *Resistance through Rituals*, London: Hutchinson.
Marks, P. (1976) 'Femininity in the classroom: an account of changing attitudes', in J. Mitchell and A. Oakley (eds) *The Rights and Wrongs of Women*, Harmondsworth: Penguin.
Nava, M. (1981) 'Girls aren't really a problem', *Schooling and Culture*, 9.
Payne, I. (1980) 'Working class in a grammar school', in D. Spender and E. Sarah (eds) *Learning to Lose: sexism and education*, London: Women's Press.
Powell, R. and Clarke, J. (1976) 'A note on marginality', in S. Hall and T. Jefferson (eds) *Resistance through Rituals*, London: Hutchinson, in association with the CCCS.
Purvis, J. (1980) 'Towards a history of women's education in nineteenth century Britain: a sociological analysis', paper presented at the International Sociological Association Conference, Paris, 7–8 August.
—— (1981) 'The double burden of class and gender in the schooling of working class girls in nineteenth century Britain', paper presented at Westhill College, Conference on the Sociology of Education, January, unpublished.
Rowbotham, S. (1973) *Woman's Consciousness, Man's World*, Harmondsworth: Penguin.
Schultz, T.W. (1970) 'The reckoning of education as human capital', in W.L. Hansen (ed.) *Education, Income and Human Capital*, New York: National Bureau of Economic Research.
Secombe, W. (1973) 'The housewife and her labour under capitalism', *New Left Review*, 83, (January–February), pp. 3–24.
Sharpe, S. (1976) *Just like a Girl*, Harmondsworth: Penguin.
Shaw, J. (1981) *Family, State and Compulsory Education*, Milton Keynes: Open University Press.
Spender, D. (1980a) 'Education or indoctrination?', in D. Spender and E. Sarah, *Learning to Lose: sexism and education*, London: Women's Press.
—— (1980b) 'Educational institutions where co-operation is called cheating', in D. Spender and E. Sarah, *Learning to Lose: sexism and education*, London: Women's Press.
Spender, D. and Sarah, E. (1980) *Learning to Lose: sexism and education*, London: Women's Press.
West, J. (1978) 'Women, sex and class', in A. Kuhn and A.M. Wolpe (eds) *Feminism and Materialism*, Boston and London: Routledge & Kegan Paul.
Westergaard, J. and Resler, H. (1975) *Class in a Capitalist Society*, London: Heinemann Educational Books.
Willis, P. (1977) *Learning to Labour*, Farnborough: Saxon House.
Wolpe, A.M. (1976) 'The official ideology of education for girls', in R. Dale, G. Esland, R. Fergusson and M. MacDonald (eds) *Education and the State: politics, patriarchy and practice*, vol. 2, Lewes: Falmer Press.
—— (1978a) 'Girls and economic survival', *British Journal of Educational Studies*, 26, 2, pp. 150–62.

—— (1978b) 'Education and the sexual division of labour', in A. Kuhn and A.M. Wolpe (eds) *Feminism and Materialism*, London: Routledge & Kegan Paul.

Woodhall, M. (1973) 'Investment in women: a reappraisal of the concept of human capital', *International Review of Education*, 19, 1, pp. 9–28.

7 Schools and families

Gender contradictions, diversity and conflict

In this article I will examine, from a feminist perspective, the approach to education and the family developed by left sociologists in the 1970s in Britain and the United States. It is now accepted by many that the mainstream left discourse on the sociology of education was constructed primarily by male academics who have continued to focus almost entirely on boys' educational experiences. This bias, fortunately, has been partially remedied by new feminist research on girls' experience in school and their transition into waged and domestic work. However, while this research is a necessary first step, it does not solve the full range of problems created by the mainstream left discourse. The standard theories are also deficient in the way they pose the relationship of the family to mass schooling and, more specifically, the relationship between class and gender in both the family and the school.

The problem has not been a lack of theorising about the relationship between class and gender, but the nature of the theories that have become entrenched. The relationship has been formulated in such a way that the separation of family and work – and with it the division of the male public world and the female domestic sphere – has been legitimated. As a result, I will argue, the family has been located outside the economy. It has been portrayed as being insignificant as a social determinant of schooling and therefore its internal dynamics have not been thought worthy of study. I will also argue that the ideology of *familism*, unlike that of vocationalism, has been inadequately treated as an aspect of social-class differentiation. I will then go on to discuss the new research on family and school relations which, in my view, has opened the door to a more sensitive and less biased political economy of education and a better grasp of the complexities of class and gender relations.

A political economy perspective

Although I will be critical of the existing political economy perspective, I think it is essential to remember the main premises of that theory. Within capitalist societies, economic, political and cultural power is distributed unequally since such societies are based upon the extraction of surplus value. Social-class relations represent the relations of exploitation and oppression within such societies. It is not surprising, therefore, that social class has been found to be statistically the most significant indicator of the length and type of an individual's education. It affects the shape of educational careers, the nature of schooling and training received, and the possibility of a higher education after compulsory schooling. It does this for both men and women, for all ethnic groups and for individuals in all geographic regions within that society.

Reid found that, in Britain,

> successful completion of some form of higher education is almost exclusively associated with membership of the non-manual or middle classes, consequently the lack of it with membership of the manual or working classes.
>
> (Reid, 1981, p. 207)

Class identity is also the basis from which individuals, albeit often unconsciously, derive their social identities, their occupational aspirations and life styles, their forms of consciousness, and their political interests and activities. Westergaard and Resler argued that in a capitalist society neither gender nor age, region nor skin colour, 'has the force, the sweeping repercussions of class inequality':

> None of them in itself produces the communality of condition which marks class position in the economic order: a common complex of life circumstances shared by the victims; a contrasting set of life circumstances held in common by the privileged; broadly common ambiguities of condition among those who are neither clearly victims nor clearly privileged.
>
> (Westergaard and Resler, 1974, p. 352)

They argue that to recognise the effects of social-class inequality and raise it to higher explanatory status than other social cleavages, such as gender and race, is not necessarily to dismiss the latter as 'unreal or unimportant'. Rather we are encouraged to recognise the *total nature of social inequality and the effect of social-class divisions upon these other social divisions*. As Westergaard and Resler point out,

> the economic divisions of class … in turn give variations of character and shape to the manifestations of inequality by sex or age, region or colour, at different levels of the class structure.
>
> (ibid., p. 352)

It is this 'structuring power' of class relations which I believe provides us with the focus for a revised political economy of education. It opens up a whole range of new questions. For example, how has male power (or hegemony) been affected by the power relations of the class structure? How have the two processes of domination – class and male hegemony – come together to shape the educational system and the ideology and practice of its pupils, students, teachers and administrators? How do individuals form their class and gender identities in sets of social relationships which are often contradictory and ambiguous? How do individuals make sense of the presence of a double division of the world, with antagonistic social classes and two antagonistic sexes?

Maintaining a political economy perspective is also important theoretically, since without an analysis of the material basis of education we can easily fall into the trap of taking for granted the official and liberal versions of the school's neutrality and its ability to act as an independent agent of social reform. It is in this context that I have criticised what I called 'the cultural theory of gender', which is the dominant paradigm in the sociology of women's education (Arnot, 1981, 1982; the latter is reprinted as Chapter 6 in this volume). At the level of description, this research is at its strongest. It gives insights to teachers, parents, pupils and educational planners into what and where the educational problems are for girls in a school system that tends, particularly in this century, to hide its own gender bias. The research analyses the internal processes of schools which discriminate against girls, which discourage them from taking high-status school subjects (e.g., science), from attending university and from entering the male world of political and economic power. Such research focuses on *how* girls come to 'underachieve' at school, why they fail to compete equally with boys for entry into high-status professions and careers, and so forth. The prescriptions for social reform which such cultural theory suggests, however, are reduced in their potency precisely because of the lack of understanding of the conditions under which female education has developed. Cultural theory fails to analyse the power basis which has kept alive the arbitrary construction of gender differences, the transmission of an ideology of natural sex differences and the maintenance of gender inequalities in education either through segregation or through differential treatment. Thus girls' underachievement appears to be strictly an *educational problem* with an *educational solution* – that of changing individual attitudes. This approach does not identify the structural basis of women's oppression and exploitation in the home and in the waged labour process, which shapes those sex-role ideologies and the sexual division of labour. This is precisely the critical cutting edge that political economy offered.

Despite these problems, research with a cultural perspective is valuable for feminists for its focus upon the actual experiences of girls and its very real sense of the injustices involved in the relationship between men and women. Feminists concerned with the oppression and exploitation of women are far more likely to be drawn to such cultural theory than to the male-dominated and developed paradigm of political economy. Up until recently, nearly all discussion of the sexism of teachers, of sexual harassment of girls and female teachers, of the sexism of school material had been located within such cultural models of education rather than in critical sociology of education. Only too often, the political economy of education has identified the structural basis of women's oppression in capitalism and then neglected or ignored the concrete reality of that oppression in the relationships between men and women, boys and girls.

This can be seen, for example, in the ways in which three major sets of social relations have been defined and discussed: the relationship between schools and the economy, the relationship between school and work, and the relationship between school and the family. In each of these areas, the mainstream left approach has avoided questions that might have been asked and which might have allowed the investigation of women and their particular conditions of living to enter the radical sociological discourse.

Schools and the economy

The political economy perspective has debated forcefully the degree of dependence and autonomy that schools enjoy within the capitalist economy. Such analyses describe the capitalist economy by the social relations of the waged labour process, particularly in the factory and occasionally in the office. Assumptions are made that economic work means paid work, that efficiency refers to productivity in the waged labour force and that there is essentially only one labour force. However, as we now realise, the family and its labour force cannot be excluded from an analysis of capitalism. The separation of work and family life (the division of production and consumption) was shaped historically by the changing demands of a capitalist system of production, to the benefit of the capital-owning bourgeoisie. This separation of work and family, reinforced through ideologies of the family and 'the home', has marginalised and 'privatised' the family to the extent that it no longer appears to have a central role in economic life. Domestic work is not defined as 'real' work and *de facto* housewives appear to be outside the 'real' world of economic life.

Sociologists of education, by defining the economic mode of production as that based on the exploitation of waged workers only, have contributed their own ideological support to this process of separation. The family, no longer defined as part of the economy, is not seen as playing any major role in the formation of school life. Because of this, crucial aspects of the relationship between families and schooling cannot be adequately explained or accounted for. These include the transfer of control over 'schooling' from the family to the state, how this transfer has shaped the custodial functions of schools and how the state has been constituted *in loco parentis* (Shaw, 1981).

The search for the social origins of education in just the 'industrial' sector produces a one-sided and simplified account of schooling. This account has the effect of ignoring the family–education couple (cf. Althusser, 1971). David (1978) has argued that this results in a marginalization of women's educational role as mothers and teachers (particularly in early schooling). The content of their pedagogic work has been defined as part of gender reproduction but not class reproduction, as it involves 'expressive' and emotional training and the development of the child's personality – characteristics unrelated, apparently, to the formation of class identity. Zaretsky (1976), on the other hand, alerted us to the centrality of such 'affective' development in the maintenance of the capitalist social formation. Chamboredon and Prévot (1975) recognised that the division between 'spontaneous' forms of pedagogy (which typify the work of mothers in child care and teachers in primary schools) and the more 'instrumental' pedagogic styles (found in secondary schools) is one which reproduces not only the sexual division of labour but also bourgeois *class culture*.

The analysis of mass schooling which limited discussion to the requirements of capital for a skilled work force or a literate electorate also could not account for the rise of girls' schooling – especially, as Davin (1979) has pointed out, since women were not in skilled jobs and did not have the vote. The rationale for providing girls with education in the nineteenth century was to transmit the bourgeois family form through schooling. Given this, it is clear that in Marxist accounts of schooling the historical difference between working-class boys' and girls' education could not be understood.

Schooling and work

The relationship between pupils' education and their future employment has concerned diverse educational theorists, from government planners to human capital theorists and left sociologists. For human capital theorists seeking to estimate the cost-effectiveness of education, the problem has been that women have tended to enter the labour force spasmodically and to receive less benefit (defined as income) than men for their comparable educational qualifications. The solution was that, since women could not be included in *manpower* estimates and *manpower* planning, they were excluded from the analysis (Woodhall, 1973). For government educationalists, the issue of a pupil's destination after school was solved in the case of girls since it was assumed they would all marry and have children and that paid work was only a secondary concern for them.

Without putting it so baldly, left-wing sociologists of education have really been making the same assumption. For them, as for the other theorists, the 'problem' of social-class mobility and the reproduction of social classes has been the question of boys' education. This paradigm marked the work of, among others, Bowles and Gintis (1976), Willis (1977) and Corrigan (1979). The relationship between girls' education and their occupational destinies was not studied as a class issue, nor was the nature and extent of their social mobility examined. The other side of the coin was that boys were only perceived as having one destination – waged work – so that schools were not investigated in terms of how far they contributed to the formation of fathers and husbands. Did schools prepare boys, through the ideology of the male breadwinner, for their roles as head of the household and patriarchal authority? Instead of investigating the *relationship* between the family and the waged labour process and how boys and girls are prepared by schools for *both* destinations in different ways, such radical analyses legitimated the artificial separation of the two spheres.

The concern with the outcomes of schooling as defined by paid employment (or unemployment) led many sociologists to concentrate their efforts on understanding the last years of secondary schooling. It is at this point in their school lives that boys are most likely to become truants, to develop their own subcultures, to acquire or not acquire certificates, and to plan their entry into an occupation. If there is any similarity between schools and 'the long shadow of work', then it would be found in these last years of secondary schooling. The fact that gender theorists had urged the significance of the early years of schooling for the formation of children's identities appeared to be largely irrelevant to the majority of radical sociologists. (Apple and King, 1977, and Sharp and Green, 1975, are interesting exceptions to this pattern.) By the end of the 1970s, the educational system had been portrayed largely by a snapshot of the final years of secondary school life, with little account taken of the earlier (or later) years of schooling. If, however, the family had been taken as a destination for boys and girls alike, then surely the theorists would have had to deal with the ways in which schooling – from the very start – affects the formation of class and gender identity.

Schooling and the family

The interest of critical sociologists of education in the relationship between the family and the school has been intermittent. In the 1960s and 1970s, a concern for working-class underachievement in schools led to theories of cultural deprivation which outlined the importance of family culture. Such theories recognised that schools transmit the culture, the educational criteria and the social expectations of the bourgeoisie. What was important for children, therefore, was the distance between their family class-culture and that of the school. Such theories emphasised the central role the family played in mediating a class-determined education. However, in criticising the thesis that working-class families were in some way 'culturally deprived' and faulty, radical sociologists turned away from the family toward more 'economic' explanations of school failure. The central focus was on how schools reinforce the privilege of the bourgeoisie and the exploitation of the working class, through preparation for paid work.

In these new accounts of schooling, pupils were portrayed as 'negotiating' the messages of their teachers, yet, while in the home, learning appeared to take place via a process of 'assimilation'. The family was seen as a depository of class culture, derived from the father's experience as a waged worker. All of the father's dependants were assumed to have acquired his class consciousness. There was an assumption that class culture and its forms of consciousness were *donated* rather than being learned in any active sense. The dynamics of family life and the conditions under which children acquire their class identities were not investigated. Rather, culture was seen as a form of *capital*, owned primarily by the bourgeoisie and *inherited* by its children, a form of property which was 'non-negotiable', but could be exchanged for educational qualifications and eventually social privilege. The result was that there was no concept of struggle within families, especially since the study of youth cultures rejected the generation gap. The emphasis upon social class forced generational studies (and gender relations) out of mainstream sociology of education. Family culture tended to be represented as an 'input' into schooling, through the apparently unproblematic construction of working-class or middle-class identities. Yet generational conflict between mothers and daughters and fathers and sons over appropriate definitions of gender are also part of the process of acquiring a class identity.

Most people know from their own experience of family life that there is conflict within families, especially over the notions of femininity and masculinity. But this insight has generally been neglected by sociologists of education. While McRobbie (1978) and Thomas (1980) show that teenage girls believe they have close friendships with their mothers, there has been no investigation of how these friendships reflect a female alliance against males and in particular against the father's authority and behaviour in the home (Newson, Richardson and Scaife, 1978). Similarly, we do not know how the sex alliance between fathers and sons can be used in family struggles.

Codes of behaviour for both girls and boys are constructed out of the ideological materials available to them, from the sets of age, gender and class relations. Contradiction characterises their experiences. Hebdige has argued (in the case of black male youth) that contradictions of location and ideology can produce a new youth 'style' which 'is not *necessarily* in touch, in any immediate sense, with [their] material position in the capitalist system' (Hebdige, 1979, p. 81). In other words, there is no automatic transference from male working-class culture to that of male youth subculture. Wilson's research shows that teenage working-class girls face a major contradiction between:

> promiscuity which appears to be advocated by the 'permissive society' and the ideal of virginity advocated by official agencies and, to a large degree, the families.
>
> (Wilson, 1978, p. 68)

The working-class girls in Wilson's study constructed their own *sexual code* which determined whom to have sex with and under what circumstances. Their self-classification distinguished between 'virgins', 'one-man girls' and 'easy lays'. Girls negotiated the form of femininity prescribed by their parents and the alternative versions offered, for example, by the mass media. The new sexual code therefore did not just grow out of their class position.

The resistance of girls to their parental culture is very often dismissed as being a marginal phenomenon. It is explained as a demonstration that the girl wishes to be 'just like a boy' (an apparently perfectly natural thing) rather than resisting the pressures to be a traditional girl. Yet, in her study of female juvenile delinquents, Shacklady-Smith (1978) shows that these girls positively reject male supremacy and family definitions of femininity. She shows how these girls develop self-conceptions of being 'tough, dominant and tomboyish' by fighting, getting drunk, having sexual intercourse and being aggressive. What they were involved in was a 'double rejection' of legal norms and the traditional stereotyped conceptions of femininity, perceived by the girls as too constraining. Here again we find a negotiation rather than an assimilation of family culture.

The school and the family can have a range of different types of relationships, which cannot be easily described either by the physical notion of distance or by the use of a dichotomy of working-class and middle-class cultures. Schools can 'add to' (by reinforcing) family culture. They can also act 'against' family and thus cause contradictions and conflict for the child. Finally, they can be a progressive force – for example, setting up new models of gender relations which are liberating for girls. It is especially this third aspect of family–school relations which has been lost in Marxist accounts of school life. Yet schools do offer some working-class girls access to higher status and 'cleaner' occupations (such as nursing and teaching) than their mothers' manual work. Schools may provide a means of breaking down gender stereotypes of women's inferiority by giving them a means to improve their relative standing *vis-à-vis* men. This was certainly the case in Fuller's (1980) study of West Indian girls in British schools. These girls were in favour of school and of obtaining academic qualifications since these would allow them to challenge the double stereotypes of 'blackness' and femininity. Similarly, we can view the increase in the numbers of middle-class girls who enter higher education as not just the increasing hold of the bourgeoisie over the university sector, but also a victory for women over their ascribed status in society. The fight for education has played a significant role in the quest for equality between the sexes, and it is a role that has been largely ignored in critical histories of education.

Family–school relations

I would now like to turn to research which focuses specifically upon family–school relations. This area contains, in my view, some of the most interesting new developments in the analysis of class and gender. What characterises this research is an interest in the consistency or inconsistency faced by members of different social classes and sexes in the messages they receive in these different contexts. As a result, I feel that the complex dynamics of the lived experience of class and gender relations are beginning to be glimpsed and that the ambiguities which mark a system such as patriarchal capitalism are being brought into focus for the first time.

Ve Henricksen (1981) offers an initial foray into the consistencies and contradictions experienced by different social classes and the two sexes. She points out the similarity of training offered to working-class and middle-class girls – a training for family life. This training encompasses the notion of *familism*, which she defines as an 'exaggerated identification with the myth that the family is the only place where a woman may experience self-fulfilment'. Girls are taught at an early age that their future means becoming mothers and housewives, and they are expected to plan their futures in accordance with this fact. Boys of whatever class are, on the other hand, pushed towards a belief in individual achievement, self-interest and material success – what Ve Henricksen calls *individuation* (in other words, the capitalist ethic). Class differences may, however, have an important effect on the strength of an individual's belief in such ideologies. For example, Gaskell's (1977–8) research in British Columbian schools showed that working-class girls were even more conservative than middle-class girls in emphasising sex roles in the home, male power, femininity and the stability of sex roles. From a class perspective, Ve Henricksen argues that whereas the middle-class children are socialised into the ideologies of social mobility and achievement in work, the working class's own culture stresses solidarity and collectivity in work, consciousness and culture. These class cultures cause dilemmas for middle-class girls, who have to juggle the dual expectations of being a wife and having a full-time job at the same time. They also cause dilemmas for working-class boys who are expected to be individually successful and to participate in the meritocratic rat race while conforming to the working-class ideals of collective action. The middle-class boy, with the dual identities of individuation and social mobility, experiences a certain consistency of demands made on him; so do working-class girls, who can find a certain compatibility in the dual demands of family life and collective working-class solidarity.

While Ve Henricksen's theory is sensitive to the contradictions which can occur within the family, she neglects to discuss the conflict which can occur *between* family and school class-cultures. She ignores the imposition of bourgeois values upon working-class children through the development of state schooling, arguing that the key reference groups for each generation are only 'family, friends and school teachers'. There is no analysis of the differences between parental attitudes, the class-based assumptions of schools and school teachers, and the particular forms of peer-group cultures developed by pupils. The contradictions between these are critical aspects of the lived experiences of boys and girls of all social classes. It is these contradictions which form the basis of the research by Australian sociologists Connell, Ashenden, Kessler and Dowsett (1982). These authors reject the view that families are self-contained and closed units, 'havens from a heartless world'. They also reject the view that families and schools are separate spheres, pointing out that pupils are not in transition from one institution to another but actually live in families while they attend school. The issue for them is the link between family circumstance and schooling. By taking into account the organisation of work, the location and type of home, and the relations between the sexes within each family, the authors conclude that families are places 'where larger structures meet and interact'. As they put their view:

> We do not mean to suggest that families are simply the pawns of outside forces any more than schools are. In both cases, class and gender relations create dilemmas (some insoluble), provide resources (or deny them), and suggest solutions (some of which don't work), to which the family or school must respond in its collective practice.
>
> (Connell et al., 1982, p. 73)

A family is, in their definition, a closely knit group which has an intense inner life and a reasonably stable organisation. Further, this group of individuals makes choices and takes certain paths through the variety of situations it has to confront – marriage, work, having children, the schooling of their children, unemployment and so forth. In terms of socialisation, therefore, Connell and his colleagues argue that a family does not form a child's character and then deliver it pre-packaged on the doorstep of the school. Rather,

> the family is what its members do, a constantly continuing and changing practice, and, as children go to and through school, that practice is reorganised around their schooling.
>
> (ibid., p. 78)

According to these sociologists, *families produce people*, rather than reproduce social relations or class cultures in the abstract, and they produce them under often 'terrible constraints', including the constraints imposed by existing class and gender relations in society. The result is not predictable in every case. But what they see as vital is for sociologists to follow the consequences of such processes of production. In the schools, the consequences can be found in the variety of strategies adopted by pupils from different family circumstances. These strategies – such as compliance, pragmatism and resistance – can all be adopted by a pupil and used with different teachers. The impact of such different strategies, nevertheless, is not one which is likely to destroy the processes of social-class reproduction.

The reproduction of female class relations

I would now like to turn briefly to the new feminist historical work on the development of mass schooling. Here a new awareness is being developed as to the particular ways in which class and gender relations come together for *girls*. What does seem to be the case historically is that girls' education went across class lines in that both middle-class and working-class girls were prepared for their domestic futures by an educational ideology that stresses service to their menfolk rather than to themselves. But the precise notions of femininity presented to middle-class and working-class girls were not the same. Middle-class girls were offered the bourgeois ideal of the 'perfect wife and mother' – an ideal which encompassed the notion of the Christian virtues of self-denial, patience and silent suffering, as well as the aristocratic values of ladylike behaviour (which meant refusing any paid or manual employment) and ladylike etiquette. What the working-class girls received was a diluted and modified vision of the 'good woman' – an image of the 'good woman', wife, mother and housekeeper who had no pretension of becoming a lady and aspiring above her station. Such an ideal envisaged working-class family caretakers who would prevent their families from slipping into crime, political ferment, disease and immorality – and who in many cases would be reliable domestic servants for their middle-class counterparts (Purvis, 1980, 1981).

This dilution of the dominant gender definition can most probably be found today in the courses for the 'least able' girls. These girls are taught the practical skills of cooking and domestic science as preparation for female roles in the family. In contrast, middle-class girls are most likely to be learning the arts and languages, social sciences and history – subjects more suitable for their role as educated mothers and domestic hostesses. It is difficult to know what differences there are between the notions of femininity expected of working-class and middle-class girls in schools today, since so much of the research neglects class differences in favour of showing how girls as a group are treated differently than boys. What research there is, such as that by Douglas (1964) and Hartley (1978), suggests that teachers label working-class and middle-class girls differently in the classroom. The higher the social class the better behaved the pupil was seen to be. Working-class girls were seen as much rougher and noisier, much less tidy, and much less able to concentrate.

Connell and his colleagues, in this context, talk about the school's role in producing rather than reproducing masculinity and femininity, through what they call *masculinizing* and *feminizing* practices. These practices are different for each social class. They argue that schools create a hierarchy of different kinds of masculinity and femininity. Rather than reproduce sex stereotypes, they establish *sets of relations* between male and female pupils which will differ by social class. Private schools, therefore, are likely to set up a different set of relations between male and female pupils than state schools. Okeley's (1978) analysis of her own educational experiences in a private English boarding school reinforces this view. What these schools reproduced, through their particular work in creating 'ladies' and 'gentlemen', was the sexual division of the bourgeoisie. When we talk about different types of school, however, we have to remember that the reproduction of *female class relations* through education takes a different shape from that of boys. For boys, the reproduction of social differences, particularly in Britain, is often described as a matter of the division between private and state schools. The type of school attended is often as good an indicator of social-class origins as father's occupation (since only the privileged minority of boys from professional and managerial classes, along with the sons of landed aristocracy and capitalists, can afford to attend private schools). These boys will go on to take advantage of the entry that such schools offer into higher education, the high-status professions, the government and, more recently, industry. The dominance of those educated privately in positions of economic and political power has, of course, been a major political issue since World War II.

The development of private education for girls has had a very different pattern, especially marked by its shorter history. The division between private and state schools has been differently constituted for boys and for girls. Class differences were weaker for girls for a variety of reasons. According to the 1969 Public Schools Commission, the founders of private girls' schools fought for state education for *all* girls. Their political ambitions stretched across the class divide in their search for equality of opportunity for all girls and the freedom of all women to enter the professions of law, medicine, teaching and public service. Second, female teachers in private schools moved freely between different types of schools; they did not accept the view that private and state schools were mutually exclusive sectors. The Association of Headmistresses, unlike that of Headmasters, represented all girls' schools whether private or state, and drew girls in from all different social origins (especially because of the lower fees). As a result, the Public Schools Commission concluded:

> These schools are not as divisive as the boys' schools. Their pupils are few in number and they do not later wear an old school tie – literally or metaphorically. The tie would be of no use to them in their future careers. No magic doors to careers are opened at the mention of any school's name, however socially distinguished the school may be. The academically distinguished schools obviously help their pupils to a place in the universities but so do those in the maintained or direct grant sectors.
>
> (Public Schools Commission, 1969, p. 67)

Educational privilege was not, therefore, a class privilege of daughters of the bourgeoisie, compared with the men of that social class. The low-level education which girls often received in both private and state schools made them uncompetitive in the labour market. The small proportion who went into higher education was a problem faced by all girls' schools, or by all schools with girls in them (ibid., p. 69).

Despite the fact that the division between state and private schools is not a major discriminator between girls of different social classes when their occupational destinies are taken into account, the type of education offered to middle-class girls does differ greatly from that offered to working-class girls. In fact, the class gap between girls has been found to be greater than between boys, when university entrance is taken into account. According to King,

> middle-class boys are the most advantaged and working-class girls the most disadvantaged, the former having twenty-one times more chance of taking a full-time university degree than the other.
>
> (King, 1971, p. 140)

Westergaard and Little pointed out that the failure of working-class girls to reach higher education is due to the fact that the resources (cultural, economic and psychological) necessary for a working-class child to overcome the obstacles on the way are very rarely extended on behalf of a girl (Westergaard and Little, 1965, p. 222).

This brief history suggests that the reproduction of female class-positions in Britain is based more firmly upon the transmission of cultural values (such as familism) than upon the vocational preparation of women for a stratified work force. The transmission of bourgeois conceptions of femininity and their dilution for girls in the working class may even be a more effective means of differentiating girls than the ideology of vocationalism for boys, since such processes of class discrimination are so well hidden.

Gender and school experience

According to Connell and his colleagues, class and gender relations are best thought of as *structuring processes* rather than 'systems'. As such, they are to be found within the dynamics of family, school and industrial life simultaneously, even if their effects differ in the different spheres. Class and gender relations have their own histories which may merge or may be independent of each other. What is important for the child is the *relationship between such processes*. For the working-class boy, for example, the construction of his masculinity would be in the context either of economic insecurity or 'hard won and cherished security':

> It means that his father's masculinity and authority is diminished by being at the bottom of the heap in his work place, and being exploited without being able to control it; and that his mother has to handle the tensions, and sometimes the violence, that result. It means that his own entry into work and the class relations of production is conditioned by the gender relations that direct him to male jobs, and construct for him an imagined future as breadwinner for a new family. And so on.
>
> (Connell et al., 1982, p. 181)

In this extract one can see how the simplified versions of the transition from school to work have been changed by a sensitivity not just to the presence of gender relations but also to the role of family life in determining the shape of an individual's identity and occupational choice.

When discussing pupils' experience of schools, Connell et al. talk about the *hegemonizing* influences of the school in a way which has much in common with the notions of male hegemony and the dominant gender code which I discussed in an earlier paper (Arnot, 1982; see Chapter 6 in this volume). In that paper I used the concept of gender code to refer to the social organisation of family and school life where the attempt is made to 'win over' each new generation to particular definitions of masculinity and femininity and to accept as natural the hierarchy of male over female. This attempt to win the consent of boys and girls to particular definitions of gender is limited by the strategies and responses adopted by pupils to the social and ideological structures of school life. Often pupils collectively will develop their own culture, creatively and actively transforming the very material of school and family life, and reshaping their meaning in ways that have more relevance and interest for them. These youth cultures may not in themselves challenge the structuring processes of gender and class relations but they do make the outcome of schooling unpredictable.

Empirical research on these youth cultures unfortunately rarely investigates the meaning masculinity has for boys. Willis's work on working-class lads stands out in this respect and reveals, furthermore, not just the essential nature of masculine identity for manual workers but also the sexism involved in that construct. Their anti-school culture is based on the celebration of sexuality – in this case an aggressive, physical machismo – which gives working-class boys a weapon to fight a class-determined education. Far more work is needed, however, before we can say we understand the ways in which class and gender relations interact and shape boys' lives in different social classes.

Thomas' (1980) work is a particularly interesting study, since it is a comparison between working-class and middle-class girls. Middle-class girls, she found, developed an *anti-academic* counter-culture in which they celebrated a femininity which was based upon notions of beauty, fashion and the requirements of female glamour occupations such as top secretary and receptionist. By individually negotiating the school's approval of traditional notions of femininity and their encouragement of girls to find jobs for themselves, these girls worked their school lives into line with their interests, asking for special courses in secretarial work, deportment, fashion and the like. They exaggerated the importance of prettiness, docility and poise. In contrast, working-class girls responded collectively rather than individually to the pressures of the school and developed an *anti-school* counter-culture. These girls stressed female sexuality to the extent that they were quickly labelled as sexually deviant. They stressed the value not of glamour jobs but of love, romance and motherhood. What such working-class girls resisted was not just the imposition of certain notions of femininity in the school but also the set of class relations which left them with very dismal occupational futures. Thomas (whose findings paralleled those of McRobbie, 1978, in her study of British working-class girls) concluded that:

> While they may share ultimately domestic occupational destinies, and may have their personal identities similarly molded by a common 'culture of femininity', girls from different social class backgrounds nevertheless experience appreciably different social, material and cultural conditions which mediate their lives and are reflected in differential class responses to notions of femininity, romance, domesticity and motherhood. In their response to school and work, too, girls draw on the specific values and traditions of their 'parent' class cultures, and these values are mirrored in their differential rates of participation and achievement in the formal educational system.
>
> (Thomas, 1980, p. 136)

Reintegrating family and work

Developing a political economy of education which takes the family seriously will not just mean that researchers should interview more parents or ask pupils how they feel about their parents as well as about their teachers. What it means above all is that we have to recognise the specificity of the family 'site' of class and gender relations and see it as the 'location' of individuals while *at school*. Such a location, like that of the school, is not static but is a complex ensemble of practices and relationships. If we want to talk about the 'lived experience' of family life, therefore, we must understand the nature of the power relations involved in the family, class culture *in the making*, and the forms of negotiation over gender identity. In the home, just as in classrooms, notions of good behaviour and rules of conduct are negotiated by the participants. Each set of social relations is important, but as Connell et al. argue, so too is the *relationship between these sets of social relations*. The family and the school are interwoven spheres of activity simultaneously responding to each other. What is critical for the individual child is how to maintain a relationship between the two spheres on a day-to-day basis. Children are required to cope with the formal and informal relations between school personnel and parents, their parents' memories of their own educational histories and the 'burden' of parental aspirations or feelings of failure. They also have to cope with teachers' assumptions about different types of families and the ways in which their teachers respond to parental involvement. The children, from this perspective, are the *mediators*, the *go-betweens* carrying the class-cultural messages of the home and the school through the school gates each day, influencing each in turn by their own practices and responses. In contrast with the relations between school and work, there is no transition from the family to the school; there is only perpetual motion. It is this motion that needs to be captured in the accounts of schooling under capitalism.

From a feminist perspective what is obviously of major concern are the contradictions and the dilemmas faced by boys and girls in trying to sort out gender messages. The researcher should ask, for example, how an adolescent girl makes sense of her experiences of sexual harassment by boys in the playground and classroom in relation to her experience as a protected daughter in the family home. Alternatively, how does she reconcile the demand that she take adult responsibility for certain domestic arrangements with being a school 'child' who is forbidden the use of such adult symbols of femininity as jewellery, fashionable clothes and make-up? How does a boy cope with being beaten academically by a girl at school and yet told by teachers and parents that he will eventually be held responsible for the family income and a dependent and subordinate wife? Such realities may seem trivial but they are the stuff that school and family life are made of. The tension for girls and boys is not how to 'obtain' or 'acquire' abstract notions of gender but how to use particular concepts of femininity and masculinity which work *in practice* in the context of social-class membership. The cultures of different social classes, manifested in different types of family life, offer only certain choices and restrict the possibilities in certain directions for the expression of gender. This does not mean that each individual of the same social class will have an identical notion of what it is to be masculine and feminine, but that all members of the same social class are more likely (than any member of another social class) to be confronted with similar situations to which they must respond.

The experience of family life, with all its contradictions and complexity, is one of experiencing sets of power relations (e.g., between men and women, parents and children, male and female siblings). That experience will be manifested in a set of *gendered practices*; that is, the *forms of expression* of particular sets of social relations. Such gendered practices will be adapted, modified and 'translated' ('recontextualised') in the setting of school corridors and classrooms. As Anyon (1983) has argued, such practices will involve a complex web of private and public forms of accommodation and resistance. The challenge for sociologists is to unravel the web, uncovering the class specificity and identifying the gendered practices.

Finally, a revised political economy of education needs to reformulate the concept of a pupil's destination after schooling. The current extent of youth unemployment has obviously meant that any simple theory of the transition from school to waged work is no longer viable, but even today we can find research on youth unemployment which does not investigate the issue as one affecting the conditions of family life or gender relations. Unemployed school leavers mostly remain living at home, with increased financial dependence upon the parents rather than the state. This has meant extra work and financial worry for the parents, more domestic work for the female members of the household and different sets of relationships between members of the family. In the case of girls, the issue of unemployment after school is a very different political issue from that of boys' unemployment. As I have argued in this paper, girls have been assumed to be 'destined', if not actively prepared by schools and families, for eventual marriage and motherhood. The experience of female unemployment, therefore, is not treated as such a serious problem as the unemployment of male school leavers who are expecting to find waged work in order to fulfil themselves. The dichotomy of family and work and its ideological underpinning in concepts of gender difference has not yet been shifted in the rhetoric of either state educational planners or radical sociologists. What is needed is to see in what ways families and schools construct a particular relationship between future work and family life and how this relationship is mediated by youth today. The reality of unemployment facing school leavers, the changing shape of family life, the pressure by women to enter waged work and male jobs – all these influence the expected relationship between domestic and waged work. What must now enter the radical discourse is a concern to assess the impact of these changes upon girls' and boys' schooling and self-perceptions. It is only by reintegrating the family and the waged labour process in our analyses of schooling that we can hope to provide an adequate and a radical critique of current class and gender relations in education.

If the family is analysed in these ways by critical sociologists, then the potential is there for an integration of feminist and political economy perspectives. An awareness among feminists studying education of the need to provide a materialistic analysis of gender relations will be complemented by a concern among critical sociologists to involve themselves in issues which directly affect women and which grow out of the family–school–work relations. For example, the concern for the age of entry of children into state schools, the concern for after-school-hours day care, school meals service, school transport, the role of the social services in treating children from 'broken' homes and single-parent families, the treatment of school absenteeism – these are all matters which affect women especially. In my view they are matters which can no longer remain outside the mainstream of radical discourse and practice.

Acknowledgement

This paper is a revised and shortened version of a paper presented at the Political Economy of Gender Relation in Education Conference, Ontario Institute for Studies in Education, Toronto, Canada. I am grateful to Alison Griffith and Paul Olson for comments on the earlier draft and for their permission to publish this version. I am also grateful to Kathleen Weiler and the editors of the *Journal of Education* for their very helpful advice.

References

Althusser, L. (1971) 'Ideology and ideological state apparatuses', in *Lenin and Philosophy and Other Essays*, London: New Left Books.

Anyon, J. (1983) 'Intersections of gender and class: accommodation and resistance by working-class and affluent females to contradictory sex role ideologies', in S. Walker and L. Barton (eds) *Gender, Class and Education*, Lewes: Falmer Press.

Apple, M.W. and King, N. (1977) 'What do schools teach?', *Curriculum Inquiry*, 6, 4, pp. 341–58.

Arnot, M. (1981) 'Culture and political economy: dual perspectives in the sociology of women's education', *Educational Analysis*, 3, 1, pp. 97–116.

—— (1982) 'Male hegemony, social class and women's education', *Journal of Education*, 164, 1, pp. 64–89.

Bowles, S. and Gintis, H. (1976) *Schooling in Capitalist America*, London: Routledge & Kegan Paul.

Chamboredon, J.C. and Prévot, J. (1975) 'Change in the social definition of early childhood and the new forms of symbolic violence', *Theory and Society*, 2, 3, pp. 331–50.

Connell, R.W., Ashenden, D.J., Kessler, S. and Dowsett, G.W. (1982) *Making the Difference: schools, families and social division*, Sydney: Allen & Unwin.

Corrigan, P. (1979) *Schooling the Smash Street Kids*, London: Macmillan.

David, M.E. (1978) 'The family–education couple: towards an analysis of the William Tyndale dispute', in G. Littlejohn et al. (eds) *Power and the State*, London: Croom Helm.

Davin, A. (1979) 'Mind you do as you are told: reading books for boarding school girls 1870–1902', *Feminist Review*, 3, pp. 80–98.

Douglas, J.W.B. (1964) *The Home and the School*, London: MacGibbon & Kee.

Fuller, M. (1980) 'Black girls in a London comprehensive school', in R. Deem (ed.) *Schooling for Women's Work*, London: Routledge & Kegan Paul.

Gaskell, J. (1977–8) 'Sex role ideology and the aspirations of high school girls', *Interchange*, 8, 3, pp. 43–53.

Hartley, D. (1978) 'Sex and social class: a case study of an infant school', *British Educational Research Journal*, 4, 2, pp. 75–81.

Hebdige, D. (1979) *Subculture: the meaning of style*, London: Methuen.

King, R. (1971) 'Unequal access in education – sex and social class', *Social and Economic Administration*, 5, 3, pp. 167–75.

McRobbie, A.L. (1978) 'Working class girls and the culture of femininity', in Women's Studies Group (eds) *Women Take Issue: aspects of women's subordination*, London: Hutchinson, in association with the CCCS.

Newson, J., Richardson, D. and Scaife, J. (1978) 'Perspectives in sex role stereotyping', in J. Chetwynd and O. Hartnett (eds) *The Sex Role System*, London: Routledge & Kegan Paul.

Okeley, J. (1978) 'Privileged, schooled and finished: boarding education for girls', in S. Ardener (ed.) *Defining Females*, London: Croom Helm.

Public Schools Commission (1969) *First Report*, vol. 1, London: HMSO.

Purvis, J. (1980) 'Towards a history of women's education in nineteenth century Britain: a sociological analysis', *Westminster Studies in Education*, 4, pp. 45–79.

—— (1981) 'The double burden of class and gender in the schooling of working class girls in nineteenth century Britain', in L. Barton and S. Walker (eds) *Schools, Teachers and Teaching*, Lewes: Falmer Press.

Reid, I. (1981) *Social Class Differences in Britain*, 2nd edn, London: Grant McIntyre.

Shacklady-Smith, L.S. (1978) 'Sexist assumptions and female delinquency: an empirical investigation', in C. Smart and B. Smart (eds) *Women, Sexuality and Social Control*, London: Routledge & Kegan Paul.

Sharp, R. and Green, A. (1975) *Education and Social Control: a study in progressive primary education*, London: Routledge & Kegan Paul.

Shaw, J. (1981) '*In loco parentis*: a relationship between parent, state and child', in R. Dale, G. Esland, R. Fergusson and M. MacDonald (eds) *Education and the State*, vol. 2, *Politics, Patriarchy and Practice*, Lewes: Falmer Press.

Thomas, C. (1980) 'Girls and counter-school culture', *Melbourne Working Papers*, no. 1., Melbourne: Department of Education, University of Melbourne.

Ve Henricksen, H. (1981) 'Class and gender: role model considerations and liberation in advanced capitalism', *Interchange*, 12, 2/3, pp. 151–64.

Westergaard, J. and Little, A. (1965) *Educational Opportunity and Social Selection in England and Wales*, Paris: OECD.

Westergaard, J. and Resler, H. (1974) *Class in a Capitalist Society*, London: Heinemann Educational Books.

Willis, P. (1977) *Learning to Labour*, Farnborough: Saxon House.

Wilson, D. (1978) 'Sexual codes and conduct: a study of teenage girls', in C. Smart and B. Smart (eds) *Women, Sexuality and Social Control*, London: Routledge & Kegan Paul.

Woodhall, M. (1973) 'Investment in women: a reappraisal of the concept of human capital', *International Review of Education*, 19, 1, pp. 9–28.

Zaretsky, E. (1976) *Capitalism, the Family and Personal Life*, New York: Harper Colophon Books.

8 A crisis in patriarchy?

State regulation of gender and feminist educational politics

Few sociological analyses of the New Right in the United Kingdom address the interconnections between the rise of the radical right and critical feminist traditions in education. A surprising fact, perhaps, given the evident hostility of Conservative politicians to feminist and anti-racist politics and their explicit references to the ending of the 'age of egalitarianism'.[1] Sophisticated analyses, such as those by Dale (1989), Ball (1990) and Whitty (1990), offer us insights into the various discourses and ideological tendencies of the Conservative government and its party advisers. From their perspective, we are encouraged to see education policy as 'infused with economic, political and ideological contradictions' (Ball, 1990, p. 211); a site of struggle between different groups for domination, prestige or economic advantage where the most significant context is the restructuring of capitalism. As Stephen Ball argues:

> The [National] curriculum ... is a particular focus for contradiction and struggle. The economic provides a context and a 'vocabulary of motives' for reform. The overall repositioning and restructuring of education in relation to production is evident.
>
> (ibid., p. 211; my addition)

No reference is made to patriarchal ideologies, nor indeed to the logic of patriarchy. The New Right is represented instead as a set of political responses to the necessity of 'restoring authority' and 'responding to the contemporary logic of capitalist development' (ibid., p. 213). As Dale earlier explained, this logic implies that educational systems are structured around three problems:

> direct support for the capital accumulation process; the provision of a wider social context not inimical to the continuing capital accumulation; and the legitimation of the work of the state and the education system.
>
> (Dale, 1989, p. 95)

Yet, given such emphasis on the effects of economic formations on educational discourses, it seems extraordinary that feminist and 'race' politics are so absent from such sociological accounts. It is hard to deny the impact of the women's movement and black community politics on the post-war economy and the considerable increase in married women's economic activity in the economic, familial and cultural spheres. But radical sociologists in the United Kingdom often failed to address these other sets of social relations and, as a result, did not incorporate into their accounts explanations of the rise of the New Right based upon new forms of racial discourses and 'moral/-traditional/familial' ideologies and policies (ten Tusscher, 1986, p. 67). According to Kenway, mainstream policy analysts:

> have rather arrogantly failed to notice that they (most often men) write largely for and about men. Insensitive to matters of gender, they have little or no apparent consciousness of how gender inflected are their theories, concerns and interests. Many mainstream/malestream policy analysts … seem unaware of an increasing body of feminist scholarship which both exposes many of the limitations of the presuppositions of the policy field and brings matters of gender into the foreground.
>
> (Kenway, 1990, p. 7)

For Jane Kenway, the solution is to develop 'gender and educational policy analysis' as a new field of study. This field, she argues, already exists in so far as one can find a diversity of research literature which focuses upon state policy-making. Such literature includes, for example, analyses of the gendered assumptions behind government policies and studies of the impact of the women's movement and feminist struggles on state policy-making processes. Contained within this new field are studies of the success and the limitations of legislation promoting equal opportunities for women. Particularly in Australia, state administrative apparatuses, through which such equality policies are implemented, are being analysed by feminists. In this context, reports on the ways in which feminists have been incorporated within the state bureaucracy as 'femocrats' are especially instructive.[2]

This chapter contributes to Kenway's new field of study. It offers a preliminary analysis of the ways in which gender issues are part of the political context behind the recent radical reorganisation of education in the United Kingdom. I intend to reconsider the circumstances which allowed for the promotion of those aspects of New Right ideology which we tend to associate with the doctrines of Margaret Thatcher's government (1979–91) – doctrines which many have described as a mixture of neo-liberal influences emphasising a free market approach and an absence of state controls, and neo-conservative influences which reassert 'an orientation to the past, traditional values, and collective loyalties' (Ball, 1990, p. 214).

The construction of Conservative education policy in the 1980s has been represented as an attempt at 'modernising' gender relations (cf. Weiner, 1989a; Arnot, 1991, 1992b) in a way that belies its patriarchal basis. Despite this rhetoric, new distinctions were made between the rights and responsibilities of male and female citizens in the public and familial spheres (Arnot, 1992a) and new forms of gender differentiation were created within areas of knowledge.[3] The reassertion of male values is particularly evident in the hierarchical reordering of school knowledge, the styles of pedagogy and modes of assessment. State educational policy was being used to construct and regulate gender relations in new ways. And the reasons, I want to argue, can be found in what ten Tusscher (1986) called the 'crisis in patriarchy' by the 1980s.[4]

The focus of this chapter is to explore the nature of that crisis in relation to state policy and practice. I begin my analysis by briefly outlining some of the debates within feminist theories of the state. These debates helped me reconsider the ways in which feminist critiques of social democratic education and state policy-making were not just interconnected but part of the same processes. In the second section I demonstrate how gender issues and women's struggles contributed to the 'crisis in patriarchy' which lay at the heart of contemporary educational reforms. I consider the ways in which feminists challenged the patriarchal relations constructed by social democracy and how such challenges encouraged particular state responses. I also explore in the final section the ways in which Conservative educational policies can be understood as attempts to retrieve and restructure male–female relations. I argue therefore, in conclusion, that feminist educational struggles cannot remain at the margins of our analyses of contemporary social reconstruction.

Theorising patriarchy and the state

Although it is now commonplace to talk about patriarchal relations as historically formed, nevertheless it is still very difficult to conceptualise the nature of the historical process which has shaped gender relations and theorise its significance. Walby's (1990) much-debated theory of patriarchy[5] suggests that we should look initially at the ways in which modern society has involved a transition from private forms of patriarchy, where women were subordinated in the household by individual men, to modern versions, where women are now allowed access to the public spheres but are subordinated to men by new forms of patriarchy.

The consequences of such a shift from private to public forms of patriarchy for education has not as yet been analysed but it suggests an interesting line of thought for educationalists to pursue (cf. Araújo, 1992). It implies that we should now view patriarchal relations within the occupational structures of teaching as part of this more general societal shift and focus our efforts on understanding the role which state educational provision played in the transformation of patriarchal relations over the last century. It suggests that we understand the changing nature of patriarchy and hence its modes of legitimation and modes of transmission.[6]

From such a perspective, we might begin to think therefore about the significance of opening up the public sphere of teaching to women and of allowing women access to 'male' forms of instrumental knowledge. Should such educational reforms now be understood as part of a broader pattern of encouraging women to enter the public sphere only to reinforce their subordinate status within new sets of patriarchal relations? Were we looking at the development of new, more public forms of patriarchy, facilitated through mass secondary and higher education in the post-war period?

Walby's theory is useful in encouraging us to focus attention not on the maintenance of the social order but rather on the nature of educational change and the shifting relationship between schooling and its social context. It encourages us to consider the ways in which patriarchal relations are recontextualised by schooling in such a way as to prepare children, perhaps, for different forms of patriarchal control. It suggests that schools may have played a part in changing our assumptions about the nature of family life and marriage in society and in contributing to the shifting dissonances of modern society.

What Walby's theory does not do, however, is illuminate the operation of the state, except in so far as she suggests a complexity of state agencies and approaches. In 1983, MacKinnon pointed out that 'feminism has no theory of the state' (MacKinnon, 1983, p. 635) – a statement that was particularly pertinent to contemporary feminist educational theory. Many feminists, especially those in social policy, political science and women's studies, have since quoted this famous opening line as the starting point for a new theoretical project. As a result, there is a considerable amount of debate on the advisability or inadvisability of developing a unitary theory of the state. Can a theory of state cater for the complexity of women's experiences of state policies and practice (see Weedon, 1987; Allen, 1990; Phillips, 1991)?

This is not the place to rehearse the complexity of these discussions and analyses. Fortunately some excellent and highly accessible summaries are now available of the different feminist theories of the state (e.g., Franzway, Court and Connell, 1989; Kenway, 1990; Watson, 1990). A reading of this literature allows us to discover the diversity of feminist interpretations of the relationship between the state and gender or sexual politics. Many of the summaries point, for example, to key distinctions between socialist, radical and liberal feminist interpretations of the impact of the state upon women. The result has been seen in the more sophisticated reinterpretations of the relationship between patriarchy as a political power structure and state formation. Few contemporary feminists today would see the state as either monolithic or simplistically 'patriarchal' or 'male'. Increasingly feminists have recognised that there are 'a series of *arenas* which constitute the state both discursively and through shifting interlocking connections and practices' (Watson, 1990, p. 7; my emphasis). As Watson observes,

> In the last decade recognition that the state is a category of abstraction which cannot simply be characterized as a unified entity has increasingly informed feminist work on the subject. There are many different varieties of state, spatially and historically. Each of these has its own combination of institutions, apparatuses, and arenas, which have their own histories, contradictions, relations and connections, internally and externally.
>
> (ibid.)

Such statements are not unfamiliar to any student of educational policy, especially those working within Marxist or Foucauldian traditions.[7] What may be less familiar, however, for many educationalists are the hard-hitting critiques of the liberal democratic state developed by feminist theorists concerned to describe the ways in which women are positioned through political discourses and practices. Carol Pateman's (1980) challenge to the tenets of liberal democracy as patriarchal in conception and in practice has reverberated around feminist social science. She has posited the existence of a 'fraternal social contract' as the central component of liberal democracy and identified gendered concepts of citizenship and male-defined notions of democracy. She has encouraged others to reassess, in light of patriarchal relations, the significance of the philosophies of 'master thinkers' such as Hegel, Rousseau and Kant (e.g., Lloyd, 1986).

Such feminist political theory encourages us to move, as Connell does, to the proposition that:

> The state is constituted within gender relations as the central institutionalisation of gendered power. Conversely, gender dynamics are a major force constructing the state, both in the historical creation of state structures and in contemporary policy.
>
> (Connell, 1990, p. 519)

This new sensitivity to the structuring influence of gender dynamics on state apparatuses, bureaucracies and discourses has encouraged new conceptual understandings about the relationship between patriarchy and the state. For example, Franzway, Court and Connell (1989) and Connell (1990) stress the capacity (although not unlimited) of the state to 'regulate' gender categories, relations and practices. The state is conceived now as 'an active player in gender politics'. It is represented as a 'significant vehicle' of both 'sexual and gender oppression and regulation' (Connell, 1990, p. 519).

A key line of argument focuses on the role which the state has played in constructing the division between public and private relations, between predominantly male and female spheres. State maintenance of these allegedly complementary but separate spheres, which are key to so many social policies including education, shapes women's oppression but also becomes (as a result) a site of 'contention and struggle' (Franzway, Court and Connell, 1989).

Such a view of the state also allows a different perspective on the internal dynamics of the state itself, its policies and practices. Men and women are to be found in different locations, and at different levels within the hierarchies of state bureaucracies and within the echelons of political power. Struggles for the right to control and shape a new 'gender regime'[8] could affect the nature of public feminist campaigns and also internal struggles within the political structures to increase women's representation and power sharing. 'The control of the machinery of government can be tactically decisive' (Connell, 1990).

Looking at the machinery of government in the United Kingdom it is difficult to contest the view that men have long controlled the policy-making process and implementation structures. A political system where women constitute only 60 out 651 (9.2 per cent) democratically elected members of parliament is hard to describe as anything other than a men's club. Connell describes the consequences well:

> State structures in recent history institutionalise the European equation between authority and a dominating masculinity: they are effectively controlled by men; and they operate a massive bias towards heterosexual men's interests.
>
> (ibid., p. 535)

Within the state, men's interests therefore, like those of capital, are 'actively constructed'. But even more critically so too are feminist demands upon the state. As Watson (1990) argues, feminist struggles have been constructed not in isolation from the state, nor necessarily external to it. Women's demands are a product of the process in which some demands have been acceded to and not others. Feminist struggles, therefore, are integral to the purposes and action of the state within modern society.

From this perspective it becomes politically important for our understanding of social change that we are able to interpret the ways in which feminist demands have been 'diluted' or even 'co-opted' through engagement with the institutions and discourses which constitute the state (ibid.). It is also vital to our analysis that the state is viewed not as a static entity but as constantly undergoing change – the contradictions and inconsistencies, the forms of contention and struggle create crisis tendencies but they also allow new political possibilities (Connell, 1990, p. 532).

In light of these strictures, let us briefly look at the role which feminist educational politics has played in the United Kingdom in the last two decades. We can consider the ways in which feminist campaigns and research have created one of the 'arenas' which constituted the 'Conservative educational revolution' (cf. Jones, 1989) of the 1990s.

Feminism, patriarchy and social democratic education

One way of comprehending the relationship between state educational policy and gender politics is to reassess the post-war period when the social democratic principles which underpin educational reforms were challenged by feminist educationalists. In the first decades after World War II, principles such as equality of opportunity (equal access) and universalism (equal or comparable provision) seemed to favour the removal of biological discourses which had shaped educational processes and outcomes since the nineteenth century. Any support for the notion of biological differences between the sexes increasingly was hidden in the new rhetoric of promoting equal education for all. The emphasis initially became one of assimilating women into mainstream male culture and educational values, at a time when the economy required their labour.

For the purposes of promoting a meritocratic society, educational policy-makers hid behind psychological discourses of differential pupil abilities. References to biological differences between the sexes were being replaced by an increasing reliance upon male/female differences in personalities, interests and above all 'educational needs' (Wolpe, 1976). Differences between male and female pupils, particularly in relation to their interest in marriage and parenthood, were discussed by policy-makers as naturally part of the different psychological make-up of girls and boys. It seemed appropriate, therefore, to work on the design of appropriate female and male subjects and curricular routes which would also suit the needs of young men and women in the post-war economy (CCCS, 1981). The organisation of the school curriculum and its timetabling, assessment and teaching styles, and the culture of the school constructed and regulated such assumed differences between male and female approaches to learning, skills and abilities; all this at the same time as concern was expressed about the failure of girls to seize post-war educational opportunities (cf. Finch, 1984). In effect, the processes of gender differentiation were being built into the warp and weft of the conventions of school life (DES, 1975; Arnot, 1983; reprinted as Chapter 5 of this volume).

By the late 1960s, the contradictions between social democratic principles and such gendered curricula, teaching and learning were increasingly evident, especially in a context where stronger and more critical versions of egalitarianism were developing.[9] The impetus for a resolution of such conflicting influences came from the women's movement, a movement which (ironically) had been nourished by welfarism and state education. Contained within the groundbreaking 1944 Education Act, with its promise of 'education for all', was the possibility of women's liberation from their domestic destinies (Burton and Weiner, 1990). Yet, when the ensuing expansion of education (particularly secondary and tertiary education) 'hurtled a generation [of women] beyond the confines of their mothers' world into the male sphere of public affairs and work', they found to their cost that no provision had been made to care for their children (Rowbotham, 1986, p. 85) and that male dominance through occupational hierarchies restricted and contained their advancement. For many, particularly white middle-class women, individual experiences of private forms of patriarchy were being supplemented (some for the first time) by the collective experience of public forms of male domination. The liberalism which framed social policy had, it seems, remained committed to the division between public and private domestic spheres. Also, traditional and unequal gender relations within the family, even if reconstructed by new social policies, were hardly being challenged by other forms of provision in the welfare state (Pascall, 1986; Dale and Foster, 1986; Williams, 1989).

By the late 1960s such tensions between women's position in the home and in the labour force, not surprisingly, were to surface and explode in the second wave of the women's liberation movement. This movement took as its project the removal of the shackles of male dominance in all spheres. At a deeper level it exposed the male–female power relations which lay beneath economic and political structures and which shaped state policies and practice. As Rowbotham (1986) comments in retrospect, the feminist project became one of extending the definitions of political or economic democracy to ever more diverse and intimate spheres. If the liberal democratic state shaped the notion of rights in relation to the public sphere, feminists demanded that they be extended into the personal sphere. On the new agenda were:

> domestic inequality, identity, control over sexuality, challenge to cultural representation, community control over state welfare and more equal access to public resources.
>
> (Rowbotham, 1986, p. 86)

In the educational world, this political awakening took various forms. By the late 1960s, women were becoming increasingly disillusioned with the failure of educational policy-makers to deliver equality of opportunity. The ideals of collectivism behind the post-war settlement appeared to have failed to support women or their particular concerns in the development of educational provision. And the gap between rhetoric and reality was becoming increasingly evident to those educational researchers who had looked at the educational outcomes and experiences of girls within the educational system. Early attempts at feminist policy analysis (e.g., Byrne, 1978) suggested that greater and more committed state intervention was needed if inequalities between men and women were to be ironed out and if the principle of equality of opportunity was to be upheld.

A range of perspectives in feminist educational thought were developed in the ensuing decades which had much in common with the political philosophies that had shaped the women's movement since the 1960s (Eisenstein, 1984). Indeed, in recent years it has become common practice for feminist educationalists to identify the various tendencies of liberal feminism, on the one hand, and radical, socialist and black feminism on the other (Middleton, 1987; Acker, 1987; Weiner and Arnot, 1987). Lesbian feminism, more developed in the United States, had a twilight existence in the context of British educational work (see recent contributions in Jones and Mahony, 1989), especially since sexuality was such a studiously avoided aspect of British school life (Kelly, 1992).

Liberal feminism, in particular, assumed pride of place within educational research traditions, teachers' initiatives and national policy-making bodies. Its success seemed initially to result from the compromises it reached between feminist principles of improving women's position in society and offering suggestions for reforms from within male-dominated structures. It asked for political commitment and goodwill rather than resources and strong state intervention; it required educating rather than constraining individuals; it was encouraging rather than punitive in approach (Arnot, 1991). What gave liberal feminism its strength was its commitment to the principle of sustained economic growth, to alleviating the shortage of skilled 'manpower' through a process of 'upskilling' (Deem, 1981). It offered a way forward by proposing that women adapt to changing economic opportunities and men are helped to come to terms with increased family responsibilities. In some respects it attempted to tie the two ends of the chain and bring the modes of teaching and learning into line with the original intentions of the post-war policy-makers of equality of educational opportunity.

Yet, despite such apparent conformity with the goals of the post-war economy, liberal feminists in their own way struck at the heart of the liberal democratic state. They challenged the versions of male meritocracy which had dominated post-war thinking (Arnot, 1983). They objected publicly and often to the ways in which, as Sullivan (1990) put it, 'gender' was arbitrarily assigned to social characteristics and roles. Liberal feminism suggested instead the need to 'degender' the public sphere.

Within that approach were the seeds of a particularly devastating attack on the dominant concept of public policy-making and system of male representation within the state. Eisenstein (1987), Kenway (1990) and Connell (1990), for example, have argued that liberal feminists, by fighting for the principle of equal rights of citizenship to be extended to women, exposed and challenged the gendered discourses and structures of government. As Connell argued, 'Liberal feminists took the concept of rights and turned it against the patriarchal model of citizenship' (Connell, 1990, p. 513). They protested at the control which men had over the political, judicial, military and cultural life of the country. Some feminists went even further by revealing the procedures and processes within the state which frame a masculine discourse of 'need' (Fraser, 1989). Recognition of the gendered nature of the state allowed liberal feminists to 'inspire a formidable and sustained politics of access' (Connell, 1990, p. 513).

The new project was to transform the world of politics, industry, culture and education by 'degendering' it.[10] Gender would no longer be ascribed and utilised as a principle of social organisation in the public sphere. Women would be encouraged to use their freedom to choose between a wider range of life styles (even if still inevitably responsible for child-rearing and the home). The Sex Discrimination Act (1975) and the equal opportunities policies (implemented in its aftermath) attempted to neutralise the consequences of capitalist economic restructuring for women by protecting their conditions of service, their rights to fair employment practice and a fair wage (Arnot, 1987). In contrast, little was done to tackle the dilemmas women faced in their dual roles, nor to promote greater equality in the home. Social and family policy significantly was not included in the Sex Discrimination Act. Paradoxically, such legislation, like comparable anti-discrimination legislation developed in Australia and the United States, could also be described as signally the moment described by Sullivan (1990) when the distinction between public and private spheres is reconfirmed and women are 'relocated' in the private sphere.

Degendering strategies, she argues, have a tendency to both 'privatise and depoliticise issues of particular relevance to women (such as abortion, maternity, child care)' (p. 174).

Much mainstream feminist educational thought in the 1970s and 1980s had in fact encapsulated the principles of social democracy which it sought to challenge. Even when, by the 1980s, feminist educational analyses became more sophisticated and attempted to identify the class and racial diversity of female experiences within education and to remove the more subtle cultural processes affecting individual advancement, one can still find a strong commitment to defending the privacy of the family, the tenets of individualism, teacher autonomy and the use of education as the means of social reform (e.g., Spender, 1981a; Thompson, 1983; Acker and Warren Piper, 1984; Whyte et al., 1985).

Most feminist teachers and educationalists have been ambivalent about the role which the state performs in relation to patriarchy. If anything, much of the Western literature on gender and education has in fact tended to ignore the role of the state. This was particularly evident in the 1970s and 1980s when sex-role socialisation theories dominated. Education writing seemed to suffer what I called (Arnot, 1981), following Bourdieu (1973), a 'misrecognition of the action of the state'. Benevolent or enlightened action was demanded of central government by liberal feminists in order, paradoxically, to transform precisely those gendered relationships which the state had historically helped to construct.

By the late 1970s, it was becoming apparent that the politics of equal access were not sufficient. The egalitarian and libertarian philosophies of the women's movement had begun to have an effect upon educational debates and research. Feminist critiques of education within social democracy bit deeper and deeper, suggesting the inability of liberalism to create social equality or social justice. Liberal philosophy at the heart of educational policy and also the specific sets of relations constructed within the liberal democratic state and its institutional arrangements would have to be transformed if social justice was to be achieved.[11] The concept of equal rights was being exchanged for a demand for 'equality of power' (Rowbotham, 1986).

More 'egalitarian' campaigns called for democratic 'freedoms' and for the full economic, political and social rights of citizenship to be extended to all subordinate groups. Apple (1989), for example, argues that in the United States the black and women's movements threatened the legitimacy of the dominant groups, especially in so far as the legitimacy of the social order was founded upon notions of *property rights*. These rights were held on the basis of ownership of property, such as economic contracts, political rights of participation and the rights of access to knowledge. In contrast, egalitarian campaigns celebrated the notion of *person rights* which invested individuals with the power to enter into those social relationships on the basis of being simply members of the social collectivity (rights which ensured equal treatment of citizenship, freedom of expression and equal access to participation in decision-making).

The feminist challenge undermined the dominance of men who, on the whole, hold those property rights and legitimate their power through their ownership of cultural capital, their access to 'legitimate' knowledge and their access to high-status academic qualifications. It is appropriate perhaps to reconsider, in the context of male power, Bourdieu's insightful comment about the role which education plays in the legitimation of class privilege:

> among all the solutions put forward throughout history to the problem of the transmission of power and privilege, there surely does not exist one that is better concealed, and therefore better adapted to societies which tend to refuse the most patent forms of the hereditary transmission of power and privileges, than that solution which the educational system provides by contributing to the reproduction of the structure of class relations and by concealing, by an apparently neutral attitude, the fact that it fills this function.
>
> (Bourdieu, 1973, p. 72)

Significantly, in the post-war period, the concept of male and female 'needs' and interests offered a much weaker base from which to legitimate patriarchal relations in comparison with the biological discourses of the nineteenth century. Increasingly, male economic and political power, like that of the dominant social classes, had had to be justified in terms of 'proven' (i.e., certified) academic merit. By attempting to reform or even replace the principles and practice of male academia, feminists mounted a deeply threatening attack on the legitimacy of male economic, political and social privilege. By uncovering, for example, the 'patriarchal paradigm' of mass schooling (cf. Spender, 1981b), the 'malestream' curricula and male-oriented teaching and assessment styles, radical, socialist and black feminists each in their own way debunked the myth of education's gender neutrality.

Another critical aspect of the increasingly confident egalitarian tradition was the challenge it presented to the liberal principles of individual rational autonomy and freedom. Male dominance of educational policy-making, the control of education and access to higher education had been premised upon the notion of freedom of choice – men had chosen such positions and careers and women, although given the chance, had chosen alternative paths. Increasingly, however, the falsity of that claim was being revealed. Even if the formal opportunity existed, a combination of informal discriminatory practices, the construction of a 'gender order'[12] and women's not unrealistic assessment of their objective possibilities in employment militated against them taking full advantage of whatever opportunities were provided.

But female and male pupils were being shaped not just by the unofficial hidden discourses of the school curriculum, nor the looming constraints of a gendered world of employment. They were also being moulded by their personal struggles within what Wood (1987) and Lees (1986) revealed as the sexual underworld of schooling. This underworld, so controlled by male sexuality, found expression in the 'spaces' created by the ideologies of individualism and personal autonomy. Within such 'freedoms' constructed through liberal discourses were to be found, for example, sexually and racially abusive language and harassment, the neglect or marginalisation of young women, patronising behaviour towards female students and reinforcement of traditional class- and race-laden notions of femininity and masculinity. Those prejudices, whether sexual, racial or class-based, were often even permitted to find expression by teachers who supported the concept of 'free speech', 'privacy' and freedom of individual action. Teachers were often unaware of the extent to which their failure to intervene in the sexual and racial conflicts of schooling constituted in itself 'a significant political act' in favour of a specific form of gender order.

Teacher sexism, ethnocentrism or classism, therefore, were only ever part of a much wider process by which large numbers of children were 'denied access' to their rights. Many of the problems faced by pupils in schools arose as a result of a range of incompatible principles. In the name of equality of opportunity, schools were encouraged to 'treat all alike' in order to overcome social disadvantages – even though those disadvantages were built into the social fabric. The development of a child's potential and their personal fulfilment were to take place within a hierarchically structured and culturally defined arena – one which was alien to the majority of children in the state system. At the same time, parents and communities who might have been able to help promote their children's welfare were disenfranchised from school participation by the strong commitment to teacher and school autonomy. What egalitarian educationalists increasingly made public were the consequences of this confused project for large groups of pupils.

Further, they asked critical questions about even those progressive ideologies born in the expansionist days of the 1960s. Co-education and child-centred pedagogies, for example, were increasingly being revealed as deeply problematic by feminist educationalists. Feminists asked whether co-education in the state secondary sector genuinely promoted a 'relaxed normality' between the sexes (cf. Arnot, 1983). Had the principle of 'proximity equals equality' really worked in the case of gender? Or were co-educational schools in effect just a different way of constructing gender relations so that young women were assimilated into the world of male educational values and brought into closer contact with the opposite sex? Were mixed schools genuinely a means of reducing the differentiation between the sexes or were they a more effective way of providing the conditions for female entry into a sex-segregated labour market? Were the values of mixed comprehensive schools constructed with sex equality in mind?

Such were the questions asked of secondary education by feminist researchers. Interestingly, their research revealed not just the limitations of the comprehensive ideal but also far more about the nature of adolescent masculinity and the ambiguity of male youth in facing a class-divided education system than had been recognised by male cultural theorists (e.g., Willis, 1977). In the picture of contemporary school life that such feminist research offers, we see the increasing confidence of young women but also the effects of an uncertain adolescent masculinity, struggling to define male gender identity in the context of economic recession and an ever more violent world. Coping with absent fathers who are positioned and controlled by their work within the public sphere, experiencing contradictory class and racially specific versions of masculinity, male pupils were shown to respond by colonising the world of secondary schools. They set, through their actions and their public forms of resistance, the terms under which female pupils defined their identities (Lees, 1986).

By the 1970s, male and female pupils were being prepared for a restructured labour force in which each sex would still have differentiated roles but where they were treated in a more equal fashion (Deem, 1981). In the new world of a mixed comprehensive secondary school in the state sector, all children would be encouraged to fulfil their academic potential. Yet what policy-makers had clearly not anticipated were the effects of subjecting the developing sexual identities of young people to the scrutiny of the opposite sex in such an apparently unprotected environment. The positive and the negative aspects of the gender relations being constructed through state secondary schools were now being revealed.

At the same time child-centred philosophy in primary education was also subjected to feminist critique, especially that of Walkerdine (1981). Here the 'spaces' for the free expression of a child's personality were encouraged by developmental psychology and psychoanalytic discourses which constructed male and female sexuality in particular ways. Pupils, especially male pupils, were encouraged to express their needs, while teachers were encouraged to develop their pupils' personalities through child-centred pedagogies. Yet, despite the apparent freedom to be found in early education, the conflictual and contested nature of gender relations revealed itself, often without teachers being aware of such undercurrents in their classrooms. In Walkerdine's view, male dominance was legitimated through the psychological discourses which shaped teachers' understandings of male sexuality. The imperative of providing for the early 'natural' expression of male heterosexuality led not only to the uninterrupted displays of male aggression but also to the particular forms of girls' resistance, which involved the exploitation of women's domestic identities. The effects of such child-centredness were not, it seems, liberatory for either sex.

What I have tried to show is that such feminist research, although often not intended as policy analysis, represented a sustained attack on post-war educational philosophies and practice. It made explicit some of the ways in which gender relations were regulated by the state through various educational institutions. Further, such research articulated women's educational needs and values, and by so doing attacked the legitimacy of centring educational provision upon male life styles and values.

The gendering of educational politics

These critiques might not, of themselves, have been as effective a threat to the status quo had not many teachers, particularly within state primary and secondary education, been attracted to feminist politics. Many women teachers have been active in setting up initiatives, campaigning for change in teacher employment, curricula content and in modes of teaching and assessment. Feminist academics and teachers have added their voices to debates about identifying pupils' special needs and targeting provision, and about democratising access into further and higher education, open and distance education. They have encouraged whole-school policy development and introduced new concerns about child abuse and sexual harassment into the language and policies of schooling (see Weiner and Arnot, 1987).

Although British teachers did not establish a consensus around a feminist pedagogy, especially in the context of compulsory schooling, many of the strategies developed in the 'freer air' of adult and higher education and especially in women's studies were adapted to school classrooms (Thompson, 1983). Feminist teachers, through their practice, have recommended various teaching methods to try to improve female pupils' subject choice and performance. Many such strategies have been similar to progressive teaching practices and notions of critical pedagogy. They have given support to educational styles which emphasised the quality of the learning experience and encouraged more 'democratic' forms of work (e.g., pupil participation and control of their own learning through mixed ability teaching, group work, course work, self-assessment, independent study and participation in school policy-making).

The different discourses of radical, socialist and black feminism by the 1980s had the effect of 'gendering' (i.e., making gender an explicit dimension of) educational policy-making. Schools and local education authorities, particularly in metropolitan areas, adopted explicit sex equality or anti-sexist policies which focused attention on female education and male-centred education (Arnot, 1987). Such policies moved away from the limited projects of improving girls' curriculum choices in science and mathematics. They focused attention on the need to 'empower' women, to discover and promote female values in education and to challenge male dominance in schools. At the same time socialist feminists added to the exposure of continuing class differentiation in education and black feminists (as part of the anti-racist movement) contributed to the 'racialisation' of educational policy-making (Troyna, 1992).

The egalitarian feminist project called for the substantial democratisation of education, through full participation and equal control of education by both sexes. It was a project, ironically, which called for more rather than less central government control, for more use of disciplinary powers and fewer 'freedoms' for sexism to exploit (Arnot, 1991). The articulation of socialist feminism and black feminism to other arenas of struggle also strengthened the demands made on the state for equality to be extended to other subordinate groups. As I have argued elsewhere (ibid.), feminist struggles were a major force in the attempts being made to restructure social democracy itself.

Radical feminist, socialist and black feminist discourses added their weight to the critiques of liberal philosophy in the late 1970s and 1980s. Not only, as Bowles and Gintis (1976) argued, was schooling shown to be affected by 'the long shadow of work' – the requirements of an advanced capitalist economy – but the contradictions between capitalism and liberalism they identified were being reconsidered from a woman's perspective. Despite the success of the education system in encouraging white middle-class women into higher education, feminist educationalists revealed how working-class and black girls remained at a considerable disadvantage. They dispelled the myth that one 'successful' woman, like one 'clever' working-class child, vindicated the educational system and attested to the extent of equality of opportunity (Payne, 1980). Despite the promise of the post-war period, state policies in education had effectively regulated gender relations. They had not liberated women from their domestic destinies, instead they had created new conditions under which young women could not avoid the effects of patriarchal relations in a sex-segregated labour market. Women were even more exposed to the impact of male control.

Increasingly, egalitarian feminists' attention focused not just on the contradictions between schooling and the ideals of equality of opportunity in the public sphere but also on the model of the heterosexual monogamous nuclear family being assumed through the discourses and practices of schooling (Phoenix, 1987; Kelly, 1992). The construction of such families as the 'norm' began to be seen not merely as unrepresentative of the reality of family life in modern Western societies, but also as inappropriate and oppressive. Sex education could begin to be used to teach pupils about a diversity of life styles, sexualities and moral values.

Yet in Britain, while the idea of pluralism is acceptable within the framework of cultural diversity, it seems to be unacceptable as a concept in the sexual context. Alternative sets of gender relations (a new 'gender regime') were represented by the right as destabilising the social order. It threatened the central function of the family as the key site for the socialisation of each new generation into dominant values. Was there perhaps a fear that feminists were not just attempting to democratise contemporary relations between husbands and wives, male and female partners, but more importantly they might be undermining the ways in which future generations would view patriarchal relations in the private and the public spheres?

One could argue, therefore, that feminism had begun to be effective in undermining in a very serious way the legitimacy of the patriarchal social order. Eisenstein put it well when she argued 'Feminism has uncovered the truth that capitalist patriarchal society cannot deliver on its liberal promises of equality or even equal rights without destabilising itself' (Eisenstein, 1987, p. 239). Patriarchal structures, especially the family and the educational system, were threatened by the egalitarianism of the women's movement. Feminist campaigns threatened the version of democracy and its failure to provide rights of citizenship to women (Heater, 1990), questioned the distinction between public and private spheres, the appropriation of the educational system by men, the criteria for the selection of knowledge and its modes of transmission, the gender regimes of schooling, the nature and values of family life and the promotion of heterosexuality as norm.

Thus if capitalism was in crisis by the 1980s, so too were patriarchal relations. The ways in which a social democratic state had regulated gender had been exposed as contradictory, especially the more the state utilised degendering discourses and strategies for the public sphere. Further, and not insignificantly, 'the myth of female classlessness' (Arnot, 1983) which had allowed for the homogenising of all girls in the post-war period was now dispelled. Women, like men, were clearly situated within class and race structures. Further, feminists had introduced a new agenda of sexual politics around normative notions of heterosexuality which were likely to be deeply worrying to those committed to traditional family life.

The New Right and the modernising of gender

It is naive to imagine, therefore, that feminist demands for sexual equality had no political impact. The developments were regarded, along with comparable projects in the area of 'race', as subversive by a central government influenced by the radical right (Klein, 1989; Davies, Holland and Minhas, 1990). Feminist campaigns were portrayed by members of the New Right as 'ideological extravagances' and as part of the 'forces in contemporary society which are deeply inimical' to the family (Centre for Policy Studies, quoted in Campbell, 1987, p. 170). Demands for sex equality were blamed for the rise in the divorce rate and single parenthood.

In retrospect, it seems extraordinary how little concern was shown in feminist education writing about the build-up of Conservative opposition. However, two factors might explain such seeming lack of interest. First, the legacy of social democracy as the main target of sociology of education proved hard to break in all aspects of the discipline. Second, in contrast with Reagan's government in the United States which supported an aggressive Moral Right political movement (Dworkin, 1978), the first Thatcher government made few explicit 'anti-feminist' statements. It did not directly attack the women's movement, repeal the anti-discrimination legislation or shut down either the Equal Opportunities Commission or the Commission for Racial Equality as some expected it would (David, 1983a). Initially Thatcher's government remained 'officially neutral' on issues such as abortion, divorce and homosexual rights (Segal, 1983).

David (1983a, 1983b, 1985), Segal (1983) and Gardiner (1983) revealed the more subtle forms of anti-feminism used by the Thatcher government in its first period of office. The initial implications of Thatcherism could apparently be found in family ideology and policy which emphasised 'Victorian values', in particular the bourgeois family-form of the male wage-earner and the dependent wife and mother. The much quoted outburst of Patrick Jenkin in 1979 (later to be Social Services Minister) that 'If the Good Lord had intended us to have equal rights to go out to work, he wouldn't have created men and women' (quoted in Gardiner, 1983, p. 195) was put a little more delicately but no less conservatively by a 1986 Institute of Economic Affairs report, when it commented: 'men will expect to specialise in market work and women will expect to specialise in household work' (quoted in Williams, 1989, p. 120).

The assumption underlying the notion that a 'woman's place is in the home' was that biological and natural instincts determined both the sexual division of labour within the family and the separation between the private and public spheres. For Roger Scruton, a leading neo-conservative educationalist, the family was, therefore, a 'natural form':

> the family is a small social unit which shares with civil society the singular quality of being non-contractual, of arising (both for the children and the parents) not out of choice but out of natural necessity.
>
> (quoted in Williams, 1989, p. 119)

The family occupied a privileged place in New Right discourses but there was little attempt in the 1980s to reconcile the confusion of conservative and liberal functions being assigned to the family or to develop any deep understanding about the actual shifts in contemporary family life (David, 1983a; Campbell, 1987). The family was held responsible for the 'defence of the individual against socialism and excessive state power' (quoted in Campbell, 1987, p. 166); on the other hand, it was the basis of private property and the location of the consumer responsible for the management of his/her financial affairs. Then again, the family was the 'centre of affections', 'the transmitter of traditions' and the necessary condition of authority (ibid.). Such functions transcended all allegiances of class and had no historical specificity – they were essentially universal.

In the context of this vision of family life, the concept of parenthood, actively promoted by The Black Papers[13] (quoted in CCCS, 1981) in their discussion of education reform, became the symbol of not just the economic values of consumerism. Parenthood represented, for neo-conservatives such as Scruton, the political and moral values of hierarchy, authority and loyalty (Williams, 1989). For neo-liberals, parenthood represented the symbol of the economic values of consumerism and a means of social stability in an aggressively competitive economy. Paradoxically, 'the family had to be maximised in order to minimise the state'. By rehabilitating the family, arguably the government could break down the 'scrounger welfare state' and through a 'moral crusade' counter the effects of sexual permissiveness that grew out of the 1960s (Campbell, 1987, p. 166).

Such family ideology, incoherent as it seems, has been interpreted by feminists as a significant attack on women's position in the employment sector and in the family. This was hardly surprising given that cuts in state welfare provision made it more likely that women would be left to cater for young children, the aged, the mentally ill and the unemployed members of the household. If this dismantling of the welfare state assumed rather than asserted the need for women to remain at home, educational policies focusing around the values of a patriarchal family life were given the responsibility of actively promoting traditional sexual divisions. Early statements by Conservative politicians suggested that all children would be encouraged to receive an education in moral values and in parental responsibilities (David, 1983a, 1983b) – thus girls would be prepared for their role as wives, mothers and carers and boys would learn the role of head of household and main wage earner.

Fears were expressed that this rekindled interest in moral education was the thin end of the wedge. It represented the first attempts 'to rescind equal opportunities policies … and to replace them with specific policies which promote sex difference' (David, 1983b). Added to other attacks on women's rights, particularly in terms of sexuality and employment, this educational approach was interpreted as an effort to restore patriarchal values. According to ten Tusscher (1986), the concern of the New Right to link monetarism and moralism, therefore, was an attempt to tackle the dual crises of the capitalist economy and patriarchy and to reunite their interests.

> Thus Thatcherism and the New Right managed to occupy the vacuum created by the breakdown of social democracy combined with the opening stemming from the perceived threat to patriarchy. This determined the nature of the New Right. It embraced the twin goals of restoring class forces in favour of capital and of restoring gender relations in favour of men.
>
> (ten Tusscher, 1986, p. 76)

However, such patriarchal discourses were not easily implemented in practice. On the one hand, the impact of the women's movement in the country – even if disorganised – had changed public opinion sufficiently to be able to curtail the extent to which the New Right could promote traditional values, especially surrounding women's domesticity. Segal (1983, p. 214) argues that the Conservative government was held back by the 'continual vigour and success of feminism in mobilising support for women's rights and equality'. Changes in women's employment since World War II had encouraged middle-class career women, some of whom could be found as female Conservative party members, fighting against any simple equation between women and motherhood.

In the event, despite harsh social policies, women did not go back *en masse* to their homes, instead they continued to carry the dual burden of being wives and workers (Wilson, 1987). The early educational initiatives were also less than successful. Curricular reforms encouraging traditional parenting roles were hard to implement within a decentralised system. Education for parenthood and sex education were unlikely vehicles for such a 'moral crusade' since these courses were not mandatory. As Wolpe observed,

> The implications of a third term of Thatcherism in the field of sex education are not straightforward … . Moral values are seen to have declined and there are moves to combat this … . What is not clear is whether the way to combat this will be through the provision of sex education, given the opposition to its inclusion in the school curriculum in some quarters.
>
> (Wolpe, 1987, p. 45)

Ironically new legislation had made sex education the responsibility of school governing bodies, who could choose to remove such a controversial topic. Courses on family living were also likely to be optional and have the low status ascribed to non-examined subjects. Far more significant to this programme of moral 'clean-up' was the legislation through Section 28 against 'promoting homosexuality' (see Kelly, 1992), although here again the impact on schools nationally was not likely to be great since so few local authorities had developed policies on sexuality.

It has become increasingly clear from recent feminist analyses that, despite the desire to re-establish traditional family structures and 'remoralise' the nation's children, the Conservative government still wished to be seen as committed, at least in rhetoric, to a version of equality of opportunity and equal rights. Conservative women sustained notions of themselves as equal to men 'in the sight of God' (Campbell, 1987). Neo-liberals in particular encouraged the notion of individual liberty, particularly economic freedom in the market place and political freedom from coercion and excessive state control. Hayek and Friedman, often quoted as leading theorists of monetarism, saw such freedom being provided by an autonomous and private family unit (equated with women's role) and being found within the public sphere (as equated with male activity). The assumption of such gender differences led feminist critics to conclude that logically 'the promise of liberty can only apply to men'. Individualism, property ownership, consumerism were men-only concepts, even if (as Ferdinand Mount, right-wing author of *The Subversive Family*', argued in 1982) 'women's rights to equality are unassailable because women are human beings' (quoted in Williams, 1989, p. 119). Indeed, as Margaret Thatcher herself argued in 1982,

> It is, of course, true that women of our generation are often still comparatively young by the time our children are grown up and therefore we have an opportunity further to develop our own talents .... For many that experience can enhance their lives and enlarge their interests.
>
> (quoted in Wilson, 1987, p. 295)

Neo-liberals encouraged the notion of individual liberty, particularly economic freedom in the market place as consumers and political freedom from coercion and excessive state control (even if they assumed such liberties would only apply to men; Segal, 1983, p. 119). The solution to this contradiction could not be found by expelling women from the market place, especially since capital still required female waged labour. Instead the notion of competitive individualism could be selectively applied to men and women who had no family responsibilities (David, 1983a, 1983b) or alternatively to women who had already fulfilled one of their roles, as homemakers, and could now re-enter the market. Such 'solutions', as Wilson argued, allowed the Conservative government to represent itself as 'the modern party':

> the theme of the Conservative party under Mrs Thatcher as the *modern* party, the party that welcomes and harnesses change and is committed to an attack on the 'old fashioned' dogmas of trades unions and an assortment of blinkered ideologues – Fabians, Marxists, feminists and the like – whose time is past and who have got fatally out of step with the world we live in.
> (Wilson, 1987, p. 205)

Such 'modernising tendencies' within Conservative party policy were to find somewhat confused expression within the various education reforms of the 1980s. Cuts in state funds (particularly in adult education, in subjects such as the arts and humanities, in discretionary grants for further education) threatened the educational and training opportunities for women (Deem, 1981). Also, the failure to fund pre-school education or further reductions to it in some localities would restrict considerably the chances of married women to fulfil that 'second role' as paid workers in anything other than part-time and low-paid employment. The DES under Thatcher's government also continued its largely indifferent stance to issues of sex equality, even though the HMI were able to offer explicit but not very strong support to those concerned about female educational experiences and achievement (Orr, 1985; Acker, 1986). Political complacency and inadequate support for gender issues in education seemed to be the main criticisms made by feminists when analysing central government policy in the 1980s (Arnot, 1987).

Strangely enough, the concept of equal rights in Conservative party thinking emerged most obviously in relation to the so-called 'new vocationalism' which attempted to restructure and 'modernise' the economy through direct state intervention. Initially critics argued that 'the new vocationalism signals the abandonment of equal opportunity as a central reference point of educational strategy' (Finn, 1985, quoted in Weiner, 1989a, p. 117). However, this analysis took little or no account of the possibilities within the Conservative educational programme of 'modernising' gender relations and the female work force.

The Manpower Services Commission (now known as the Training Agency) in contrast with the DES had appeared to take more interest in equal opportunities issues (Arnot, 1992b). Although it largely ignored the extent of gender differentiation in its youth training schemes and, as a result, had dismally failed to break down sexual divisions (Fawcett Society, 1985; Wickham, 1987), the attempt to ensure that all Technical and Vocational Educational Initiatives (TVEI) in secondary schools tackled equal opportunities between the sexes could be interpreted as a significant attempt to 'reshape' gender relations in education. The promotion of equal opportunities within such vocational initiatives, according to Weiner (1989a), had economic as well as political benefits, especially in relation to the needs of the capitalist economy for a 'free (i.e., unsegmented) labour market' and 'a flexible work force, undifferentiated by sex'. In other words,

> liberal/progressive ideas concerning freedom for girls and women to move upwards in educational and occupational hierarchies have become synonymous with 'liberal', 'laissez-faire' ideas about labour market freedom.
> (Weiner, 1989a, p. 121)

Ironically the funding criteria which made it compulsory that all TVEI projects promote equal opportunities came to represent one of their most progressive aspects, even though help and support from the MSC/Training Agency was thin on the ground. A full evaluation of the strategies adopted by TVEI to promote equal opportunities was even commissioned and published (Bridgwood and Betteridge, 1989). In practice, the experience gained by schools suggested that equal opportunities could not be based on principles of individualism and free choice. Increasingly schools were developing their own form of a common compulsory curriculum: they were also pushed into challenging (although slowly at first) the gendered nature of school knowledge, the naming of subjects and the occupational associations of particular courses (Millman and Weiner, 1987).

This experience, together with a long history of calls from the Left and from feminists such as Byrne (1985) for a common curriculum to tackle social inequality, perhaps prepared the ground for a muted response to the introduction of the National Curriculum. But also ideological disunity and the lack of consistent committed political support (Loach, 1987) and perhaps an overemphasis on personal politics (Rowbotham, 1986) could have weakened feminist campaigns. In the event, despite years of academic research and policy development in schools and colleges, feminist opposition to the Education Reform Act was neither public nor organised. When responses to the Education Reform Bill were collected, the voices of women were not heard (Haviland, 1989). Apart from within those organisations in which women had struggled successfully (e.g., NUT, NATE), feminist educational concerns ironically were represented by the Equal Opportunities Commission (already becoming increasingly partisan in its appointments).

The absence of a coherent feminist response either by sociologists or by women's education groups and networks may perhaps also be explained by the confusion over the likely effects of the legislation. The impact of a combination of centralised control of the curriculum and a blatant lack of concern with the form of pedagogy (other than formal assessment) was not immediately obvious. Early commentators (Kant, 1987; Myers, 1989; Arnot, 1989a) interpreted the legislation as yet another instance of 'missed opportunities' to tackle sex discrimination in education rather than a case of virulent anti-feminism. Having said that, clearly feminists were aware that the list of subjects to be included in the National Curriculum, based on a traditionally 'male' grammar school curriculum, provided early evidence of an androcentric structure. While girls could benefit from the compulsory science and technology, many of them were likely to choose the least intensive or more traditionally 'feminine' options within these subjects; girls' schools were also threatened by lack of sufficient resources, especially for technology.

National Curriculum planning could theoretically challenge male biases in subject content. Yet, as evidence emerged of the low level of female representation on subject working groups, the lack of reference to gender research, no consultation with women's groups and derisory reporting on the issue by the National Curriculum Council (Arnot, 1989b; Davies, Holland and Minhas, 1990; Weiner, 1990), it became clear that masculinist and racial biases within most subjects were not going to be challenged officially. Indeed working groups have not, to date, taken a major stand on promoting anti-sexist or anti-racist curricula content – arguably subject content and pedagogy has regressed to outmoded styles, reasserting male-centred forms of knowledge (Burton and Weiner, 1990).

The ideological significance of the National Curriculum in terms of gender, therefore, is somewhat unclear. If this centralised control of the curriculum represented a victory of the neo-conservatives, then why were precisely those courses closest to parental education (i.e., child care and domestic science) demoted to the margins of the curriculum? The downgrading of these 'female' domestic courses could be seen either as fortuitous for girls, releasing them from domestic ideologies, or alternatively as a signal of the Conservative government's lack of concern for the subjects in which girls achieve. Certainly it is not clear that family values have shaped the selection of subjects nor indeed that subject working groups were actively encouraged to find ways of valuing family life, in anything like the same way as they were pressured to celebrate English history and nationhood (Jenkinson, 1990). Apart from failing to refer to anti-sexist or anti-racist education, the National Curriculum supposedly leaves schools with the duty to choose their own pedagogy and to find ways of 'promoting equal opportunities'.

Such ideological tensions within the government concerning equal opportunities can also be glimpsed in the approach adopted by the National Curriculum Council. Equal opportunities, for example, was listed as only one of two cross-curriculum dimensions for schools to develop as part of the whole curriculum. At the same time, its chief executive Duncan Graham indicated that gender was too 'delicate' an issue to merit a task group, and therefore the production of specific non-statutory guidance for schools (Arnot, 1989b). This approach, coupled with the fact that there was no official commitment to monitor sex bias in assessment, to train governors in sex discrimination legislation nor to encourage the teaching profession to improve its expectations of female pupils or reassess teaching styles, was unlikely to win support from those committed to sex equality.

In effect, centralised intervention appears to have reinforced male control of education policy-making and to have delegated the implementation of sex equality to teachers (Arnot, 1989b). While at first glance this may seem beneficial, the evidence provided by sociological research on teachers' attitudes to gender difference suggests that, although there is likely to be considerable rhetoric about the importance of equal opportunities policies, in practice little will be put into effect. In other words, the rump of teacher autonomy still allowed within the new educational system may well serve to marginalise gender issues and to sustain continued discriminatory behaviour.

Conclusion

The effects of the Education Reform Act on women have yet to be evaluated. Current sociological understandings of the policy intentions and expected outcomes of the Education Reform Act and the National Curriculum have tended to ignore the significance of the gender dimension, preferring to focus predominantly on the relationship between schooling, the state, ideology and the economy (e.g., Ball, 1990; Whitty, 1990). These accounts sit well within the tradition of the British Left, who have failed to 'understand the nature of the New Right through their gender blind analysis' (ten Tusscher, 1986, p. 67). They have failed to consider whether the New Right in the United Kingdom had any similarity with the New Right in the United States. This latter movement, as Andrea Dworkin found in her influential study, was a 'social and political movement controlled almost totally by men and as such it was fundamentally anti-feminist in stance' (Dworkin, 1978, p. 235).

The gender analysis offered here demonstrates, I hope, that the context for the emergence and success of the New Right was not just a 'crisis in capitalism'. Feminism, along with anti-racism, had thrown liberalism itself into crisis. This challenge was particularly true in education, where feminist educationalists and researchers were shattering the illusions of the social democratic project. Many of the fundamental beliefs in equality of opportunity, universalism, co-education, comprehensivisation and progressive teaching styles had been challenged by gender research. Further, the more that power relations in education were being exposed, the greater the demands for gender, class and race equality and the more outspoken the calls for increased state intervention to limit liberal so-called 'freedoms' and to help restructure domestic relations in the name of social equality (Arnot, 1991).

Thatcherism, if it existed at all as a coherent political philosophy, was not synonymous with the moral right nor indeed with pure neo-liberalism. It attempted to respond to the interests of capital and patriarchy, and also the threat to British nationhood. However, as far as women were concerned, since Thatcherism reasserted a form of competitive individualism and attempted to reinforce sexual divisions within and between public/private domains, it did not represent, as Hall (1988) argued, a significant break from social democratic thought.

In the event, the strength of the women's movement in shaping public opinion over the last two decades restricted the options available to the New Right to respond to such crises. Despite the attempt at a 'moral crusade', there has not been a concerted ideological attack on wage-earning women *per se*. Instead we find an assault on the working classes in an apparent attempt to raise productivity, increase profits and weaken collective organisation, especially trade unions. As Wilson (1987) has shown, the range of strategies adopted by the Conservative government in the 1980s had the effect of incorporating women into the labour force but under the worst possible terms – by reducing their protection, raising unemployment rates and failing to establish child care provision, thus adding to their domestic burdens.

The new vocationalism and modernising influences in education arguably promised women more opportunities to extend their occupational horizons. The National Curriculum, at least in its early formulations, would make available to girls traditionally male subjects and professional scientific and technological careers. The effects of such reforms, however, are most likely to be felt by middle-class women whose opportunities could be enhanced through consumer choice in education and increased concern about access and training. Working-class women and black and ethnic-minority women, in contrast, are likely to find their opportunities even further reduced and their rights to choose their own work patterns restricted by Conservative economic and family policies. It is not difficult to predict that there will be a widening class gap between women. Miles and Middleton, for example, observe that 'the Education Reform Act will not be neutral in its effects on different classes and ethnic groups'. Thus,

> We have seen … that this openly inegalitarian government is not averse to equal opportunities measures in so far as these may enlarge the pool of talent from which employers may draw. But highly paid and prestigious jobs are, by definition, within such an order, relatively scarce so that the achievement of parity between the sexes will still leave the inequalities between women (as well as those between men) unimpaired.
>
> (Miles and Middleton, 1990, p. 201)

The key issue for sociologists should, therefore, be an investigation of the processes involved in the attentuation of class relations in the context of gender and race. Such analyses would need to draw upon the insights which gender research brings to bear on social democracy, on the nature of the public/private division, on the impact of school organisation and gender dynamics within schools. Research into such themes will also no doubt take into account the new era of centralised control which extends even further male power over educational policy-making and hence greater control over a predominantly female teaching force; open enrolment and opting out which raises yet again the question of parental choice of single-sex or co-educational schools, particularly in relation to separate schools; and local management of schools which will highlight the priorities of educational managers and affect the development of equality policies. Sociological research which takes account of gender, race and class will provide valuable insights into whether full 'entitlement' is either possible or being achieved by such educational reform.

Another Conservative government strategy has been to neutralise feminist educational campaigns through new forms of assimilation. The National

Curriculum, while apparently offering equal entitlement, re-established male cultural priorities and values. It reasserted male hierarchies of knowledge, selected subjects in which men excelled, disposed of subjects traditionally the preserve of working-class girls (Arnot, 1989a) and is currently revaluing modes of teaching, learning and assessment which privilege middle-class male students. How this new 'gender code' (MacDonald, 1980) will shape the masculinising and feminising process of schooling in the next generation of children is another important topic for sociological investigation. Not surprisingly, feminist educationalists were confused in their response to Conservative government education reforms. Discontent over curricular choices was reduced by the introduction of a compulsory common curriculum, even if differentiated options and levels within subjects are re-emerging. Teacher autonomy has again been used to justify the refusal to offer political commitment to sex equality in the new reforms. Teachers have again been given the responsibility to initiate social reform. Emphasis upon democratising higher education has diffused public concern about the disadvantages experienced by working-class, black and female students.

Clearly a new agenda was set. New sets of gender relations were constructed through education which are likely to work in favour of white female and male middle-class students. The state was actively engaged in restoring patriarchal relations, but in different form and with different consequences to those of the post-war period. Without an understanding of that project, it is unlikely that we can adequately read the significance of shifts in contemporary society. Let us hope that Segal was right when she argued that:

> Thatcherism … has not successfully crushed a feminist consciousness which is aware of the oppression of women's lives as vulnerable and exploited workers and as hopelessly overburdened housewives, mothers and daughters.
>
> (Segal, 1983, p. 214)

Feminist research still has a valuable role to play maintaining that consciousness within the sociology of education, but equally important is the integration of that perspective into mainstream sociological theorising and evaluation of these educational reforms.

Notes

1 Mr Kenneth Baker, then Secretary of State for Education and Science, in 1988 was quoted as saying that the age of egalitarianism is now over (cf. Arnot, 1991).
2 See, for example, Eisenstein (1990) and Yeatman (1990).
3 National Curriculum subjects such as technology have various options within them. Science, on the other hand, can be studied for a single or double GCSE award (reflecting the time given to the subject on the timetable). In technology, girls are likely to continue opting for design and, in science, girls are likely to choose the double award.

4 Public debates about the decline of marriage, the extent of illegitimacy and teenage motherhood, single parenthood, divorce rates, increase in youth crime and so on, often blame women and also the women's liberation movement.
5 Acker's (1989) response reveals the continuing concern over the concept of patriarchy and the importance of not diverting attention away from the significance of gender as part of the fundamental constitution of all social life, by suggesting that patriarchy is a separate stucture operating alongside that of the economy.
6 Elsewhere (Arnot, 1983) I posited the notion of different modes of transmission of gender relations through schooling, drawing upon Basil Bernstein's theory of educational codes. The value of this concept is that it highlights the fact that gender relations can be transmitted through different forms of social control and different curricular arrangements.
7 A number of writers have outlined theories of the state in relation to education. A good early summary was that by Dale (1986). More recent discussion can be found in Dale (1989) and Ball (1990).
8 In my earlier work I discussed schooling in terms of constructing a particular gender order or gender code. These concepts had many similarities with the concept of gender regime discussed by Connell et al. (1982). The emphasis here is upon the production of gender difference through school structures and culture.
9 The development of egalitarian thought in the post-war period was analysed by the Centre for Contemporary Cultural Studies (1981). Gaby Weiner and I attempted to document the egalitarian tradition among feminists in the last two decades (see Weiner and Arnot, 1987).
10 I have drawn the concept of 'degendering' discourses from the insightful analysis by Sullivan (1990) of Australian equal opportunities legislation. It ties in well with contemporary discussion in the United Kingdom about 'deracialisation' and 'racialisation' of educational policy in the same period (Troyna, 1992).
11 Gaby Weiner and I argued that egalitarian approaches, such as those of radical, lesbian, socialist and black feminism,

> each in their own way, wished for no less than the transformation of the educational system. They had no wish to ameliorate the existing inadequate education system; they wanted to transform its power base.
>
> (Weiner and Arnot, 1987, p. 357)

12 See Note 8.
13 The Black Papers were a series of occasional publications produced by the Critical Quarterly Society (CQS) which, in the 1970s, became famous for their attacks on modern teaching methods, Plowden philosophy and comprehensive schools, and their view that educational standards were in decline.

References and further reading

Acker, J. (1989) 'The problem with patriarchy', *Sociology*, 23, 2, pp. 235–40.

Acker, S. (1986) 'What do feminists want from education?', in A. Hartnett and M. Naish (eds) *Education and Society Today*, Lewes: Falmer Press.

—— (1987) 'Feminist theory and the study of gender and education', *International Review of Education*, 33, 4, pp. 419–35.

Acker, S. and Warren Piper, D.W. (eds) (1984) *Is Higher Education Fair to Women?*, London: SRHE-Nelson.

Allen, J. (1990) 'Does feminism need a theory of the state?', in S. Watson (ed.) *Playing the State: Australian feminist interventions*, London: Verso.

Apple, M.W. (1989) 'How equality has been redefined in the Conservative Restoration', in W.G. Secada (ed.) *Equity in Education*, Lewes: Falmer Press.

Araújo, H.C. (1992) 'The emergence of a New Orthodoxy: public debates on women's capacities and education in Portugal (1880–1910)', *Gender and Education*, 4, 1/2, pp. 7–24.

Arnot, M. (1981) 'Culture and political economy: dual perspectives in the sociology of women's education', *Educational Analysis*, 3, 1, pp. 97–116.

—— (1983) 'A cloud over co-education: an analysis of the forms of transmission of class and gender relations', in S. Walker and L. Barton (eds) *Gender, Class and Education*, Lewes: Falmer Press.

—— (1986) *Race, Gender and Education Policy Making*, Module 4 E333, Milton Keynes: Open University.

—— (1987) 'Political lip-service or radical education reform? Central government responses to sex equality as a policy issue', in M. Arnot and G. Weiner (eds) *Gender and the Politics of Schooling*, London: Hutchinson.

—— (1989a) 'Crisis of challenge: equal opportunities and the National Curriculum', *NUT Education Review*, 3, 2, pp. 7–13.

—— (1989b) 'Consultation or legitimation? Race and gender politics and the making of the National Curriculum', *Critical Social Policy*, 27, pp. 20–38.

—— (1991) 'Equality and democracy: a decade of struggle over education', *British Journal of Sociology of Education*, 12, 4, pp. 447–66.

—— (1992a) 'Feminist perspectives on education for citizenship', paper presented at the International Sociology of Education Conference: 'Citizenship, Democracy and the Role of the Teacher', Westhill College, Birmingham.

—— (1992b) 'Feminism, education and the New Right', in M. Arnot and L. Barton (eds) *Voicing Concerns: sociological perspectives on contemporary education reforms*, Oxford: Triangle Books.

Ball, S.J. (1990) *Politics and Policy Making in Education*, London: Routledge.

Bourdieu, P. (1973) 'Cultural reproduction and social reproduction', in R. Brown (ed.) *Knowledge, Education and Cultural Change*, London: Tavistock.

Bowles, S. and Gintis, H. (1976) *Schooling in Capitalist America*, New York: Basic Books.

Bridgwood, A. and Betteridge, J. (1989) *Equal Opportunities for Boys and Girls with TVEI*, Windsor: NFER/Training Agency.

Burton, L. and Weiner, G. (1990) 'Social justice and the National Curriculum', *Research Papers in Education*, 5, pp. 203–27.

Byrne, E. (1978) *Women in Education*, London: Tavistock.

—— (1985) 'Equality or equity? A European view', in M. Arnot (ed.) *Race and Gender: equal opportunities policies in education*, Oxford: Pergamon Press.

Campbell, B. (1987) *The Iron Ladies: Why Do Women Vote Tory?*, London: Virago.

Centre for Contemporary Cultural Studies (CCCS) (1981) *Unpopular Education: schooling for social democracy in England since 1944*, London: Hutchinson.

Connell, R.W. (1990) 'The state, gender and sexual politics', *Theory and Society*, 19, pp. 507–44.

Connell, R.W., Ashenden, D.J., Kessler, S. and Dowsett, G.W. (1982) *Making the Difference: schools, families and social division*, Sydney: Allen & Unwin.

Dale, J. and Foster, P. (1986) *Feminists and State Welfare*, London: Routledge & Kegan Paul.

Dale, R. (1986) 'Perspectives on policy making', Part 2, Module 1 E333, *Introducing Education Policy: Principles and Perspectives*, Milton Keynes: Open University Press.

—— (1989) *The State and Education Policy*, Milton Keynes: Open University Press.

David, M.E. (1983a) 'Sex education and social policy: new moral economy?', in S. Walker and L. Barton (eds) *Gender, Class and Education*, Lewes: Falmer Press.

—— (1983b) 'Teaching and preaching sexual morality: the New Right's anti-feminism in Britain and the USA', *Journal of Education*, 166, 1, pp. 63–76.

—— (1985) 'Motherhood and social policy – a matter of education', *Critical Social Policy*, 12, Spring, pp. 28–43.

Davies, A.M., Holland, J. and Minhas, R. (1990) *Equal Opportunities in the New Era*, London: Hillcole Group, Paper 2.

Deem, R. (1981) 'State policy and ideology in the education of women, 1944–1980', *British Journal of Sociology of Education*, 22, pp. 131–44.

DES (1975) *Curricular Differences for Boys and Girls*, Education Survey 21, London: HMSO.

Dworkin, A. (1978) *Right-Wing Women*, London: Women's Press.

Eisenstein, H. (1984) *Contemporary Feminist Thought*, London: Counterpoint Unwin Paperback.

—— (1990) 'Femocrats, official feminism and the uses of power', in S. Watson (ed.) *Playing the State: Australian feminist interventions*, London: Verso.

Eisenstein, Z. (1987) 'Liberalism, feminism and the Reagan state: the neoconservative assault on (sexual) equality', in R. Miliband, L. Panitch and J. Saville (eds) *Socialist Register*, London: Merlin Press.

Fawcett Society and the National Joint Committee of Working Women's Organisations (1985) *The Class of 84*, London: Fawcett Society.

Finch, J. (1984) *Education and Social Policy*, London: Longman.

Franzway, S., Court, D. and Connell, R.W. (1989) *Staking a Claim: feminism, bureaucracy and the state*, Cambridge: Polity Press.

Fraser, N. (1989) *Unruly Practices: power, discourse and gender in contemporary social theory*, Cambridge: Polity Press.

Gardiner, J. (1983) 'Women, recession and the Tories', in S. Hall and M. Jacques (eds) *The Politics of Thatcherism*, London: Lawrence & Wishart.

Hall, S. (1988) *The Hard Road to Renewal: Thatcherism and the Crisis of the Left*, London: Verso.

Haviland, J. (1989) *Take Care Mr Baker!*, London: Fourth Estate.

Heater, D. (1990) *Citizenship: The Civic Ideal in World History, Policies and Education*, London: Longman.

Jenkinson, F. (1990) *Multicultural Education and the National Curriculum*, unpublished M.Phil. thesis, University of Cambridge.

Jones, C. and Mahony, P. (eds) (1989) *Learning Our Lines: Sexuality and Social Control in Education*, London: Women's Press.

Jones, K. (1989) *Right Turn: The Conservative Revolution in Education*, London: Hutchinson/Radius.

Kant, L. (1987) 'National Curriculum: nationally equal', *NUT Education Review*, 1, 2 (Autumn), pp. 41–4.

Kelly, L. (1992) 'Not in front of the children: responding to right wing agendas on sexuality and education', in M. Arnot and L. Barton (eds) *Voicing Concerns: sociological perspectives on contemporary education reforms*, Oxford: Triangle Books.

Kenway, J. (1990) *Gender and Education Policy: a call for new directions*, Victoria: Deakin University.

Kessler, S., Ashenden, D., Connell, B. and Dowsett, G. (1987) 'Gender relations in secondary schooling', in M. Arnot and G. Weiner (eds) *Gender and the Politics of Schooling*, London: Hutchinson.

Klein, G. (1989) 'New Right – new era', *NUT Education Review*, 3, 2 (Autumn), pp. 14–19.

Lees, S. (1986) *Losing Out: Sexuality and Adolescent Girls*, London: Hutchinson.

Loach, L. (1987) 'Can feminism survive a third term?', *Feminist Review*, 27, pp. 27–36.

Lloyd, G. (1986) 'Selfhood, war and masculinity', in C. Pateman and E. Gross (eds) *Feminist Challenges: social and political theory*, Sydney: Allen & Unwin.

MacDonald, M. (1980) 'Socio-cultural reproduction and women's education', in R. Deem (ed.) *Schooling for Women's Work*, London: Routledge & Kegan Paul.

MacKinnon, C. (1983) 'Feminism, Marxism, method and the state: toward feminist jurisprudence', *Signs*, 8, pp. 635–8.

Middleton, S. (1987) 'The sociology of women's education', in M. Arnot and G. Weiner (eds) *Gender and the Politics of Schooling*, London: Hutchinson.

Miles, S. and Middleton, C. (1990) 'Girls' education in the balance', in M. Flude and M. Hammer (eds) *The Education Reform Act 1988; origins and implications*, London: Falmer Press.

Millman, V. and Weiner, G. (1987) 'Engineering equal opportunities: the case of TVEI', in D. Gleeson (ed.) *A Critical Appraisal of TVEI*, London: Routledge.

Myers, K. (1989) 'High heels in the market place', *Education*, 16 June, pp. 559–60.

Orr, P. (1985) 'Sex bias in schools: national perspectives', in J. Whyte, R. Deem, L. Kant and M. Cruickshank (eds) *Girl Friendly Schooling*, London: Methuen.

Pascall, G. (1986) *Social Policy: a feminist analysis*, London: Tavistock.

Pateman, C. (1980) *The Disorder of Women*, Cambridge: Polity Press.

Payne, I. (1980) 'A working class girl in a grammar school', in E. Sarah and D. Spender (eds) *Learning to Lose*, London: Women's Press.

Phillips, A. (1991) *Engendering Democracy*, Cambridge: Polity Press.

Phoenix, A. (1987) 'Theories of gender and black families', in G. Weiner and M. Arnot (eds) *Gender Under Scrutiny: new inquiries in education*, London: Hutchinson.

Rowbotham, S. (1986) 'Feminism and democracy', in D. Held and C. Pollitt (eds) *New Forms of Democracy*, London: Sage.

Segal, L. (1983) 'The heat in the kitchen', in S. Hall and P. Jacques (eds) *The Politics of Thatcherism*, London: Lawrence & Wishart.

Spender, D. (1981a) 'Education: the patriarchal paradigm and the response to feminism', in Spender, D. (ed.) *Men's Studies Modified*, Oxford: Pergamon Press.

—— (ed.) (1981b) *Men's Studies Modified*, Oxford: Pergamon Press.

Stanworth, M. (1983) *Gender and Schooling*, London: Hutchinson.

Sullivan, B. (1990) 'Sex equality and the Australian body politic', in S. Watson (ed.) *Playing the State: Australian feminist interventions*, London: Verso.

ten Tusscher, T. (1986) 'Patriarchy, capitalism and the New Right', in J. Evans, J. Hills, K. Hunt, T. ten Tusscher, U. Vogel and G. Waylen (eds) *Feminism and Political Theory*, London: Sage.

Thompson, J. (1983) *Learning Liberation: Women's Response to Men's Education*, London: Croom Helm.

Troyna, B. (1992) 'Can you see the join? An historical analysis of multicultural and anti-racist education policies', in D. Gill, B. Mayor and M. Blair (eds) *Racism and Education: structures and strategies*, London: Sage.

Walby, S. (1990) *Theorizing Patriarchy*, Oxford: Basil Blackwell.

Walkerdine, V. (1981) 'Sex, power and pedagogy', *Screen Education*, 38, pp. 14–23.

Watson, S. (1990) 'The state of play: an introduction', in S. Watson (ed.) *Playing the State: Australian feminist interventions*, London: Verso.

Weedon, C. (1987) *Feminist Practice and Post-structuralist Theory*, Oxford: Basil Blackwell.

Weiner, G. (1989a) 'Feminism, equal opportunities and vocationalism: the changing context', in H. Burchell and V. Millman (eds) *Changing Perspectives on Gender*, Milton Keynes: Open University Press.

—— (1989b) 'Professional self knowledge versus social justice: a critical analysis of the teacher-research movement', *British Educational Research Journal*, 15, pp. 41–53.

—— (1990) 'The future for social justice in the 1990s', *Education Review*, 4, pp. 56–9.

Weiner, G. and Arnot, M. (1987) 'Teachers and gender politics', in M. Arnot and G. Weiner (eds) *Gender and the Politics of Schooling*, London: Hutchinson.

Whitty, G. (1990) 'The New Right and the National Curriculum: state control or market forces?', in M. Flude and M. Hammer (eds) *The Education Reform Act 1988: its origins and implications*, London: Falmer Press.

Whyte, J., Deem, R., Kant, L. and Cruickshank, M. (eds) (1985) *Girl Friendly Schooling*, London: Methuen.

Wickham, A. (1987) *Women and Training*, Milton Keynes: Open University Press.

Williams, F. (1989) *Social Policy: a critical introduction*, Cambridge: Polity Press.

Willis, P. (1977) *Learning to Labour*, Farnborough: Saxon House.

Wilson, E. (1980) *Only Halfway to Paradise*, London: Tavistock.

—— (1987) 'Thatcherism and women: after seven years', in R. Milliband, I. Panitch and J. Saville (eds) *Socialist Register*, London: Merlin Press.

Wolpe, A.M. (1976) 'The official ideology of education for girls', in M. Flude and J. Ahier (eds) *Educability, Schools and Ideology*, London: Croom Helm.

—— (1987) 'Sex in schools: back to the future', *Feminist Review*, 27 (Autumn), pp. 37–48.

Wood, J. (1987) 'Groping towards sexism: boys' sex talk', in G. Weiner and M. Arnot (eds) *Gender Under Scrutiny: new inquiries in education*, London: Hutchinson.

Yeatman, A. (1990) *Bureaucrats and Technocrats and Femocrats*, Sydney: Allen & Unwin.

9 Sociological understandings of contemporary gender transformations in schooling in the UK

> A new agenda is being set. New sets of gender relations are being constructed through education which are likely to work in favour of white female and male middle class students. The state is actively engaged in restoring patriarchal relations but in different form and with different consequences to those of the post-war period. Without an understanding of that project, it is unlikely that we can adequately read the significance of shifts in contemporary society.
>
> (Arnot, 1993, p. 206)

In 1993, it was clear that the impact of New Right economic, educational and social reforms on gender relations would be considerable and complex. Given the contradictory agenda set by the neo-conservative and neo-liberal wings of the Conservative government under Margaret Thatcher (Arnot, 1993; Arnot, David and Weiner, 1998), it seemed likely that traditional gender relations would not simply be sustained within the new era but would also be transformed. Economic policies were likely to have differential impact on male and female patterns of employment and educational and social policies would almost certainly affect middle-class and working-class pupils in unequal ways. Central to this reform agenda was the restructuring of the pivotal relationships between schooling, families and the economy, and the role of the state within such relationships. It was probable, therefore, that the 1980s and 1990s would witness a social transformation of gender relations. As I shall argue, the restructuring of society and of schools in the late twentieth century substantially changed the modalities of gender transmission and its 'gendered' products in quite fundamental ways.

The story of gender and education in the United Kingdom, at least on the surface, appears as a story about the extraordinary success of post-war egalitarian movements. Up to sixteen years of age, a number of the major gender gaps in subject choices, examination performance and entry patterns in primary, secondary and tertiary education closed. Such is the success of girls in the school system in the United Kingdom that every summer journalists go into a frenzy as they seek to establish the latest changes in examination performances between girls and boys at sixteen (GCSE) and at eighteen (A-levels). The main focus has been the extent to which the gender balance has shifted, with girls catching up and overtaking boys in traditionally male subjects such as mathematics and science and boys continuing to perform relatively poorly in traditionally female subjects such as English and modern languages. Sociologists might ponder over this extraordinary media debate, with its incitement of government to act in the name of boys and retrieve boys' advantage. To some extent it represents a moral panic that is associated with uneven economic and political cleavages of late modernity (Epstein, Hey and Maw, 1998; Raphael Reed, 1999). But there are also other interesting questions to ask of this national phenomenon.

In this article, I consider the shifting patterns of gender performance in education through the lens of social reproduction theory.[1] From this theoretical perspective, such gender patterns of performance reflect a historical transformation of the *gender codes* (cf. MacDonald, 1980) of schooling – the principles which govern the production, reproduction and transmission of gender relations and gender hierarchies. I shall argue that the patterns of gender performance signify a new *gender order* (Connell, 1987) – a symbolic order which is embedded in the social relations of power and control in society. As Quicke argued, behind the differences in gender performance lie major political issues:

> because these [gender] differences are not 'innocent' but reflect asymmetrical power relations where men historically have been in the ascendancy.
> (Quicke, 1999, pp. 96)

Gender patterns in education are central aspects of the relationship of education and society and transformations in society.

The structure of this article is as follows: first, I describe the changing forms of gender transmission through education by drawing upon the findings of two major reports: *Educational Reforms on Gender Equality in Schools* (Arnot, David and Weiner, 1996) commissioned by the Equal Opportunities Commission and *A Review of Recent Research on Gender and Educational Performance* (Arnot et al., 1998) commissioned by the UK school inspectorate (Office for Standards in Education).[2] Second, I explore the interconnections between social and educational change in the last twenty-five years, rehearsing and developing some of the main arguments put forward by Miriam David, Gaby Weiner and me in *Closing the Gender Gap: postwar education and social change* (Arnot, David and Weiner, 1998).

Shifting gender patterns of educational performance

In the period between the late 1980s and 2000, gender patterns of educational performance caught the public eye and caused consternation in relation to the maintenance of the social order. Of central significance was evidence of boys' failure to improve their performance at the same rate as girls, from very young ages. Boys' educational performance at sixteen did not seem to be improving in comparison with girls. At the same time, girls became 'space invaders' –

entering into and conquering male academic space, especially in science and mathematics (Foster, 2000). Of great concern was the invasion of such public space in which male hegemonic control of women was premised. The threat of boys' disaffection and disengagement also raised the spectre of a male underclass – the so-called 'underwolves' (Wilkinson, 1994) – who would not be able to participate in the engine of social progress associated with increased performance and certification.

While public concern focuses on boys' experiences, of greater significance to sociologists is the change in gender relations represented by the divergent male and female patterns of performance. Although gender differences have been reduced in some quarters, in other sectors traditional gender divisions have been maintained, if not strengthened. The boundaries between male and female spheres have not necessarily broken down, but rather have been modified and adapted to new educational and social climates. The dominant gender codes in education have been transformed as the relations of power and control between men and women change in line with new globalised and marketised economic and social structures. These changes, as I illustrate below, are to be found primarily in the redistribution of educational credentials and the divergent modes of gender transmission found in compulsory and post-compulsory education.

The redistribution of educational credentials

Examination results at sixteen and eighteen in the UK in the last twenty-five years vividly demonstrate the redistribution of educational credentials. In the 1970s, girls in the UK acquired more higher-grade qualifications at sixteen than boys (Arnot, 1986), but many failed to make the transition into post-compulsory education. Fewer girls than boys achieved the three good A-levels which would have given them access to higher education. The English educational system (especially its elite institutions) appeared reluctant to allow women access to high-status education, even though the economy required much higher numbers of scientists, engineers and skilled labour. In the 1980s, it was relatively rare for girls to study science and mathematics, to perform well in these subjects and study them at university level. Since the early 1980s, however, gender patterns of performance of sixteen-year-old school leavers have changed substantially. While the number of qualifications taken by pupils increased for the majority of pupils, by the 1990s a new pattern of female academic success was established. Girls had overcome their disadvantage and had pulled ahead. In the summer of 2001, 10 per cent more girls than boys in England and Wales achieved five GCSE with A*–C grades. Girls had turned the tide of credentialism, at least temporarily, in their favour.

Key to the shift (if not inversion) of this post-war pattern of educational performance within the period of compulsory schooling (aged five to sixteen) was a range of curriculum reforms introduced by the Conservative government under Margaret Thatcher (Arnot et al., 1998). The introduction in 1984 of a new common examination, the General Certificate of Secondary Education, which is now taken by nearly all pupils in England and Wales, reduced the extensive differentiation between vocational and academic courses and routes. Pupils were encouraged to take a greater range of subjects and to work with new, more flexible styles of teaching and examining. This curricular reform redistributed educational credentials not only from the elite to the masses but also, and not intentionally, in favour of girls (Arnot, David and Weiner, 1996). As Figure 1 demonstrates, boys outperformed girls up to the 1960s by about 5 per cent – and for the next fifteen years boys and girls were performing at almost equivalent levels. However, from 1987 only about eighty boys to every hundred girls achieved five high grade passes at 16+. Boys had clearly lost their advantage in terms of school credentials.

A similar redistribution of educational credentials is evident in the post-compulsory sector. After sixteen, girls match (if not better) boys' performance. Figure 2 demonstrates the near elimination of the difference in male and female performance at A/AS-level subjects in the last few years. Although slightly more boys than girls (taking two or more A/AS-levels) achieved the highest number of point scores in relation to their A-level grades, this gap became

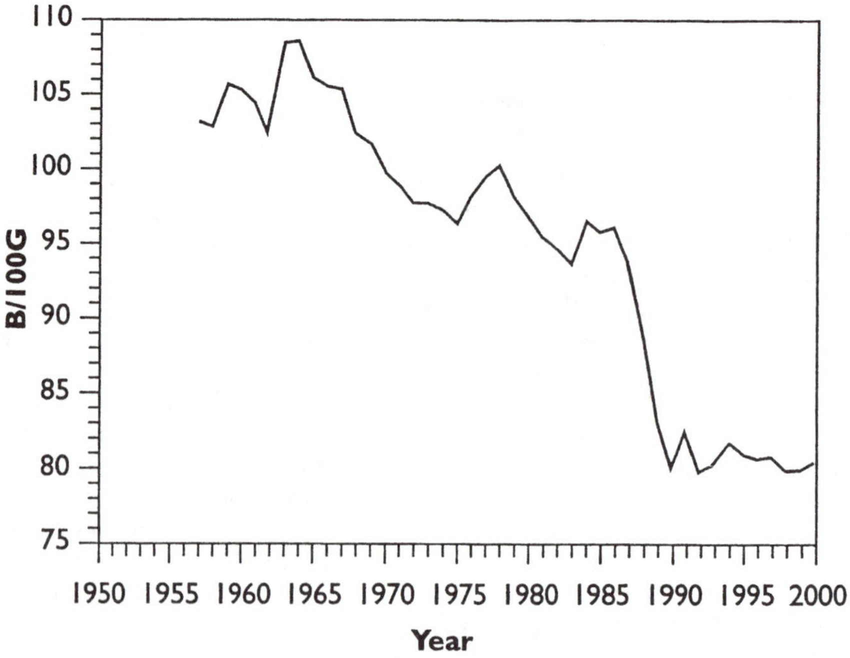

Figure 1 Number of boys obtaining 5+ Higher Grade Passes (A*–C) in any subject in 16+ Examinations per 100 girls, England, 1955–2000

Source: Marks, 2001, p.15, Figure 12.

Note: A question remains about the comparability of data collected before and after 1974, when the school-leaving age was raised.

minimal in 1995 (boys averaged 14.5 points and girls averaged 14.1) (Arnot et al., 1998, p. 16). More recent statistics reveal that girls are in the lead at A-level (1.9 per cent ahead at grades A–E and 0.8 per cent ahead at grade A). The new AS-levels, which were taken for the first time in 2001, put girls ahead with a 4.2 per cent lead and a 3.2 per cent lead at grade A. This gap was larger than that for 'legacy A-levels' (the name given to the traditional A-level) (Joint Council for General Qualifications, 2001).

Girls' raised level of performance at sixteen and eighteen contributed to the rise in the number of students undertaking full-time and part-time post-sixteen

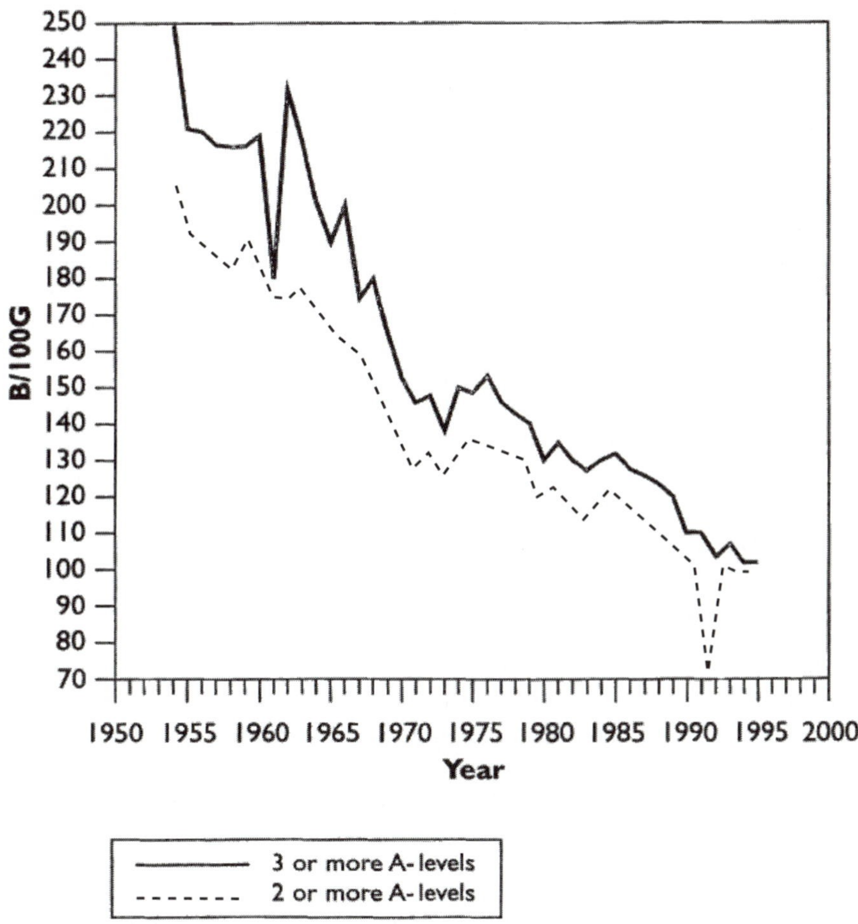

Figure 2 Number of boys obtaining 2+ and 3+ A-level results per 100 girls, England, 1955–1995

Source: Marks, 2001, p. 16, Figure 13

courses. The figures have leapt from two-thirds (66 per cent) of the age group to around four-fifths (80 per cent) in the last decade. In 1995, three-quarters of female students were on full-time, post-sixteen courses compared with 69 per cent of boys. In the ten years after 1985, young women raised their entry on such courses from one in five (20 per cent) to around two-fifths (39 per cent) (Arnot et al., 1998, p. 16).

In turn, the increase in the proportion of young people staying on after sixteen has meant that numbers on full-time and part-time courses post-eighteen have more than doubled and girls now match male entry figures. In 1985, only 26 per cent of young women were in post-eighteen courses, compared with 34 per cent of young men; ten years later the figures were roughly equal (49 per cent to 47 per cent respectively). Both young men and women also more than doubled their numbers in higher education in those ten years, but here again young women overtook young men such that, in 1995, proportions entering higher education were 20 per cent and 19 per cent respectively (ibid.).

These changes in the gender distribution of educational credentials in the last twenty years have been associated with two features: the continuing strong performance of girls in English and their success in improving their results in science and mathematics. The OFSTED review cites the few studies that have tracked boys and girls through primary or through secondary schools, all of which indicate that girls make better progress than boys in reading, mathematics and verbal/non-verbal reasoning (Arnot et al., 1998). Data collected from national assessments at the age of seven (Key Stage 1) demonstrate that girls get off to a better start at reading than boys and that the lead they establish in English is maintained at Key Stage 2 (age eleven) and Key Stage 3 (age fourteen) (Arnot et al., 1998). Indeed, a sizeable gap between boys and girls in reading and English is sustained throughout compulsory schooling. By 2000, approximately 15 per cent more girls than boys obtained A*–C grade in English GCSE (DfEE, 2000). The fact that boys have not reduced this female 'advantage' is one of the principal reasons why they have lost overall ground in compulsory schooling in comparison with girls.

At the same time, girls in England and Wales have caught up with boys in mathematics and science. In 1995, seven-year-old girls had a head-start in mathematics (81 per cent of girls reached the expected level compared with 77 per cent of boys) and 86 per cent of girls and 83 per cent of boys reached the expected level in science. Girls' greater success in science and mathematics at GCSE helped them invert the patterns of gender inequalities in school-leaving examinations at sixteen. The proportion of girls who achieved A*–A grades in mathematics in that year was only 2 per cent lower than the proportion of boys, and 44 per cent of girls (compared with 45 per cent of boys) reached A*–C grades. In combined science, 48 per cent of girls (compared with 47 per cent of boys) achieved A*–C grade. Using a statistical construct of a 'gender gap', Figure 3 illustrates these patterns of performance between 1985 and 1995.[3]

In the mid- to late 1980s, the reduction of gender inequalities in performance at A/AS-level (taken at eighteen years), although not as great as that

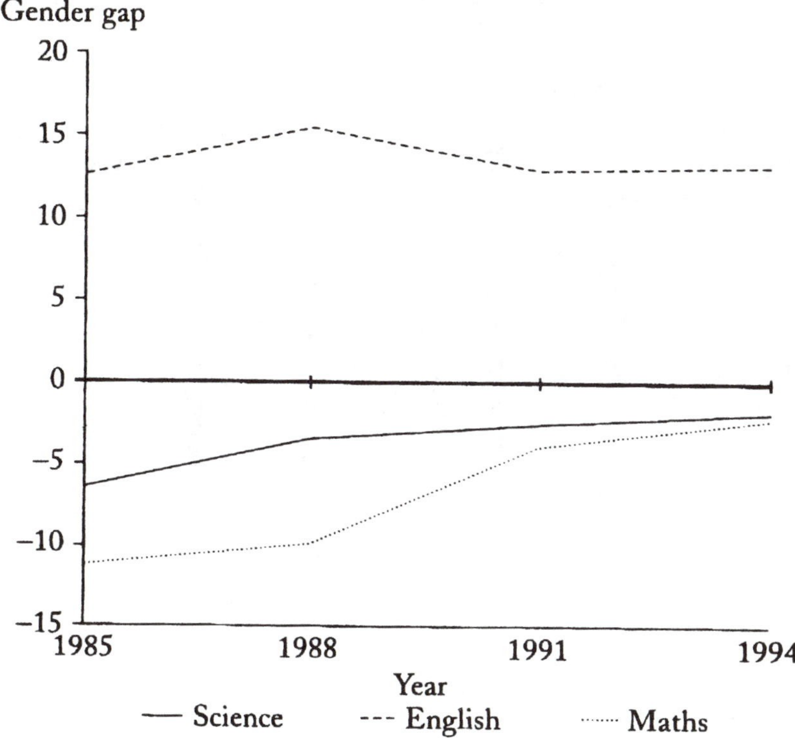

Figure 3 The gender gap in relative performance for core National Curriculum subjects, 1985–94

Source: Arnot, David and Weiner, 1996, p. 30, Figure 3.7

found in GCSEs, was also evident in national statistics (Arnot et al., 1998). Girls gradually closed the gaps in performance at A–B grades in the sciences (biology, chemistry and physics), as well as in subjects such as English and modern foreign languages. However Table 2 below indicates that the picture is quite complicated, since in 2000 comparatively large proportions of girls achieved high grades in biology, computer studies, geography, history and English, but a higher proportion of boys than girls performed well in chemistry, physics, mathematics and, interestingly, French.

Modalities of gender transmission

It would be as misleading to read these performance patterns simply as the breaking down of gender dualisms or male power as it would be to associate it simply with male 'underachievement'. There are now major differences in the patterns associated with female education in *compulsory* and *post-compulsory*

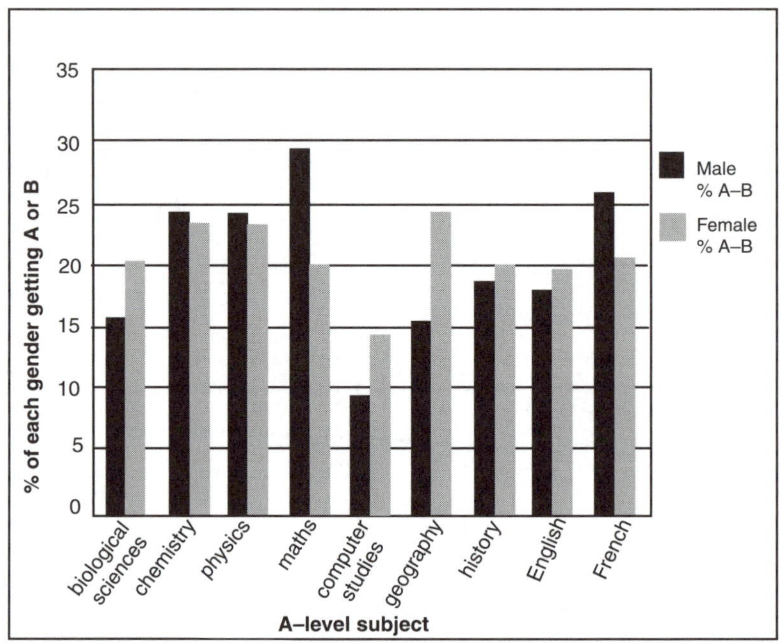

Table 2 Proportion of male and female students achieving A or B grades at A-level by subject in 2000, England

Source: http://www.standards.dfee.gov.uk/genderandachievement/2000_data_5.html

education. The last two decades have demonstrated the official *desegregation* of subject choices in school-leaving qualifications at sixteen; on the other hand, they have been associated with the *masculinisation* of science and technology in the post-compulsory sector (Arnot et al., 1998). Thus, while within compulsory education the segregation of gender spheres and male hierarchies has been weakened, traditional gender relations in post-compulsory education have been largely strengthened. Put in Bernsteinian terms (Bernstein, 1971), there are two different 'modalities' of transmitting gender relations within the educational system – one for the majority educated up to sixteen and the other for those who proceed to further and higher education. Thus two contradictory trends in the patterns of subject choice have emerged in these data – one of which suggests the dismantling of traditional gender classifications, while the other suggests the reinforcement of male hegemony. Let us explore each in turn.

In the compulsory sector, until the early 1980s, boys and girls occupied almost completely different educational tracks. Since that time, gender boundaries between traditionally male and female subjects have been weakened, with most of these gender differences in subject take-up substantially reduced. Between 1985 and 1995, the male dominance of subjects such as physics, geography, CDT and technology decreased and a more balanced entry pattern has been sustained in English, art and design, mathematics and history. The data generated by the EOC project (Arnot, David and Weiner, 1996) showed that the gender gap in subject entry was found to be on the increase in only five of eighteen GCSE subjects (see Table 3). On the whole, the picture was one of *desegregation* of subject choice up to sixteen.

However, Table 3 also demonstrates that, despite the weakening of most subject boundaries, the pattern of male advantage at sixteen can still be found in the sizeable gaps in the entry into higher-status male subjects at GCSE (e.g.,

Table 3 Changes in the gender gap in entry to different subjects at GCSE, 1984-94

Size of gap in 1994	*Boys predominate*	*Balanced entry*	*Girls predominate*	*Trend in gap over last decade*
Large (30%+)	Physics			Decreasing
	CDT			Decreasing
	Economics			Increasing
			Home economics	Decreasing
			Social studies	Increasing
			Vocational studies	Increasing
Sizeable (15–30%)	Chemistry			Increasing
	Computer studies			Increasing
Small (5–15%)	Technology			Decreasing
	Geography			Decreasing
			Modern foreign languages	Decreasing
			English literature	Decreasing
No gap (<5% either way)	Science			Decreasing
			Biology	Decreasing
		English		No change
		Mathematics		No change
		History		No change
		Art and design		No change

Source: Arnot et al., 1998, p. 13, Table 1.2

physics and chemistry). Far more boys than girls are among the elite minority of pupils, often in private schools, who take the single sciences at GCSE (most pupils study combined sciences). In 1995, 28,000 boys took physics GCSE compared with only 15,000 girls (the comparable figures for chemistry were 28,000 and 16,000 respectively) (ibid., p. 10). Thus, although gender boundaries between areas of knowledge have been substantially weakened for the majority, this is the not the case for elite male groups in society who start to specialise in such subjects prior to A-level.

In the post-compulsory sector, the dominance of boys in science, technology and mathematics at A-level increased further in this period. Between 1984 and 1994, many of the gender gaps in entry were sizeable. Over 30 per cent more boys than girls chose physics, mathematics, computer studies, technology, economics and CDT, and in many of these instances this gender gap had increased. Far larger proportions of girls than boys chose conventional female subjects, such as English and modern foreign languages (although here boys had made inroads), and more girls chose biology, social studies and art and design (see Table 4).

These national statistics on educational performance demonstrate that, despite the near equalisation in the proportions of academically successful male and female students achieving A-levels and high grades in these examinations (and hence the pathway to university), male educational advantage was not only sustained but increased in the worlds of science and technology. Thus male students, especially after sixteen, have considerable control over these particular highly valued forms of educational knowledge.[4]

Male students' success and the 'masculinisation' of technology and the sciences at A-level also continue to be a feature of vocational and academic courses in further and higher education. Official statistics for the Advanced General National Vocational Qualification (GNVQ) demonstrate how some subjects (such as health and social care, leisure and tourism, IT) are 'almost exclusively male or female'.[5] The OFSTED review concluded that:

> gender stereotyping in the mid-nineties among 16–19 age group in terms of the subjects studied for vocational qualifications is just as strong as at A-level.
>
> (Arnot et al., 1998, p. 18)

Young men are more likely to choose science and engineering in further and higher education (Cheng, Payne and Witherspoon, 1995; Felstead, Goodwin and Green, 1995; UCAS, 2000). The impressive improvement in girls' performance in science and mathematics in 16+ examinations arguably should have transformed the performance patterns of those academically able students heading for university. Instead, male dominance of the 'hard' sciences strengthened its hold.

The redistribution of educational credentials towards female students is, therefore, neither uniform nor complete. On the one hand, a higher proportion

Table 4 Changes in the gender gap in entry to different subjects at A-level, 1984–94

Size of gap in 1994	*Boys predominate*	*Balanced entry*	*Girls predominate*	*Trend in gap over last decade*
Large (30%+)	Physics			Increasing
	Mathematics			No change
	Computer studies			No change
	Technology			Increasing
	Economics			Increasing
	CDT			Increasing
			English	Decreasing
			Modern foreign languages	Decreasing
Sizeable (15–30%)	Chemistry			No change
	Geography			No change
			Biology	Decreasing
			Social studies	Increasing
			Art and design	Decreasing
Small (5–15)	None		None	None
No gap (<5 % either way)			History	Decreasing

Source: Arnot et al., 1998, p. 16, Table 1.5

of female students achieve higher-grade qualifications in nearly all GCSE subjects. They acquire higher qualifications than boys in the period of *compulsory* schooling. On the other hand, the academically able boy who stays on at school to complete A-levels (used for university entrance) performs particularly well. At the same time, sex segregation in subject choice, whilst reduced in compulsory education, remains embedded in the subsequent phases. In the next section, I explore how and why such contradictory trends and complex structures of transmission came to be established in the UK.

The challenge to Victorian values

It would be naive to attribute these shifts in gender performance in the UK solely to educational reform. Although the 1988 Education Reform Act has been signalled as the most radical reform of the school system since the 1944

Education Act, restructuring every aspect of educational provision and practice, its political impetus in relation to gender was not necessarily new. Gender change had its roots in a far longer and more deeply embedded challenge to nineteenth-century liberal ideas concerning the role of men and women in society (Arnot, David and Weiner, 1998). Despite calls for a return to domestic, family virtues and structures, Margaret Thatcher's government failed to turn the tides of change that were symptomatic of nineteenth- and twentieth-century gender struggles. She failed, we argue, to put the genie back in the bottle (ibid.). In the second part of this article, I describe these shifts, particularly in the relationship between the family, schooling and the state which played a key role in restructuring gender relations in education.

In *Closing the Gender Gap*, we suggest that what lies at the heart of these post-war educational changes in gender was a challenge to the hegemony of nineteenth-century (Victorian) gender values as the dominant structuring principle which shaped the selection, organisation and transmission of knowledge. The shift away from such values represents a historical break with the foundations of the modern educational system which was established in the nineteenth century and was closely associated with the historical rise of the bourgeoisie (upper middle classes) (Arnot, 1982). Key to this Victorian model of the world (its gender code of strong boundaries and hierarchies and little opportunity for negotiated identities) was the powerful ideological distinction between public and private spheres. Historians in the United Kingdom and the United States (Burstyn, 1980; Dyhouse, 1981) have provided us with excellent detailed analyses of how such a distinction functioned to shape masculinity and femininity. As Bourdieu (1977) argued, the male world was constructed around the centrifugal public world focused upon war, politics and work while the female centripetal private spheres circled around psychology, the hearth and intimacy. This distinction between public and private spheres, as feminist political theorists have reminded us, became part of the liberal democratic concept of the social contract (Arnot and Dillabough, 2000). Underlying this social contract, which defined the social order, was the disorder represented by women (Pateman, 1988). Thus women were defined as outside the social order – and as a threat to it. Further underlying the social contract was the sexual contract with women subservient to men. Women were not dominant even in their own sphere.

Such Victorian values had a deep effect on the content and structuring of female education. If women were understood to be subordinate to men both intellectually, emotionally, physically and socially, their schooling was considered to be dangerous. Women were associated with nature and emotion, men with reason and intellect. Such were the strength of these views that women were seen as incapable of learning sciences (a view that can still be found in the UK today). As a result, until well into the 1970s women were offered a domestically oriented inferior education. Education for girls was seen as supporting natural female interests, needs and choices with respect to personal/domestic life (Arnot, 1983). Even twenty years after World War II, girls in England were still being offered or being channelled into choosing subjects which prepared them for a nurturing, domestic role. Child care, domestic science and sewing were added to a diet of social sciences and humanities. It is hard to remember that, when the Sex Discrimination Act (1975) was passed, the majority of girls were sitting examinations in this narrow cluster of subjects, taught mainly by women teachers and going on to the mainly female vocational courses (beauty care, hairdressing, service work).

Such gender ideologies also involved women in supporting the developing educational system as mothers, but also critically as teachers. Thus, the educational system assumed the ready supply of female labour, with appropriate nurturing qualities, a disposition that was appropriate for the inculcation of the masses and low aspirations in terms of career development (Walkerdine, 1983). The mass educational system was built upon the labour of female citizens who, as Jo-Anne Dillabough (2000) argues, were never counted as 'productive worker citizens' but rather as public representatives of the private sphere involved in the domestication of the future generation of citizens. Female teachers and teacher educators were seen as offering an extended form of vocational domestic work in the name of the nation. They were portrayed as 'Mothers of the Nation'.

But history recounts how the imposition of this bourgeois model of family life by a liberal democratic school system was never entirely acceptable to women, even in the nineteenth century. The patterns of educational transmission and performance today are the product of counter-hegemonic struggles against, and other challenges to, such models (Arnot, 1993). Victorian gender values, we argue, were challenged by claims in the name of (a) women's rights; (b) post-war philosophies of meritocracy; (c) the second wave of the women's movement, and more specifically what has been called 'education feminism' (Stone, 1994); and (d) the individualism of the New Right. Below I outline briefly some of the arguments which we put forward in *Closing the Gender Gap* (Arnot, David and Weiner, 1998).

In the name of women's rights

The challenge to Victorian domestic ideology was initiated most forcefully in nineteenth-century campaigns for women's rights. Drawing on the principles established by Mary Wollstonecraft's *Vindication of the Rights of Woman* (1792), feminist campaigners took as their central motif the humanistic claim that women would be treated and should act as autonomous beings. While clearly establishing women's right to an independent existence and indeed an education in their own name, women campaigners were nevertheless confronted with what is now called 'Wollstonecraft's dilemma' (Phillips, 1991) – should women ask for the same or different treatment to men? In educational terms, should women have equal or separate but equal education to men? In the event, the dilemma was resolved in different ways for different social classes. Historians of education remind us how one of the key campaigns was gaining access for women to high-status secondary education and to universities in the late nineteenth and early twentieth century. It was not until 1948 that the last bastions of male privilege fell and women were allowed to take the same degrees as men in Cambridge University. This battle for equal rights and equal treatment of men and women still has resonance today.

The real thrust of the educational reforms associated with the notion of women's rights affected the elite rather than the mass population. What it led to, we argued, was the rise of a *female graduate elite* – initially through private or state single-sex girls' grammar schools and also through the expansion of university places in the 1960s. Key to the rise of such an elite was the adaptation of elite girls' education to the concept of individual achievement. In the past, such girls had been educated to become the wives and mothers of the male upper middle classes (Arnot, 1983). They could rely for the reproduction of their class position on marrying into the same social class of successful men. However, by the mid-twentieth century, the status of upper-middle-class men was becoming unstable, threatened by the transformations in the economy, the rise of new scientifically based professions and the rise of credentialism (Tolson, 1977; Connell, 1997). While elite male schooling changed the class-based qualities of gentry masculinity to include elements of competitive individualism and specialist (often scientific/technological) expertise, women of this class were being educated to take responsibility for achieving and sustaining their own class position (through university education and full-time careers).

The biographies and ethnographic accounts of the schooldays of upper-class and upper-middle-class schoolgirls in the 1950s reveal the new concerns of private girls' schools to promote a notion of upper-middle-class femininity which emphasised academic success. Marriage and future domesticity were seen as poor investment for their schooling. The statistics of school performance document the growth in white middle-class girls' attainment over and above that of boys in the same social grouping, with girls taking up many of the new places in higher education and, on occasion, even surpassing men in entry in the ancient universities. However, there was a price to be paid for winning women's rights in these highly competitive male spheres: research points to the high levels of anxiety experienced by elite schoolgirls, the increased pressure from parents to deliver clusters of A-grades. It is not clear whether such short-term examination successes are matched by long-term confidence or success, especially since such women are still likely to encounter major obstacles in the labour market.

These transformations in class reproduction are associated with the internal restructuring of the professional middle classes, with women reshaping the conditions of employment and family life, challenging gender hierarchies and also economic and social forms of male control. The challenge to middle-class concepts of femininity encouraged 'a gender blind approach' to education, weakening gender boundaries and hierarchies of knowledge. As a result, the language of mass not just elite schooling was to become more gender neutral, especially when equality of the sexes was promoted within the discourses of meritocracy.

The meritocratic challenge

Another challenge to the structuring of the educational system in line with male interests was the promotion of meritocracy and equal opportunities, associated in the UK with the establishment of the welfare state in the post-war period. The dual repertoire of economic expansion and an egalitarian concern for social welfare which we call social democracy (1940–70s) weakened the homologous classifications of male public and female private spheres through the post-war expansion of women's work and the opening up of educational opportunities for all.

It is one of the ironies of post-war history that Victorian family values, paradoxically, were undermined at precisely the point when they were built into the nature and shape of the welfare state. The development of the health and educational systems after the war, the social security system and taxation system were premised upon models of the male head of household. Proponents of welfare stressed the value and importance of traditional families and especially the role of the mother in keeping the family cared for, educated and orderly. Mothers were held responsible for any breakdown in law and order and their children's physical, psychological or educational problems.

But while these images were being constructed, the welfare state was taking large numbers of women out of the home to work in the new welfare occupations which depended on their labour. The rise of female employment (particularly of mothers) after the war brought with it calls for child care, calls for better female education, for better conditions for female employment. Further, women started to organise politically to claim the rights invested in the concept of the welfare state. They claimed what Marshall (1950) called their *social rights* (over and above political and economic rights). The paradox, we argue in our book, is that the social democratic period set in train a sequence of social changes that fundamentally transformed the nature of patriarchal family life. And yet, while all this was happening, men were still encouraged to see themselves as heads of households with their main responsibility being as main wage earner. The welfare reformers asked little of fathers in terms of taking responsibility for their children (care, education). They did not ask fathers to support their wives at work, nor their children at school. The impact of the welfare state was, therefore, considerably different for each sex.

In retrospect, the principle of meritocracy had its limitations. Despite the expansion of educational opportunities and the commitment to notions of parity of esteem and equality of opportunity, the educational system in this period maintained rather than undermined a patriarchal order and gendered differences in outcomes. Gender differentiations were deep and extensive, supported as they were by school staff and management structures and a distribution of power within the educational system which gave men control over educational policy. Discriminatory practices within educational institutions and school cultures promoted what Spender (1987) called 'patriarchal educational paradigms'. Arguably these were the mechanisms by which a male hegemony and female subordination were being maintained (Arnot, 1982). Educational expansion, on its own, had not necessarily challenged the taken-for-granted cultural and disciplinary regimes of schools and their close association with the sexual division of labour.

A more substantial and critical challenge to the modernist educational project and its conventional gender codes – its boundaries between public and private, its hierarchical knowledge structures and its forms of moral surveillance – was mounted not through the state but rather through what Stone (1994) called 'education feminism' – the women's movement within the educational system. Of major significance were the counter-hegemonic actions of teachers (Weiler, 1988) caught up in this political reform movement.

Education feminism

In the UK, education feminism took a particular form since the state had not openly challenged gender inequality. I argued that central government's approach to addressing gender inequalities had been characterised by lip-service rather than strong commitment (Arnot, 1987). Early attempts to use legislation to remove sex discrimination in education had been half-hearted and deeply problematic, based as it was on case law rather than constitutional rights. The legislation had promoted greater awareness but, given the decentralised nature of the English educational system, there was little top-down reform of schooling in the name of gender equality. Until the late 1980s, teachers were the key agents of change in the UK. They had control over the curriculum and considerable professional autonomy. Further, when social inequality became a matter of public concern, the responsibility for tackling it was delegated (or left) to teachers. Given this power and with their own experiences of discrimination themselves, women teachers were a natural audience for the ideas of the women's movement. 'Education feminism' within schools in the UK developed as a 'bottom-up' grassroots movement which captured the imagination of large numbers of women teachers, many of whom would have been on the lowest rungs of the teaching profession.

Since the influence of education feminism was patchy, leading as it did to small-scale school-based initiatives, it has appeared to have had little national impact. Moore suggests that it is highly implausible and unlikely that 'the success of girls could be attributed to the success of equal opportunities good practice' (Moore, 1996, p. 150). First, the association of changing educational practice and changing group attainment levels was not repeated elsewhere; second, the initiatives associated with this movement were not applied on a sufficient scale or for long enough to have an impact; third, there could even have been an inverse relationship of equal opportunities to school success since elite schools, which have contributed substantially to female educational success in the UK, arguably were less affected by feminist reforms. Finally, equal opportunities work was theoretically flawed and had not been evaluated properly. While not dismissing the significance of feminism for girls' success, Moore's argument sees its effects as mediated through class and racial inequalities, and through 'changing occupational aspirations, labour market conditions and family structures' (ibid.). Ideological position, educational attainments and social opportunities, he argues, are related paradoxically not serially. However, this thesis fails to recognise the extent to which feminism mobilised teachers as agents of change. Connell's comment reflects precisely the stance taken by the women's movement: 'it is teachers' work as teachers that is central to the remaking of the social patterns investing education' (Connell, 1985, p. 4).

As part of a counter-hegemonic movement, feminist teachers challenged the ways in which gender categories were constructed, reproduced and transmitted through schooling. They challenged the principles of the social order – the gendered principles for the distribution of power and social control – and the framing of a unitary social identity 'woman'. Feminism had essentially destabilised the category of femininity for a generation of young women by making the process of problematisation critical to identity formation. Being female became associated not with a static class-based categorisation but with a dynamic process of 'becoming'. Women, therefore, were encouraged to become actors within a set of social relations that were described as arbitrary not given. In Bernsteinian terms, the new integrative gender code would be one of weak gender categorisations and weak framing (−C−F). Research by a range of sociologists on young women's identities and aspirations[6] provides ample evidence for the transformative effects of such feminist praxis.

In *Closing the Gender Gap*, we argue that Western feminism was able to sustain its force by its institutional adaptability. It exploited the forms of voluntarism under the conditions of social democracy when teachers were assumed to have autonomy and arenas of curriculum discretion. It manipulated, where possible, the managerialism of the Conservative government's reforms – integrating equality of opportunity notions into debates about standards, performance and good schools. Gender issues were mainstreamed into concerns about quality of teaching, about improving school management, about effectiveness in teaching and in learning, and about addressing diversity and difference. School improvement as a theme was integral to the project of egalitarianism and vice versa. Indeed, as social inclusion became the antidote to excessive competitiveness, performativity and materialism, so feminist ideas about co-operation, collaboration, therapeutic models of counselling and person-centred management also became attractive. These concepts, along with 'feminisation of work place' and work cultures (Crompton, 1993) and interest in caring concepts of citizenship, are often taken as indicative of the mainstreaming of female culture.

Interestingly, sociological ethnographies have revealed major discursive shifts in young women's thinking in this period. In contrast, there has been comparatively little evidence of such shifts recorded among young men in the UK. The voices of young men captured by ethnographers demonstrate, if anything, the importance of traditional concepts of masculinity, especially in so far as it affects male bonds and friendships. Change appeared to come to young men less through the counter-hegemonic actions of egalitarian reformers or feminist campaigners than through changes in the structural relationships between schooling and the economy, especially through the policies of the Conservative governments of the 1980s and 1990s (Haywood and Mac an Ghaill, 1996). The policies of the New Right were more likely than feminist teachers to challenge boys' traditional gender identities. Paradoxically, as I argue below, despite supporting Victorian gender structures, the Conservative government of the 1980s and 1990s undermined the male role as head of household and breadwinner and created the educational conditions for change in gender relations.

The individualism of the New Right

Various crises throughout the 1970s – in the economy, in employment and in international competitiveness – led to a break-down in the political consensus about education in a social democracy. As we describe in our book, by the end of the 1970s there were criticisms of the welfare state and education was particularly attacked for not having helped sustain economic growth. The New Right targeted both for revision. On the one hand, they encouraged economic restructuring and, on the other, they initiated the destruction of communities based on industrial employment. Accompanying the growth of banking services and the re-emergence of the City of London as a global finance capital was a parallel decline in manufacturing industries and occupations, once central to the British economy. For example, in 1946 construction, mining and manufacturing industries provided 45 per cent of employment and service industries 36 per cent of jobs. In 1989, the three great industrial sectors made up just 25 per cent of jobs in the country, while the service sector accounted for 15 million jobs (almost 70 per cent of employment) (Arnot, David and Weiner, 1996).

The challenge to male working class hegemony was economic. During this era, traditional working-class communities lost their soul, with high levels of male unemployment and the need for women to support the family. The effect on family life was devastating. Women were often left as single parents in families without a male head of household. Traditional middle-class male work was also undermined through the restructuring of the service sector and the traditional professions, with many industries experiencing bankruptcies and redundancies. Boys therefore had to adapt to an increasingly insecure and different economic environment where the traditional transitions between school and work were broken (Pye, Haywood and Mac an Ghaill, 1996), where collectivism was replaced by individualism and self-help. The response of boys from different social groupings to post-Fordist schools and economy has been well researched in the UK. The evidence suggests that, on the whole, boys responded by sustaining strong gender boundaries except in those cases where they choose to move in the direction of new entrepreneurial cultures where such distinctions are less clear. In these cases, boys need to cope with learning subjects and courses that traditionally had been seen as female (media studies, business and commerce, languages). But for the majority, supporting traditional class-based male identities appears to be the norm. Young black and white men in the UK have been found to hold firmly onto romantic notions of traditional family values and the male breadwinning role, even though many can now speak the language of equal opportunities and women's rights. The pressures of social change, particularly it seems the weakening of the collective economic and familial bases of traditional masculinities, appear in the investment of manhood in physique (body, sport/fitness), sexual prowess and traditional patterns of male employment (Connell, 1989, 1997; Mac an Ghaill, 1988, 1994, 1996; Sewell, 1997).

The challenge to traditional gender power relations also received considerable support, paradoxically, from educational reforms which emphasised individual choice, competition and performance. As we have seen, by restructuring the educational system, the Conservative government, unintentionally and unwittingly also reshaped the modality of gender transmission (Arnot, 1993). New high-tech industry did not necessarily require a conventionally sex-segregated labour force and indeed the vocational courses which the Conservative government introduced into schools in the early 1980s highlighted this fact by using special funding to promote equal opportunities for both sexes.[7] The Education Reform Act intervened in gender relations by institutionalising a National Curriculum with its entitlement of nine subjects for all pupils – girls would now have to study science, mathematics and technology. A symbolic nail in the coffin for Victorian gender relations can also be found in this compulsory curriculum: it did not include domestic science for girls. In 1988, 42 per cent of girls had taken this subject – in 1993, only 15 per cent of girls were studying domestic science. The pattern from the 1970s, where boys and girls in England had almost separate educations and where boys had dominated the high-status subjects (e.g., mathematics and science), was dramatically changed. The new legislation, reinforced by the earlier introduction of the GCSE examination, appeared to remove most of the sex segregation of subjects up to sixteen from the public eye. Gender-differentiated choices were now made *within* subjects, through ability sets, tiered examinations and choices of modules – patterns that were hidden within individualising school practices. Statistics on male and female choices of subject components still demonstrated gender differences, but these statistics are unlikely to be part of the new public narrative around male and female education.

Gender orders, schooling and society

To conclude: girls' educational performance has been read by the UK media as a major challenge to male hegemony, asserting that now 'the future is female'. At one level, such media hype is right. There is evidence of a shift in the principles which govern gender power relations and their modes of transmission. The reproduction of gender relations is no longer through the dual system of male and female education which was established in the nineteenth century and perpetuated in schooling for the masses. The principle of gender differentiation which shaped the class-divided school system is now clearly neither as explicit nor as legitimate. It is more likely to be hidden within the individualising processes of learning than to be found in the formal structures of schooling.

Paradoxically, although male educational forms were being strengthened by the introduction of a National Curriculum (which was premised upon the curricula associated with elite male education), this reform undermined the strongly gender-differentiated curriculum of the 1970s. Gender differentiation which had been shaped by nineteenth-century educational ideals of the patriarchal family was less relevant to an educational system that was focused on standards, excellence and choice. Major gender differentiations, in effect, were delayed until after the end of compulsory education when the impact of the labour market had greatest effect. Within the new National Curriculum, girls could legitimately gain an advantage in terms of the acquisition of educational credentials and, encouraged by the ethos of the women's movement, could challenge conventional notions of gender difference. Thus, although the *educational codes* of schooling returned to the strong classificatory practices and strong control mechanisms (+C+F), the new *integrative gender codes* (−C−F) encouraged the redistribution of educational credentials and the negotiation of gender identities within education. The effects were, on the one hand, the rise in female performance and, on the other, the continuing strong effects of social class and ethnic differentiation (demonstrated by Gillborn and Mirza, 2000). Put sociologically, the principles which shaped the *distribution* of knowledge were changed even if the gendered hierarchies of knowledge remained intact. Within a newly structured educational system which aims to inculcate individualised learning and competence, the new gender order in the UK is more likely to be found in the micro-inequalities of schooling and in the more subtle differentiated curriculum tracks (Arnot, 2000).

Elite male dominance of the sciences and technology remains within and across class and was sustained more overtly in the post-compulsory sector. Here feminist presence had historically been much less than in the secondary and primary sectors of schooling. In the post-compulsory sector, with its transitions into further study and employment, the dominant modality of gender transmission (+C+F) remained, although girls have certainly carried forward their success in improving their academic performance. This may well be a class rather than a gender factor. Here, the redistribution of educational credentials have challenged but not necessarily removed the principles of gender classification and hence power relations.

The structures and processes of gender transmission for the elite, on the whole, have been retained. Boys from the dominant social classes could sustain what Connell (1987) argued were versions of 'gentry masculinity', based on scientific expertise and credentials. Ownership of such knowledge supported closure mechanisms for entry into high-status professional work and managerial positions of authority and control. Gender classifications at the top of the social hierarchy are transmitted conventionally and with great effect. Upper-middle-class girls have proved that they can achieve in the scientific worlds, but they still choose not to enter the scientific/technological spheres of employment. The language of individualisation becomes the means by which consent is achieved to male control of the environment, scientific policy-making and government. Thus the male hegemony of dominant social classes still retains its power.

There was no evidence that the range of economic and social reforms instigated by the Conservative government of the 1980s and the New Labour policies of the 1990s have fundamentally undermined the discriminatory practices governing male and female employment. Thus, although girls appeared to be strengthening their economic and social position by gaining access to higher-status male subjects and were seen to be doing well in them in the weakened gender boundaries of the school, there was no guarantee that such academic capital could be converted and indeed would be converted into academic and economic privilege. Thus, despite media panics, despite egalitarian social movements which attempted to redistribute male power, male dominance of academic capital is still intact. The conditions for sustaining male power, although different, are still in place.

Sociological analysis can help us understand the significance of gender relations and the role of education as a means of social reproduction. It points to the complex interaction of macro- and micro-influences on education, the interconnections between family and schooling and schooling and the economy. This gendered analysis has indicated the importance of exploring the ways in which social change impinges on social relations within and across such economic categories. In many ways, gender relations are symbolic of change in the forms of social control in our society.

Acknowledgements

The first version of this paper was presented at the UK–Japan Education Forum at Waseda University, Toyko, in 2000. I am very grateful to the Forum for allowing me to publish it here. My thanks to Miriam David and Gaby Weiner for allowing me to reproduce in this article material from our co-authored book *Closing the Gender Gap*, and to John Gray, Mary James and Jean Rudduck for permission to quote material from the OFSTED report which we co-wrote. I am also grateful to Rob Moore for engaging so generously in dialogue with me. The interpretations of the material and any errors are my responsibility.

Notes

1 By social reproduction theory I mean the development of theoretical understandings of the role of education in the production, reproduction and transmission of class, race and gender relations (see MacDonald, 1980, for a fuller discussion)
2 Other reports were produced for Wales (Salisbury, 1996), Scotland (Turner, Riddell and Brown, 1995) and Australia (Collins, Kenway and McLeod, 2000; Teese et al., 1995).
3 By comparing the gender gap in performance and the gender gap in entry it is possible to identify which sex is achieving particularly well or badly. If the size of performance gender gap is greater than the entry gender gap, the sex which is predominant in relation to entry is better than could be normally anticipated. The graphs for each subject show whether the performance gap is in favour of girls (+) or in favour of boys (−). Equality in terms of performance between the sexes would be indicated if the line approaches zero (Arnot, David and Weiner, 1996, p. 27, Appendix). The size of the gender gap in English (above the line) demonstrates the extent to which girls have sustained their advantage in this subject. In contrast, the reduction in the size of the gender gap in science and mathematics over the ten years, illustrates how boys' advantage in these subjects is being reduced. In 1985 there was a clear advantage in favour of boys; by 1994 the size of this advantage had reduced almost to zero in both subjects.
4 Data for 1995, for example, suggest that at A-level boys remain top academic achievers. More male students (10 per cent) than female students (7 per cent) secured the highest number of points (30+) accrued from A-level grades in different subjects.
5 Young women frequently choose business and commerce, hairdressing and beauty and caring service courses related to the female-identified sector of the labour market. Or, at university, women choose social studies, arts and humanities degrees.
6 For example, Griffin, 1985, 1989; Wallace, 1987; Weis, 1990; Mirza, 1992; Lees, 1993; Chisholm and du Bois-Reynaud, 1993; Bates, 1993; Sharpe, 1994; Basit, 1996; Skeggs, 1997.
7 See, for example, Haywood and Mac an Ghaill (1996) and Pye, Haywood and Mac an Ghaill (1996) for a discussion of how male trainees experience the relationship between school and work.

References and further reading

Arnot, M. (1982) 'Male hegemony, social class and women's education', *Journal of Education*, 164, 1, pp. 64–89.

—— (1983) 'A cloud over co-education: an analysis of the forms of transmission of class and gender relations', in S. Walker and L. Barton (eds) *Gender, Class and Education*, Lewes: Falmer Press.

—— (1986) 'State education policy and girls' educational experiences', in V. Beechey and E. Whitelegg (eds) *Women in Britain Today*, Milton Keynes: Open University Press.

—— (1987) 'Political lip-service or radical reform? Central government responses to sex equality as a policy issue', in M. Arnot and G. Weiner (eds) *Gender and the Politics of Schooling*, London: Hutchinson.

—— (1993) 'A crisis in patriarchy? British feminist education politics and state regulation of gender', in M. Arnot and K. Weiler (eds) *Feminism and Social Justice in Education: international perspectives*, London: Falmer Press.

—— (2000) 'Gender relations and schooling in the new century: conflicts and challenges', *Compare*, 30, 3, pp. 293–302.

Arnot, M. and Dillabough, J. (2000) (eds) *Challenging Democracy: international perspectives on gender, education and citizenship*, London: RoutledgeFalmer.

Arnot, M., David, M. and Weiner, G. (1996) *Educational Reforms and Gender Equality in Schools*, Research Discussion Series no. 17, Manchester: Equal Opportunities Commission.

—— (1998) *Closing the Gender Gap: postwar education and social change*, Cambridge: Polity Press.

Arnot, M., Gray, J., James, M. and Rudduck, J. (1998) *A Review of Recent Research on Gender and Educational Performance*, OFSTED Research Series, London: The Stationery Office.

Basit, T.N. (1996) 'I'd hate to be just a housewife: career aspirations of British Muslim girls', *British Journal of Guidance and Counselling*, 24, 2, pp. 227–42.

Bates, I. (1993) 'A job which is right for me? Social class, gender and individualisation', in I. Bates and G. Riseborough (eds) *Youth and Inequality*, Buckingham: Open University Press.

Bernstein, B. (1971) 'On the classification and framing of educational knowledge', in M. Young (ed.) *Knowledge and Control: new directions for the sociology of education*, London: Collier-Macmillan.

Bourdieu, P. (1977) 'The economics of linguistic exchange', *Social Science Information*, 16, 6, pp. 645–68.

Burstyn, J. (1980) *Victorian Education and the Ideal of Womanhood*, London: Croom Helm.

Burton, L. and Weiner, G. (1990) 'Social justice and the National Curriculum', *Research Papers in Education*, 5, 3, pp. 203–28.

Cheng, Y., Payne, J. and Witherspoon, S. (1995) *Science and Mathematics in Full-time Education after 16*, Youth Cohort Report no. 36, London: Department for Education and Employment.

Chisholm, L. and du Bois-Reynaud, M. (1993) 'Youth transitions, gender and social change', *Sociology*, 27, 2, pp. 259–79.

Collins, C., Kenway, J. and McLeod, J. (2000) *Factors Influencing the Educational Performance of Males and Females in School and their Initial Destinations after Leaving School*, Commonwealth Department of Education, Training and Youth Affairs, Deakin University.

Connell, R.W. (1985) *Teachers' Work*, London: Allen & Unwin.

—— (1987) *Gender and Power: society, the person and sexual politics*, Cambridge: Polity Press.

—— (1989) 'Cool guys, swots and wimps: the inter-play of masculinity and education', *Oxford Review of Education*, 15, 3, pp. 291–303.

—— (1990) 'The state, gender and sexual politics', *Theory and Society*, 19, pp. 507–44.

—— (1997) 'The big picture: masculinities in recent world history', in A.H. Halsey, H. Lauder, P. Brown and A.S. Wells (eds) *Education, Culture, Economy and Society*, Oxford: Oxford University Press.

Crompton, R. (1993) *Class and Stratification: an introduction to current debates*, Cambridge: Polity Press.

DfEE (2000) http://www.standards.dfee.gov.uk/genderandachievement/2000_data_5.html

Dillabough, J. (2000) 'Women in teacher education: their struggles for inclusion as "citizen-workers" in late modernity', in M. Arnot and J. Dillabough (eds) *Challenging Democracy: international perspectives on gender, education and citizenship*, London: RoutledgeFalmer.

Dyhouse, C. (1981) *Girls Growing up in Late Victorian and Edwardian England*, London: Routledge & Kegan Paul.

Epstein, D., Elwood, J., Hey, V. and Maw, J. (eds) (1998) *Failing Boys, Issues in Gender and Achievement*, Buckingham: Open University Press.

Felstead, A., Goodwin, J. and Green, F. (1995) *Measuring up to the National Training Targets: women's attainment of vocational qualifications*, Research Report, Centre for Labour Market Studies, University of Leicester.

Foster, V. (2000) 'Is female educational "success" destabilising the male-learner citizen?', in M. Arnot and J. Dillabough (eds) *Challenging Democracy: international perspectives on gender, education and citizenship*, London: RoutledgeFalmer.

Gillborn, D. and Mirza, H.S. (2000) *Educational Inequality: mapping race, class and gender*, London: OFSTED.

Griffin, C. (1985) *Typical Girls? Young women from school to the job market*, London: Routledge & Kegan Paul.

—— (1989) 'I'm not a woman's libber, but … . Feminism, consciousness and identity', in S. Skevington and D. Baker (eds) *The Social Identity of Women*, London: Sage.

Haywood, C. and Mac an Ghaill, M. (1996) 'What about the boys? Regendered local labour markets and the recomposition of working class masculinities', *British Journal of Education and Work*, 9, 1, pp. 19–30.

Hillman, J. and Pearce, N. (1998) *Wasted Youth: raising achievement and falling social exclusion*, London: Institute for Public Policy Research.

Joint Council for General Qualifications (2001) News Releases: 'A Bumper Year for Examinations – over 1.65 million results', 15 August.

Lees, S. (1993) *Sugar and Spice: sexuality and adolescent girls*, Harmondsworth: Penguin.

Lowe, R. (1997) *Schooling and Social Change, 1964–1990*, London: Routledge.

Mac an Ghaill, M. (1988) *Young, Gifted and Black*, Buckingham: Open University Press.

—— (1994) *The Making of Men: masculinities, sexualities and schooling*, Buckingham: Open University Press.

—— (ed.) (1996) *Understanding Masculinities*, Milton Keynes: Open University Press.

MacDonald, M. (1980) 'Socio-cultural reproduction and women's education', in R. Deem (ed.) *Schooling for Women's Work*, London: Routledge & Kegan Paul.

Marks, J. (2001) *Girls Know Better: educational attainments of boys and girls*, London: Civitas (Institute for the Study of Civil Society).

Marshall, T.H. (1950) *Citizenship and Social Class and Other Essays*, Cambridge: Cambridge University Press.

Mirza, H. (1992) *Young, Female and Black*, London: Routledge.

Moore, R. (1996) 'Back to the future: the problem of change and the possibilities of advance in the sociology of education', *British Journal of Sociology of Education*, 17, 2, pp. 145–61.

Pateman, C. (1988) *The Sexual Contract*, Cambridge: Polity Press.

Phillips, A. (1991) *Engendering Democracy*, Cambridge: Polity Press.

Purvis, J. (1985) *The History of Women's Education*, Buckingham: Open University Press.

Pye, D., Haywood, C. and Mac an Ghaill, M. (1996) 'The training state, de-industrialisation and the production of white working class trainee identities', *International Studies in Sociology of Education*, 6, 2, pp. 133–46.

Quicke, J. (1999) *A Curriculum for Life*, Buckingham: Open University Press.

Raphael Reed, L. (1999) 'Troubling boys and disturbing discourses on masculinity and schooling: a feminist exploration of current debates and interventions concerning boys in school', *Gender and Education*, 11, 1, pp. 93–110.

Salisbury, J. (1996) *Educational Reforms and Gender Equality in Welsh Schools*, Cardiff: Equal Opportunities Commission.

Salisbury, J. and Jackson, D. (1996) *Challenging Macho Values: practical ways of working with adolescent boys*, London: Falmer Press.

Sewell, T. (1997) *Black Masculinities and Schooling*, London: Trentham Books.

Sharpe, S. (1994) *Just Like a Girl: how girls learn to be women*, 2nd edn, Harmondsworth: Penguin.

Skeggs, B. (1997) *Formations of Class and Gender*, London: Sage.

Spender, D. (1987) 'Education: the patriarchal paradigm and the response to feminism', in M. Arnot and G. Weiner (eds) *Gender and the Politics of Schooling*, London: Hutchinson.

Stone, L. (ed.) (1994) *The Education Feminism Reader*, London: Routledge.

Teese, R., Davies, M., Charlton, M. and Polesel, J. (1995) *Who Wins at School? Boys and girls in Australian secondary education*, Department of Education Policy and Management, University of Melbourne.

Tolson, A. (1977) *The Limits of Masculinity*, London: Tavistock.

Turner, E., Riddell, S. and Brown, M. (1995) *Gender Equality in Scottish Schools: the impact of recent educational reforms*, Glasgow: Equal Opportunities Commission.

UCAS (2000) http://www.ucas.ac.uk/figures/archive/gender/index.html

Walkerdine, V. (1983) 'It's only natural: rethinking child-centred pedagogy', in A.M. Wolpe and J. Donald (eds) *Is There Anyone Here from Education?*, London: Pluto.

Wallace, C. (1987) 'From girls and boys to women and men: the social reproduction of gender', in M. Arnot and G. Weiner (eds) *Gender and the Politics of Schooling*, London: Hutchinson.

Weiler, K. (1988) *Women Teaching for Change*, New York: Bergin & Harvey.

Weiner, G. (1993) 'Shell-shock or sisterhood? English school history and feminist practice', in M. Arnot and K. Weiler (eds) *Feminism and Social Justice in Education: international perspectives*, London: Falmer Press.

Weiner, G. and Arnot, M. (1987) 'Teachers and gender politics', in M. Arnot and G. Weiner (eds) *Gender and the Politics of Schooling*, London: Hutchinson.

Weis, L. (1990) *Working Class without Work: high school students in a de-industrialising economy*, New York: Routledge.

Wilkinson, H. (1994) *No Turning Back: generations and the genderquake*, London: Demos.

Wollstonecraft, M. (1792) *A Vindication of the Rights of Woman*, Harmondsworth: Penguin; reprinted 1985.

10 *Schooling in Capitalist America* revisited

Social class, gender and race inequalities in the UK

Twenty-five years after the publication of Sam Bowles and Herb Gintis' seminal text, I would like to pay tribute to the importance of *Schooling in Capitalist America* (1976) as one of the most significant and groundbreaking texts within the sociology of education in the post-war period. My first encounter with it was in 1976, the year the book was published, when I joined the *Schooling and Society* team at the Open University in England. My colleagues, Roger Dale and Geoff Esland, who had discovered the book on their travels in the US, arranged for it to be published in the UK. Our careers were shaped by the exposure of Sam Bowles and Herb Gintis' arguments, along with other neo-Marxist theories of education, to critical debate. Because we used the book as compulsory reading for the 2,000 teachers who took the course each year, we were pilloried in the press and even in Parliament for Marxist bias. We had apparently perverted the liberal project of education, exposing its economic determinants in a cynical and pessimistic way.

Despite all the criticisms of methodology, theory and interpretation of the text, we took the view in our own book *Schooling and Capitalism* (Dale, Esland and MacDonald, 1976) that the relationship between education and the economy posited by these authors was one of the most serious and original interventions in educational thinking at the time. It provided the agenda for sociology of education for the next ten years, focusing attention on the structures and processes of social reproduction, raising questions about the role of the state within and between education and the economy, and querying the nature of class conflict and resistance within this relationship.

My second encounter with *Schooling in Capitalist America* was in 1980 when I was asked, for the first time, to write an article on gender relations and education. I chose to engage critically with theories of social reproduction using this new political lens (see Chapter 2 of this volume). I argued then, and I want still to argue today, that while Bowles and Gintis were fundamentally correct in their analysis they were also importantly wrong in other respects. They had failed to capture the complexity of the education–economy relationship because they had failed to recognise the primacy and significance of gender and race relations. Schooling, and the economy, had patriarchal and race relations as deeply embedded within them as they had social-class relations. The passing and somewhat fragmentary references to gender and race in the public and private spheres (which was not unusual at the time) would mean that the analysis of *intra-class differentiations*, *conflicts and change* had not been built into the account.

In this, my third encounter, I want to argue that in some sense the thesis presented in *Schooling in Capitalist America* has proved, in one respect, to be more salient and, in another, to be even more limited. In the case of the first, I will argue that the education–economy relationship has become even closer than before and yet, as I shall show, in terms of gender relations, schooling rather than being determined by economic forces has contributed in a major way to the transformation of gender relations within and across social classes and ethnic groups. Key to this tension are the discursive shifts in the contemporary social identities of young people, combined with the rise of credentialism in the new generation. As social-class theorists Marshall (1997), Marshall, Swift and Roberts (1997) and historians such as Roy Lowe (1997) recognise in relation to gender, we are at a point historically of greatest contradiction. Far greater proportions of young people achieve school certification and enter higher education, and the emphasis is upon pupils becoming more flexible and committed learners. At the same time, the pattern of social-class, racial and gender inequalities in the labour market are as prevalent and determining as before. These social contradictions, a much neglected theme within social reproduction theory of the mid-1970s, should be at the core of sociology of education and it is in this context that gender and class relations must now be understood.

In this chapter, I shall talk briefly about class reproduction and the education–economy link, and then move on to the findings of research on shifting gender inequalities in education and what this might mean for a re-reading of Bowles and Gintis' thesis.

Class reproduction theory

Bowles and Gintis' thesis was that the 'long shadow of work' stretched back from the industrial sectors into the very structure and processes of schooling. Using the correspondence principle to highlight the social and educational stratification of the school system, they argued that schools, rather than serving meritocracy, were instead preparing a future generation of workers for their place within the industrial order. They highlighted the ways in which the social relations of production were mirrored in the social relations of schooling with different intended outcomes. This analysis relied heavily upon the political and economic relationship established historically between the educational system and the emerging forms of corporate capitalism. Education was understood, in all its diversity, to be the central agency for the social reproduction of the class structure, thus challenging the liberal mythology of equality of opportunity and social progress.

The significance granted to the education–economy relationship within capitalist formations was not only correct but far-reaching in its implications.

Indeed, in the last twenty-five years, we have seen a deepening of the 'long shadow of work' into mass schooling in the US, and also in the UK and other corporate capitalist economies. In the UK, the so-called 'secret garden of the curriculum' has been transformed through state intervention. The curriculum has been made compulsory by the state to meet the needs of standardisation and mass upskilling in relation to literacy and numeracy. More recently, schools have been encouraged to adapt the compulsory curriculum to meet the needs of flexibilisation and individual diversification (DfEE, 2001). Economic imperatives have also led to the introduction, through financial incentives, of new vocational curricula, new entrepreneurialism in school curricula in the 1980s, the promotion of ICT in schools – making technology a core subject in secondary schools – and a wealth of new vocational qualifications (NVQs, GNVQs) which were meant to offer parity of esteem to, and transferability between, vocational subjects and traditional academic subjects. Higher education has been expanded and new initiatives around lifelong learning have attempted to address the needs of post-Fordist economies for flexibility in the work force (Macrae, Maguire and Ball, 1997).

These economic imperatives have been matched by major restructuring at the organisational level of schooling from the early years through to tertiary education and adult education. Marketisation as a principle has promoted the notion of educational products, delivery systems for the curriculum, evaluation of learning outcomes, inspection systems and a high level of competitiveness between individual pupils, members of staff and institutions as a whole. Schools are more not less regulated, despite the narratives of devolution, deregulation, autonomy and promotion of popular control and parental choice in relation to schools.

Associated with such reform agendas have been severe social-class inequalities in educational performance and employment prospects. Despite the rise in credentials of the new generation of pupils, and despite the increase in access to higher education, the gap between the working class and upper middle (professional) classes in the UK is still substantial. For example, patterns of class inequality in secondary education have been sustained throughout the last twenty-five years even though students are leaving with far more qualifications than ever before (Gillborn and Mirza, 2000). In 1993, the National Commission of Education confirmed that children from the professional middle class do far better on average in examinations at sixteen in the UK. Furlong and Cartmel's (1997, p. 21) study of Scottish school-leaver patterns suggests that only a small proportion of working-class young adults reached the highest attainment band (three or more Highers). Under 20 per cent of working-class youth achieved this level compared with 40–50 per cent of young people in the professional and managerial classes.

McCulloch's (1998) review of the theory and practice of working-class secondary education in the UK reveals the resilience of class antagonisms and differentiation across two centuries. He found that:

> social differentiation has been a major and resilient underlying influence in secondary education, from the efforts to bridge the divide between the secondary education associated with the middle classes and the elementary education of the working class that were characteristic of the late nineteenth century, to the establishment of the tripartite system that underpinned secondary education for all in the twentieth century. Division, hierarchy and social inequality have been basic continuities in educational provision.
>
> (McCulloch, 1998, p. 157)

The values of a class society which were associated with Victorian nineteenth-century industrial order, the welfare state of the post-war period and the affluent society of the 1950s and 1960s have left a legacy of 'deep seated conflicts and contradictions' (ibid., p. 158). There was a belief that some strategies could promote the upward social mobility of able children from the working classes, and some even attempted to find 'an authentic and respectable' alternative model of education for all working-class children. However, according to McCulloch, neither of these approaches fundamentally challenged the tradition of social differentiation which had been built into the warp and weft of schooling and is still one of the key principles of educational provision. Thus, 'class-based provision has persisted through changing circumstances, surviving relatively unscathed the educational and social reforms of the twentieth century' (ibid., p. 159). 'Division, hierarchy and social inequality', as Bowles and Gintis had pointed out in the American context, had been built effectively into the English system of secondary education.

Despite such continuity, different mechanisms are now in use to sustain class patterns of education. For example, New Right (and arguably New Labour) strategies such as the so-called 'marketisation' of education and the promotion of parental choice of schools have affected the form of class reproduction through education. As Ball (1990), David, West and Ribbens (1994), Gewirtz, Ball and Bowe (1995), Reay and Ball (1997) and Reay (1998), for example, have shown in their research, 'choice' is a concept which differentiates between social classes and effectively hides the fact that it does so. Middle-class families are able to use their material and symbolic advantages to increase their privileges through market strategies and high-status choices, while working-class families choose schools, courses and higher-education routes according to different principles that rationally reflect their much-reduced material circumstances. The class strategies of the professional classes have revealed their flexibility as well as their success at class reproduction.

Partly as a result of the class inequalities in schooling, and partly as a result of government reforms of higher education, there has also been little substantial change in the class inequalities associated with university education. There had been little change over the years in the proportion of entrants who come into higher education from working-class families. In 1963, the Robbins Report found that undergraduates were six times more likely to come from non-manual backgrounds than from manual backgrounds. Marshall, Swift and Roberts (1997), using data from 11,000 young people from 1960 onwards, found that, even though young people from working-class families have become more likely to secure ordinary qualifications, persistent inequalities can be found in access to degree-level qualifications. Farrant (1981) showed that between 1962 and 1977, although there had been a 7.5 per cent increase in middle-class student numbers, there was only a 1.8 per cent increase in working-class student numbers – a pattern also confirmed by Egerton and Halsey's (1993) major study of access to higher education. Using a sample of 25,000 people born in three different cohorts (1985, 1986, 1987), they confirmed that, despite the fact that the proportion of each social class entering higher education had increased, there was a pattern of relative social-class disadvantage (despite decreasing disadvantage for women). Plummer (2000, p. 38) quotes UCCA 1992 figures which show that students from the middle classes (I, II and IIIa) represented some 71 per cent of applications and 75 per cent of university places. In contrast, students from manual working-class backgrounds (III, IV and V) represented 20 per cent of applicants and 18 per cent of places. Only 1 per cent of applications came from students from Class V (unskilled manual classes) and they were allocated 1 per cent of places. Thus the last twenty years of higher-education expansion, with the doubling of student numbers, has had relatively little impact on entrants from the working classes. Broadly speaking, approximately 80 per cent of children from low-income groups do not go to university or college in the UK while 80 per cent of higher-income children do (*TES*, 6 November 1998, quoted in Plummer, 2000, p. 38).[1] This class gap has been aggravated in the UK by the removal of grants to cover university fees and maintenance (Reay et al., 2001). Here again, class reproduction has not only been secured but strengthened.

Finally, there also has been much debate about the impact of education on social mobility and employment. Saunders (1997) argued that Britain is now more meritocratic and that academic ability and merit are important determinants of economic position. However, other evidence from class theorists such as Marshall, Swift and Roberts (1997) suggests that – even though there is some social mobility in Britain and in other industrialised nations – when educational attainment is held constant, social origins still exert important influence on class destinations. Using data from 4,000 individuals in 1981, 1987 and 1992, these authors found that class injustice is still present in terms of occupational success. They concluded that:

> the reality of modern Britain is that people from different class origins have unequal chances not only of educational but also of occupational success, despite taking actual credentials into consideration; and that these class processes are evident among men and women alike.
>
> (Marshall, Swift and Roberts, 1997, p. 85)

Class differences have been the enduring feature of the educational system from the nineteenth century through to the early twenty-first century. The educational mechanisms through which such class inequalities are reproduced (although different from those used in the mid-1970s) are therefore in line with the structuring principles of correspondence theory. However, the correspondence between schooling and the field of production has become that much more nuanced and differentiated *within* social classes. Students are being differentiated now through new, more subtle forms of tracking (setting) and through diverse achievement patterns. As Power (2000) argues, educational pathways through public and private schools and through higher- and low-status universities and degrees contribute to the horizontal differentiation not just of working and middle classes but also of the middle classes themselves. Such differentiations separate out those who take up traditional careers within the professional middle classes and those who employ their cultural capital.

Bowles and Gintis' theory, while powerful in its structural analysis, was unfortunately weakened by its failure to engage with the nature of class culture, identities and class formation. By limiting their analysis primarily to economic factors, Bowles and Gintis failed to discern what Diane Reay called 'the myriad ways in which social class differences contribute to social inequalities' (Reay, 2000, p. 259; see also Mahony and Zmroczek, 1997). Social class, as we now know it, is about the 'dynamic mobile aspects of identity' (ibid.). In this context, we can begin to think not just about class reproduction, but also *class formation* and the role of production, consumption, community and family values within the latter processes. Furlong and Cartmel (1997) argue that most class analyses in education veer between political arithmetic traditions and approaches which focus on the processes of social reproduction and have rested upon 'fairly traditional conceptualisations of class'. Today these conceptualisations are 'increasingly inappropriate for a post-Fordist society', especially when talking about youth, since youth cultures now cross class boundaries and may no longer reflect class divisions as strongly as they did ten years ago (cf. Mac an Ghaill, 1994; Sharpe, 1994). The processes of social reproduction implicated in such theories would now need to take account of the fact that the transitions from school to work on which the correspondence principle was premised are more protracted and complex – what Beck called 'elongated transitions' (Beck, 1992, p. 7). Young people as a result have grown up in different social conditions from their parents and their identities will be shaped as much by the processes of individualisation and risk (cf. Beck, 1992) as by traditional class relationships.

However, Carter (1997) suggests that even recent post-Fordist analyses of the education–economy relationship fail to take account of social changes concerning gender and ethnicity/race. Mid- and late twentieth-century capitalism was built upon particular racialised and gendered patterns and on particular linkages between public and private worlds. Without recognition of non-class social divisions, such economic analyses run with 'an overly simplified and homogenised view of the social world' (Carter, 1997, p. 50). Gender and race relations, thus, offer clear-cut examples of the limitations of social reproduction and later post-Fordist analyses. One of the most interesting challenges to Bowles and Gintis' thesis, if it is to sustain its relevance, I want to argue, is whether it can conceptualise and work with the shifting patterns, for example, of female education and employment in contemporary society.[2] In the next section I shall draw upon my 1980 critique of *Schooling in Capitalist America* and the body of evidence collected over the last ten years about girls' educational performance and occupational position in the UK to reassess their theory of social reproduction.

Gender relations and social reproduction of class

My argument (MacDonald, 1980; see Chapter 1 in this volume) with Bowles and Gintis' theory of schooling and the economy initially was that, although Bowles and Gintis recognised the segmentation and segregation of the primary and secondary labour markets and the allocation of what they called 'the most oppressed groups' (blacks, Puerto Ricans, Chicanos, Native Americans) to the secondary labour market, they failed to analyse the gendered aspects of labour-market segmentation as one of the most significant features of the capitalist formation. Therefore, they could not take adequate account of the significance of the sexual division of labour in the home and in the work place as key to the segmentation of the labour force, nor did they recognise the ways in which patriarchal power structures had shaped the social relations of production. Gender relations (like race relations) were reduced to the status of integration of 'exogenous ideological factors' not dissimilar to other social prejudices which had been adapted and used by capitalism. Thus no material basis for male power was identified, nor was there sufficient recognition of the strength of gender relations as strong determining influences in shaping the school system.

As a result, Bowles and Gintis failed to grapple with the complex relationship between the public and private sphere which critically affected the relationship between the family, schooling and the production processes. The reproduction of family–work relations through schooling was significant for both men and women's position in the occupational structure. As Butler and Savage (1995) argue, men's occupational status and mobility was conditional upon channelling women into inferior low-status work situations with no career-like trajectory. Also, the reproduction of male class position through work deeply affected family forms and their control of women.

The family–education couple, as David (1978) argued at the time, was central to the processes of class and gender reproduction. Bowles and Gintis addressed this by arguing that 'there was a significant correspondence between the authority relations of capitalism and family childrearing', particularly in so far as:

> the male-dominated family with its characteristically age-graded patterns of power and privilege, replicates many aspects of the hierarchy of production in the firm.
>
> (Bowles and Gintis, 1976, p. 141)

They argued that families also produce sex-typing, which encourages women to take up their inferior status in the wage-labour system. However, the thesis failed to notice the much more significant role that families play in relation to class reproduction, through the formation of identity, authority relations, class cultures and forms of resistance to schooling and through the mediation of different material circumstances. Arguably, the social relations of the family historically have been as determining an influence on the shape of schooling, its authority relations, its shaping of the concept of teacher and the curriculum. The 'long shadow' of the family has influenced what Bernstein (1975) called 'the expressive order of the school', or what Bourdieu (1993) called its 'institutional habitus'.

In 1976, when *Schooling in Capitalist America* was published, women were not expected to bear the costs of their reproduction – as a result they were educated to be dependent upon men and were given salaries or wages which reflected that dependency. In fact, the hiring of female labour was deeply contradictory for capitalism, given the requirements to sustain the social order. Family stability could ensure the socialisation of its members in the legal and moral order associated with production, the nurturance of the future work force and the psychological and physical well-being of adult workers. For these reasons, schooling played a key role in sustaining patriarchal domestic relations and women's dual position in both waged and domestic work. In the early 1980s, I argued that any theory of correspondence of schooling and the economy required an analysis of the particular relationship between men and women's education and *both* their destinations within family and work (Arnot, 1984). I also argued that the special circumstances of female education could not be subsumed within the normative male models of class, education and occupational destination. At the time, while the education of men appeared to involve *direct* forms of reproduction described by Bowles and Gintis, the education of women was *indirect* – their class position apparently ensured through an education which stressed the importance of marriage, temporary/casual 'traditionally female-type' employment and motherhood (see Chapter 1 in this volume). The way in which such indirect reproduction worked was primarily through the domestication of women using a curriculum and school experience that had little of the same resonances associated with the male personality traits, occupational routes and educational trajectories described by Bowles and Gintis.

The class cultures of young people before and during their schooling, as sociologists later showed, were the result of pupils acting as go-betweens – as mediators between family class cultures and the cultures of employment, not just the product of the latter (Connell et al., 1982). Middle-class family cultures were understood as bearers of economic, social and symbolic resources or capital which brought social advantage within the school system, especially if coupled with material resources. As New Right agendas called upon family values and parental concerns, the unequal distribution of such symbolic resources (the forms of economic, cultural and social capital) between working-class and middle-class families became the central mechanism by which social inequalities were sustained at each major transition point in education. Families, not just children, have been brought inside (rather than left outside) the modalities of social reproduction.

Since the key role of the family and of gender relations within class reproduction had been underplayed in *Schooling in Capitalist America*, the thesis was not conceptually powerful enough to address the nature and extent of social and educational change. Family change has become more not less crucial to our understanding of social change and the ways in which education functions within the social structure. Indeed, Beck (1992) argues that gender transformations in the family are symbolic of the shift in economic orders and the development of what he called 'the risk society'. In our book (Arnot, David and Weiner, 1999), we confirm just how critical family change was to the transformation of girls' education in the late twentieth century. Contestation of Victorian family values was a linchpin in girls' struggle for the right to gain equal access to full and high-status employment and economic independence. In our analysis of the transformation of girls' education in the last twenty years in the UK, we highlight the ways in which family change, alongside political reforms and economic restructuring, transformed existing 'modalities' of class reproduction for girls. We describe (a) the rise of the female graduate elite and (b) the restructuring of working-class girls' preparation for their class position. Although in these cases the class position of women is secured, the role of education in the social reproduction of gender and class relations is not the same as that described in *Schooling in Capitalist America*. Below, I discuss each of these themes in turn.

The rise of a female graduate elite

One significant advance in education in post-war British society was the expansion of what we called a 'female graduate elite'. Halsey (1997) describes how, between 1970 and 1989, the number of male undergraduates rose by 20 per cent while the number of female students on full-time courses rose by 114 per cent. Many of these students were likely to come from the predominantly white, professional middle classes, having attended selective state or independent schools. The adaptation of selective and independent fee-paying girls' schools to new economic and social opportunities and the compromises reached with feminism in the twentieth century offer interesting examples of increasing incorporation into the correspondence principle. Such schools historically played a particular role in the stratification of the work force described by Bowles and Gintis. Their role was to prepare young women of the upper class and upper middle class for marriage into those social classes. However, by the mid- to late twentieth century, they were preparing elite schoolgirls for formal qualifications and entry into higher-level professional work. Liberation became synonymous with personal autonomy, individualism and a career in high-status professions.

The social reproduction of the middle-class woman had been ensured in the past primarily through marriage rather than qualifications or skill training. The domestic sphere, therefore, dominated over the public sphere. Delamont suggests that such schools had educated the daughters of the upper class and upper middle class to be 'the most influential group in rearing and marrying men who are the most successful products of the British educational system' (Delamont, 1989, p. 5). The ideology of achievement presented to girls with academic aspirations involved imitating and encouraging masculine and masculinist habits of intellectual self-assertion and rational thinking (Evans, 1991, p. 20). Evans recalls the impossibility in the 1950s of accommodating the two-fold aim of trying to 'find a man' and acquiring learning: rather, she suggests,

> The world of the traditional grammar school provided an apparently perfectly coherent and congruent training ground for the managers – and their wives – of the new Elizabethan world.
>
> (Evans, 1991, p. 40)

Yet girls' stories about their lives in such schools reveal the successful exploitation of precisely the post-war (male) meritocratic ethos that Bowles and Gintis discussed and the development of elite education within an individualistic world. At the same time, these schools were also affected by feminist discourses, even if only those concerning equal rights to the same class status.

The ethnographic studies of mainly white, elite girls point to the fact that when they place themselves at the centre of their ambitions, they threaten a world in which marriage is the main instrument of class reproduction. Girls from this social group were increasingly encouraged, through high academic achievement, to take responsibility for their own class reproduction. However, there was also the danger that they might become downwardly mobile by choosing occupations unsuitable for their class status. Initially channelled away from powerful positions in control of finance, economy and politics, according to Connell et al. (1982) upper- and middle-class young women were encouraged to enter what were termed 'the semi-professions' (e.g., teaching, nursing), which seemed less able to threaten the reproduction of the patriarchal order. The voices of elite schoolgirls show the elaborate mechanisms that were in place to encourage their ambitions beyond that of becoming leisured housewives, yet also to police the boundaries of their aspirations so that they did not challenge the male dominance of the status quo.

Class differences among women have historically been expressed in terms of exclusionary distinctions between different forms of femininity – for example, the working-class 'good woman' and the upper- and middle-class 'perfect lady' (Purvis, 1989). In several studies of elite-educated girls, specific forms of femininity produced anxiety about how to sustain social distinctions between elite girls and girls from other social groups. Key markers (geographic, cultural, class) allowed the girls to define their superiority. In this context, although girls' individualism remained based upon a subversion of the patriarchal order, it was also associated with a series of damning comparisons with other girls, inscribed in Kenway's study as non-ladylike, 'lazy', 'dirty', 'having poor speech' and being sexually promiscuous (Kenway, 1990). Fine class distinctions based upon consumption patterns such as fashion and holidays were also used by the girls to differentiate various cliques within their schools. Girls at the Ladies School in Perth were categorised as either 'boarding' or 'day' girls, 'trendies' or 'rejects' (ibid., pp. 141–6).

By the late 1990s, elite girls appeared to be aiming for and achieving the highest educational levels both at school and university, regardless of whether this alienated young men. In this sense, they had become incorporated finally into the educational forms associated with male forms of class reproduction. By developing careers, middle-class women are effectively shifting the relations between public and private spheres in ways that have, according to Crompton (1995), major implications for class formation (and reproduction).

First, middle-class girls' level of formal qualifications has risen very rapidly. It was anticipated that these trends would result in more women moving into middle-class positions in the primary labour market and that they would make an impact on the vertical segregation of the market. However, gender parity has not been achieved by any means. While more women have entered the professional middle classes, they are more likely to be found in 'practitioner roles' (Butler and Savage, 1995, p. 65), in specialist niches which require the possession of specific expertise rather than managerial 'careerist' roles which offer positions of authority and control. The new scenario means that there will be new gendered internal demarcations but, while women may predominate in such occupations, men are still likely to dominate. Sex-typing of jobs and the patterns of sex discrimination mean that middle-class women are still confronted by the glass ceiling. The impact of this new female graduate elite, some argue, is more likely to be found in the increase in changed management practices such as flexible working patterns, the shift from 'a predominantly masculine to a more heterogenously gendered aggregation of occupations' and internal resegregation by sex within different middle-class occupations (Crompton, 1995, p. 72).

According to Anne Witz (1995), women's entry into middle-class employment in recent years has also challenged middle-class men's closure strategies which used to be based upon credentialism. Male mobility in the past had depended largely on the mobilisation of cultural educational assets (rather than property or organisational assets), access to which is patriarchally structured. It also depended on female immobility. Witz argues that:

> the collective exclusion of women from the institutional means of acquiring specialist knowledge throughout the nineteenth century and well into the twentieth century is now well documented … and the dispropor-

> tionate increase in the numbers of women occupying expanding service-class positions today has been one result of the opening up of higher education to middle-class women since the 1940s. Thus, one key historical way of restricting access to service-class positions has been the use of credentialist tactics by men of this class.
>
> (Witz, 1995, p. 49)

To say that class relations within middle-class families are static from the point of view of these women would also be an error. Clearly *within*-class cultures are being transformed by new sets of gender relations. Professional women are likely to make different demands on family life. They have fewer children, later in life, and expect different forms of support from men (hence the high divorce rate) and contribute far more directly to the processes of class formation through *economic capital* rather than domestic pedagogic work (Bourdieu, 1977).

The rise of the professional woman therefore has challenged the model of the male breadwinner within the middle-class household. As Witz argued, the professional middle classes relied on home-based mothers and upon male power – in the future there will be interesting possibilities of coalition and conflict in terms of intra- and inter-class relationships. Professional middle-class women encourage new models of middle-class solidarism, new relationships between public and private spheres, and new models of masculinity and femininity (Crompton, 1993). At the same time, the incomes of professional women also facilitate home ownership and increased family consumption, and they provide cultural capital in their own right (especially in relation to the value of education). The expansion of educational and hence work opportunities for professional middle-class women, therefore,

> may have the effect of widening the gulf between the most materially advantaged and disadvantaged households in Britain.
>
> (Crompton and Sanderson, 1990, p. 166, quoted in Witz, 1995, p. 55)

Thus, in the future, social class inequalities in the UK are likely to be critically associated with the unequal earning power and status of working-class and professional women.

Working-class girls' identities: from romanticism to pragmatism

The social reproduction of working-class girls' labour market position has differed in form and complexity from that of upper-middle-class girls. White working-class girls' schooling had more in common with working-class boys' achievement patterns than with elite girls. Recently, Gillborn and Mirza (2000) demonstrated that while gender differences in educational achievement are small rationally, substantial social-class inequalities in education have been present over the last ten years. However, they also argue that, when class is controlled for, there are still significant attainment differences between different ethnic groups. Both male and female black middle-class pupils performed little better than their white peers from the manual working classes. They argue that social-class disadvantage has only a limited effect on ethnic groups. The 'race' gap in educational performance is not only large but is even increasing in some contexts.

Working-class girls and boys have been particularly affected both by government policies which undermine traditional working-class communities and by educational reforms in the name of egalitarianism. As a result, Miriam David, Gaby Weiner and I argued (1999), the role which education plays within their lives as schoolgirls has changed. Schooling still provides an *indirect* mode of social reproduction (MacDonald, 1980; see Chapter 1 in this volume), but not in the same way as it did in the 1970s, since it now creates major contradictions between education and female economic positioning. Key to this shift has been the transformation of the social relations of schooling and the curriculum introduced by New Right performance discourses but also the introduction of different meritocratic discourses.

Schools as institutions have played a key role in challenging the gendered curriculum and traditional female pathways into social-class destinations. Thus, while the forms of labour market segmentation, particularly the vertical and horizontal segregation of male and female work in the secondary labour market, have remained resistant to change, nevertheless there has been a shift in the forms (modalities) of social reproduction. Therefore, as Lowe (1997) pointed out, the qualifications for women in the UK are at the highest they have ever been, yet at the same time the pattern of sex segregation in the labour market has not only been sustained but, in some cases, it has been even more divisive and oppressive to women than previously. Considerable tension now exists between female aspirations for autonomy and personal freedom and the reality of their material circumstances. Paradoxically, as Skeggs (1997) and other youth researchers show, girls overcome this contradiction by using the discourse of individualisation and choice.

Using the data from studies of working-class girls over the last twenty-five years, we see how the education–economy relationship has been affected by economic restructuring. For middle-class girls, the transition to adulthood lies within known parameters, even if the pathway is individualised, highly competitive and pressurised. For aspiring working-class girls, a vision of the future is less available. 'Distinctive orientations' have been found among schoolgirls towards formal education, employment and personal life goals (Chisholm and du Bois-Reynaud, 1993). Working-class girls' voices captured by researchers have suggested the possibilities of, in Bernsteinian terms, 'an interruption' in the processes of social reproduction – a transitional phase which disrupts, yet also sustains, the maintenance of the status quo.

The role of schools in the reproduction of working-class women's occupational/class position is, therefore, more contradictory than that suggested by the correspondence principle. In the 1970s, schools promoted – at least rhetorically – equality of opportunity, yet they also transmitted traditional notions of feminine sexuality and a domestically oriented curriculum. Social-class reproduction through education, therefore, was through the transmission of middle-class family values which dictated a moral/academic curriculum that was suitable for child care and domesticity for working-class girls. White working-class girls appeared to have come to terms with their class fate through, as Angela McRobbie found, a 'remarkable if complex homogeneity' that involved the 'ultimate if not wholesale endorsement of the traditional female role and of femininity, simply because to these girls, these seemed to be perfectly natural' (McRobbie, 1978, p. 97).

The white young working-class women who were interviewed by McRobbie and Garber (1975) and McRobbie (1978) spoke of the prospect of a romanticised future. To Claire Wallace (1987) a decade later, such girls still appeared to be 'inordinately preoccupied with romance'. The impression was given that white working-class girls were immersed in the ideology of romance and glamour as an expression of female sexuality, celebrating what they took to be their fate – marriage and motherhood – but in ways that offered realistic assessments of what marriage consisted of and that avoided thinking about the domestic drudgery of the home. Marriage in this context seemed to be used both to confer status and to express individuality and sexuality. There was little evidence of the personality traits associated with subordination – rather there was a celebration of an alternative occupational and sexual future.

In the mid-1980s, sex segregation of the labour market and working-class women's position within the secondary market was ensured through the identification of white working-class girls' identification with *female* work – they were not prepared to take up male employment which was seen as hard, manual, dirty and noisy. Despite rising unemployment, femininity for most girls was still more linked to boyfriends, marriage and motherhood than the wage packet (Griffin, 1985, p. 99). In that sense, schools were effectively helping prepare girls for the conditions of the labour market through indirect rather than direct modes of social reproduction (MacDonald, 1980).

By the end of the 1980s, however, there was evidence that this seemingly intransigent set of girls was on the move as a result both of shifts within the labour force and of changes within the family. The restructuring of the economy and in particular the severe reduction of the industrial manufacturing base had led to high rates of working-class male unemployment and the destruction of working-class communities (Arnot, David and Weiner, 1999). Working-class girls could no longer rely upon the economic support of their menfolk as breadwinners, fathers and husbands. In this context, the concepts of individualisation and of female autonomy had particular material and symbolic resonance.

In 1987, Wallace reported that young working-class women were displaying what she termed 'unromantic realism' – an unromantic perception of the relationship between men and women and women's destiny. Girls had begun to distance themselves from centuries of emotional and financial dependency on men. Similarly, the Ealing girls interviewed by Sue Sharpe in the early 1990s seemed to find it unthinkable to give up work automatically after marriage, or indeed after children. Their mothers' occupations, often seen as limiting and 'boring', were of little interest. Girls wanted more interesting job-content and higher levels of satisfaction. At the same time, as Sharpe commented, compared with previous generations: 'girls are less hampered by fears of maternal deprivation but guilt can still be provoked and nursery provision remains sadly lacking' (Sharpe, 1994, p. 220). The notion of education for individual social mobility appeared to be taking hold, even if only as an aspiration.

Other groups of similarly less-privileged girls already appear to have held longer-term perceptions about education, work and independence. Education was a means of moving across class as well as breaking out of traditional gender and racial classifications. Since the 1980s, studies (Sillitoe and Meltzer, 1985; Eggleston et al., 1986) indicated that young, black women obtained numerically more qualifications than other groups, though often in FE colleges rather than schools. In contrast to the teachers who perceived them as 'diffident and devious', the young women interviewed by Mac an Ghaill in 1988 reported exploiting the school system to help in coping with the realities of what they saw as increased competition for scarce local jobs. Examination qualifications, they believed, would provide them with exchange value in the labour market and an opportunity to escape conventional forms of black female work (Mac an Ghaill, 1988, p. 32):

> Ye can't get anywhere without qualifications. We have to be better than the whites if we want to get away from the usual cleaning jobs an shop work we're offered. I sometimes think that they built the hospitals, railways an all that to keep us working (Joanne).
>
> (ibid., p. 33)

The group of African-Caribbean girls interviewed by Heidi Mirza in the late 1980s also talked about their families' encouragement in helping them to use the educational system as a means of upward mobility, albeit collective rather than individual, out of their class and racialised positions. Their expressed desire for social mobility was interpreted by Mirza as an orientation towards 'strategic careers' that challenged gender stratification in pragmatic and rational ways (Mirza, 1992).

The high proportion of African-Caribbean schoolgirls who opted for non-traditional courses such as plumbing, electronics and carpentry provides evidence of their greater gender independence when compared with their white, female peers. African-Caribbean girls appeared to have 'relative autonomy' in pioneering new school and career pathways, and in choosing economic independence over dependence on men. Femininity in their language was not tied to dominant 'Eurocentric attitudes about gender oppositions' (Mirza, 1992, p. 159). 'Getting on' (cf. Brown, 1987) for such girls meant 'staying on' at school, with many transferring to further and higher education and aspiring to high-status professions.

Access to the caring professions, such as nursing and social work, was one means of gaining occupational mobility (Bhavnani, 1991). Such jobs, girls claimed, would also allow them to move up and out of their mothers' low-status factory or office work, and provide financial benefits and status for black women and their families. Many young black women, however, faced major forms of sexual and racial discrimination and were often 'downwardly mobile' (Wallace, 1987). White women, as Butler and Savage argue, have been 'better placed to benefit from widened educational opportunities and have moved close to making up half of the labour force' (Butler and Savage, 1995, p. 79). Black women, in contrast, face considerable disadvantages in employment. All indicators suggest that racial as well as gender discrimination is still built into the labour market.

Nevertheless, in 1996 Basit found high aspirations among a group of British-Asian Muslim fifteen- and sixteen-year-old girls she interviewed who did not want to be 'just a housewife'. Although many of their fathers were unemployed or in working-class occupations, they felt supported by their families in their wishes to become lawyers, doctors, accountants and pharmacists, or to start their own businesses. Debnath's study of young working-class Bangladeshi women in the East End of London also reported high aspirations, even if it meant leaving the community (Debnath, 1999). Such studies suggest that girls from different Asian communities, whatever their class, ethnic or religious backgrounds, hope to have careers and incomes in their own right and in middle-class occupations (Bhavnani, 1991).

Two major (and not unconnected) discursive shifts affected the interrelations between education and the class structure as far as white and black working-class girls were concerned – *feminism* and *individualisation*. The impact of *feminism* on young women's lives cannot easily be explained through correspondence theory, nor indeed through a theory of social reproduction which does not take account of cultural and political discursive shifts. Such political movements signal not just a strong sense of agency but also the complex relationship between culture, identity and class formation. In the 1990s, Sharpe found that a group of working-class schoolgirls from various ethnic backgrounds 'resoundingly admitted' the impact that feminism had on women's role, status and equal opportunities in employment:

> The ways girls see themselves and their lives have altered with the social and economic change of the intervening twenty years, reflecting changes in the structure and stability and a rise in the status of women – at least in women's eyes.
>
> (Sharpe, 1994, p. 220)

According to Sharpe, more schoolgirls preferred 'being a girl' than twenty years earlier, having rejected conventional views about gender difference and male dominance, and having seemingly acquired a greater sense of women's worth, individuality and independence. Differences between white and African-Caribbean girls, in terms of valuing qualifications and staying on at school, had *decreased*, as white working-class girls seemed more recently to have come to share African-Caribbean and Asian girls' understanding of the possibilities of education as a means of achieving autonomy and independence.

Although Griffin (1989), for example, found in her study of working-class girls that many began with 'I'm not a woman's libber, but … ', at the same time they often appeared to draw on feminism to understand their own lives and the diverse and contradictory discourses which are available to them. Traditional class-based discourses of gender still remain, yet working-class girls have to now synthesise their experience of gender relations, a plethora of different and often contradictory forms (and images) of femininity in the mass media (Skeggs, 1997), and feminist programmes of reform which encourage new political and educational affiliations.

The complex interconnections between the *individualisation* of young women and the reproduction of their class position in the labour market are captured vividly by sociologists who focus on the transition from school to work. Paradoxically, many young working-class women will convert their academic capital into traditional working-class jobs. They do not have the power to convert their academic capital into economic capital in the labour market, nor, in contrast with the female upper middle classes, are they able to challenge the sex-segregated structures in the secondary sector of the labour market. Instead, and with great pragmatism, training courses which draw upon the domestic and caring skills learnt in the home are used by working-class girls as 'domestic apprenticeships' (Skeggs, 1988). The outcomes are a training in dependency, low pay and 'realistic' expectations of their futures (Buswell, 1992, p. 94). Thus, when Bates asked groups of young working-class women about these training courses, the processes of individual self-realisation and greater emphasis upon autonomy and 'self-actualisation' seemed unable to dislocate traditional forms of class and gender reproduction. On the contrary, class and gender reproduction appeared to be reinscribed by 'the care girls' as they consciously 'chose' traditional and low-status work as carers (Bates, 1993a). Bates discovered that they had reconstructed their individual biographies (e.g., family experiences) so as better to adapt to the occupational cultures they faced. For example, they redefined low-skilled, often 'dirty' or difficult, occupations as 'tough female work' and as appropriate for them since they were 'no bleeding whining Minnies' (ibid., p. 28). According to Bates:

> Reflexive individualism facilitated not the fulfilment of [Kay's] 'original' ambitions (she had wanted to be a secretary), but a re-invention of ambitions in line with labour market prospects.
>
> (ibid., p. 23)

In this instance, the process of using values of personal reflexivity and self-actualisation (individualisation) facilitated the reconstruction of social injustice as justice and the conversion of 'fate' to choice or, in one trainee's term, as a 'job which is right for me'.

In contrast, those girls on fashion and design courses who spoke to Bates about their ambitions to have designer careers revealed many of the features of individualisation but less of the pragmatism of the other group. They aspired to have their own design studio and to enter a world of glamour where there were opportunities for individual creativity, the prospect of 'loads of money' and the appeal of owning a business. As Bates argues:

> In other words, it offered all the attractions of a post-Fordist, individualist, enterprise career path that could be carved out in an international arena, transcending the generally more fettered forms of female labour. It was a high risk step into the future, reflecting ambitions formed in the context of a melange of interrelated late/post modern social influences: individualisation; the cult of the 'designer'; youth sub-cultures which centre their creativity on dress; ideologies of equal opportunities and 'post-feminism'.
>
> (Bates, 1993b, p. 72)

Shifting patterns of class formation

It would seem that two trends have become visible *within* female class relations in the latter part of the twentieth century. The role of schooling has been transformed within the lives of both middle-class and working-class girls, affected as they have been by shifting economic realities and opportunities and by the discursive, cultural shifts associated with late modernity. Here both feminism, as a political movement, and reflexive individualisation have been referred to. However, as Skeggs points out, the complexity associated with identity formation in the late twentieth century is much more complex.

I have argued so far that upper-middle-class girls and their particular form of schooling (often in private single-sex girls' schools) appear to have been incorporated more fully within the forms of class reproduction associated with upper-middle-class men. This form of schooling offers a training, as Bowles and Gintis suggested, in leadership and the confidence to aspire to high-status professions. Girls from these backgrounds are now expected to ensure their own class status through qualifications, higher education and entry into one of the top professions. At the same time, middle-class values around notions of femininity, like those of *gentry masculinity* (described by Connell, 1997) are still priorities within schooling. Rather than being marginal, they frame the career routes within primary labour markets and professional occupations, differentiating men and women within the professional classes.

Within this elite sector the diffusion of individualising discourses has given middle-class girls considerable educational advantage, but when found within the working classes they have different resonances and repercussions. Beck (1992) saw clearly that the process of individualisation which used to be claimed largely for the developing bourgeoisie is now affecting all other social groups. Entry into the labour market now requires individual mobility, ascribed biographies have become transformed into reflexive biographies, and traditional categories such as class and estates (traditional modes of capitalist social stratification) are relinquished. To this extent, all social groups are being incorporated into the imperatives of capitalism. Although individualisation represents an emancipation from feudal relations and also class, neighbourhood, occupation and culture, and although social-class identities are no longer at the core of social identities, nevertheless social-class power does not disappear just because traditional ways of life fade away. If Beck is right, then the identification with, and positioning within, individualising discourses could possibly be seen as yet another variation of the processes of working-class 'embourgeoisement'.

It is interesting to note that, in their famous study entitled *The Affluent Worker*, Goldthorpe et al. (1969, p. 24) argued that full 'embourgeoisement' occured only if the working classes acquired all *three* of the following elements:

The Economic (income living standards)
The Normative (new social outlook and values)
The Relational (being accepted as equal by middle-class society)

Although the working classes in the 1960s had raised their incomes in certain occupations, they had only acquired one of these three elements of middle-class culture and status. The taking up of middle-class life styles did not replace social-class differences, nor indeed was it a process of assimilation of working-class communities. Thus,

> A break with working-class traditionalism need not take the form of a shift in the direction of 'middle classness' and that evidence of the former cannot therefore be taken as evidence of the latter.
>
> (ibid., p. 159)

Today, Diane Reay argues that the 'permeation' of new middle-class values within the working classes has been 'disastrous' (Reay, 1997, p. 23), precisely because it has displaced collectivist understandings of the self in relation to the social group. The 'triumph of individualism' (ibid., p. 20) has threatened the collective inclinations and identities of working-class groups. They are in retreat or denial. The working classes are no longer entitled to a 'sense of unfairness' since everything is the reponsibility of individuals – everything 'from their financial situation, the state of their health to their children's schooling has been repackaged under late capitalism' and is understood to be the responsibility of the individual alone rather than society. The dilemmas of a middle-class education and the adoption of middle-class individualising values are even greater than before since there are few 'politicising scripts of class oppression' to counter such views (ibid., p. 23). Chisholm argues that 'to take one's own fate in one's hands is personally emancipatory but it is not socially emancipatory' (Chisholm, 1995, p. 47). Partial autonomies are purchased at some cost for the working-class girl. As Diane Reay comments:

> If you have grown up working class you know that the solution to class inequalities does not lie in making the working classes middle class but in working at dismantling and sharing out the economic, social and cultural capital that goes with middle class status.
>
> (Reay, 1997, p. 23)

In effect, working-class girls today are encouraged to adopt the normative outlook and values of the upper middle classes (i.e., individualisation) without any of their economic power and, indeed, without being accepted as part of the middle class. In the context of sex-segregated labour markets and vulnerable communities, it is more likely that the language of individualisation becomes a mechanism for legitimating gender divisions and class inequalities rather than a mechanism for 'liberation' or 'embourgeoisement' in its fullest sense. Unlike their upper-middle-class sisters, for working-class girls, this discourse with its normative middle-class elements (deferred gratification, social mobility) thus becomes the mechanism for their class reproduction. In this context, the relationship between schooling and the economy, therefore, is much more complex than allowed by 'the correspondence principle'.

Conclusions

Sociologists of education are now faced with the task of relating theories of late modernity and of class dominance. The arguments put forward by Bowles and Gintis in 1976 do not easily square with Beck's (1992) thesis, since Beck argues that not only has the economic order been fundamentally transformed but so too are the mechanisms of social reproduction. Beck argues that people are beginning to be 'set free' from the social forms connected with industrial society. Through a process of *detraditionalisation*, class culture and class consciousness (like gender and family roles) will pale in significance and it will 'happen in a social surge of individualisation' (ibid., p. 87). Even if relations of inequality remain relatively stable, the modernist links between family and occupation will break down. Individuals will have to plan their own individual labour market biographies.

Beck argues that a new history of social class is emerging through the collective experience of individualisation and atomisation. The social-class society described by Bowles and Gintis, with its segmentations and stratifications, its forms of alienation and collective struggles over education, will be replaced by *the individualisation of social inequality* – a class society which is constituted by an 'individualised society of employees' (Beck, 1992, p. 100). Concepts of social mobility will be 'meaningless and disappear'. Inequalities, rather than being reproduced by appropriate 'personality traits', will become 'psychological dispositions'. Social inequality will be considered to be 'classless', since unemployment will be transformed into notions of personal failure rather than class failure, gender status and social-class status will be relinquished, the spirit of individualisation will lead to families in which negotiation is the norm, and individuals themselves will be the key agents of social reproduction, mediating their lives through the processes of 'life planning and organisation'.

However, not everyone is prepared to go so far down this path. Furlong, for example, takes the view that, although 'there is evidence that class cultures are weakening and that the subjective experience of risk is present throughout the class structures' (Furlong, 1998, p. 596), there is also evidence that class identities are being reconstructed within particular geographic and social spaces (Cohen, 1997; Skelton and Valentine, 1998). Instead, there is a complex interface of material and discursive locations and dispositions which is perhaps best described by Roberts, Clark and Wallace's (1994) concept of *structured individualisation*. These processes of structured individualisation are embedded not just within the economic and cultural spheres, but also within the family, the site of class and gender formations. The experience of this process therefore differs in important ways in terms of social class, gender and ethnicity.

Significantly, shifting female class relations and their associated family relations are beginning to contribute to mainstream social-class theory. Goldthorpe and others do now recognise that the specific location of women in the occupational structure affects the distribution of men's life-chances. The rather tentative conclusions of Marshall et al. are an example of this shift in approach to gender issues:

> class systems are structured by sex in ways that clearly affect the distribution of life-chances, class formation and class action among both women and men alike … [T]he mobility chances of men are themselves dependent on a pronounced degree of sexual differentiation in the social division of labour, that is at the level of the class structure as a whole. Classes and class phenomena are conditioned by the peculiar pattern of women's participation (however intermittent) in the market for paid labour.
>
> (Marshall et al., 1988, p. 73, quoted in Witz, 1995, p. 42)

Anne Witz rightly argues that it is difficult to ignore the ways in which gender is implicated in the reproduction of the class system. Gender matters in education and in employment and the family are central to the notion of class formation and hence reproduction through education. Gender achievement patterns in education have major implications for intra- and indeed inter-class solidarity. What is needed, therefore, is a thorough rethink of contemporary conceptualisations of class formation so as to appreciate its gender dynamics.

> [W]e need a new concept of class formation in order to describe the processes and mechanisms whereby occupational structures of 'places'

> emerge and gendered 'persons' come to be associated with them over time, and indeed how these two processes are not necessarily sequential.
>
> (Witz, 1995, p. 43)

In this chapter I have demonstrated that recent research supports Bowles and Gintis' argument about the 'enduring relevance' of social-class analysis, albeit in more sophisticated form, for understanding the contemporary structures of industrial society (Bonney, 1998, p. 601). There does not appear to be any diminishing of social-class differences in the twentieth century – the inequalities of educational opportunities remain. As Bonney argues:

> Contrary to liberal theories of industrialism, the expansion of advanced educational places is no guarantor of increased relative educational and social openness in social class terms.
>
> (ibid., p. 602)

At the same time, the onus is upon Bowles and Gintis, and those who return to their work, to take up the challenges offered by feminist class theory and feminist educational research.

Acknowledgements

I would like to thank Alan Sadovnik and Susan Semel for inviting me to participate in the twenty-fifth anniversary symposium at the American Research Association Conference, Seattle, in 2001, Sam Bowles for his response to my paper at the conference and Jo-Anne Dillabough and Diane Reay for their comments on the drafts. I would also like to thank Miriam David and Gaby Weiner for allowing me to draw upon some of the arguments and, on occasion, the text of *Closing the Gender Gap*, which we co-authored. The errors and misinterpretations are mine alone.

Notes

1 There is similar under-representation of ethnic minorities in higher education in the UK (Skellington with Norris, 1992).
2 Other social-class theorists have been seriously challenged to address gender theory (see, for example, Butler and Savage, 1995; Marshall, Swift and Roberts, 1997; Devine, 1998).

References and further reading

Arnot, M. (1982) 'Male hegemony, social class and women's education', *Journal of Education*, 164, 1, pp. 64–89.

—— (1984) 'A feminist perspective on the relationship between family life and school life', *Journal of Education*, 166, 1, pp. 5–24.

Arnot, M., David, M. and Weiner, G. (1999) *Closing the Gender Gap: postwar educational and social change*, Cambridge: Polity Press.

Ball, S.J. (1990) *Politics and Policy Making in Education: explorations in policy sociology*, London: Routledge.

Basit, T.N. (1996) 'I'd hate to be just a housewife: career aspirations of British Muslim girls', *British Journal of Guidance and Counselling*, 24, 2, pp. 227–42.

Bates, I. (1993a) 'A job which is right for me? Social class, gender and individualisation', in I. Bates and G. Riseborough (eds) *Youth and Inequality*, Buckingham: Open University Press.

—— (1993b) '"When I have my own studio": the making and shaping of designer careers', in I. Bates and G. Riseborough (eds) *Youth and Inequality*, Buckingham: Open University Press.

Beck, U. (1992) *Risk Society: towards a new modernity*, London: Sage.

Bernstein, B. (1975) *Class, Codes and Control*, vol. 3, London: Routledge & Kegan Paul.

Bhavnani, R. (1991) *Black Women in the Labour Market: a research review*, Manchester: Equal Opportunities Commission.

Bonney, N. (1998) 'The class war continues', *Sociology*, 32, 3, pp. 601–5.

Bourdieu, P. (1977) *Outline of a Theory of Practice*, Cambridge: Cambridge University Press.

—— (1993) *Sociology in Question*, London: Sage.

Bowles, S. and Gintis, H. (1976) *Schooling in Capitalist America: educational reform and the contradictions of economic life*, London: Routledge & Kegan Paul.

Brown, P. (1987) *Schooling Ordinary Kids: inequality, unemployment and the new vocationalism*, London: Tavistock.

Buswell, C. (1992) 'Training girls to be low paid women', in C. Glendinning and J. Millar (eds) *Women and Poverty in Britain: the 1990s*, Hemel Hempstead: Harvester Wheatsheaf.

Butler, T. and Savage, M. (eds) (1995) *Social Change and the Middle Classes*, London: UCL Press.

Carter, J. (1997) 'Post-Fordism and the theorisation of educational change: what's in a name?', *British Journal of Sociology of Education*, 18, 1, pp. 45–61.

Chisholm, L. (1995) 'Cultural semantics: occupations and gender discourse', in P. Atkinson, B. Davies and S. Delamont (eds) *Discourse and Reproduction: Essays in honour of Basil Bernstein*, Creskill, NJ: Hampton Press.

Chisholm, L. and du Bois-Reynaud, M. (1993) 'Youth transitions, gender and social change', *Sociology*, 27, 2, pp. 259–79.

Cohen, P. (1997) *Rethinking the Youth Question: education, labour and cultural studies*, London: Macmillan.

Cole, M. (ed.) (1988) *Bowles and Gintis Revisited: correspondence and contradiction in educational theory*, Lewes: Falmer Press.

Connell, R.W. (1997) 'The big picture: masculinities in recent world history', in A.H. Halsey, H. Lauder, P. Brown and A.S. Wells (eds) *Education, Culture, Economy and Society*, Oxford: Oxford University Press.

Connell, R.W., Ashenden, D.J., Kessler, S. and Dowsett, G.W. (1982) *Making the Difference: schools, families and social division*, Sydney: Allen & Unwin.

Crompton, R. (1993) *Class and Stratification: an introduction to current debates*, Cambridge: Polity Press.

—— (1995) 'Women's employment and the middle class', in T. Butler and M. Savage (eds) *Social Change and the Middle Classes*, London: UCL Press.

Dale, R., Esland, G. and MacDonald, M. (eds) (1976) *Schooling and Capitalism*, London: Routledge & Kegan Paul.

David, M.E. (1978) 'The family–education couple: towards an analysis of the William Tyndale dispute', in G. Littlejohn, B. Smart, J. Wakeford and N. Yuval Davis (eds) *Power and the State*, London: Croom Helm, pp. 158–96.

—— (1980) *The State, the Family and Education*, London: Routledge & Kegan Paul.

—— (1993) *Parents, Gender and Education Reform*, Cambridge: Polity Press.

David, M.E., West, A. and Ribbens, J. (1994) *Mothers' Intuition: choosing secondary schools*, London: Falmer Press.

Debnath, E. (1999) *Youth, Gender and Community Change: a case study of young Bangladeshis in Tower Hamlets*, unpublished Ph.D. dissertation, University of Cambridge.

Delamont, S. (1989) *Knowledgeable Women*, London: Routledge.

Devine, F. (1998) 'Class analysis and the stability of class relations', *Sociology*, 32, 1, pp. 23–42.

DfEE (2001) *Schools:* Building on Success*, Green Paper (Cm 5050), Norwich: The Stationery Office.

Egerton, M. and Halsey, A.H. (1993) 'Trends by social class and gender in access to higher education in Britain', *Oxford Review of Education*, 19, 2, pp. 183–96.

Eggleston, J., Dunn, J., Anjali, M. and Wright, C. (1986) *Education for Some: the educational and vocational experiences of 15–18 year olds, members of minority ethnic groups*, Stoke-on-Trent: Trentham Books.

Evans, M. (1991) *A Good School: life at a girls' grammar school in the 1950s*, London: Women's Press.

Farrant, J. (1981) 'Trends in admissions', in O. Fulton (ed.) *Access to Higher Education*, Guildford: SHRE.

Furlong, A. (1998) 'Youth and social class: change and continuity', *British Journal of Sociology of Education*, 19, 4, pp. 591–7.

Furlong, A. and Cartmel, F. (1997) *Young People and Social Change: individualisation and risk in late modernity*, Buckingham: Open University Press.

Gewirtz, S., Ball, S. and Bowe, R. (1995) *Markets, Choice and Equity in Education*, Buckingham: Open University Press.

Gillborn, D. and Mirza, H. (2000) *Educational Inequality: mapping race, class and gender*, London: OFSTED.

Goldthorpe, J.H., Lockwood, D., Bechhofer, F. and Platt, J. (1969) *The Affluent Worker in the Class Structure*, Cambridge: Cambridge University Press.

Great Britain. Committee on Higher Education (1963) *Higher Education* (the Robbins Report), 1961–63, 14 vols, London: HMSO.

Griffin, C. (1985) *Typical Girls? Young women from school to the job market*, London: Routledge & Kegan Paul.

—— (1989) 'I'm not a woman's libber, but … . Feminism, consciousness and identity', in S. Skevington and D. Baker (eds) *The Social Identity of Women*, London: Sage.

Halsey, A. (1997) 'Trends in Access and Equity in Higher Education: Britain in an international perspective', in A. Halsey, H. Lauder, P. Brown and A. Stuart-Wells (eds) *Education: Culture, Economy and Society*, Oxford: Oxford University Press.

Hillman, J. and Pearce, N. (1998) *'Wasted Youth': disaffection and non participation amongst 14–19 year olds in education*, London: Institute for Public Policy Research.

Kenway, S. (1990) 'Privileged girls, private schools and the culture of success', in J. Kenway and S. Willis (eds) *Hearts and Minds: self esteem and the schooling of girls*, London: Falmer Press.

Lowe, R. (1997) *Schooling and Social Change, 1964–1990*, London: Routledge.

Lucey, H. and Walkerdine, V. (2000) 'Boys' underachievement: social class and changing masculinities', in T. Cox (ed.) *Combating Educational Disadvantage*, London: Falmer Press.

Mac an Ghaill, M. (1988) *Young, Gifted and Black*, Milton Keynes: Open University Press.

—— (1994) *The Making of Men: masculinities, sexualities and schooling*, Buckingham: Open University Press.

MacDonald, M. (1980) 'Socio-cultural reproduction and women's education', in R. Deem (ed.) *Schooling for Women's Work*, London: Routledge & Kegan Paul.

—— (1981) *Class, Gender and Education*, Units 10/11 E353, Milton Keynes: Open University Press.

Macrae, S., Maguire, M. and Ball, S. (1997) 'Whose "learning" society? A tentative deconstruction', *Journal of Educational Policy*, 12, 6, pp. 499–509.

Mahony, P. and Zmroczek, C. (eds) (1997) *Class Matters: women's perspectives on social class*, London: Taylor & Francis.

Mann, C. (1998) 'The impact of working class mothers on the educational success of their adolescent daughters at a time of social change', *British Journal of Sociology of Education*, 19, 2, pp. 211–26.

Marshall, G. (1997) *Repositioning Class: social inequality in industrial societies*, London: Sage.

Marshall, G., Newby, H., Rose, D. and Vogler, C. (1988) *Social Class in Modern Britain*, London: Hutchinson.

Marshall, G., Swift, A. and Roberts, S. (1997) *Against the Odds? Social class and social justice in industrial societies*, Oxford: Clarendon Press.

McCulloch, G. (1998) *Failing the Ordinary Child? The theory and practice of working class secondary education*, Buckingham: Open University Press.

McRobbie, A. (1978) 'Working class girls and the culture of femininity', in Women's Studies Group, *Women Take Issue: aspects of women's subordination*, London: Hutchinson, in association with the CCCS.

McRobbie, A. and Garber, J. (1975) 'Girls and subcultures: an exploration', in S. Hall and T. Jefferson (eds) *Resistance through Rituals: youth subcultures in postwar Britain*, London: Hutchinson.

Mirza, H. (1992) *Young, Black and Female*, London: Routledge.

Moore, R. (1996) 'Back to the future: the problem of change and the possibilities of advance in sociology of education', *British Journal of Sociology of Education*, 17, 2, pp. 145–61.

Power, S. (2000) 'Educational pathways into the middle class(es)', *British Journal of Sociology of Education*, 21, 2, pp. 133–45.

Plummer, G. (2000) *Failing Working Class Girls*, London: Trentham Books.

Purvis, J. (1989) *Hard Lessons: the lives and education of working class women in nineteenth century England*, Cambridge: Polity Press.

Reay, D. (1997) 'The double bind of the "working class" feminist academic: the success of failure or the failure of success?', in P. Mahony and C. Zmroczek (eds) *Class Matters: women's perspectives on social class*, London: Taylor & Francis.

—— (1998) 'Engendering social reproduction: mothers in the marketplace', *British Journal of Sociology of Education*, 19, 2, pp. 195–209.

—— (2000) 'Rethinking social class: qualitative perspectives on class and gender', *Sociology*, 32, 2, pp. 259–75.

Reay, D. and Ball, S.J. (1997) '"Spoilt for choice": the working classes and educational markets', *Oxford Review of Education*, 23, 1, pp. 89–101.

Reay, D., Ball, S., David, M. and Davies, J. (2001) 'Choices of Degree or degrees of choice? Social class, race and the higher education choice process', *Sociology*, 35, 4, pp. 855–74.

Roberts, K., Clark, S.C. and Wallace, C. (1994) 'Flexibility and individualism: a comparison of transitions into employment in England and Germany', *Sociology* 28, 1, pp. 31–54.

Saunders, P. (1997) 'Is Britain a meritocracy?', in B. Cosin and M. Hales (eds) *Families, Education and Social Differences*, London: Routledge.

Sharpe, S. (1994) *Just Like a Girl: how girls learn to be women*, Harmondsworth: Penguin.

Sillitoe, K. and Meltzer, H. (1985) *The West Indian School Leaver*, vol. 1, *Starting Work*, London: OPCS, Social Survey Division, HMSO.

Skeggs, B. (1988) 'Gender reproduction and further education: domestic apprenticeships', *British Journal of Sociology of Education*, 9, 2, pp. 131–49.

—— (1997) *Formations of Class and Gender*, London: Sage.

Skellington, R. with Norris, P. (1992) 'Race', in *Britain Today*, London: Sage.

Skelton, T. and Valentine, G. (eds) (1998) *Cool Places: geographies of youth subcultures*, London: Routledge.

UCCA (1993) *Statistical Supplement, 1991–2*, London: UCCA.

Wallace, C. (1987) 'From girls and boys to women and men: the social reproduction of gender', in M. Arnot and G. Weiner (eds) *Gender and the Politics of Schooling*, London: Hutchinson.

Weis, L. (1990) *Working Class without Work: high school students in the de-industrialising economy*, New York: Routledge.

Witz, A. (1995) 'Gender and service class formation', in T. Butler and M. Savage (eds) *Social Change and the Middle Classes*, London: UCL Press.

11 Basil Bernstein's sociology of pedagogy

Female dialogues and feminist elaborations

Although not 'primarily known for writing about gender' (Delamont, 1995, p. 323), Basil Bernstein's theory of pedagogy has played a fascinating role in the development of gender theory in sociological studies of education. First, there is an international group of feminist academics who have chosen to position themselves within this male-defined and -controlled intellectual field by engaging with Bernstein's theoretical project – an exploration of the modes of educational transmission and production. Second, there are female scholars who would not necessarily wish to be labelled as feminist yet have used Bernstein's theory to explore gender relations and difference in the family and various educational contexts. Third, there is the gendering of theory that occurs not merely through male academic discourses but also when women scholars construct their own sociological theory. In this context, female theorists of pedagogy who draw upon Bernstein's conceptual framework or research problematic are interesting in their own right. Preparing this chapter seemed a golden opportunity to ask these different groups of female academics, many quite noted in their field, if they could describe the nature of their engagement with Bernstein's work. This chapter explores the subjective positioning of women academics in relation to male theory and considers how such intellectual encounters contribute to the development of gender theory.

Not surprisingly, given the complex and abstract nature of Bernstein's theory, the group of female academics I made contact with constituted a small, highly selected group. They are located in countries as culturally diverse as Australia, Colombia, Japan, Portugal, Spain, South Africa, the United States and the United Kingdom. Many in the group (including myself) had been graduate students of Bernstein and have since become colleagues or had come across his work in their graduate years. I asked everyone the same questions: Could they describe how they discovered Bernstein's theory? What was the nature of the encounter? Which texts and/or concepts influenced them the most? How did they come to apply his theory to their work? How did they see the relationship between Bernstein's theories of education and the study of gender and feminism?

Although not all of the group addressed every question, what was immediately striking was how extraordinarily delighted most were to be asked such questions, even by an intrusive stranger. Despite the personal nature of the questions, almost everyone quickly and enthusiastically came back with answers.[1] Clearly these academic encounters with Bernstein's theory had been personally meaningful. The conceptual work had been hard, but it had also been rewarding. The fascination with Bernstein's theory was not constructed in these accounts as a matter of belief, a conversion to a fashion or fad, but rather a commitment to theoretical/conceptual thinking. The female academics came across as reflexive and highly sophisticated, committed researchers who were unlikely to shrink from any intellectual challenge. The power of their responses was indicative of the strength rather than the oppressed status of these female scholars.

The focus of this chapter, therefore, is not a critique of Bernsteinian theory. Nor do I make any claims on the basis of this evidence about whether the female engagements with Bernstein's theory of pedagogy are characteristically different from male engagements with his work. That would take more research. Here I try, in a preliminary way, to analyse such female engagements by focusing upon the relation of women to Bernstein's theory of educational transmission or, more particularly, his sociology of pedagogy.

Since there is no way I can do justice to the wealth of material I received, I have selected two key themes and illustrated them with relevant quotations. In the first section, I begin by exploring the perceived power and attraction of Bernsteinian theory. What emerges from the accounts I received are the different forms of power associated with such theory. I discuss the *transgressive nature* of the theory, describing its *educative* and *transformative power*. I also delve into the particular dialogue between feminism and Bernstein himself, and his responses to such intellectual encounters. In the second half of the chapter, I briefly describe how gender research has developed in relation to Bernstein's theory of pedagogy, focusing especially on code modalities, pedagogic discourses and devices, and feminist pedagogy. Here I draw mainly upon feminist writers or gender researchers, but I have also added the insights of those academics who have not specifically addressed feminist writing or gender theory in their own work. Knowledge of Bernstein's theory has allowed this last group to describe the potential of Bernsteinian concepts for theories of gender, a potential not necessarily recognised by feminist sociologists.

The power and the attraction of Bernsteinian theory

In a 1999 interview with Bernstein, Joseph Solomon argues that Bernstein's theory is famous for 'its complex, formal, generative character' (Bernstein and Solomon, 1999, p. 265) since it:

> (1) systematically encompasses and connects, in one device, different contexts of experience, such as work, family and education, and different levels of regulation: from class relations and the state, through curriculum and pedagogy, down to the level of individual subjects;

> (2) aims at the creation of a language to provide consistent sociological descriptions of practices or regulation and conceptual tools for research;
> (3) contains from its outset, variation and change, actual or potential, at and between all levels of the device.
>
> (Bernstein and Solomon, 1999, p. 266)

It is 'a complex theoretical discourse' that has been treated, on the whole, by the English-speaking intellectual community with suspicion – a fact noted by many a commentator.[2] This suspicion, however, may be derived less from the comprehensiveness and formal nature of the theory than from its *transgressive* nature. Drawing upon Durkheimian traditions, Bernstein himself argues that the mixing of categories is precisely the point of danger and transition, symbolising the moments when the distribution and the mechanisms of power are exposed. At such moments, when there is a blurring of key distinctions and categorisations, the transgression itself represents a dangerous pollution, a weakening of the borders between the sacred and the profane. However, the effect is not necessarily negative; indeed, transgression can become its own source of power, which generates instability but also its own processes of resolution. There is the potential either to transform the power base or to encourage a reinstatement of its force. The effect can be exciting, filled as it is with creative possibilities (Bernstein, 1996).

Bernstein might well have been talking about the positioning of his own work in the interstices of sociological, educational and sociolinguistic theories. His sociology of pedagogy is characterised, as he himself hoped, by the absence of a field of study or professional identification (Bernstein, 2000). Perhaps as a result of this 'non-positioning', his sociolinguistic work on elaborated and restricted codes caused consternation and controversy, with serious consequences for the interpretation of his findings. Mary Douglas, for a long time a colleague of Bernstein, was quick to notice that the power and 'threatening' element of his work was to be found in its transgressive nature. In *Implicit Meanings*, Douglas reflects on Bernstein's position in sociology, arguing that he is 'neither fish, flesh nor fowl'. She writes:

> Some tribes reject and fear anomalous beasts, some revere them. In sociology, Professor Bernstein is to some a fearsome scaly monster, cutting across all the tidy categories. The light he sheds on thoughts we would prefer to keep veiled is often cruel. No wonder he holds an anomalous place in his profession.
>
> (Douglas, 1975, p. 174, quoted in Delamont, 1995, p. 324)

Bernstein has also been described as 'a thorn in the flesh of sociology' and an 'enfant terrible', not just because of his research on social class and language but perhaps also because he adopted 'a post-Durkheimian structuralism in an era of Fabian functionalism' (Atkinson, 1985, quoted in Delamont, 2000, p. 101). Although Bernstein was recognised as the *leading* contemporary UK sociologist of education, and was holder of the prestigious Karl Mannheim Chair at the London Institute of Education, his work could never easily be placed within the fashionable intellectual categorisations of sociology or sociology of education. In the 1970s and 1980s, for example, his theories of cultural reproduction sat uncomfortably between the academic camps of political economy and micro-interactional theory (Delamont, 2000). His unique combination of the concepts of power and control as guiding principles of all forms of educational transmission meant that he was able to integrate macro- and micro-sociological concepts. He was also able to appeal, latterly, for the importance of integrating structure, culture, language and discourse.

As one respondent explained, the attraction of Bernstein's theory was both the 'order' represented by structuralism and its oppositional nature:

> I like the structuralism of it, the oppositional analysis. I love drawing quadrants. It's probably the concentration on form rather than content. I like the fact that he doesn't succumb to what's fashionable and sticks out on a limb.

Bernstein's emphasis upon structural principles and rules suggested a modernist approach. However, by the 1990s, when the tensions between modernist and post-modernist approaches were at their height, Bernstein's theory again appeared to override such labelling. One respondent noted that Bernstein's theory transgressed the boundaries between academic and personal in ways that were in tune with the subjectivity and reflexivity of the new era. Describing her work with Bernstein as 'one of the most intellectually stimulating years of my life', she commented:

> There was a continuous tension between constructions based on Basil's empirical data and reflections on language through the basic tenets of post-modernism. There was, of course, the rejection by Basil of any classification and my idea that he was not a structuralist but post-structuralist. I thought at the time that there was a contradiction in the way he classified himself intellectually [despite his definite stand against 'intellectuals'] as empirical and objective. [At the same time] one could and did share his artistic feeling for life and perceive the definitive influence of existentialism in his experience that I think, in a very deep way, is related to his work. He would not deny the statement that his work is a metaphor of his very inner self, of his vital experience. I had a daring insight also that he was in a sense a post-modernist because of the role he attributed to language as a device that, in its inner dispositions, structures society. He has an idea of the ontological being of language as an abstract text without words whose principles of classification and framing regulate the relations of society.
>
> (my addition)

The insecurity associated with transgression offers the possibility of heretical or unthinkable knowledge, but it also offers, for the follower, the opportunity to become 'interpreters' of this 'new' message. The follower becomes the disciple who can develop privileged readings of the text or even the man. On the one hand, according to one respondent, Bernstein fills the role of 'guru' at the same time as representing a 'folk devil'. In her teacher-training course, Bernstein's language research was characterised as amounting to 'social-class stereotyping. That was it.' Such negative representations of his research had to be overcome before engagement could occur. Particularly for those working within the English-speaking academic community, the conditions and rules of engagement, therefore, involved an active distancing from the prejudices and processes of marginalisation within the dominant academic community. It involved essentially 'taking a stand'.

Reading the accounts of different intellectual journeys, I observed that the justification for such engagements with Bernstein's work was often made in terms of personal connections, whether as his graduate student or a research colleague, or in the perceived relevance of his theory to an individual's personal or professional life. For one respondent, the personal experience of finding Bernstein's theory felt 'a bit like coming home intellectually. It felt that here, at last, was someone who understood how my mind worked and did not object to that!' The links between such transgressive theory and marginalised positions/identities is another such theme. My own experience as one of his students suggests that there might be a connection between the intellectual capital gained by working with such theory as theory and being positioned as an 'outsider' or 'other'. For example, reflecting on my own involvement with Bernsteinian theory, I wrote:

> My interest in Bernstein's work stems from far more complex personal and academic influences. I have often wondered whether it was my (Polish) Catholic upbringing, which urged me to make sense of the world according to structures, rituals and order or whether it was my father's Jewish family culture, which emphasised that knowledge is a precious inheritance and a source of wealth that made me choose the path I eventually took through the maze of sociological theory … . A structural analysis seemed, from where I started, not just attractive but essential to an understanding of the patterns of social inequalities and power relations in society.
>
> (Arnot, 1995, p. 298)

The power of Bernstein's theory was also described as its ability to speak to the personal experience of being female and working class, both subordinate social categories:

> I found his *Class, Codes and Control*, volume 3 in particular, really powerful because it spoke to my experience of education and social class. I also found his concepts of personal and positional modes of interaction very useful but

> I also thought the notions of elaborated and restricted codes were trying to say really important things. I know they were seen to be *heretical* but in spite of that – and they were misrepresented – I felt that the thinking behind the concepts was really interesting and (yet again) spoke to my experience.
>
> (my emphasis)

Other women talked about how Bernstein's theory made sense of their experiences as mothers and female teachers, and speculated that women may be attracted to his theory precisely because, as one person worded it,

> He understands the educative process so much more fully. His recognition of the contemporary new middle-class mother as pedagogue is one example. Perhaps his understanding of going to the doctor as pedagogic encounters is another, or maybe it's something to do with power and invisibility, or maybe not.

Another respondent described how she was:

> immediately curious and began thinking about my own five years of primary school teaching experience. Bernstein's work enabled me to think abstractly about or theorise the day-to-day work of teaching.

Bernstein himself, when asked, described the attraction of the journey into his theory as constituting, for some, the 'rebiographising of the subject' where:

> [the] subject emerges at the end of the attraction, perhaps with a new inner coherence or with a strong anti-transference, or just a thankfulness that the journey is over.[3]

In the 1970s, intellectual theory was put to new radical uses in education that were not that distant from the factors that shaped the emergence of the new middle classes, which Bernstein himself had described so well in volume 3 of his *Class, Codes and Control*. Knowledge in this new context, he argued, involved not only a form of symbolic 'property' but rather a process of 'radical personalising' (Bernstein, 1977c). Bernstein's theory might, therefore, have offered female academics the possibility of gaining access to and being repositioned within the field of higher education. Thus, finding different ways of seeing the world could also lead to the gaining of new forms of intellectual property. Mastery of such a powerful explanatory theory offered the opportunity of acquiring a form of symbolic capital within a largely empirical and, some say, undertheorised discipline. It gave more than just theoretical insights; it offered a high-status form of knowledge to those female academics who were very likely to need it in a male competitive world. What Bernstein's theoretical framework represented was a new language of description to those seeking to redescribe (if not to transform) power relations in society. And for some feminists, as I shall show, there was much to be gained from such an engagement *against*, but also *within*, the educational establishment. The power of Bernstein's theory was not just transgressive but also educative. The female reader became transformed, in effect, into the pedagogical subject.

Educative power

Bernstein's theory is described by female academics as 'powerful' from the first moment of its discovery. The respondents articulate, in vivid fashion, their feelings of being drawn into the complexity and difficulty of the task. The moment of discovery is thus talked about in emotive terms, described as 'eye opening', a 'source of inspiration', a 'thrill' and a moment of 'absolute fascination that came after coming to terms with ambivalence about his work'. Others talk about being 'immediately curious'. In one publication, Sally Power described her engagement, writing:

> It would be something of an exaggeration to say that reading Basil Bernstein changed my life. But it is true to say that his paper 'On the classification and framing of education knowledge' (Bernstein, 1977a) altered the way I looked at education. Even though it had been published for over ten years and was widely recognised as a seminal text by the time I came across it, it seemed to offer a perspective that was not only entirely novel but also eminently convincing.
>
> (Power, 1998, p. 11)

Such initial encounters appear to have turned into long-term commitments. Indeed, as respondents remark, reading Bernstein's theory becomes in itself a sign of commitment and connection. The student becomes the disciple returning to the text again and again, thinking of ways in which it might be interpreted, applied and developed. As one respondent commented,

> I continued to work with Bernstein's ideas long after the thesis was finished and with the passage of time I think I have understood his work better and better. It's a bit like peeling back the layers of an onion – the peeling away of one layer reveals yet another.

Such engagements involve progressive forms of revelation as the rules that govern the text are exposed and understood. Repeated attempts to engage with Bernstein's work encourage an even deeper commitment to try and dispel some of the myths and misunderstandings surrounding it. As one person described this process,

> Reading and rereading his work provides me every time with insights that stimulate new critical perspectives. The criticism and controversies his work has raised is to a certain degree the result of a lack of real understanding of many of his concepts and, therefore, of his theory of pedagogical discourse which, in my opinion, is the *only* encompassing and coherent social theory of pedagogical discourse that has been articulated.

Many would sympathise with the view that reading and rereading Bernstein can be an overwhelming experience. The comprehensiveness of its goals, the all-encompassing nature of its explanations in themselves can blot out the need for any other reference point. Clearly some authors become 'only Bernsteinian', while others try to hold on to other theoretical frameworks such as those of Pierre Bourdieu, Serge Moscovici, Michel Foucault and Antonio Gramsci. Noticeably rare are examples of feminist theories being brought in to complement Bernstein's conceptual framework. Often it is safer, as one respondent commented, to stay with only a few concepts (such as languages of description, code theory or positional/personal modes of control), since there is a tendency to get lost in Bernstein's theory, 'a sort of tunnel which is very rewarding but leaves you wondering how to get back to the other stuff'. Safety, for some, comes with using his theory for the analysis of existing data rather than using it for the theoretical framing of data collection.

To engage with Bernstein's highly structured and abstract theory is also to become a pedagogic subject oneself, to become a learner in which the control of knowledge, in Bernsteinian terms, is tightly framed. For some women academics, this may reinforce their sense of vulnerability. Sara Delamont (2000), for example, criticises sociologists for their miscomprehension, which is based upon not having 'done their homework'. Women academics who are often located in subordinate positions in the academic field may sustain a high level of risk in using such theory, either because they are seen as inexpert theoreticians or because they are seen to be 'servicing' grand male metanarratives. Such uncertainty always risks the question: Is such an intellectual encounter ever equal?

What is interesting is how far women academics are able to change their relationship to this theoretical knowledge by actively owning such theory and promoting it in various national contexts. Despite being in peripheral positions in the academy, sometimes in multidisciplinary arenas, many of the respondents appeared to be engaged in the task of (re)positioning Bernstein's theory within the intellectual field (see, for example, my own early work – MacDonald, 1977). Such repositioning can occur through textbook-writing that, as Bernstein himself noticed, concentrates on the more formal mechanisms of his theory. Such 'secondary servicing' (Bernstein, 1990, pp. 8–9) is at least altruistic. Other recontextualisation processes, according to Bernstein, are less fair to the original theory. 'Schizzing', for example, occurs when the original body of work is split (normally in two) with one half subject to what he termed 'discursive repression'. Alternatively, theory is 'overdetermined' when exposition and the original author's voice are kept to a minimum in deference to the criticism of others. Finally, there is 'creative replacing', which occurs when the author is replaced altogether by the critic and a wholly imaginary text is created.

Applying Bernstein's conceptual framework to the analysis of empirical data, however, is more common among the female academics I contacted than any of these negative stances. The danger here is that such applications can lead to a highly selective use of his theory, especially if concepts are taken out of context, and to a celebratory rather than critical approach to his works. A number have noted that there has been a lack of serious engagement with the limits of Bernsteinian theory. As one respondent commented, this may be the result of the negative ways (described above) in which Bernstein himself constructed such dialogue – a point reinforced particularly by feminist critics who expressed a wish for more positive professional and personal recognition of their contribution from Bernstein himself. The following comment captures these dilemmas:

> Partly because he is so possessive of his ideas, people tend to polarise around him. They either love his work or don't bother with it. Admirers' accounts, then, can often be hagiographies rather than really useful critiques that take his ideas forward. He also tends to develop his ideas inwardly, forever refining them or making them more complex, rather than linking them to other work.

Despite all these considerations, many of the women I contacted described the key personal role they see themselves as playing in encouraging attention to the qualities of Bernstein's theory, its national/international relevance[4] and the potential of its conceptual framework for research programmes. While promoting the stature of the theory, Bernstein's own stature is also recognised. Thus his work is described as 'the *only* encompassing and coherent social theory of pedagogic discourse that has been articulated' while he is '*the* central theorist of education'. The personal and the theoretical, therefore, appear to be inseparable elements of such female engagements. By organising conferences, nominating him for honorary degrees, teaching his theory abroad and arranging high-profile visits, female academics have played their part in developing the influence of Bernstein's work. Thus women academics have become (at least in theory, but not always in practice) integral to the development of an international community of Bernsteinian scholars who are gradually coming together through conferences and publications. Women's relationships to Bernstein's theory can therefore position them as powerful.

Transformative power

Transgressive theories are not powerless – in fact, as I have argued, just the reverse. On the one hand, they have the potential to challenge hegemonic conceptions of the social order by exposing the principles that underlie it. On the other hand, transgressive theories, as we have seen, can have the power to convert and discipline thought. The connection between transgressive theory and socially transformative power is, therefore, highly complex. For a number of women respondents, the explanatory power of Bernstein's theory in relation to gender issues in education was sufficient justification for its use. As one respondent commented, 'I think our role as academics is to understand the world, not necessarily to change it.' Bernstein's theory helped her understand the nature of education rather than simply to address 'inequities in access or outcome, which is where so much sociology gets bogged down'. For others, such as Parlo Singh and Allan Luke, the explanatory power of Bernstein's theory of pedagogy could be put to political use within a social movement that required more sophistication and grounding. In their introduction to *Pedagogy, Symbolic Control and Identity* (Bernstein, 1996), these authors argue that feminism as a political project is better served with a deeper structuralist analysis that can move through a 'relay of power' and control relations, achieved through the structuring of pedagogic communication' (Singh and Luke, 1996, p. xiii) rather than by an analysis that makes claims about the biases against girls and yet fails to enable teachers or researchers to challenge the structural historical conditions that produce such bias. The purposes of Bernsteinian theory could, therefore, be related to feminist political agendas, even if it could not be simplified into programmatic strategies.

One of the key issues for feminists seeking social transformation is whether Bernstein's theory should be regarded as male-centred theory, which would therefore preclude such an application to feminist concerns. Below, I consider this argument and discuss how Bernstein himself saw the epistemological basis of knowledge and the significance of feminism as a type of knowledge structure.

Male-centred theory and feminism as 'voice'

The relationship of feminism to male theory is always problematic and complex, not just at the personal level but also as an intellectual project. While it is one thing to develop Bernstein's conceptual framework in the context of linguistic and educational theory, it is another to import his insights into a political discourse whose purpose is the deconstruction of male power. In light of this, we may ask: Can Bernstein's theory override the concerns that feminism has about the use of male epistemology? To what extent can it be put into service as a form of political critique of gender power when it could be seen as the product of a male voice? Can it effectively expose gender relations in their totality?

First, Paul Atkinson (1997) argues that for those committed to any political project, the apparent neutrality of Bernstein's conceptual framework can cause difficulties.[5] He remarks that sociologists of education, not least those concerned with gender, have criticised Bernstein's notion of pedagogy for being a 'transparent and neutral ether'. Thus the 'medium appeared to have no political substance of its own' (Atkinson, 1997, p. 117). At the same time, feminists might be suspicious of Bernstein's strong focus on social-class relations with the typical exclusion of female/gender concerns. Yet Atkinson argues that Bernstein's project, pre-dating to some extent current post-structuralist and post-modernist concerns about multiple identities and intertextuality, was far broader than a concern for one social category. Bernstein saw:

> the need to address pedagogic discourses as a device for the allocation and reproduction of social types, generative narratives of identity and difference. A sociology of pedagogy addresses a wider array of analytic themes than even the taken for granted trinity of race, class and gender.
>
> (ibid., p. 6)

The responses of feminist sociologists of education (and even those who would not place themselves within this category) to this debate are instructive. One respondent distinguished between two sets of feminist responses, both of which failed to grasp the intellectual power of Bernsteinian theory:

> The feminism/Bernstein issue is complex. For feminists who won't accept using 'the master's tools' then Bernstein's theory is clearly as male as that of Foucault, Lyotard. He is an old-fashioned structuralist whilst they have moved on to post-modernism and post-structuralism. For feminists who don't mind where an idea comes from if it is useful – what S. Brodribb calls 'ragpickers in the waste bin of male ideas' – Bernstein's theory is a powerful tool.

These responses of education feminists may have something to do with the ways in which Bernstein addressed feminist concerns about gender power.

Bernstein would be the first to accept that gender is a concern 'different from the focus of the theory' (Bernstein, 1995, p. 385). When asked directly, he replied:

> I do not think that consciously gender or feminist theory had much direct effect on my own work. This work seemed to have its own inevitability. What mattered most was whether it developed the elegance of the models.
>
> (personal communication with the author, 2000)

However, his failure to address explicitly feminist theory led to certain frustrations. Sara Delamont (1995), Susan Semel (1995) and I (Arnot, 1995) each indicated where gender connections could have been developed but were not. Such neglect, we have argued, raised questions about the male-centredness of Bernstein's conceptual framework. For example, as I have argued (Arnot, 1995), the use of classifications, polarisations, dichotomies and codes to describe symbolic orders and the modalities of social control suggests the fragmentation and emotional distancing that Chodorow (1978) and Gilligan (1987), among others, have found to be associated with male-ordered worlds. The abstraction and structural aspects of Bernstein's theory also appear to be far removed from the 'connectedness' and the integration of relations between public and emotional, sexual and private selves associated with female experience (e.g., Belenky et al., 1986; Gilligan, 1987; Hill Collins, 1990).

Interestingly, support for this view can be found in the comments of one respondent who reflected that she found Bernstein's 'dichotomous structuralisms antithetical to her own thinking', even though she 'intentionally resisted arguments that Bernstein's ideas and theories are gender linked'. Similar levels of ambivalence were also expressed about Bernstein's male styles of writing by a feminist sociologist who commented:

> I think the issue around his theories and feminism is very difficult because all his work gives primacy to social class. He often writes specifically about males, generally ignoring issues of gender, and has what I identify as a 'macho style' of writing. Like many great male theorists he has the audacity, the confidence to name the world. We women, including feminists, are much more tentative about our claims to knowledge. However, the very process of answering this question made me start to think that there are strong gendered as well as classed aspects to personal and positional orientations and that the concepts would probably work very well in relation to gender.

Some educational researchers argued that it was precisely the manifestation of the inner workings of the theory, the 'transparency' of Bernstein's theory, that allows them to use (rather than reject) the theory to challenge gender power-relations. As one respondent wrote,

> To my mind Bernstein doesn't theorise gendered relations per se, but he does indicate how gender relations embedded within pedagogic contexts revolve around the ways of knowing and ways of displaying knowledge. Again though I tend to get to Bernstein's theory through the data I am looking at, rather than using Bernstein to find the data. I think that Bernstein's work provides a way in to what otherwise might seem like masculine territory, heavy duty theorising from which women sometimes are imagined as barred. I think it provides a way in because it is quite *transparent* about how it comes into being, though whether I would have seen this *transparency* without having worked with him personally I don't know. I have found his way of thinking a tremendous resource. Bernstein's work highlights gender relations between mobile categories constructed in multiple dimensions and not necessarily taking centre stage though always

> there. This opens up where one looks for gender and how one thinks about the possibilities for transformation.
>
> (emphasis added)

For many of the women academics I questioned, the mastery of powerful explanatory discourses, generating *independent* and *universalistic* forms of knowledge which signal a disconnection rather than a dependence on social and political frameworks, appears to be precisely the basis of attraction to Bernsteinian theory. One respondent explained:

> The appeal of Bernstein's work lies in the complex social questions it attempts to address and the particular manner in which he set out to do so. One could list a range of theories and concepts, classification and framing, vertical and horizontal discourse, the pedagogic device, which are enormously powerful. But Bernstein appeals to me at a deeper level because of a systematic probing of the workings of symbolic control and most particularly how knowledge is structured, transmitted and acquired and how identities are produced at both macro- and micro-levels.

Another respondent, who claimed to have made 'no serious study of feminist writing', suggested that what she called 'domestication' was to be found precisely in 'local' specialised voices, such as the idea of women's ways of knowing. Again it was the universalistic and explanatory nature of Bernstein's theory that, in her view, had the most chance of encouraging women's development/freedom:

> Perhaps what I can say here is that I have, since my mid-teens, resisted domestication – relationally, spatially and intellectually. Power (and for me this probably means universalistic) ideas have always appealed to me for this reason. From a distance away it seems that many feminist writers – those, for example, who argue for 'women's ways of knowing' – celebrate the *local*, and particularly over the *general and universalistic*, and Bernstein would probably have something to say about that.

Nevertheless, reflecting on her own work, she argues that it is possible that two different forms of knowledge might be found within the educational system:

> One form is concerned with the 'outer', with practices in schools, which in turn can be subdivided into principled, general, context independent specialised forms (for example, theories of learning) and more context dependent tacit forms (associated with classroom practice). We could describe this as a performance mode of pedagogy.
>
> The other knowledge form is concerned with the inner self-reflective, the therapeutic, which is more particular, and localised (and associated with a competence mode of pedagogy). Now to what extent is the context

> independent and universalistic associated with the masculine and the dependent, self-reflexive, local and personal context associated with the feminine?
>
> In theory and practice I prioritise the universalistic over the locally reflective because for me the latter constitutes a form of domestication which deprives students, and most particularly women, of mastery of powerful theoretical discourses.

This theme of specialist voices, indeed of women's voice and its status within male theory, is critical to feminist engagements with theory. Sara Delamont, for example, drew on Dorothy Smith's (1979) insight that the social organisation of discourse-positions determines who can participate, be recognised and produce work – in other words those who have a right to a voice. Bernstein, challenged by this remark, replied that the 'issue of masculine theorising colonising feminist research', and thus speaking yet again through it, brings up:

> the question of what the credentials for speaking about others are and who is in a position to grant or withhold the licence … licensing and credentials are intrinsic to the intellectual field. In an important sense, gender relations are understood through inevitable projections, the deconstruction of which is trapped by the different specialisations of identity and power relations. Although projections are not particular to gender, they may well be crucially implicated in such studies and more implicated in some than others. And it is this that research may like to pursue.
>
> (Bernstein, 1995, p. 417)

From Bernstein's perspective, there is no such thing as female- or male-centred theory. Gender classifications, and indeed 'voices', are the consequence of a set of generative principles that underlie the social order. His theory, from an epistemological perspective, therefore precedes voice and cannot simply be described as masculine discourse. He argued that his theory, precisely because of its abstract exploration of generative principles, is a form of conceptualisation that can be used to describe and analyse women's positioning in various fields (the economic and symbolic). However, he also admitted that this conceptualisation can be neglectful of women's position – not by its failure to recognise such positioning but by the fact that the theory has strongly controlled the mechanisms (framed) to be used to discuss women's position. He explained:

> Implicit in S. Delamont's chapter, and in a different way in M. Arnot's, is the criticism – justified – that the specialisation, ambiguities and power position of women play a central role in the theory yet this role is understated. Women certainly are likely to be over-represented in dominant positions in the field of symbolic control compared with their positions in the economic field. However, the conceptualising of these fields is realised in a language which articulates simple–complex with respect to its classifi-

> cations; differentiation with respect to functions; and location, hierarchy and discourse with respect to actors. There are no gender voices: a presence without a voice in one field and an absence of voice in the other. The issue is neither a question of the presence or absence of voices, nor a question of their distribution within a field at any level of its function. It is a question of the regulation (framing) of the gender *message*, of the tension between the tacit, the explicit and the yet to be spoken.
>
> (Bernstein, 1995, p. 418)

Recently, however, Bernstein's ambivalence about his own relationship to his theory was revealed. He argued that 'to know whose voice is speaking is the beginning of one's voice' (Bernstein, 1996, p. 12). Indeed, as he admitted in his interview with Solomon, 'My preference here is to be as explicit as possible – then at least my voice can be deconstructed' (Bernstein and Solomon, 1999, p. 275).

Bernstein openly admitted in one of his last publications that his engagement with feminist writing could be developed, especially when considering women's role in education. He commented:

> Semel, along with Arnot and Delamont, is right to point out that although the changing role of women in cultural reproduction is not entirely absent in the work, it has not taken advantage of developments in feminist theories.
>
> (Bernstein, 1995, pp. 418–19)

He tended to use the changing role of women and their relationship to the women's movement as exemplars in his theory of social change. In *Pedagogy, Symbolic Control and Identity*, for example, there are a number of references to feminism or the women's movement, particularly in so far as they represent the launching of what he called 'prospective identities'. Not that different from the promotion of evangelist or fundamentalist identities that focus on the 'consummation of the self', he suggested that the women's movement can be understood as seeking an individual's conversion through the cultural resurgence of what he calls oppositional 'rituals of inwardness'. These symbolic and discursive shifts involve the *recentring* of identities, presupposing a change in the basis for collective recognition and relation. Such social movements are generated from specialist social bases that cut across social groupings, although sometimes they can signify class fractions. Often found in the field of symbolic control (rather than economic fields), prospective identities may well create a 'generalised basis for resistance' but they are also associated with the reorganisation of capitalism and pedagogic discourses (Bernstein, 1996, p. 79).

Alerted to this theme, Singh and Luke suggest that (in ways not dissimilar to those of Anthony Giddens or Ulrich Beck) Bernstein understands the significance of the weakening of traditional biological or social identities (age, race, sexuality, gender or social class). They become weak resources for the 'construction of identities with stable collectivities' (Singh and Luke, 1996, p. xiii). New feminist identities based more on 'confessional narratives' can potentially sever the links between the symbolic and social structures. Some forms of feminism focus upon the experiential outcomes of socially segmented functions in which are developed specialised activities and practices. Such *horizontal discourse* is a discourse of the everyday mundane world in contrast to the *vertical discourses* of formal education. The recontextualising of horizontal discourse often gives rise to supposedly emancipatory integrative pedagogies which:

> may be seen as a crucial resource for pedadogic populism in name of empowering or unsilencing voices to combat the elitism and alleged authoritarianism of vertical discourse. This move at the level of the school is paralleled by the confessional narratives of Feminist and Black studies in Higher education. The 'new' ethnography celebrates horizontal discourse through extensive use of quotations which serve as experiential evidence. The 'ethno' is 'unreconstructed' voiced informant; what is missing is the graphic (Moore and Muller, 1998).
>
> (Bernstein, 1999, p. 169)

This analysis suggests that feminist knowledge structures may not necessarily be liberatory if they are limited to such epistemologically weak horizontal knowledge forms and integrative pedagogies (especially those which rely on voice). The radical question which Bernstein raised is under what conditions can feminism adopt a more powerful 'vertical' knowledge structure which generates theory before voice (Moore and Muller, 1998).

Despite these complex and underexplored differences between Bernsteinian and feminist epistemologies, Bernstein's theory has nevertheless been used to develop a 'feminist' analysis of gender power in education. Initially, Bernstein's concepts of educational codes were influential. Here his conceptual distinctions, particularly between power and control, have been important tools in the deconstruction of 'patriarchal paradigms' in education (Spender, 1981) and for the analysis of gender data on learning, achievement and identity (e.g., Middleton, 1982, 1987; Singh, 1993; Moss, 1993, 1999; Chisholm, 1995; Fontes and Morais, 1996). Since the 1980s, a strong feminist interest in his theory of the new middle classes and women's position in different pedagogic developments can also be identified (e.g., David, 1993; Reay, 1995; Semel, 1995; Delamont, 2000). And since the publication of two more volumes of articles (1990, 1996), Bernstein's theory of pedagogic discourse has been used by female academics to study the fine detail of the transmission of gender relations in the classroom. The *capacity of* Bernstein's theory to account for gender relations as a mode of pedagogic transmission is the focal point of such feminist theoretical work. In the remaining part of this chapter, I briefly describe how feminists have engaged with (a) his theory of gender codes, (b) female pedagogic work and (c) the gendering of pedagogic discourses.

Constructing a theory of gender pedagogy

Almost all the respondents, when asked, described the seminal influence of Bernstein's 1971 paper 'On the classification and framing of educational knowledge', which drew upon Durkheimian principles of mechanical and organic solidarity and Marxist theory concerning the distribution of power and the social division of labour. In his much-quoted opening, Bernstein laid out his basic premise:

> How a society selects, classifies, distributes, transmits and evaluates the education knowledge it considers to be public, reflects both the distribution of power and the principles of social control.
>
> (Bernstein, 1977a, p. 85)

Key to Bernstein's analysis of the social order constructed through what he called the three message systems in education – curriculum, pedagogy and evaluation – were the concepts of *classification* and *framing*. Although initially Bernstein's project was understood as a theory of the cultural reproduction of social-class relations, the phraseology used in this article was purposively general. *Classification* of knowledge, as a conceptual device, referred to the 'relationships' among categories, not (as Bernstein pointed out) to *what* is classified. Classification specifically referred to the degree of boundary maintenance between contents (ibid., p. 88) signifying the distribution of power. Similarly the concept of *framing* was used to refer to the 'context in which knowledge is transmitted and received' – the pedagogical relationship of teacher and taught, irrespective of class, race, gender or age. The key factor here was 'the strength of the boundary between what may be transmitted and what may not be transmitted in the pedagogical relationship' (ibid., p. 88). Framing, therefore, referred to the degree of control the teacher or the pupil possesses over 'the selection, organisation, pacing and timing of the knowledge transmitted and received in the pedagogical relationship' (ibid., p. 89).

The potential was there to explore the idea, as one respondent wrote, that:

> the strong classifications of gender within society, together with the tacit acquisition of rules that reproduce such classifications, can be analysed and explained through Bernsteinian theory.

The concepts of classification and framing, therefore, encouraged new ways of making sense of the gendered cultures of schooling. They demanded that a distinction be made between the impact of patriarchal relations as a power relation and the forms of control exerted upon different groups of male and female children – a distinction that was not evident in feminist educational research in the early 1980s. It suggested the significance of investigating not only the content of the curriculum but also the underlying symbolic messages contained within the hierarchy and stratification of male and female forms of knowledge, the selection and classification of male and female subjects, and their status in the curriculum. The possibilities existed that gender codes related to educational codes (especially those of social class) and that, therefore, different educational codes could be gendered (MacDonald, 1980, 1981).[6]

Like all reproduction theories, Bernstein's theory of educational codes was criticised by feminists for its implied determinism and, therefore, its failure to demonstrate either the conditions in which gender conflict occurs or the mechanisms for social change (e.g., Yates, 1987; Weiler, 1987). As a result, those researching school conflict and the resistance, negotiation and coping strategies of youth have tended not to engage with Bernstein's theory. Bernstein (1977c) made a critical point when he stated that the recognition of principles does not determine the *realisation* (that is, the practice), it can only set limits on it. In a key passage he explained:

> The structural relationships, implicitly and explicitly, carry the power and control messages *and* shape, in part, the forms of response to them at the level of inter-action. Because relationships are structural, *it does not mean that the initially received objective reality is without contradiction or a seamless fabric, nor that there is uniform shared subjective meaning.*
>
> (Bernstein, 1977c, p. 155; my emphasis)

Further he argued that:

> in the process of acquisition of specific codes, principles of order are taken over but also at the same time tacit principles of the disordering of that order.
>
> (Bernstein, 1990, p. 3)

Bernstein clearly took a view that individuals were active in their own socialisation. They acquired the ground rules of a particular social order but also responded to it. Bernstein's discussion of the processes of *recontextualisation* found within educational institutions held particular promise in this context, focusing attention on the complex cultural relationships between family and schooling (MacDonald, 1981). On the one hand, he problematised the relationship between family and school cultures (rather than assuming a linear model of socialisation) and, on the other, his theory suggested that it might be important to look at how the forms of appropriate behaviours for each sex in the family and community are converted into the gender-appropriate academic disciplines. Bernstein also argued that an important key to any system of social maintenance would be the *different modalities of social control* used by different sets of power relations (see Arnot, 1983a).

As one respondent argued, such code modalities, a much under-researched concept, could well have been developed in terms of gender:

> I think that the study of code modalities differentiating along gender lines in pedagogic practice is of crucial importance … one of the issues that I

> left unanswered in my own Ph.D. and in retrospect one that I would very much like to have undertaken is correlating variations in the code modality with variations in the cultural capital of girls and boys in individualised teacher–pupil interactions, in order to investigate how different meanings/text articulations produce different patterns of subjectivity according to gender.

Although not at this level of classroom learning, a number of connections between gender and different modes of transmission have been made. In 1982, for example, Sue Middleton applied Bernstein's theory of collection and integrated codes to the development of feminist research and teaching. Her analysis of the political impetus behind Women's Studies led her to conclude:

> The low status of integrated codes is seen as related to the devaluation of both women and qualities seen as 'feminine' in patriarchal capitalist societies. The construction of the integrated code should not be seen as a positive reflection of 'femininity' under capitalism according to a correspondence principle. Rather it should be seen as a penetration by an oppressed group of the conditions which oppress them.
>
> (Middleton, 1982, p. 14)

Middleton's research shows that Bernstein's theory was relevant to epistemological questions about the nature of feminist knowledge and pedagogic styles. In her later paper, Middleton (1987) extended the analysis of integrated codes to explain the 'double marginality' of feminist academics in the oligarchically administered and fragmented structure of a university.

Bernstein himself connected the role of gender to different modes of transmission, first through his sociolinguistic research and second through his analysis of what he called 'invisible pedagogies' particularly associated with the middle-class mother's domestic pedagogic work. The concept of invisible pedagogies, as Atkinson (1997) argued, drew upon Bernstein's early recognition of the various new forms of psychotherapy becoming available to different social actors. He saw that the emerging 'therapeutic relationships' had specific requirements that were directly counterposed to the use of restricted codes. The new relationships being forged were person-oriented, increasing the pressure on individuals 'to structure and restructure their experiences in a verbally unique way' (Bernstein, quoted in Atkinson, 1997, p. 115). As Atkinson notes, Bernstein recognised that these new symbolic means were 'distributed differentially through class and gender orders' (ibid., p. 116). He argues that:

> European feminists have avoided the close inspection of language in use in favour of less grounded approaches to language and semiotics. Nevertheless, the basis has always been there for a discipline rapprochement between the two intellectual strands and characteristically Bernstein's work points the way. Had choice and circumstance been different, he could have embarked

> on detailed investigations of the class-related and gendered basis of symbolic resources and the narrative orderings of the self.
>
> (ibid., p. 117)

Susan Semel, in her analysis of the history of progressive schools in the United States, argues that code theory and in particular Bernstein's theory of invisible pedagogies could have connected more closely with feminist theory. Key to her analysis were the ways in which the new middle-class women delivered such pedagogies but in autocratic ways. Delamont also suggests that Bernstein's central idea that 'the new middle class is the controller of others by virtue of its manipulation of symbols rather than by the ownership and management of property' (Delamont, 1995, p. 327), although 'tantalisingly brief', nevertheless hints at differences in the role of the mother *within* social-class groupings. By positing an argument about the personalised organic solidarity unforeseen by Emile Durkheim, Bernstein had hinted at an extended individualism which, in the family context, could lead to increased variety and the processes of 'cultural interruption' rather than cultural reproduction (ibid., p. 328). This theoretical insight can throw light on the presence of a 'muted group' of women in the intelligentsia and bourgeoisie and can be linked to the rise of middle-class girls' education and their increasing academic success. The intersections of class and gender are then understood to occur within the privileged as well as the working classes. As Delamont notes,

> The emerging and changing intelligentsia have developed an education to produce a new kind of woman. The changes in the nature of the product offered to the girls are interrelated with changes in the sexual division of labour and the gender makeup of elite occupations.
>
> (ibid., p. 334)

A number of female sociologists and sociolinguists interested in the connections between family cultures and structures, the structure of language and communication, and processes of class/gender reproduction have taken Bernstein's theory into new empirical ground. For example, Ruqaiya Hasan's (1993) sociolinguistic research on the semantic properties of messages between mothers and their children suggests, as Bernstein himself had found in his early research, that there is variation between social classes and variations in mothers' discourse in relation to the children's sex. Other links between Bernstein's theories of pedagogy and parenting can be found in Carol Vincent and Simon Warren's (1998) work on 'becoming a better parent'. Using the concept of visible and invisible pedagogies to think about the nature of accredited courses developed under the rubric of 'parent education', these authors found that the mode of transmission bears some resemblance to the 'reproduction of the middle class home and mothering'. As Bernstein himself comments, 'women transformed maternal caring and preparing into a scientific activity' (Bernstein, 1973, quoted in Atkinson, 1985, p. 162). The growing interest in using his theory of positional and personal family types to understand different gendered and class understandings and patterns of secondary school choice is also significant (see, for example, David, 1993; David, West and Ribbens, 1994; Reay, 1995; Reay and Ball, 1998). All these projects, in their different ways, contextualise and challenge the assumed superiority and 'rationality' of middle-class language and culture and reveal internal gendered variations within social-class categories.

Clearly there is a major line of feminist research here in terms of the pedagogic role of women in the family and schooling systems. As many have noted, these possibilities of linking social class and gender relations through Bernsteinian theory remain relatively underdeveloped.

Pedagogic discourses

The relationship of Bernstein's theory of pedagogy to gender theories of the curriculum is also underdeveloped. His theory has been used, for example, in studies of science and IT education, language education, school- and home-based literacy and teacher education, although the gender aspects have not always been brought out.[7] In Bernstein's (1990) recent work, the theory of pedagogic discourse has become central. This discourse is said to be generated by a social logic of hierarchically arranged rules: *distributive* rules which distribute specialised knowledges to different social groups or social categories; *recontextualising* rules which provide the principles for delocating, relocating and refocusing discourses external to pedagogical discourse and submitting them to its own ordering principle according to the distributive rules; and finally *evaluative* rules that provide the criteria to be transmitted and to be acquired. Bernstein considers that pedagogic discourse consists of the rules and practices that construct order, relation and identity, on the one hand, and conduct, character and manner, on the other. He argues that it is the regulative, rather than the instructional, discourse that is the dominant discourse in this context.[8]

Parlo Singh's and Gemma Moss's different projects are good examples of the application of Bernsteinian theory in relation to gender identities and classroom learning. Singh applied the notion of regulative discourses to her research on computing lessons in primary schools. In an original and fascinating account, she describes the struggle and conflict between male and female pupils seeking to position themselves within the social relations of the classroom. Using Bernstein's concept of a pedagogic device, she describes 'technocratic masculinity' as the mechanism used by male pupils and supported by the classroom teacher to define particular concepts of classroom knowledge and competency. Boys are constructed as risk-taking, experimental and technically competent, while girls struggle to overcome their image as inactive passive rule-followers. In addition Bernstein's concept of 'inner voice' allows Singh to differentiate between girls' hidden resistance and sense of worth and their 'outer voice' which, in this context, positions them as 'nice', good carriers of messages and as domestic and subservient.

Singh clearly values Bernstein's conceptual framework as a means of identifying the ways in which classroom practice is structured by a hierarchy of discourses, many of which mask conflict. Her empirical data demonstrates the gender struggle over control of the *pedagogic device* (that is, control over the classroom's distributive, recontextualising and evaluative rules (criteria)) and the ways in which the discourse silences and marginalises some groups (in this case, girls). Male students are able to gain positions of power because they 'select, sequence, organise and transmit technological knowledge aims' in a form that is valued and recognised within what she calls 'the fiction of technological patriarchy' (Singh, 1993, p. 51). Her contribution, according to Bernstein (1996), was more than the 'imaginative' application of the rules of the pedagogic device – it revealed the 'inadequacy' of his theory 'to describe and interpret the process of production, fixing and canalising of desire and as a consequence the theory was unable to show how girls internalised voices to construct their own representation of the feminine (Singh, 1993)' (Bernstein, 1996, p. 122). Gemma Moss's study of literacy draws upon Bernstein's more recent distinctions between vertical and horizontal discourses when investigating the relationship between girls' romance reading outside school and the pedagogic discourses used in school literacy. Her analysis suggests that girls appropriate the conditions and credentials that are markers of an official vertical discourse. The boundary between school forms of knowledge and those of the informal domain 'intermingle' in these girls' cultural practices.

A different example of a feminist engagement with Bernstein's theory of pedagogy discourse can be found in the rather unlikely setting of feminist pedagogy. Jennifer Gore (1993), for example, developed her interest in the concepts of power 'which underlie, for example, notions of empowerment, emancipatory or liberatory authority' using Bernstein's argument that 'there is no fundamental analysis of the internal logic (in the sense of regulating principles) of pedagogical discourse' and, as a result, pedagogy is most often considered a carrier or relay for power relations external to itself (Bernstein, 1990). Gore's attention, therefore, was drawn to the potential relevance of his concept of pedagogic device, which:

> entails a detailed analysis of the specific practices which actualise power relations of the pedagogy regime. Without attention to the internal relations (I would argue 'the specific practices') of pedagogy, students can leave feminist or critical pedagogy classes more deeply entrenched in an unsympathetic relation to the material presented than when they entered. That is, it is not just the relation of the subject to the text, but the who (agent), the what (content) and the how (process) that influence what is learned or acquired.
>
> (Gore, 1993, p. 127)

Bernstein's argument that 'transformations of a text occur in the pedagogical process as the text is "recontextualised" from producer to teacher and from teacher to student' (ibid.) is also relevant to the recontextualising moments of feminist pedagogy that, according to Gore, should be linked together. As she points out:

> For the purposes of my thesis, Bernstein's elaboration of this process is important in its support of the call for greater reflexivity about both the pedagogies argued for and the pedagogies of arguments made.
>
> (ibid.)

Bernstein's theory, like that of Pierre Bourdieu and Jean-Claude Passeron (1977), cannot be directly relevant to critical feminist pedagogy, however, since (Gore argues) they are too bound to the conventional associations of power and knowledge:

> They do not provide the means for self-criticism unlike Foucault's construction of regime of truth as this kind of analysis of pedagogy maintains the intellectual in the privileged position as 'bearer of universal values'.
>
> (ibid., p. 61)

In contrast with Gore's analysis, the political advantages of Bernstein's theories in relation to feminist pedagogy and practice, according to another respondent, are precisely because 'attention falls on the social relations in situated contextualised practices'. Explaining this point, she writes:

> While I would regard myself as a feminist, I don't read the literature extensively nor do I write in feminist areas. I believe that links can be drawn at two levels, the conceptual and the empirical. Concerning the conceptual, I believe that there is a problem in much contemporary feminist work, particularly post-structuralist, and specifically theories of performativity (Judith Butler) and theories of radical democratic politics (Chantal Mouffe). The problem is that such theories use the problematic of discourse (that sexed identities emerge out of articulations of meaning and power within the social field) in order to establish the ontological grounds on which sexual difference rests in our societies but in so doing they leave aside crucial sociological questions. Namely, they do not ask the question of how sexual identities emerge in concrete practices, in specifically social and political contexts, and how such identities are linked to institutional structures of social control …
>
> The important lesson from Bernstein? In the work on feminism as well as on pedagogy, attention crucially falls on the *social relations in situated contextualised practices*. The aim is to develop sensitive conceptual tools (code modalities) that are able to read in detail the specific grammar of any regulative regime and its social effects upon specific categories of social subjects, and on the basis of this reading to re-articulate the available modalities of power and control which expand the meaning horizons of all

social subjects, and which allow for possible but not yet available identifications. A Bernsteinian logic would thus help in providing the necessary plane of sociological analysis, currently missing from 'high' feminist theory.

Conclusions

This chapter has focused on female and feminist engagements with Bernstein's sociology of pedagogy. This, of course, is not nearly the whole picture, since there have been a number of substantial applications of his theory of identities. The research conducted on male and female youth, their orientations toward schooling (Power et al., 1998), their forms of class and gender resistance (Aggleton, 1987), their construction of gendered occupational and domestic divisions (Holland, 1981, 1986), and girls' construction of occupational and cultural semantics and gender discourses (Chisholm, 1995), demonstrates the power of Bernsteinian theory to codify and theorise experiential and perspectival data. These gender applications would require another essay.

The female engagements with Bernstein's theory of pedagogy discussed in this chapter have been shown to be active, intellectual and powerful. The research described here has been largely celebratory, challenging preconceptions about the relevance of Bernstein's theory. But it has also elaborated Bernstein's theory and developed its applicability in relation to a range of gender issues. Three issues emerge. First, on the surface it seems as if the abstract and universal language of description developed by Bernstein has, to some extent, overcome concerns among some feminists about using male-centred theory. For other women academics, this was less of an issue. Second, key epistemological differences nevertheless remain between feminism and Bernsteinian theory. Some feminist theorists would consider gender categories to be essential and determining forces, shaping all knowledge forms. In terms of Bernsteinian theory, the epistemological conditions for male-centred theory lie in the underlying generative structures. The content of categories is less important than the power that shapes such categories. Gender, therefore, is less a form of power than a set of social relations formed by relations of power. From this perspective, there is no such thing as male-centred theory. There are, however, certain conditions that generate a male or female voice. One respondent summed up the views of so many of the women who replied to my questions when she commented:

> Bernstein's models are essentially beyond gender. The social structures and process to which his ideas are applied in terms of being analytic instruments are deeply gendered. But the ideas and models themselves never seemed so to me. Perhaps this is precisely the reason why women, rather than men, have indeed been attracted to his work and have, directly or indirectly, profited from their engagement with it.

Finally, this chapter has argued that gender relations and women's position within the educational system still remain undertheorised in Bernsteinian theory. While the class analysis is appreciated by most scholars concerned with gender, it draws attention away from the key role that gender plays in shaping educational systems and experiences within it. The potential is clearly there to develop feminist research and research on gender within the problematic of Bernstein's sociology of pedagogy.

Acknowledgements

It is hard to express my appreciation of the help which Basil Bernstein gave me in writing this chapter in the last months of his life. Even though terminally ill, with the kind help and support of Marion his wife, he read and reread versions of the chapter right up to the end, offering further explanations of his position in relation to gender theory and feminism. He had already given me access to all the female colleagues with whom he had worked and, as I later learned, had encouraged them to participate in this project. He took great care not to change the arguments in the paper in which he showed great interest, appreciating the difficulties I faced in summarising the range of views expressed by various authors. I was and still am deeply indebted to him for his loyalty and support and for the intellectual engagement he offered over the last twenty-five years, and feel his loss both personally and academically. Writing this chapter at the end of his life was a moment of closure for both of us.

At the same time, the chapter would not have been written without the generous help given to me by the following colleagues who took the trouble to answer my long list of questions. I would like to thank Cecilia Balcazar, Courtney Cazden, Lynne Chisholm, Lilie Chouliaraki, Frances Christie, Miriam David, Sara Delamont, Bessie Dendrinos, Mary Douglas, Paula Ensor, Ruqaiya Hasan, Janet Holland, Sue Middleton, Ana-Marie Morais, Gemma Moss, Isobel Neves, Sally Power, Diane Reay, Susan Semel, Parlo Singh, Mitsuko Tendo and Carol Vincent. I have listed examples of each author's work in the bibliography but have kept the quotations from the letters I received anonymous. After Bernstein's death, many wrote to me again saying how glad they were to have been able to express their appreciation of their collaboration with him through this chapter. I would like to thank Kathleen Weiler for giving us the opportunity by commissioning the work and for her considerable patience and encouragement in working with this project. I would also like to thank Rob Moore for his insightful comments. The views expressed in this article and any misinterpretations of a respondent's view or indeed of Bernstein's theory are mine alone.

Notes

1 Ethically and methodologically I thought it inappropriate to 'push' respondents to reply to my queries. In the case of Bernstein's work, feminists have tended to commit themselves to his project or conceptual framework or not use it at all. There is no substantive critical feminist analysis of his work to date, only partial discussions of its relevance or applicability to feminist research. It is difficult, therefore, to describe feminist 'disengagements' from the material I collected.

2 Solomon argues that the Anglo-Saxon English speaking world was suspicious of Bernstein's work even though it was indigenous. It has none of the characteristics of indigenous sociological theorising. Delamont goes further and argues that the treatment by the British sociological establishment was not only disgraceful by its neglect of its most extraordinary intellect but that Bernstein's experience was indicative of the peripheral status accorded to the educational system and family in social theory. Had Bernstein developed his theory of social class more extensively, she argues, he might have been granted more recognition. A remarkable shift now appears to be happening with the publication of two *Festschriften* (Atkinson, Davies and Delamont, 1995; Sadovnik, 1995) and a number of key international conferences focused only on his work in, for example, the UK and Portugal.

3 Personal communication with the author. When I asked Bernstein why he thought women in contrast with men might be attracted to his work, he offered this view. Clearly for him gender plays a key role in personal and academic relationships which are not just affected by the staffing structure of higher education but also by the intimate or distant relationship of staff to forms of property. He comments that:

> what has to be understood is the gender stratification of access to and acquisition of types of discourse with different potentials for men and women.

Bernstein also considers that male researchers see their future in teaching rather than research careers. As a consequence they are more concerned with the intellectual field of sociology, its various positions and their evaluation, than women who may well reject or be sceptical of what they see as this field's gender orientation. Thus the men are passing through contract research into teaching. Whatever women's desires may be, the objective picture in no way gives much encouragement to the fulfilment of this desire. The women then are more orientated to the research (which suits the Research Director) and to engagement with research problems as sites for funding. Their concerns with theory, although clearly still epistemological, may well be concerned with its viability as a research instrument. Further, as conceptualising is regarded as a privileging activity, usually male, there are likely to be competitive relations both between men and women and the Director of Research. Thus men are constructed to be 'other'-orientated with respect to discourse (the study of the intellectual field), future work (teaching) and present work (commitment). Bernstein's interest in psychoanalysis and therapeutic relationships also suggests that female–male academic interactions might also have been more fruitfully analysed in terms of dialogue where the processes of 'separation' are not required for women as in the case of men. Women might, therefore, be more prepared to admit allegiance with another's theory.

4 Respondents described how they had promoted Bernstein's work in Colombia, Portugal, Australia, New Zealand, the United Kingdom, the United States, South Africa and so on. A number of women contributed to Sadovnik (1995) and Atkinson, Davies and Delamont (1995).

5 For a substantial critique of the cultural premises of Bernsteinian theory, see Margaret Archer's suggestion that:

> [Bernstein] has driven his methodological path too brutally through the tangled webs of socio-educational structures and educo-social interaction, and that those who follow down it will thus be riding roughshod over both the structures of educational systems and the processes of educational politics which mediate between schooling and society.
>
> (Archer, 1995, p. 212)

Bernstein replied to Archer's criticisms by pointing to a range of his papers which, from 1981, indicated the importance of the educational system and the process of educational politics (Bernstein, 1995).

6 The concept of classification and frame can be found in Delamont's (1989) analysis of ethnographic data from a girls' elite independent school, where she attempts to construct a new theoretical framework combining Bernstein's theory with Mary Douglas's concept of group and grid. See also the theory of gender codes (MacDonald, 1980, 1981) and Tendo (2000).

7 For an example of the principles governing gender distribution of knowledge at government and curriculum levels, see Fontes and Morais (1996); Morais, Fontinhas and Neves (1992); Ensor (1999); and Christie (1998). The application of pedagogic discourse theory to teacher education can also be found in Ensor (1999).

8 In this way the regulative discourses of the educational systems relay that of the state's educational and public policies through the positions, practices and activities of the state's Official Recontextualising Field. How effective this field is depends on the degree and area of autonomy given to other recontextualising fields.

References and further reading

Adlam, D.J. with Turner, G.J. and Lineker, L. (1997) *Code in Context*, London: Routledge.

Aggleton, P. (1987) *Rebels Without a Cause? Middle class youth and the transition from school to work*, Lewes: Falmer Press.

Archer, M. (1995) 'The neglect of the educational system by Bernstein', in A.R. Sadovnik (ed.) *Knowledge and Pedagogy: the sociology of Basil Bernstein*, Norwood, NJ: Ablex Publishing Corporation.

Arnot, M. (1983a) 'A cloud over co-education: an analysis of the forms of transmission of class and gender relations', in S. Walker. and L. Barton (eds) *Gender, Class and Education*, Lewes: Falmer Press.

—— (1983b) 'Male hegemony: social class and women's education', *Boston University Journal of Education*, 164, pp. 64–89.

—— (1984) 'A feminist perspective on the relationship between family life and school life', *Journal of Education*, 166, 1, pp. 5–24.

—— (1995) 'Bernstein's theory of educational codes and feminist theories of education: a personal view', in A.R. Sadovnik (ed.) *Knowledge and Pedagogy: the sociology of Basil Bernstein*, Norwood, NJ: Ablex Publishing Corporation.

Atkinson, P. (1985) *Language, Structure and Reproduction*, London: Routledge.

—— (1997) 'Review symposium', *British Journal of Sociology of Education*, 18, 1, pp. 115–28.

Atkinson, P., Davies, B. and Delamont, S. (eds) (1995) *Discourse and Reproduction: essays in honour of Basil Bernstein*, Cresskill, NJ: Hampton Press.

Belenky, M.F, Clinchy, B.M., Goldberger, N.R. and Tarule, J.M. (1986) *Women's Ways of Knowing*, New York: Basic Books.

Bernstein, B. (1977a) 'On the classification and framing of educational knowledge', in *Class, Codes and Control*, vol. 3, London: Routledge & Kegan Paul

—— (1977b) 'Class and pedagogies: visible and invisible', in *Class, Codes and Control*, vol. 3, London: Routledge & Kegan Paul.

—— (1977c) *Class, Codes and Control*, vol. 3, London: Routledge & Kegan Paul.

—— (1990) *The Structuring of Pedagogic Discourse*, vol. 4, *Class, Codes and Control*, London: Routledge.

—— (1995) 'A response', in A.R. Sadovnik (ed.) *Knowledge and Pedagogy: the sociology of Basil Bernstein*, Norwood, NJ: Ablex Publishing Corporation.

—— (1996) *Pedagogy, Symbolic Control and Identity: theory, research, critique*, London: Taylor & Francis.

—— (1999) 'Vertical and horizontal discourse: an essay', *British Journal of Sociology of Education*, 20, 2, pp. 157–73.

—— (2000) 'From pedagogies to knowledges', unpublished presentation to the Lisbon Conference.

Bernstein, B. and Solomon, J. (1999) 'Pedagogy, identity and the construction of a theory of symbolic control', Basil Bernstein questioned by Joseph Solomon, *British Journal of Sociology of Education*, 20, 2, pp. 265–79.

Bourdieu, P. and Passeron, J.C. (1977) *Reproduction in Education, Society and Culture*, London: Sage.

Cazden, C. (1999) 'The visible and invisible pedagogies of reading recovery', in A.J. Watson and L.R. Giocelli (eds) *Accepting the Literacy Challenge*, Sydney: Scholastic Australia.

Chisholm, L. (1995) 'Cultural semantics: occupations and gender discourse', in P. Atkinson, W.B. Davies and S. Delamont (eds) *Discourse and Reproduction*, Cresskill, NJ: Hampton Press.

Chodorow, N. (1978) *The Reproduction of Mothering*, Berkeley: University of California Press.

Chouliaraki, L. (1998) 'Reputation in "regulation" pedagogic discourse: individualised teacher–pupil talk', *Discourse and Society*, 9, 1, pp. 5–32.

Christie, F. (1998) 'Science and apprenticeship: the pedagagic discourse', in J.R. Martin and R. Veel (eds) *Reading Science: critical and functional perspectives on discourses of science*, London: Routledge.

David, M.E. (1993) *Parents, Gender and Educational Reform*, Cambridge: Polity Press.

David, M.E., West, A. and Ribbens, J. (1994) *Mother's Intuition? Choosing secondary schools*, London: Falmer Press.

Delamont, S. (1989) *Knowledgeable Women: structuralism and the reproduction of élites*, London: Routledge.

—— (1995) 'Bernstein and the analysis of gender inequality: considerations and applications', in A.R. Sadovnik (ed.) *Knowledge and Pedagogy: the sociology of Basil Bernstein*, Norwood, NJ: Ablex Publishing Corporation.

—— (2000) 'The anomalous beasts: hooligans and the sociology of education', *Sociology*, 34, 1, pp. 95–111.

Dendrinos, B. (2001) 'Idological positioning EFL learners via instrumental texts' in *Language Education: The politics of ELT*, Athens: National and Kapodistrian University of Athens.

Diamond, A. (1991) 'Gender and education: public policy and pedagogic practice', *British Journal of Sociology of Education*, 12, 2, pp. 141–62.

Douglas, M. (1975) *Implicit Meanings*, London: Routledge & Kegan Paul.

Ensor, P. (1999) 'The myth of transfer? Teacher education, classroom teaching and the recontextualising of pedagogic practices', *Pythagoras*, 50, December, pp. 2–12.

Fontes, A. and Morais, A.M. (1996) 'Women's scientific education: influence of different socio-political contexts', in O. Valente et al. (eds) *Teacher Training and Values*, Lisbon: Education Department in the Science Faculty, in conjunction with the ATEE.

Gilligan, C. (1987) 'Women's place in men's life cycle', in S. Harding (ed.) *Feminism and Methodology*, Bloomington: Indiana University Press and Milton Keynes: Open University Press.

Gore, J.M. (1993) *The Struggle for Pedagogies: critical and feminist discourses as regimes of truth*, New York: Routledge.

Harding, S. (ed.) (1987) *Feminism and Methodology*, Bloomington: Indiana University Press and Milton Keynes: Open University Press.

Hasan, R. (1993) 'Contexts for meaning', in J.E. Alatis (ed.) *Language Communication and Social Meaning*, Washington, D.C.: Georgetown University Press.

Hill Collins, P. (1990) *Black Feminist Thought: knowledge, consciousness and the politics of empowerment*, London: HarperCollins.

Holland, J. (1981) 'Social class and changes in the orientations to meanings', *Sociology*, 15, 1, pp. 1–18.

—— (1986) 'Social class differences in adolescents: conception of the domestic and industrial division of labour', *Core*, 10, 1.

Lather, P. (1991) *Getting Smart*, New York: Routledge.

MacDonald, M. (1977) *The Curriculum and Cultural Reproduction*, Units 18/19 E202, Milton Keynes: Open University Press.

—— (1980) 'Socio-cultural reproduction and women's education', in R. Deem (ed.) *Schooling for Women's Work*, London: Routledge & Kegan Paul.

—— (1981) 'Schooling and the reproduction of class and gender relations', in L. Barton, R. Meighan and S. Walker (eds) *Schooling, Ideology and the Curriculum*, Lewes: Falmer Press.

Middleton, S. (1982) 'Women's studies at Waikato: a case study in the classification and framing of educational knowledge', *Delta*, 31, pp. 3–17.

—— (1987) 'Feminist educators in a university setting: a case study in the politics of "educational knowledge"', *Discourse*, 8, 1, pp. 25–47.

Moore, R. and Muller, J. (1998) 'The discourse of "voice" and the problem of knowledge and identity in the sociology of education', *British Journal of Sociology of Education*, 20, 2, pp. 189–206.

Morais, A., Fontinhas, F. and Neves, I. (1992) 'Recognition and realisation rules in acquiring school science – the contribution of pedagogy and social background of students', *British Journal of Sociology of Education*, 13, 2, pp. 247–70.

Moss, G. (1993) 'Girls tell teenage romance: four reading histories', in D. Buckingham (ed.) *Reading Audiences: young people and the media*, Manchester: Manchester University Press.

—— (1999) 'Literacy and the social organisation of knowledge in and outside school', Virtual Seminar 2, International Association of Applied Linguistics, http://138.25.75.6/AILA/virtsem2.mos

Power, S. (1998) 'Researching the "pastoral" and the "academic": an ethnographic exploration of Bernstein's sociology of the curriculum', in G. Walford (ed.) *Doing Research about Education*, London: Falmer Press.

Power, S., Whitty, G., Edwards, T. and Wigfall, V. (1998) 'Schools, families and academically able students: contrasting modes of involvement in secondary education', *British Journal of Sociology of Education*, 19, 2, pp. 157–76.

Reay, D. (1995) 'A silent majority: mothers in parental involvement', in R. Edwards and J. Ribbens (eds) *Women in Families and Households: qualitative research*, *Women's Studies International Forum Special*, 18, pp. 337–48.

Reay, D. and Ball, S.J. (1998) 'Making their minds up: family dynamics of school choice', *British Educational Research Journal*, 24, 4, pp. 431–48.

Sadovnik, A.R. (ed.) (1995) *Knowledge and Pedagogy: the sociology of Basil Bernstein*, Norwood, NJ: Ablex Publishing Corporation.

Semel, S.F. (1995) 'Basil Bernstein's theory of pedagogic practice and the history of American progressive education: three case studies', in A.R. Sadovnik (ed.) *Knowledge and Pedagogy: the sociology of Basil Bernstein*, Norwood, NJ: Ablex Publishing Corporation.

Singh, P. (1993) 'Institutional discourse and practice: a case study of the social construction of technological competence in the primary classroom', *British Journal of Sociology of Education*, 14, 1, pp. 39–58.

Singh, P. and Luke, A. (1995) 'Introduction', in B. Bernstein, *Pedagogy, Symbolic Control and Identity*, 1st edn, London: Taylor & Francis.

Smith, H.D.E. (1979) 'A sociology for women', in T. Sherman and E.T. Beck (eds) *The Prism of Sex*, Madison: University of Wisconsin Press.

—— (1987) 'Women's perspective as a radical critique of sociology', in S. Harding (ed.) *Feminism and Methodology*, Bloomington: Indiana University Press and Milton Keynes: Open University Press.

Spender, D. (ed.) (1981) *Men's Studies Modified*, Oxford: Pergamon Press.

Stanley, L. (1990) 'Method, methodology and epistemology in feminist research processes', in *Feminist Praxis*, London: Routledge.

Stanley, L. and Wise, S. (1983) *Breaking Out: feminist consciousness and feminist research*, London: Routledge & Kegan Paul.

Tendo, M. (2000) 'Re-examining Bernstein's power and control theory: from a gender code perspective', *Journal of Educational Sociology*, 67, October, pp. 83–99.

Vincent, C. and Warren, S. (1998) 'Becoming a "better" parent? Motherhood, education and transition', *British Journal of Sociology of Education*, 19, 2, pp. 177–93.

Weiler, K. (1987) *Women Teaching for Change: gender, class and power*, South Hadley, MA: Bergin & Garvey.

Yates, L. (1987) 'Curriculum theory and non-sexist education', unpublished doctoral dissertation, School of Education, La Trobe University, Australia.

12 Gender relations and schooling in the new century

Conflicts and challenges

One of the most powerful global forces in the nineteenth and twentieth centuries was the value ascribed by Western European nations to the gendering of separate spheres in society. Men, as main breadwinners, were associated with a masculinised public/civic sphere and women were represented as symbolic of family and private life (Arnot and Dillabough, 1999). This concept of separate but complementary gender spheres was used to domesticate both colonised peoples and women. Significantly, it shaped the organisational structures and content of a wide variety of national educational systems. Such values, especially in the context of the British domestic and colonial educational policy, contradicted the validity of liberal democratic designs for modern school systems which emphasised individual autonomy and a broad and balanced curriculum for all. In many countries, gender differentiation within education became a key principle shaping the selection, distribution and evaluation of educational knowledge for young men and women.

In the late twentieth century, however, major transformations in gender relations can be seen in the way men and women related to each other in the public sphere and in the family sphere in many Western European countries (Dench, 1997). Women's contribution to the economy has grown rapidly, in part as a result of educational expansion and the growth in female credentials. The family structure has also been transformed by the diversity of life styles in contemporary society. Such is the tide of change that even those conservative reformers, in countries like the UK, who sought to retain traditional gender relations failed and, unintentionally, their policies may even have contributed to the shifting relations between the sexes (Arnot, David and Weiner, 1999). Social change, gender change and educational change are locked together in complex and often unpredictable ways. Describing the various challenges and future scenarios that schools are likely to face becomes, therefore, a difficult task not least because it begs the question of whether schools can actively shape the future or merely respond to its exigencies.

In this brief paper I highlight, first, the challenges which schools now face in relation to egalitarianism (in relation to gender, ethnicity and social class). Second, using the UK experience, I consider the ways in which young men and women have responded to social change and predict the conflicts which schools will encounter in meeting their needs in the future. Finally, I broaden the debate by considering how schools in developed and developing economies will need to engage with the far wider gendered processes of individualisation and globalisation.

Challenges from within

Traditionally schools were the modernist project *par excellence* since, as Durkheim (1956) argued, they were designed precisely to create a diversely skilled occupational force and to transmit a *conscience collective* which bound individuals to the moral order. The basis of this moral order, as feminist educational theorists have shown, was deeply oppressive to women, preventing them from gaining access to power. Schools sustained a gender order which granted men privileged access to cultural and academic capital and hence to economic and political power. Nation-states have used educational systems, therefore, not just to sustain territorial and political boundaries but to encourage gendered citizenship identities which were circumscribed by male dominance (Pateman, 1988).

In nations with developed welfare states, schools were meant to act in a limited capacity to transform social relations in the name of egalitarianism, while still contributing to the promotion of economic growth through the certification of each new generation. Neo-liberalism destabilised this (albeit always problematic) agenda by emphasising new concepts of standards, vocationalism and individualism. Egalitarianism as a result was transformed by reworking the concept of individual rights into a notion of individualised difference and diversity. Schools, in the future, are likely to feel pressure to take account of differentiations *within* rather than *between* subordinated and powerful groups. The traditional categories of educational achievement and underachievement such as 'race', class and gender could be replaced by individual educational careers and the tailoring of courses to 'personal choices'. Thus schools will be expected to meet the demands of 'flexibilisation' of learning which will be represented as a new form of egalitarianism.

The demands for more individualised learning processes will also lead to more subtle forms of gender differentiation. The machineries which construct and treat educational failure may become more rather than less sophisticated in their sifting of each new cohort. Research in the UK (Gillborn and Youdell, 2000) identifies teachers' diagnostic techniques which, under competitive marketised regimes, sort out those children who have the 'potential' to improve and are, therefore, 'suitable cases for treatment' (a decision not unlike medical concepts of triage). Working-class boys who rebel or show signs of disengagement are already the most likely victims of this process. Girls, with their apparent 'liking' of school, may pass this test more easily.

In the future, schools could address these 'micro-inequalities' of education if they understood themselves less as a socially bounded institution and more as a particular constellation of sites, spaces and opportunities for learning. The power and influence of an educational system in the past was, to some extent, guaranteed by its institutional autonomies and structures. The panopticon which Foucault (1977) described so well vested schools with the duties of surveillance and regulation – the need to normalise children. Arguably this process of normalisation could be used to normalise new sets of gender relations – those characterised by fluidity and diversity. Feminist post-structural research reminds us that more attention should be paid to the 'micro-politics' of power which are as significant as macro-formations. Gender plays, for example, are power plays within schools (Davies, 1993; Thorne, 1993; Francis, 1998) that construct powerful girls or powerful boys at different points at different moments in time and in space. The complexity of social interaction, therefore, belies any simple notion of gender socialisation and any simple reform strategy in the new era. The experience of 'growing up' in the future may well be one of 'growing out' of traditional gender identities. Schools will need to listen to male and female pupils to learn how far and in what ways boys and girls have different ways of knowing and of learning and a diversity of gender identities (Arnot, David and Weiner, 1999).

These challenges involve substantial reforms of the modernist educational project of the last two centuries. The most likely scenario is that the voices of young people themselves, rather than the campaigns of teachers, parents and educational policy-makers, will be the driving force for educational change. Young people will ask to be treated as citizens in their own right and to have a political voice. If that happens, then central to a school's concerns will be the different experiences of young men and women negotiating the processes of individualisation and globalisation affecting society. Below I consider girls' experiences first, and then those of boys.

Girls and social change

The women's movement, coupled with the development of welfare states and global restructuring of the economy, has had considerable impact on young women in many developed and developing nations. The extent of change among schoolgirls depends on how far customary concepts of femininity have been problematised and how far traditional forms of male power have been challenged in the family, the economy and the school. What feminism offers women is the possibility of throwing off their historical oppression and enhancing their lives by achieving certain levels of autonomy. Schooling plays a critical part in that process of liberation.

Women's educational success in Western economies is a tribute to the power of feminism as a social movement in the broadest sense. In many European countries, young women appear to be 'on the move' (Chisholm and du Bois-Reynaud, 1993). They have improved their standing in schools and in further and higher education. This change has been associated with major shifts in attitudes towards the public and private sphere. Although often 'disidentifying' (Skeggs, 1997) with feminist ideas, young British women have been found to 'now reject the idea that a man's place is at work and a woman's place is at home' (Wilkinson, 1994, p. 239). Their gender values have disrupted the continuity of generations. They appear to be responding to the challenge of the new forms of modernity by transforming traditional class-based femininities and sexual relations and replacing these with more personalised and more reflexive processes of decision-making (for a summary of research, see Arnot, David and Weiner, 1999).

One of the major spurs for girls to succeed in male worlds has been the presence of a compulsory curriculum. With little opportunity to choose, and with much encouragement from teachers, girls have made their way into science and mathematics, and have shown that they can excel (ibid.). Schools will have to meet the challenge of sustaining a delicate and difficult balance between the needs for flexibilisation discussed above and the need to keep a compulsory curriculum so as to ensure gender equality.

In the Western world, schools also face the difficult task of sustaining female educational successes when only limited inroads have been made in dismantling the sexual divisions of labour. The persistent and extensive sex segregation of the labour market (integrated into class and race inequalities) casts a long shadow across the school system. This means that male and female curricular and career choices almost inevitably are gendered and class- and ethnically-based choices. This disjuncture between female educational success and female patterns of work is a key issue for schools, for higher education and for the economy in the future. Women may become downwardly socially mobile, not converting their educational qualifications into the equivalent in terms of job status (Abbot and Sapsford, 1987). While there is little pressure on schools today to ensure their young women are more occupationally mobile, this may change in the future if the wastage of female talent is recognised. The equalisation of male and female chances in the labour market could then become a critical issue for schools.

Although there is evidence, for example in the UK, that some black and white working-class girls have improved their educational achievements over and above that of boys in the same class, there is also evidence that substantial class and racial differences between women are being maintained. These differences mirror the gap between women's education in the developed and developing world, drawing attention to the power of poverty as a determining factor of life chances. Women in developing nations have to contend with high levels of illiteracy, poverty and gender discrimination (Stromquist, 1997). The 'failing working-class girl' is a feature common to advanced and developing nations alike (King and Hill, 1993; Measor, 1994). The sexual division of domestic labour can hold back young women's chances of achieving success at school and staying on long enough to obtain higher qualifications – it can also trap young women into 'safe havens' of 'women's work'. Male material and symbolic dominance is thus masked by the 'choices' women make, whether it is early school-leaving, domestically oriented occupational choices or domesticity. Clearly more assertive interventions into poverty and patriarchy would need to be considered in the future if women's economic development is to be promoted.

One strategy for schools would be to work with women in the community who, as political activists, engage daily with such problems. The concept of 'poor mothering', which has labelled and demonised the women who are raising families under adverse conditions, has to take much of the blame for neglecting this source of empowerment (Hill Collins, 1990). Mirza and Reay (2000) demonstrate from the experience of African-Caribbean women educators and girls in the UK that the processes of individualisation are not necessarily incompatible with notions of collective solidarity and the 'pulling up' of the community. Upward social mobility can involve a social not just an individual project. The question for schools and feminists is how to encourage collectivism in the face of individualisation and social fragmentation.

Masculinity and male futures

Another trend in the twenty-first century is likely to be increasing concern about male patterns of education, even though men are privileged in terms of access and control of high-status knowledge, educational routes, institutions and employment (Weiner, Arnot and David, 1997). The elite in society are still the male elite, despite women's advances. At the same time, men's position is not secure. As Connell (1997, p. 611) argued, in Western economies there has been a 'displacement, splitting and remaking of gentry masculinity', as well as a transformation of working-class masculinities as a result of deindustrialisation and global restructuring.

Media discourses construct the 'future as female' – pointing especially to the adaptability of women to the new economic conditions, their advantage over communication skills, their access to service industries and their flexibility in work. Current debates suggest that, in the future, schools in advanced economies will need to address a 'crisis in masculinity'. Although discursively constructed around the unease and anxiety associated with women's encroachment on the elite male public sphere, these debates reopen questions about the relationship of schooling to masculinity – a concern with which, for example, British and Australian feminists and gender theorists are starting to engage (Epstein et al., 1998; Gilbert and Gilbert, 1998).

In Western economies, the experience of young men differs from that of young women in the same social class. Economic restructuring has dismantled many of the traditional male preserves within manufacturing economies (Furlong and Cartmel, 1997). Previous transitions from school to work which were taken-for-granted aspects of the transfer from boyhood to manhood have been disrupted and young men are forced to contemplate the realities of an accelerating 'diploma disease'. In economies where new jobs may be seen by the boys as being on the wrong side of the male/female divide, young black and white working-class men could become increasingly disaffected and displaced. In an alienating economic and social climate, and indeed in a shifting gender climate, boys may celebrate hyper-masculine identities (Mac an Ghaill, 1994; Connell, 1997).

As Beck (1992) argues, in a risk society young men may well find themselves attempting to cling on to traditional male roles, traditional family structures and local (territorial and community) identities.

> All the factors which dislodge women from their traditional role are missing on the male side. In the context of male life, fatherhood and career, economic independence and familial life are not contradictions that have to be fought for and held together against the conditions in the family and society: instead their compatibility with the traditional male role is prescribed and protected. But this meant that individualisation … strengthens masculine role behaviour.
>
> (Beck, 1992, p. 112)

Schools, therefore, may wish to ask whether traditional class, racial and gender identities are in the best academic and vocational interests of boys. The ways in which boys 'distance' themselves from femininity (by sustaining notions of gender dualism – Davies, 1993) restrict, it seems, their abilities and performance in terms of literacy and language-related subjects (Quicke, 1999). In a society which is communication rich, there is no doubt that this male illiteracy is an important problem. Also, although male youth cultures sustain boys' confidence and pride in the context of disenfranchisement and social exclusion, they also hurtle these young men outside the boundaries of society. It is only by challenging masculinity that schools in the future will be able to offer disengaged youth the chance to grapple with economic (and gender) change. Whether those schools which are dominated by a male-centred culture and ethos will actively take on this project, we can only speculate.

Another issue strongly but not exclusively associated with masculinity is that of violence. As Davies (2000) argues, a civil school for a civil society is one which has no violence. Violence, whether symbolic or material, involves the dehumanisation of young people (and their teachers) and has no place in a civilised society. Critical educationalists searching for new forms of pedagogy in the twentieth century have manifestly failed to control violence in society or within the school walls. Evidence from young pupils in both developed and developing nations points to the levels of violence they have to negotiate within the school, the community and the society – even from very young ages (Beynon, 1989). Current levels of racial violence, sexual violence and homophobic violence stand as testimony against any notions of progress or modernisation.

An almost impossible challenge for schools, given the levels of violence and national and global conflict, is to try to become safe spaces in which children can grow. Beck (2000) argues that, in the future, conflict resolution is likely to be the major focus of learning. Without such skills it is not clear how globalisation will be 'policed', nor indeed how individuals as citizens will be contained when 'institutionalised individualism' becomes the ethos of society. Yet without safety there can be no equality. Schools, if they exist in the future, would need to carve out a new communitarian function which prepares individuals for the new demands of citizenry. In this context they will need to prioritise the containment of violence not just because it is a breach of disciplinary codes but as a priority in relation to an individual's rights.

Social change/gender futures

Schools will be under pressure to help young people cope effectively with massive social change even though the requirements for social stability are also likely to be great. In the 'second age of modernity' (Beck, 2000) not only will 'relations between and beyond national states and societies' be changed, but so too will the 'quality of the social and political'. What will become critical in this new age will be reflexive individualisation – a process in which individuals will no longer locate themselves in traditional communities, with traditional identities of class, gender, ethnicity. Men and women will need to put themselves at the centre of their life plan and actively engage in constructing their own biographies. Ascribed statuses, he argues, such as class, gender and regionality will pale into insignificance. New alliances will be formed on the basis of shared common risks. The shift in gender relations which has occurred within advanced industrial economies has been dramatic and, he thinks, irreversible. It marks the beginning of a liberation from the feudally ascribed roles for the sexes, with all their associated antagonisms. As a result, Beck argues, 'the position of men and women is becoming increasingly unequal, more conscious and less legitimated' (Beck, 1992, p. 104).

Arguably the effects on men and women in different positions in the social hierarchy and within different nation-states will be different (Arnot, David and Weiner, 1999). In Western European democracies, the women's movement has already challenged the automatic right of men to power in public life and the assignation of women to private spheres. They have delegitimised the social order by challenging conventional notions of masculinity and femininity. When the liberal democratic social orders were premised on what Carol Pateman (1988) called a 'civic brotherhood', women were subordinated on the grounds of their intellectual, moral, emotional and biological inferiority. In the twenty-first century, women are likely to assert their right to full (not partial or absent) political and economic power. They may no longer be content to service the economy, the state and men, and need massive added incentives to become the wives, mothers, nurses and teachers of the new generation. In this context, the separation between public and private spheres which supported patriarchal formations within nation-states could well appear obsolete.

Young women may also attempt to uncouple themselves from economic and social dependency upon men. In the future, women may no longer rely on men to offer support for child-rearing and family income. They wish to focus on their own life plans, irrespective of heterosexual relationships. Educational qualifications in this context become vital aspects of the economic survival of young women and their children. Schools and families will be challenged to identify new positive masculine identities in private and public life and new purposes for male education. Feminist theorists have argued for the importance of teaching a caring ethic as the basis for a more humanistic and equal society (see Arnot and Dillabough, 1999).

The forces of globalisation will affect future gender relations, introducing new political and economic dimensions, only some of which are currently being gleaned (Henry et al., 1999; Blackmore, 1999; Brine, 1999; Kenway with Langmead, 2000). Globalisation carries with it new economic requirements, not least flexibilisation of work structures, migration and mobility, new international agencies and structures, and new political and social identities (Beck, 2000). In this 'second age of modernity', which demands what Beck argues is a form of reflexive 'cosmopoliticisation', women (and ethnic groups, immigrants and other marginalised groups in the national space and developing nations) may be privileged because, as an excluded group, they are likely to be more self-aware and therefore more able to become new world citizens. The international women's movements may well come into their own in this new age.

In the twenty-first century, school systems across the world will have to address highly complex sets of gender relations which, released from the strait-jacket of nineteenth-century values, will need to find global forms of expression. The related processes of individualisation and globalisation are likely to have major consequences for gender relaions, particularly in terms of economic transformations but also in terms of personal identifications and political action. The danger is that these processes of social change will force even further apart those who have resources (what Bourdieu and Passeron, 1977, called economic, social and intellectual capital) and those who do not. New social inequalities, especially between rich and poor nations, could be created. As individualisation and globalisation transform nation-state politics, women's and men's experiences may well be not only more unequal but very different. The story is getting more not less complex as we progress into the future. The challenge for feminism and indeed for the school system is how to define gender equality in educational and social terms in this new order.

References and further reading

Abbot, P. and Sapsford, R. (1987) *Women and Social Class*, London: Tavistock.

Arnot, M. and Dillabough, J. (1999) 'Feminist politics and democratic values in education', *Curriculum Inquiry*, 29, 2, pp. 159–90.

Arnot, M., David, M. and Weiner, G. (1999) *Closing the Gender Gap: postwar education and social change*, Cambridge: Polity Press.

Beck, U. (1992) *Risk Society: towards a new modernity*, London: Sage.

—— (2000) 'The cosmopolitan perspective; sociology of the second age of modernity', *British Journal of Sociology*, 51, 1, pp. 79–105.

Beynon, J. (1989) 'A school for men: an ethnographic case study of routine violence in schooling', in S. Walker and L. Barton (eds) *Politics and the Processes of Schooling*, Milton Keynes: Open University Press.

Blackmore, J. (1999) 'Localisation/globalisation and the midwife state: strategic dilemmas for state feminism in education?', *Discourse: studies in the cultural politics of education*, 154, 1, pp. 33–54.

Bourdieu, P. and Passeron, J. (1977) *Reproduction in Education, Culture and Society*, London: Sage.

Brine, J. (1999) *Under Educating Women: globalising inequality*, Buckingham: Open University Press.

Chisholm, L. and du Bois-Reynaud, M. (1993) 'Youth transitions, gender and social change', *Sociology*, 27, 2, pp. 259–79.

Connell, R.W. (1997) 'The big picture: masculinities in recent world history', in A.H. Halsey, H. Lauder, P. Brown and A.S. Wells (eds) *Education, Culture and Economy*, Oxford: Oxford University Press.

Connolly, P. (1998) *Racism, Gender Identities and Young Children: social relations in a multi-ethnic, inner-city primary school*, London: Routledge.

Davies, B. (1993) *Frogs and Snails and Feminist Tales*, Sydney: Allen & Unwin.

Davies, L. (2000) 'The civil school and civil society: gender, democracy and development', in M. Arnot and J. Dillabough (eds) *Challenging Democracy: international perspectives on gender, education and citizenship*, London: RoutledgeFalmer.

Dench, G. (1997) *Rewriting the Sexual Contract*, London: Institute of Community Studies.

Durkheim, E. (1956) *Education and Sociology*, New York: Free Press.

Epstein, D., Elwood, J., Hey, V. and Maw, J. (eds) (1998) *Failing Boys, Issues in Gender and Achievement*, Buckingham: Open University Press.

Foster, V. (1996) 'Space Invaders: desire and threat in the schooling of girls', *Discourse: Studies in the Cultural Politics of Education*, 17, 1, pp. 43–63.

Foucault, M. (1977) *Discipline and Punish: the birth of the prison*, London: Allen Lane.

Francis, B. (1998) *Power Plays: primary school children's constructions of gender, power and adult work*, Stoke-on-Trent: Trentham Books.

Furlong, A. and Cartmel, F. (1997) *Young People and Social Change: individualisation and risk in late modernity*, Buckingham: Open University Press.

Gilbert, R. and Gilbert, P. (1998) *Masculinity Goes to School*, London: Routledge.

Gillborn, D. and Youdell, D. (2000) *Rationing Education: policy, practice, reform and equity*, Buckingham: Open University Press.

Henry, M., Lingard, B., Rizvi, F. and Taylor, S. (1999) 'Working with/against globalisation in education', *Journal of Education Policy*, 14, 1, pp. 85–97.

Hill Collins, P. (1990) *Black Feminist Thought: knowledge, consciousness and the politics of empowerment*, London: Routledge.

Kenway, J. with Langmead, D. (2000) 'Cyber-feminism and citizenship? Challenging the political imaginary', in M. Arnot and J. Dillabough (eds) *Challenging Democracy: international perspectives on gender, education and citizenship*, London: RoutledgeFalmer.

King, A.M.N. and Hill, M.A. (eds) (1993) *Women's Education in Developing Countries: barriers, benefits and policies*, The World Bank/Johns Hopkins University Press.

Mac an Ghaill, M. (1994) *The Making of Men*, Buckingham: Open University Press.

Measor, L. (ed.) (1994) 'Gender, education and development', *Gender and Education*, special issue, 6, 2.

Mirza, H. and Reay, D. (2000) 'Black women educators and the third space', in M. Arnot and J. Dillabough (eds) *Challenging Democracy: international perspectives on gender, education and citizenship*, London: RoutledgeFalmer.

Pateman, C. (1988) *The Sexual Contract*, Cambridge: Polity Press.

Quicke, J. (1999) *A Curriculum for Life*, Buckingham: Open University Press.

Skeggs, B. (1997) *Formations of Class and Gender*, London: Sage.

Stromquist, N. (1997) *Literacy for Citizenship: gender and classroom dynamics in Brazil*, New York: SUNY Press.

Thorne, B. (1993) *Gender Play: girls and boys in school*, Buckingham: Open University Press.

Unterhalter, E. (2000) 'Transnational visions of the 1990s: contrasting views of women, education and citizenship', in M. Arnot and J. Dillabough (eds) *Challenging Democracy: international perspectives on gender, education and citizenship*, London: RoutledgeFalmer.

Weiner, G., Arnot, M. and David, M. (1997) 'Is the future female? Female success, male disadvantage and changing gender relations in education', in A.H. Halsey, H. Lauder, P. Brown and A. Stuart-Wells (eds) *Education, Culture, Economy and Society*, Oxford: Oxford University Press.

Weis, L. (1990) *Working Class without Work: high school students in a de-industrialising economy*, New York: Routledge.

Wilkinson, H. (1994) *No Turning Back: generations and the genderquake*, London: Demos.

Index